Shojo Beat

love ★ com

16

Story & Art by
Aya Nakahara

love ★ com

contents 16

The Story So Far...

Risa and Ôtani are their class's lopsided comedy duo... and they've become a couple! Ôtani has been accepted into a teachers' college, while Risa plans to become a fashion stylist.

Meanwhile, life goes on. While visiting a tropical island for Mighty Sensei's wedding, Risa gets hot and bothered over sharing a hotel room with Ôtani. But after seeing the...er...natural way Mighty and Jody express their love, Risa learns to take it easy.

Now graduation is just around the corner, and Risa and her friends have all landed on the graduation committee. Charged with the task of coming up with a memorable farewell for the class, they take a video camera around the school. They get some shots of the warm friendships Ôtani will leave behind on his basketball team and then move on to the rest of the class...

♥ To really get all the details, check out *Lovely Complex* volumes 1–15, available at bookstores everywhere!!

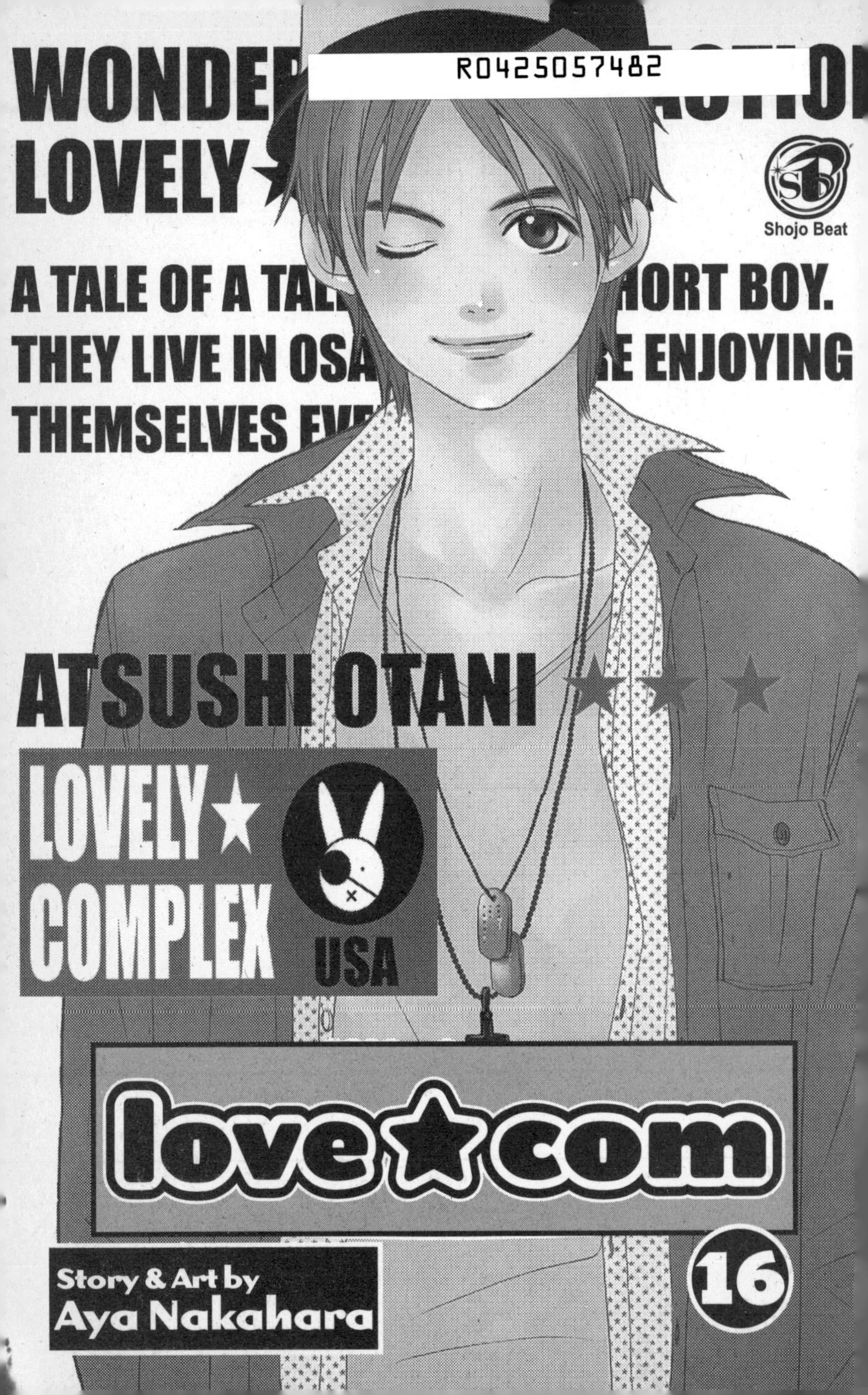
WONDER
LOVELY★
Shojo Beat
A TALE OF A TAL
HORT BOY.
THEY LIVE IN OSA
E ENJOYING
THEMSELVES EVE
ATSUSHI OTANI ★★★
LOVELY★ COMPLEX
USA
love★com
16
Story & Art by
Aya Nakahara

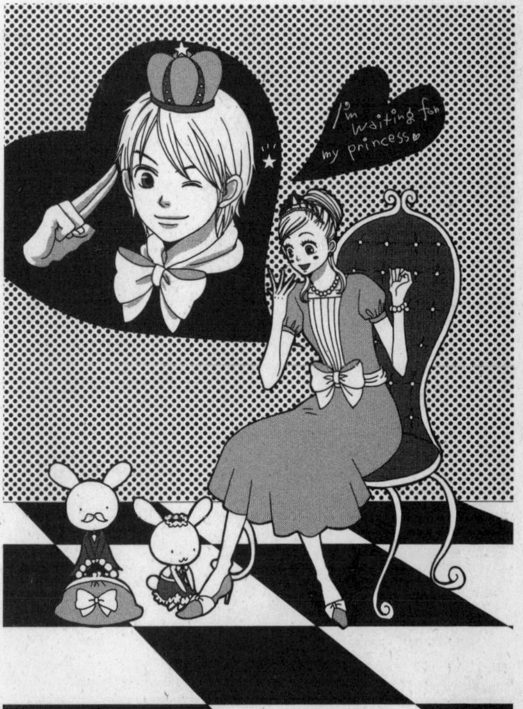
I'm waiting for my princess

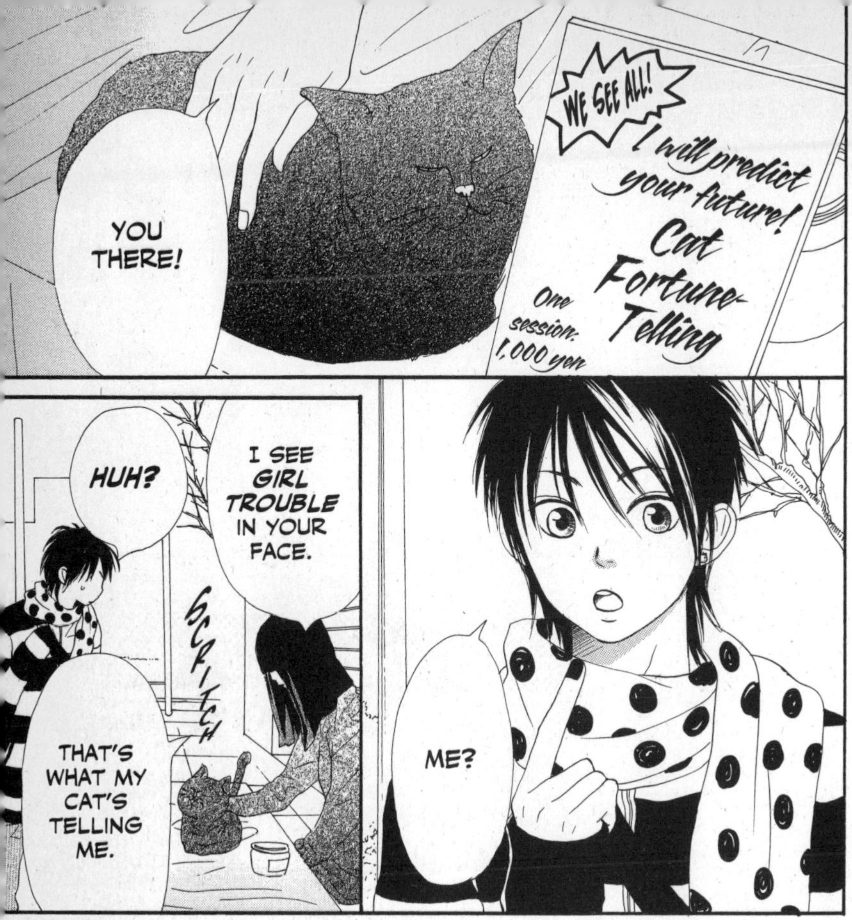
YOU THERE!
WE SEE ALL!
I will predict your future!
Cat Fortune-Telling
One session: 1,000 yen
ME?
I SEE GIRL TROUBLE IN YOUR FACE.
HUH?
SCRITCH
THAT'S WHAT MY CAT'S TELLING ME.

CHAPTER 60

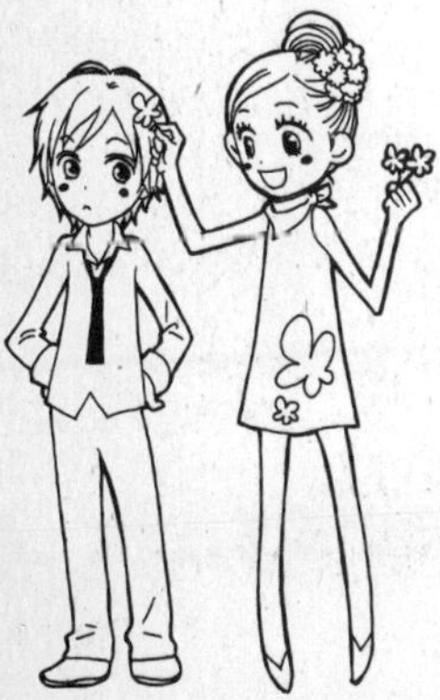

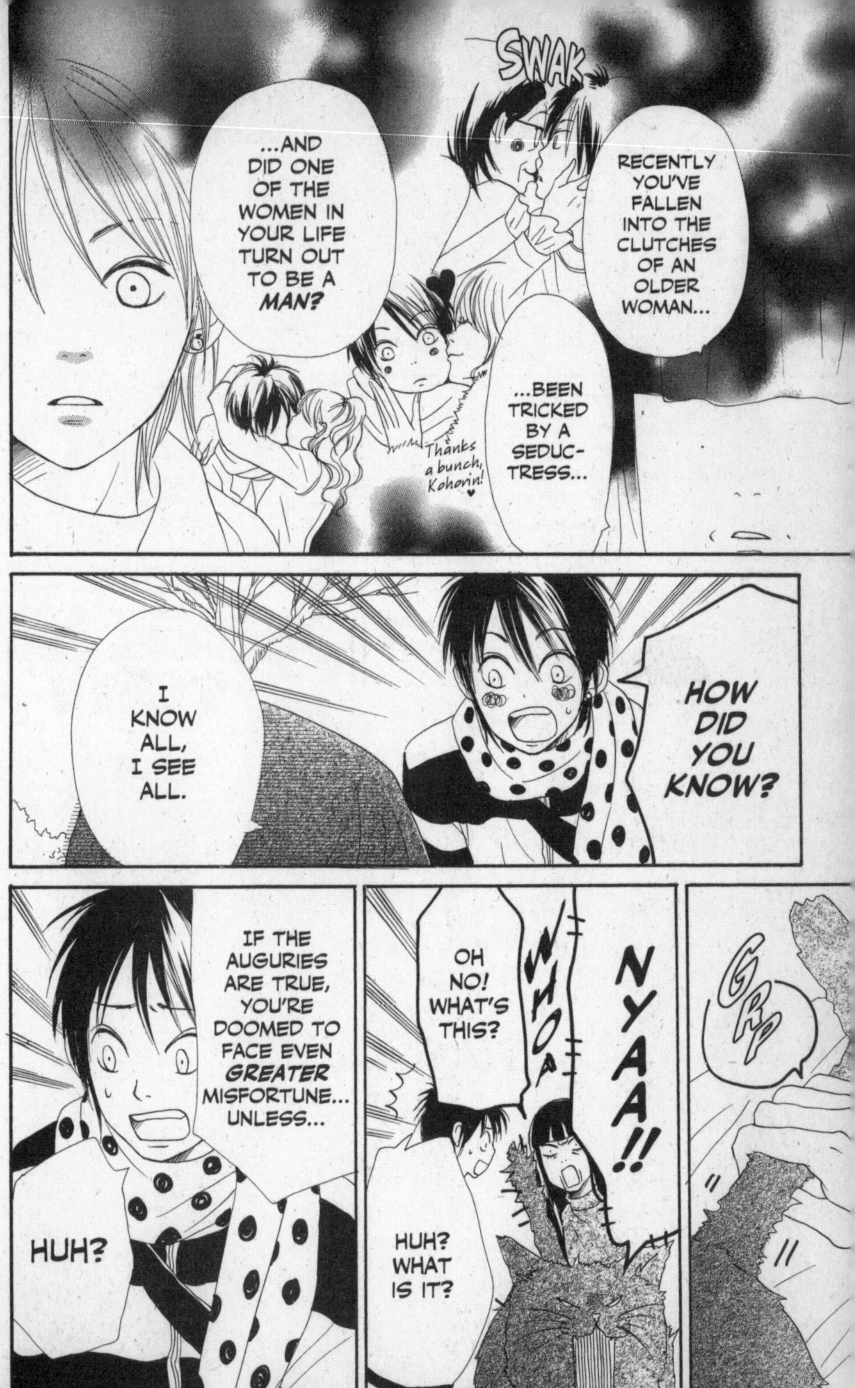
SWAK
RECENTLY YOU'VE FALLEN INTO THE CLUTCHES OF AN OLDER WOMAN...
...BEEN TRICKED BY A SEDUCTRESS...
Thanks a bunch, Kohorin! ♥
...AND DID ONE OF THE WOMEN IN YOUR LIFE TURN OUT TO BE A *MAN?*
HOW DID YOU KNOW?
I KNOW ALL, I SEE ALL.
GRP
NYAA!!
WHOA
OH NO! WHAT'S THIS?
HUH? WHAT IS IT?
IF THE AUGURIES ARE TRUE, YOU'RE DOOMED TO FACE EVEN *GREATER* MISFORTUNE... UNLESS...
HUH?

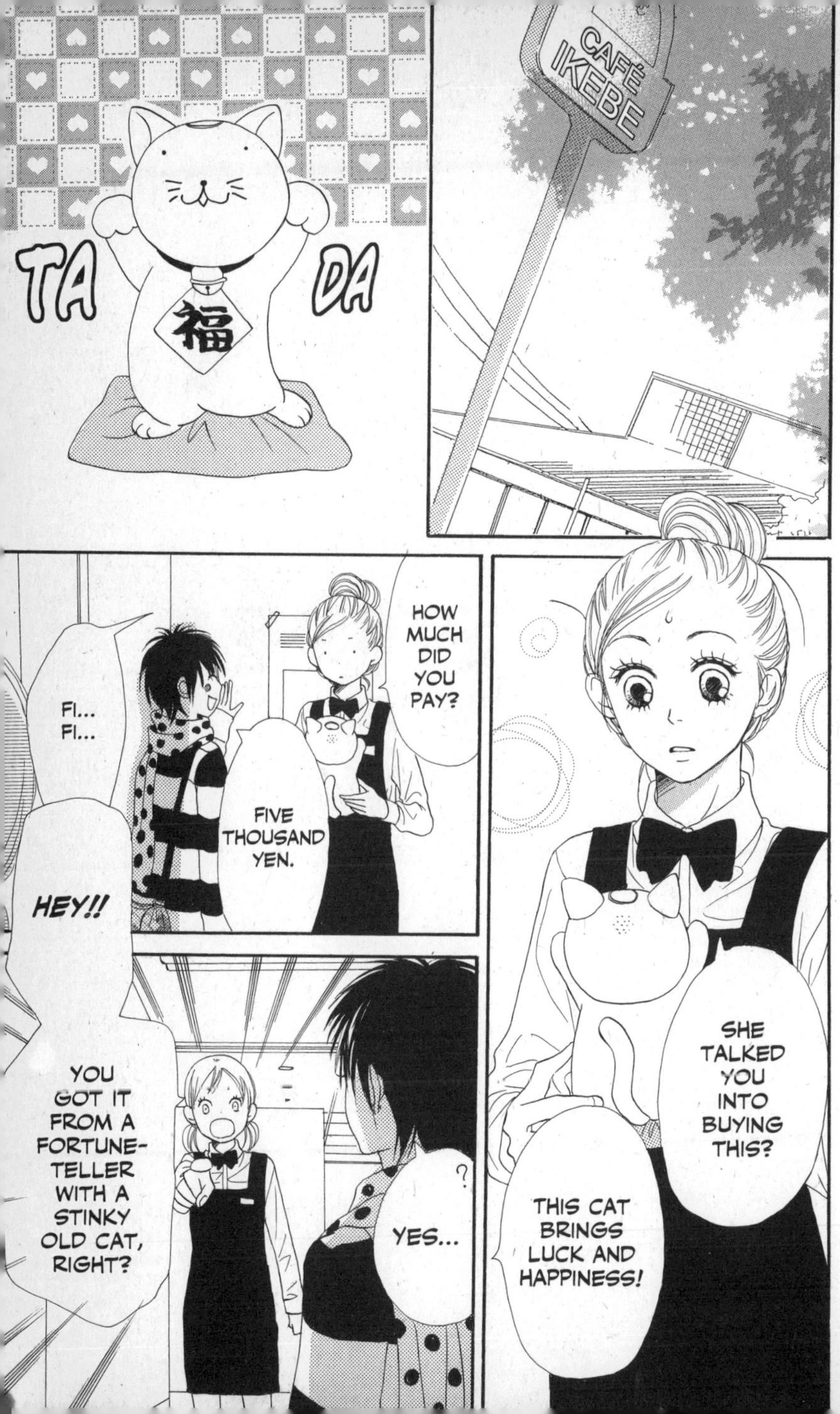
CAFÉ IKEBE
TA DA
福
SHE TALKED YOU INTO BUYING THIS?
THIS CAT BRINGS LUCK AND HAPPINESS!
HOW MUCH DID YOU PAY?
FIVE THOUSAND YEN.
FI... FI...
HEY!!
YOU GOT IT FROM A FORTUNE-TELLER WITH A STINKY OLD CAT, RIGHT?
?
YES...

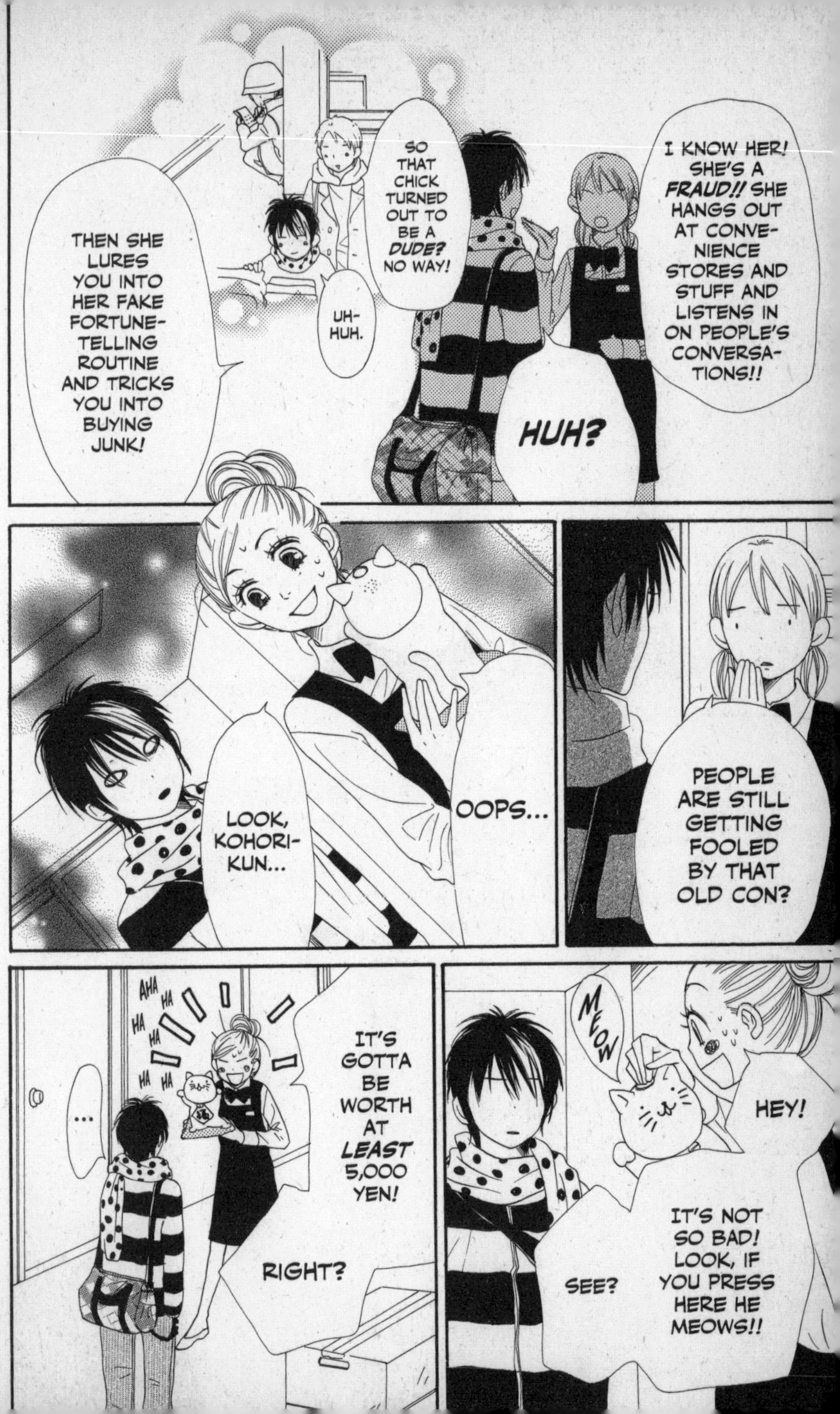
I KNOW HER! SHE'S A FRAUD!! SHE HANGS OUT AT CONVENIENCE STORES AND STUFF AND LISTENS IN ON PEOPLE'S CONVERSATIONS!!
HUH?
SO THAT CHICK TURNED OUT TO BE A DUDE? NO WAY!
UH-HUH.
THEN SHE LURES YOU INTO HER FAKE FORTUNE-TELLING ROUTINE AND TRICKS YOU INTO BUYING JUNK!
PEOPLE ARE STILL GETTING FOOLED BY THAT OLD CON?
OOPS...
LOOK, KOHORI-KUN...
HEY!
MEOW
IT'S NOT SO BAD! LOOK, IF YOU PRESS HERE HE MEOWS!!
SEE?
IT'S GOTTA BE WORTH AT LEAST 5,000 YEN!
AHA HA HA HA HA HA
...
RIGHT?

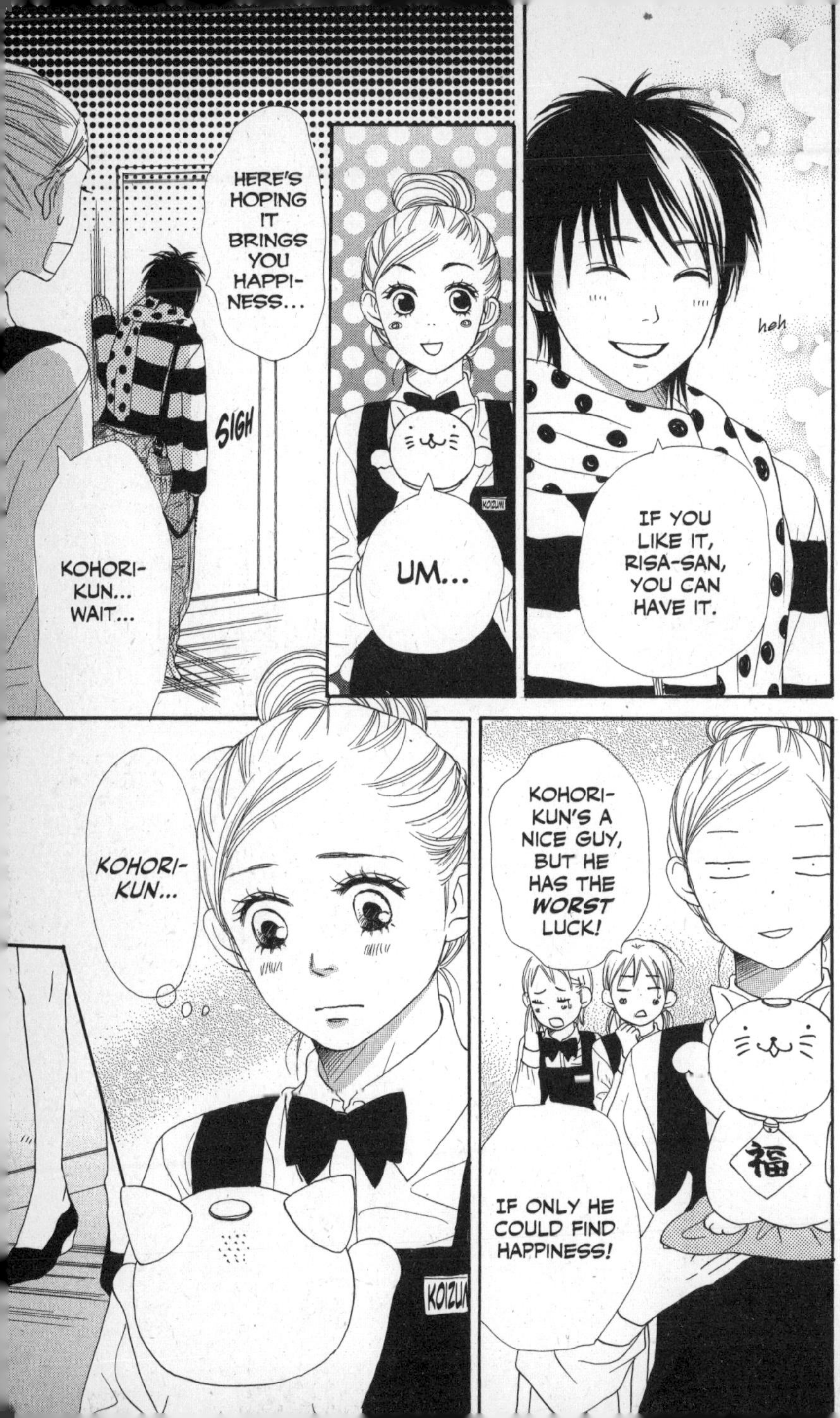
heh
IF YOU LIKE IT, RISA-SAN, YOU CAN HAVE IT.
UM...
HERE'S HOPING IT BRINGS YOU HAPPINESS...
SIGH
KOHORI-KUN... WAIT...
KOHORI-KUN'S A NICE GUY, BUT HE HAS THE WORST LUCK!
福
IF ONLY HE COULD FIND HAPPINESS!
KOHORI-KUN...

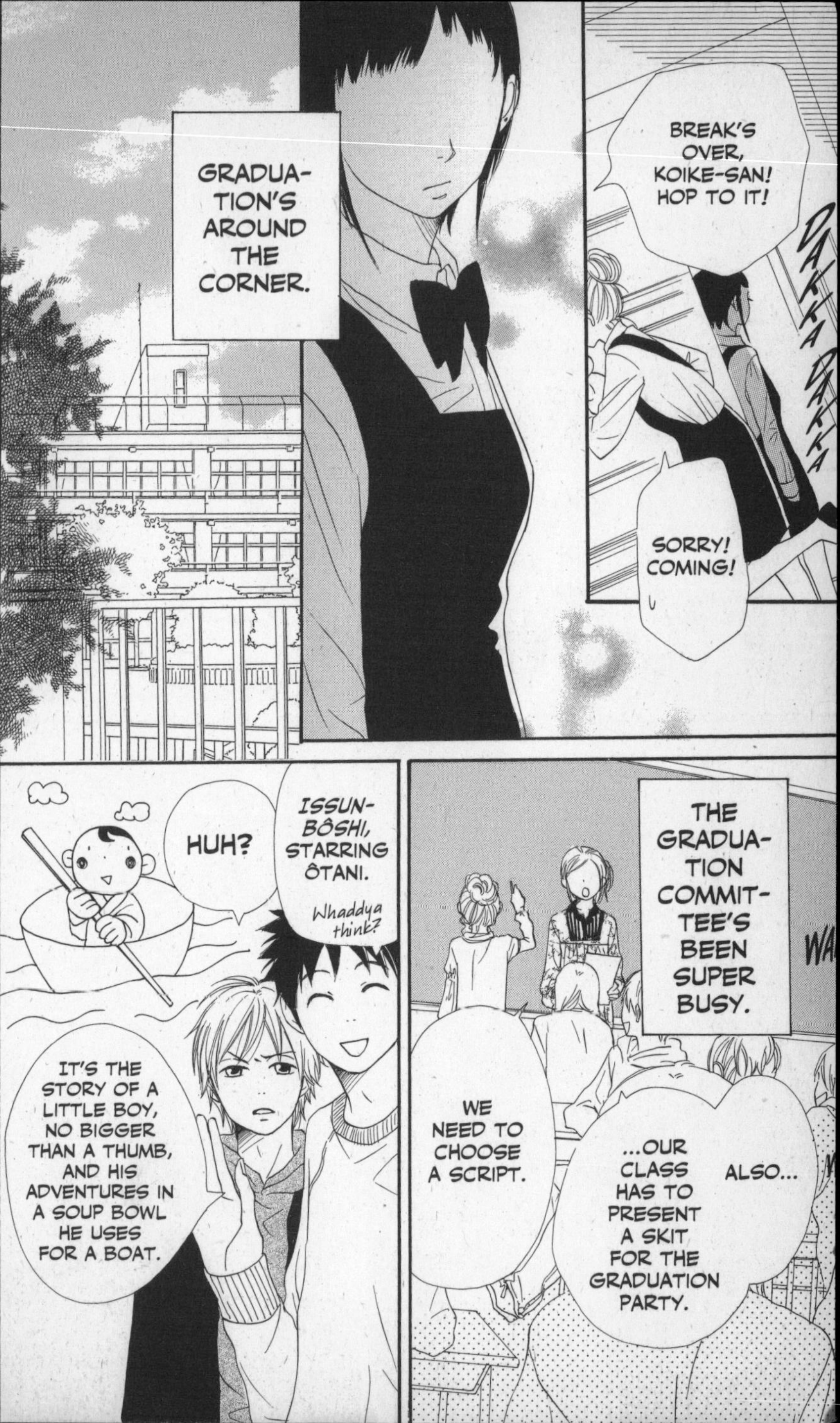
BREAK'S OVER, KOIKE-SAN! HOP TO IT!
DAKKA DAKKA
SORRY! COMING!
GRADUA-TION'S AROUND THE CORNER.
THE GRADUA-TION COMMIT-TEE'S BEEN SUPER BUSY.
ALSO...
...OUR CLASS HAS TO PRESENT A SKIT FOR THE GRADUATION PARTY.
WE NEED TO CHOOSE A SCRIPT.
ISSUN-BÔSHI, STARRING ÔTANI.
Whaddya think?
HUH?
IT'S THE STORY OF A LITTLE BOY, NO BIGGER THAN A THUMB, AND HIS ADVENTURES IN A SOUP BOWL HE USES FOR A BOAT.

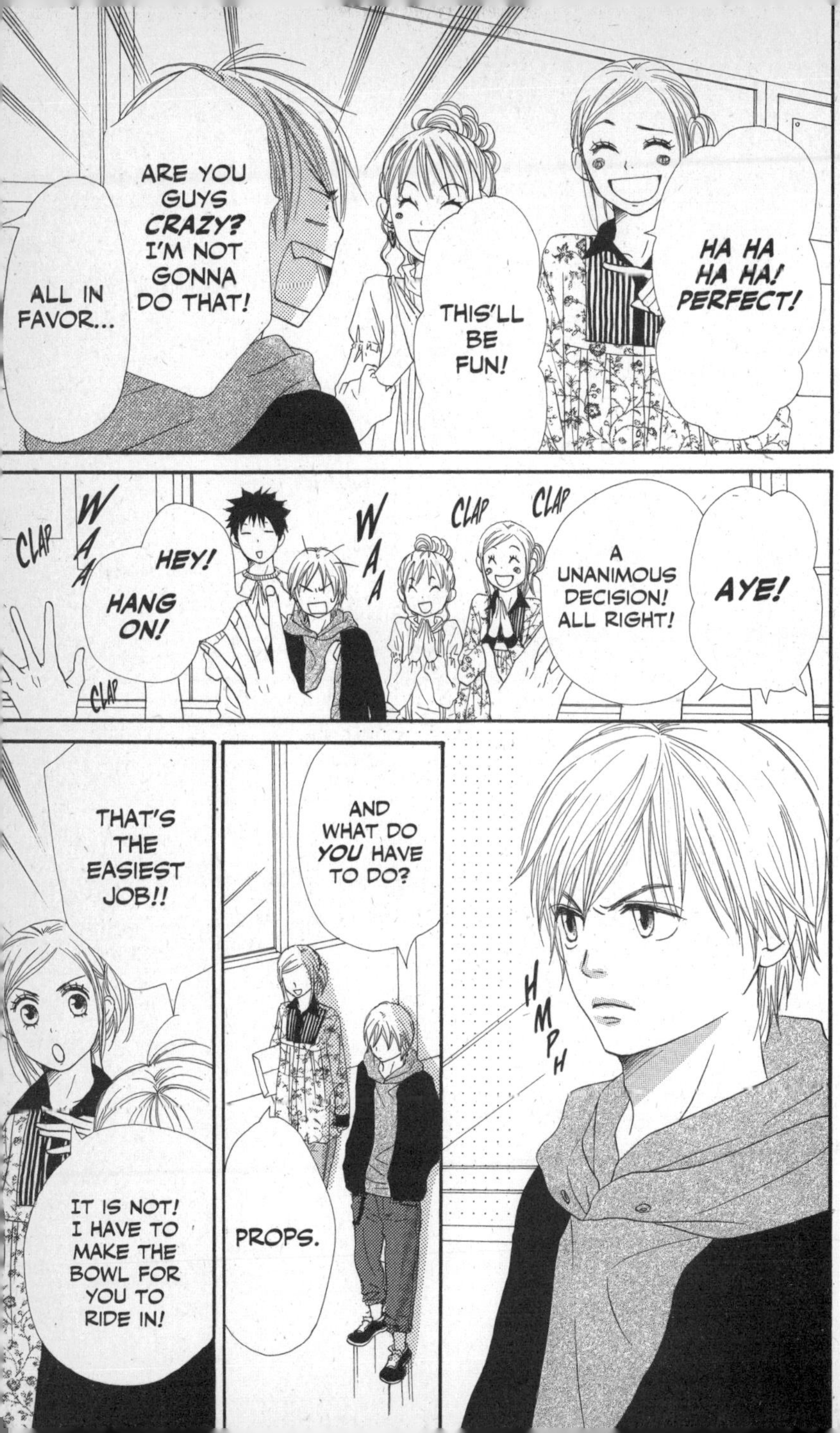
HA HA HA HA! PERFECT!
THIS'LL BE FUN!
ARE YOU GUYS CRAZY? I'M NOT GONNA DO THAT!
ALL IN FAVOR...
AYE!
A UNANIMOUS DECISION! ALL RIGHT!
CLAP
CLAP
WAAA
HEY! HANG ON!
WAAA
CLAP
CLAP
HMPH
AND WHAT DO YOU HAVE TO DO?
PROPS.
THAT'S THE EASIEST JOB!!
IT IS NOT! I HAVE TO MAKE THE BOWL FOR YOU TO RIDE IN!

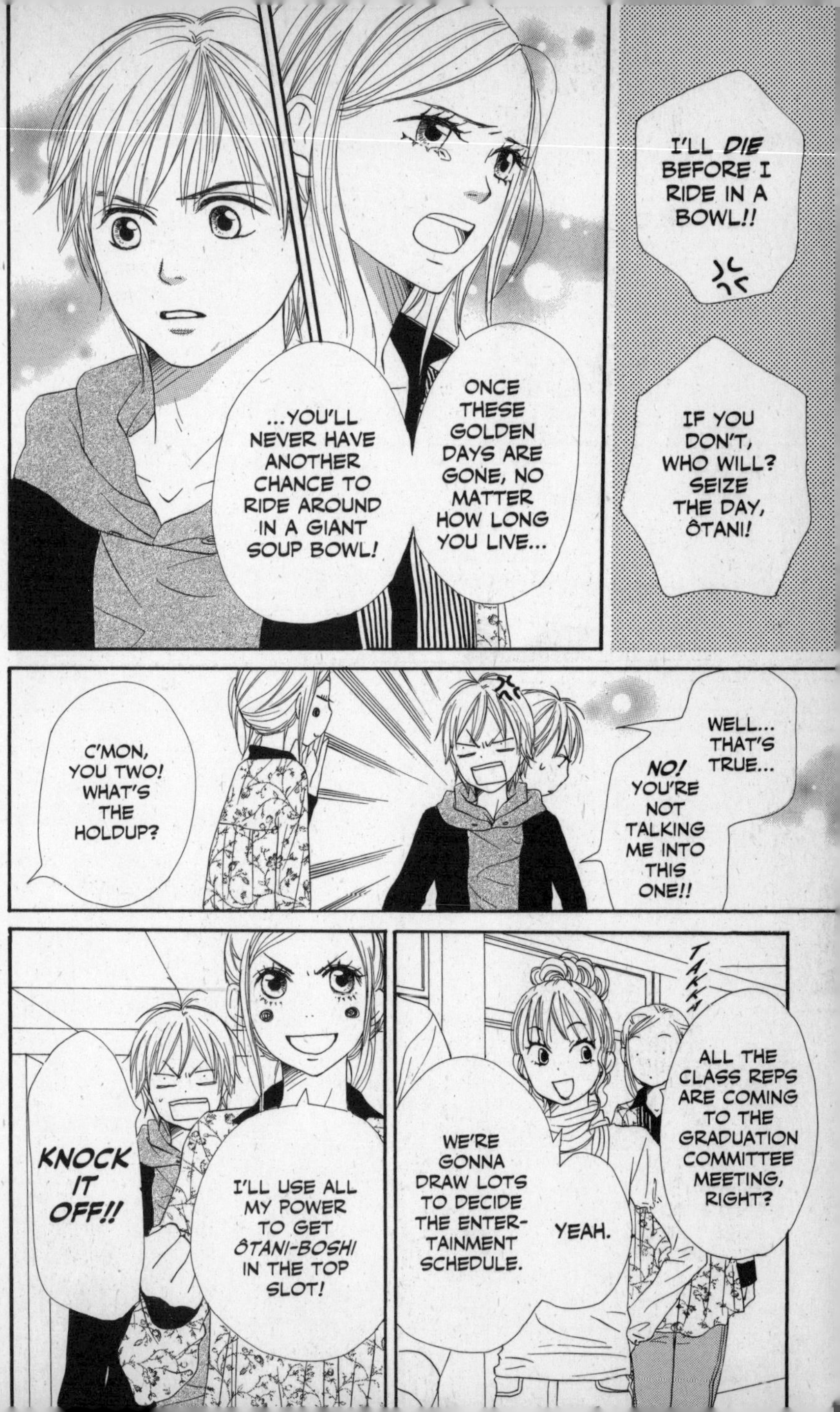
I'LL *DIE* BEFORE I RIDE IN A BOWL!!
IF YOU DON'T, WHO WILL? SEIZE THE DAY, ÔTANI!
ONCE THESE GOLDEN DAYS ARE GONE, NO MATTER HOW LONG YOU LIVE...
...YOU'LL NEVER HAVE ANOTHER CHANCE TO RIDE AROUND IN A GIANT SOUP BOWL!
WELL... THAT'S TRUE...
NO! YOU'RE NOT TALKING ME INTO THIS ONE!!
C'MON, YOU TWO! WHAT'S THE HOLDUP?
TAKKA
ALL THE CLASS REPS ARE COMING TO THE GRADUATION COMMITTEE MEETING, RIGHT?
YEAH.
WE'RE GONNA DRAW LOTS TO DECIDE THE ENTERTAINMENT SCHEDULE.
I'LL USE ALL MY POWER TO GET *ÔTANI-BOSHI* IN THE TOP SLOT!
KNOCK IT OFF!!

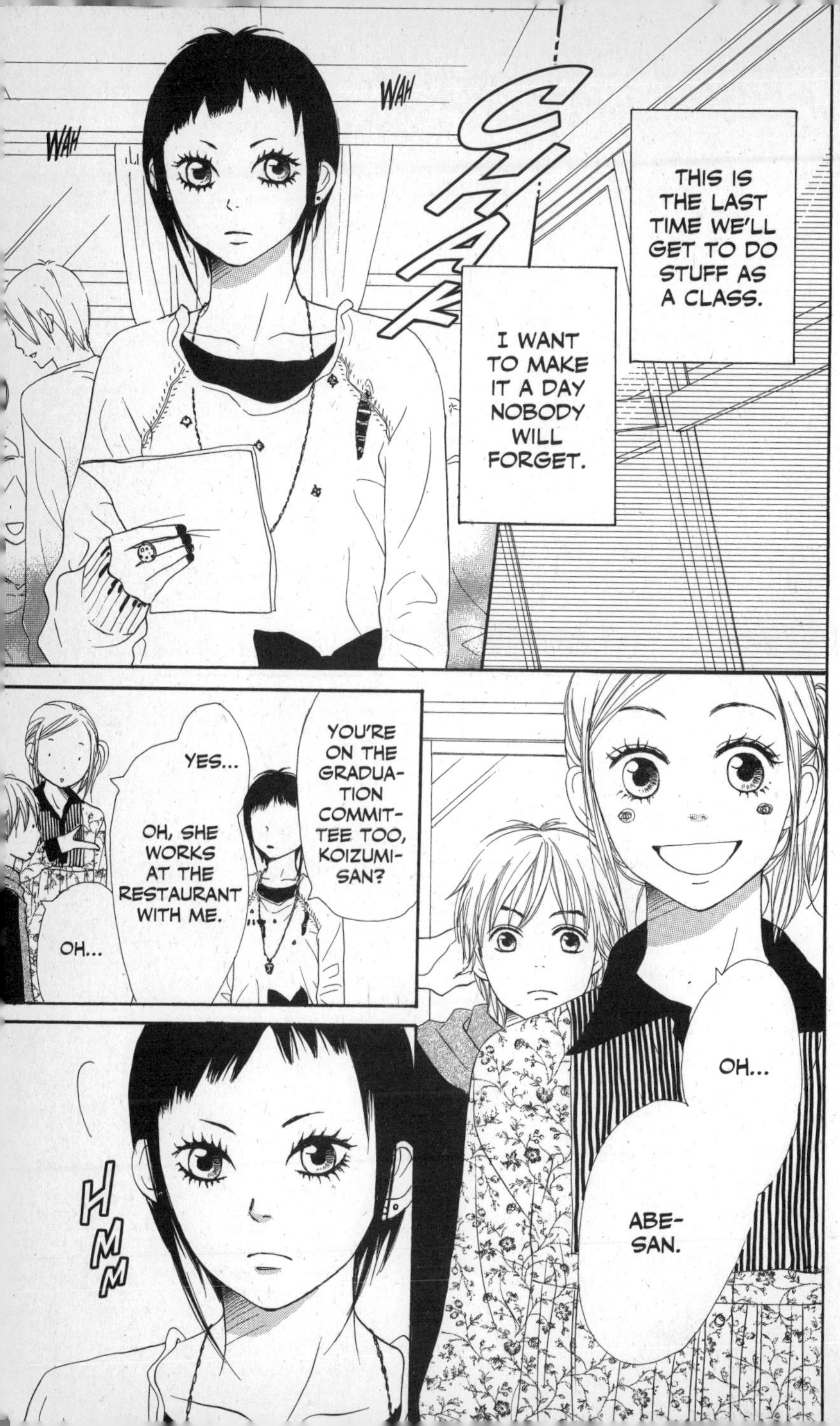
THIS IS THE LAST TIME WE'LL GET TO DO STUFF AS A CLASS.
I WANT TO MAKE IT A DAY NOBODY WILL FORGET.
CHAK
WAH
WAH
OH...
ABE-SAN.
YOU'RE ON THE GRADUATION COMMITTEE TOO, KOIZUMI-SAN?
YES...
OH, SHE WORKS AT THE RESTAURANT WITH ME.
OH...
HMM

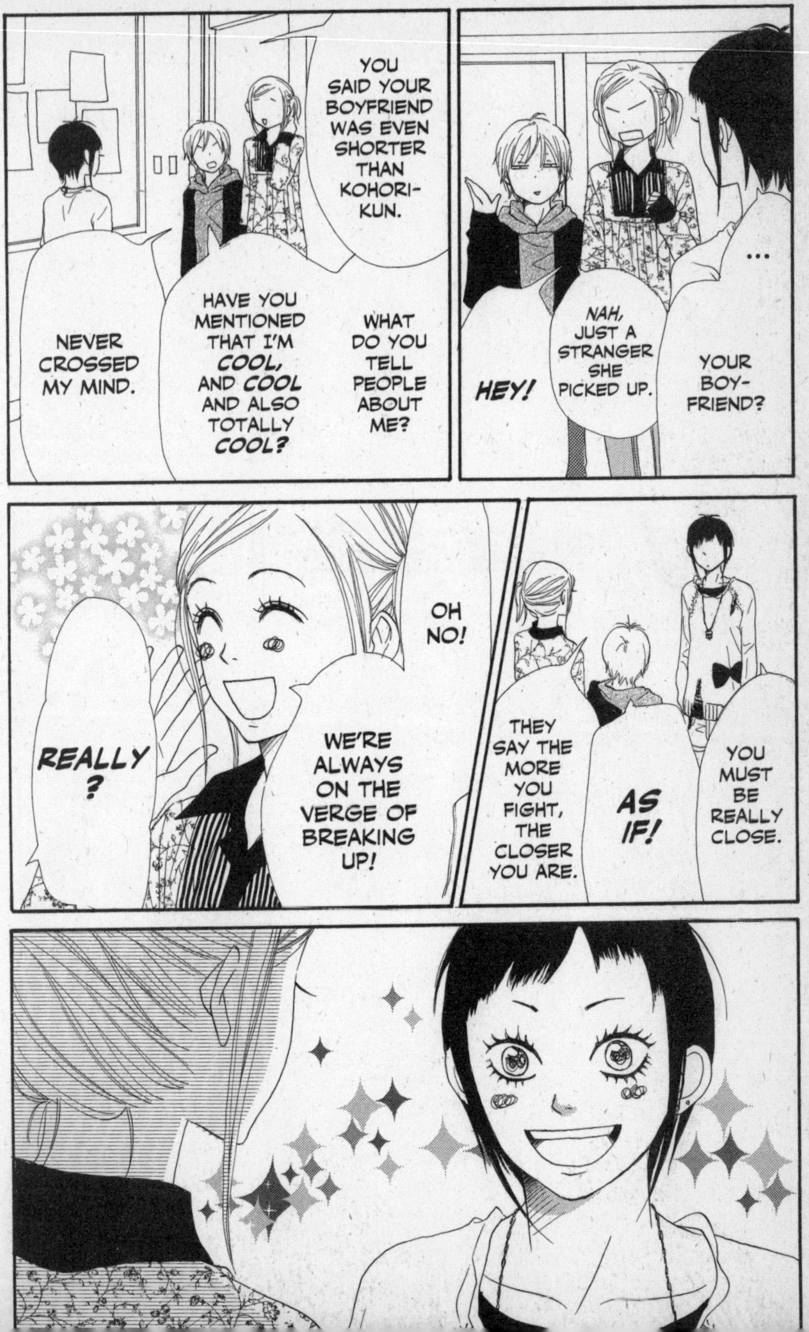
...
YOUR BOY-FRIEND?
NAH, JUST A STRANGER SHE PICKED UP.
HEY!
YOU SAID YOUR BOYFRIEND WAS EVEN SHORTER THAN KOHORI-KUN.
WHAT DO YOU TELL PEOPLE ABOUT ME?
HAVE YOU MENTIONED THAT I'M *COOL,* AND *COOL* AND ALSO TOTALLY *COOL?*
NEVER CROSSED MY MIND.
YOU MUST BE REALLY CLOSE.
AS IF!
THEY SAY THE MORE YOU FIGHT, THE CLOSER YOU ARE.
OH NO!
WE'RE ALWAYS ON THE VERGE OF BREAKING UP!
REALLY?

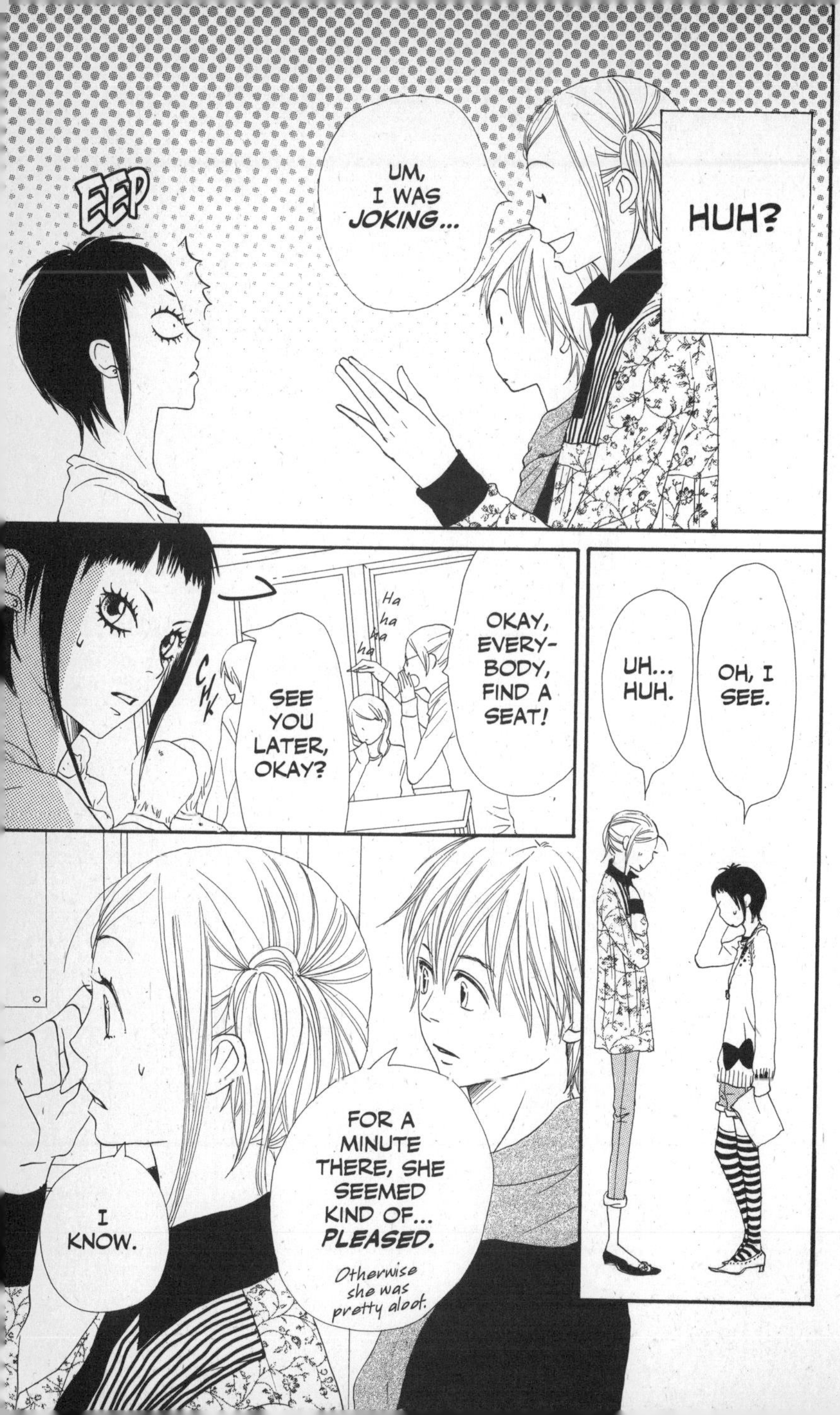
HUH?
UM, I WAS JOKING...
EEP
OH, I SEE.
UH... HUH.
OKAY, EVERY-BODY, FIND A SEAT!
Ha ha ha ha
SEE YOU LATER, OKAY?
CHK
FOR A MINUTE THERE, SHE SEEMED KIND OF... PLEASED.
Otherwise she was pretty aloof.
I KNOW.

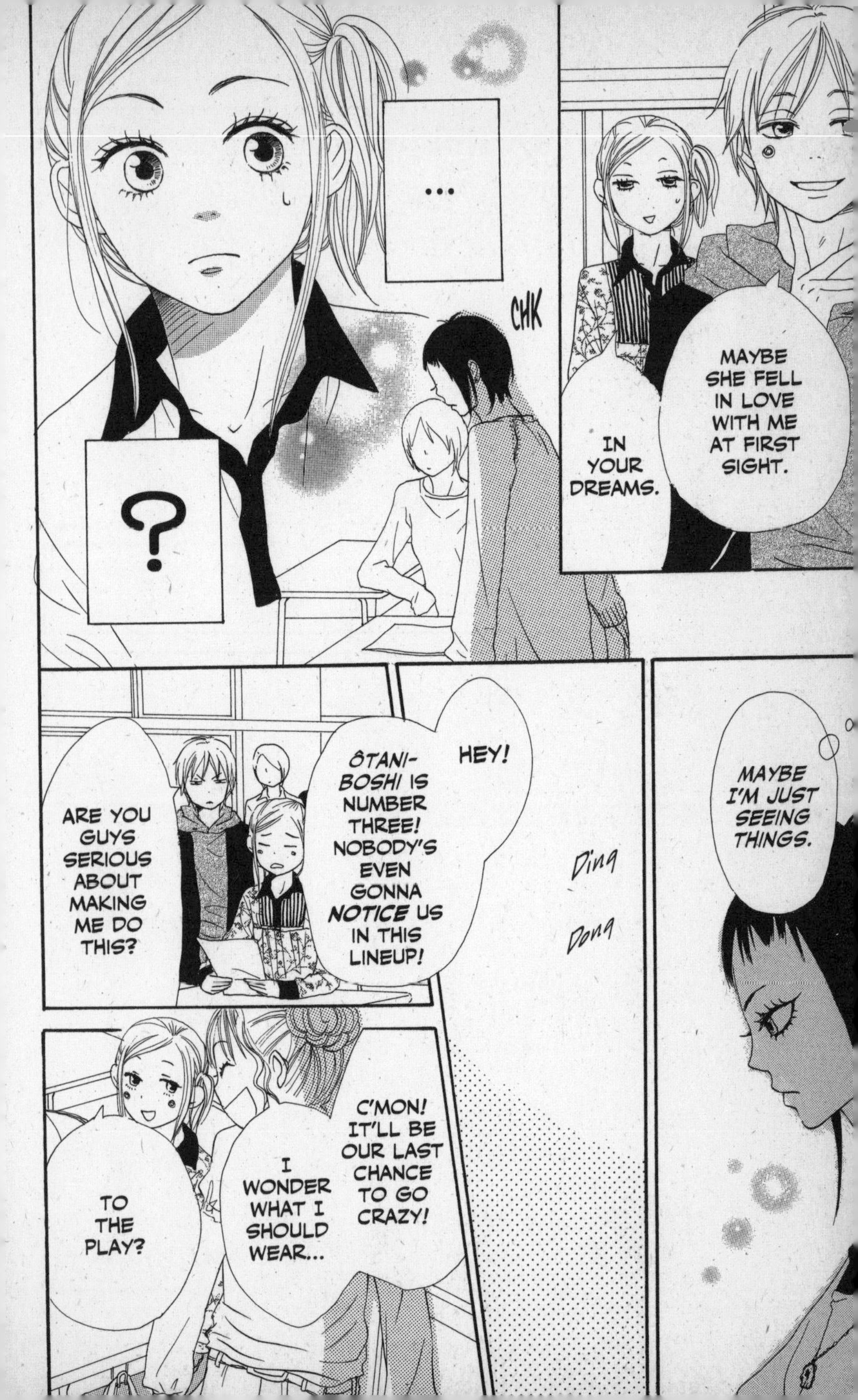
MAYBE SHE FELL IN LOVE WITH ME AT FIRST SIGHT.
IN YOUR DREAMS.
...
CHK
?
MAYBE I'M JUST SEEING THINGS.
Ding
Dong
HEY!
ÔTANI-BOSHI IS NUMBER THREE! NOBODY'S EVEN GONNA *NOTICE* US IN THIS LINEUP!
ARE YOU GUYS SERIOUS ABOUT MAKING ME DO THIS?
C'MON! IT'LL BE OUR LAST CHANCE TO GO CRAZY!
I WONDER WHAT I SHOULD WEAR...
TO THE PLAY?

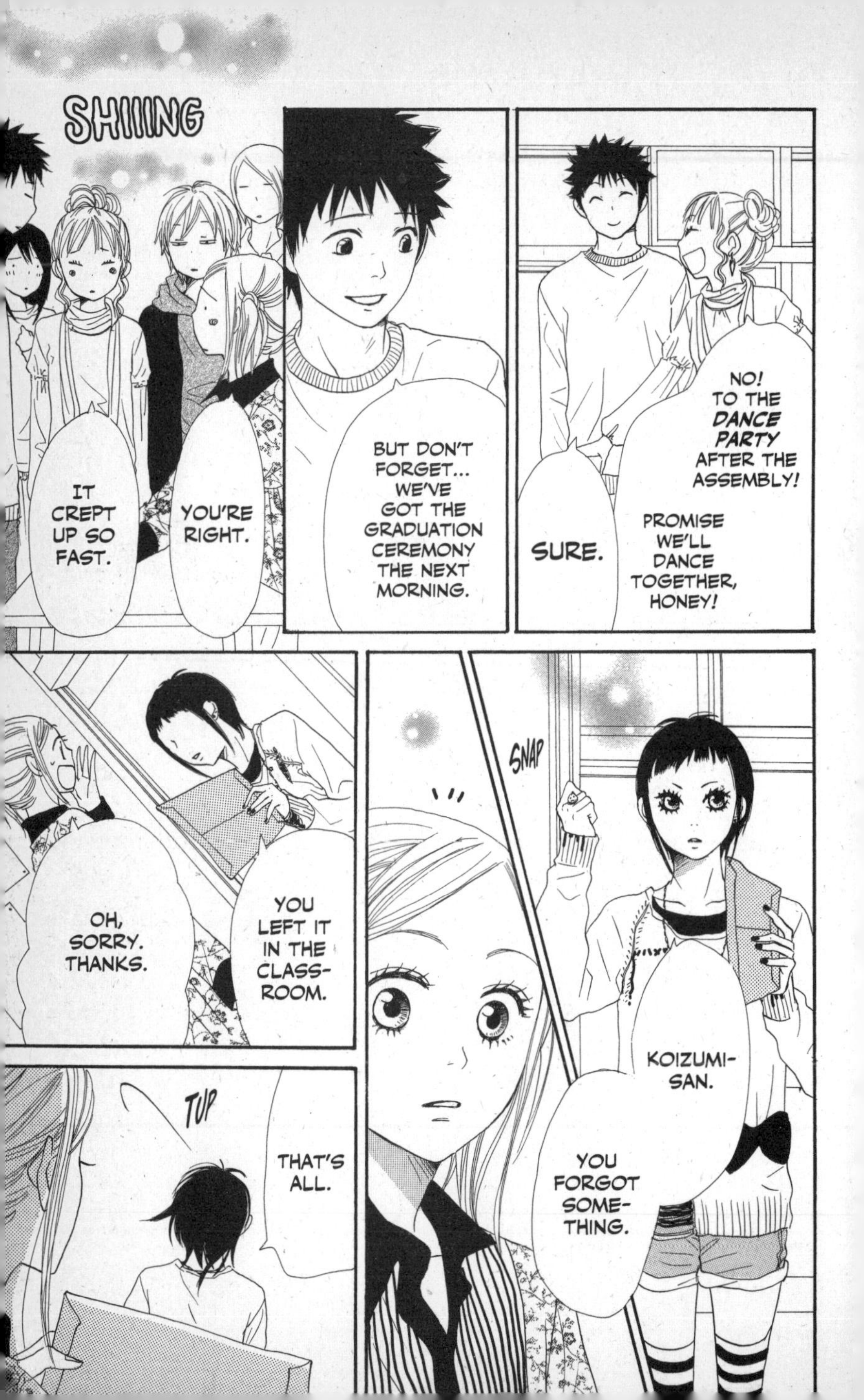
NO! TO THE DANCE PARTY AFTER THE ASSEMBLY!
PROMISE WE'LL DANCE TOGETHER, HONEY!
SURE.
BUT DON'T FORGET... WE'VE GOT THE GRADUATION CEREMONY THE NEXT MORNING.
SHIIING
YOU'RE RIGHT.
IT CREPT UP SO FAST.
SNAP
KOIZUMI-SAN.
YOU FORGOT SOMETHING.
YOU LEFT IT IN THE CLASSROOM.
OH, SORRY. THANKS.
TUP
THAT'S ALL.

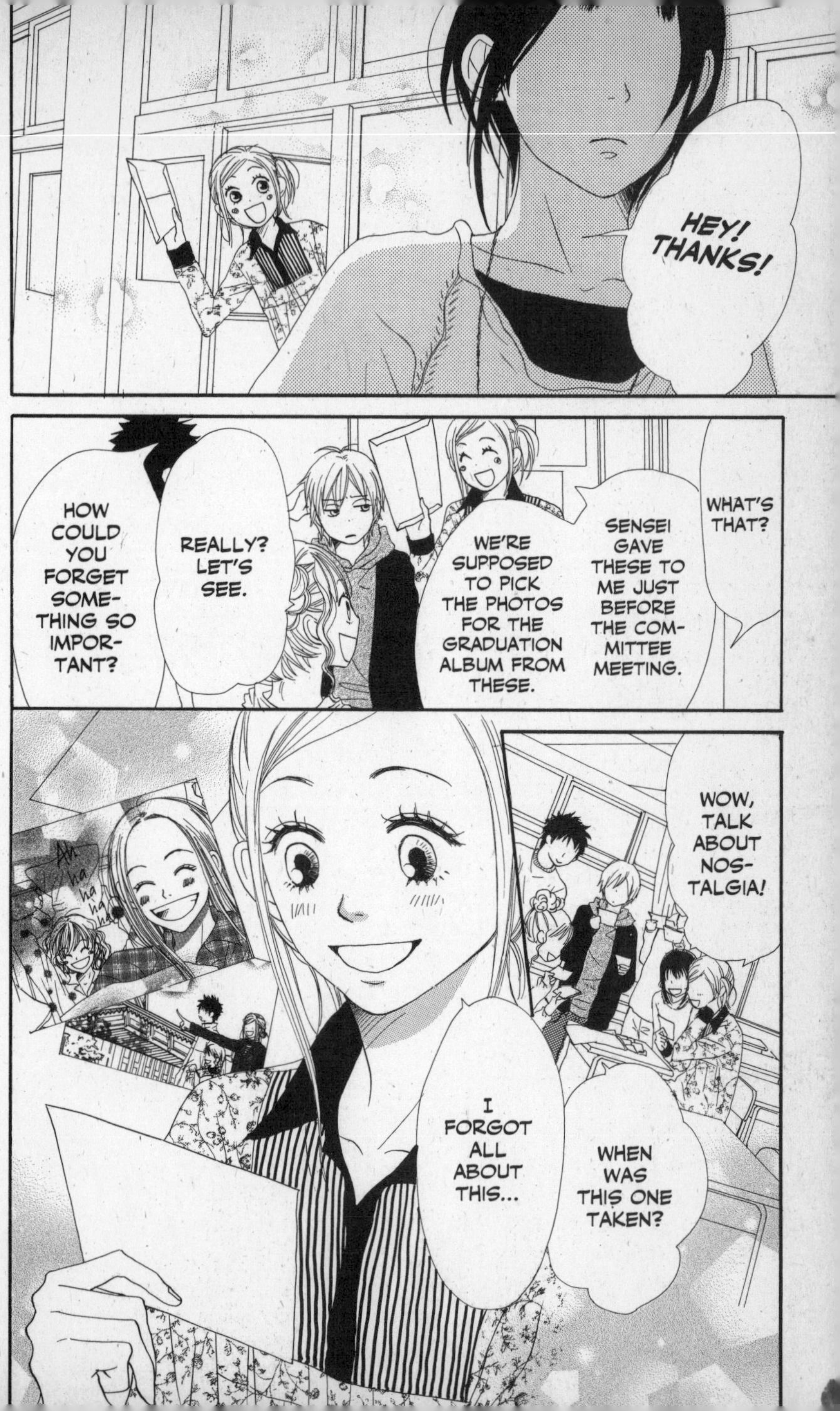
HEY! THANKS!
WHAT'S THAT?
SENSEI GAVE THESE TO ME JUST BEFORE THE COM-MITTEE MEETING.
WE'RE SUPPOSED TO PICK THE PHOTOS FOR THE GRADUATION ALBUM FROM THESE.
REALLY? LET'S SEE.
HOW COULD YOU FORGET SOME-THING SO IMPOR-TANT?
WOW, TALK ABOUT NOS-TALGIA!
Ah ha ha ha ha
WHEN WAS THIS ONE TAKEN?
I FORGOT ALL ABOUT THIS...

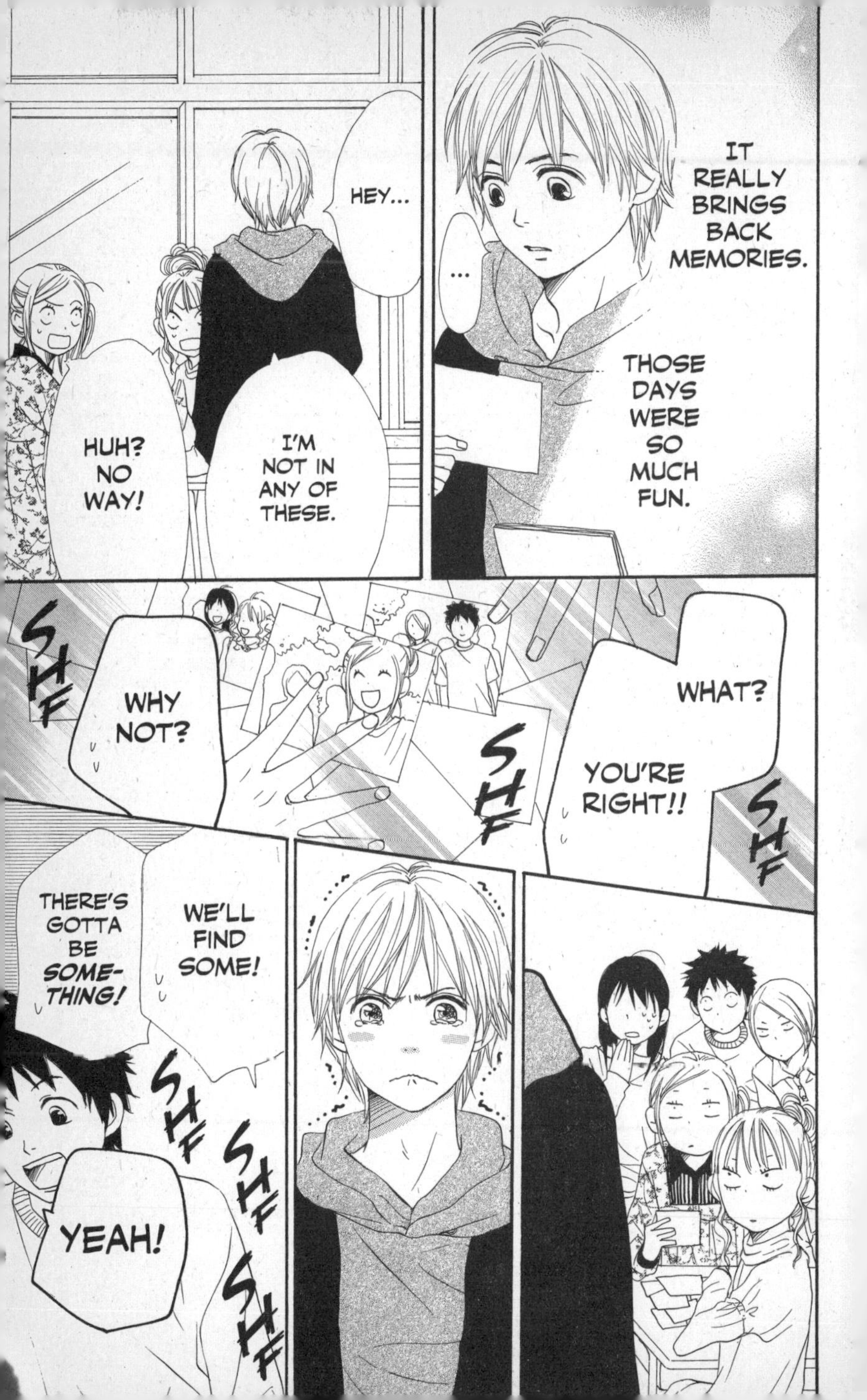
IT REALLY BRINGS BACK MEMORIES.
...
THOSE DAYS WERE SO MUCH FUN.
HEY...
I'M NOT IN ANY OF THESE.
HUH? NO WAY!
SHF
WHAT? YOU'RE RIGHT!!
SHF
WHY NOT?
SHF
WE'LL FIND SOME!
THERE'S GOTTA BE SOME-THING!
SHF
SHF
YEAH!
SHF

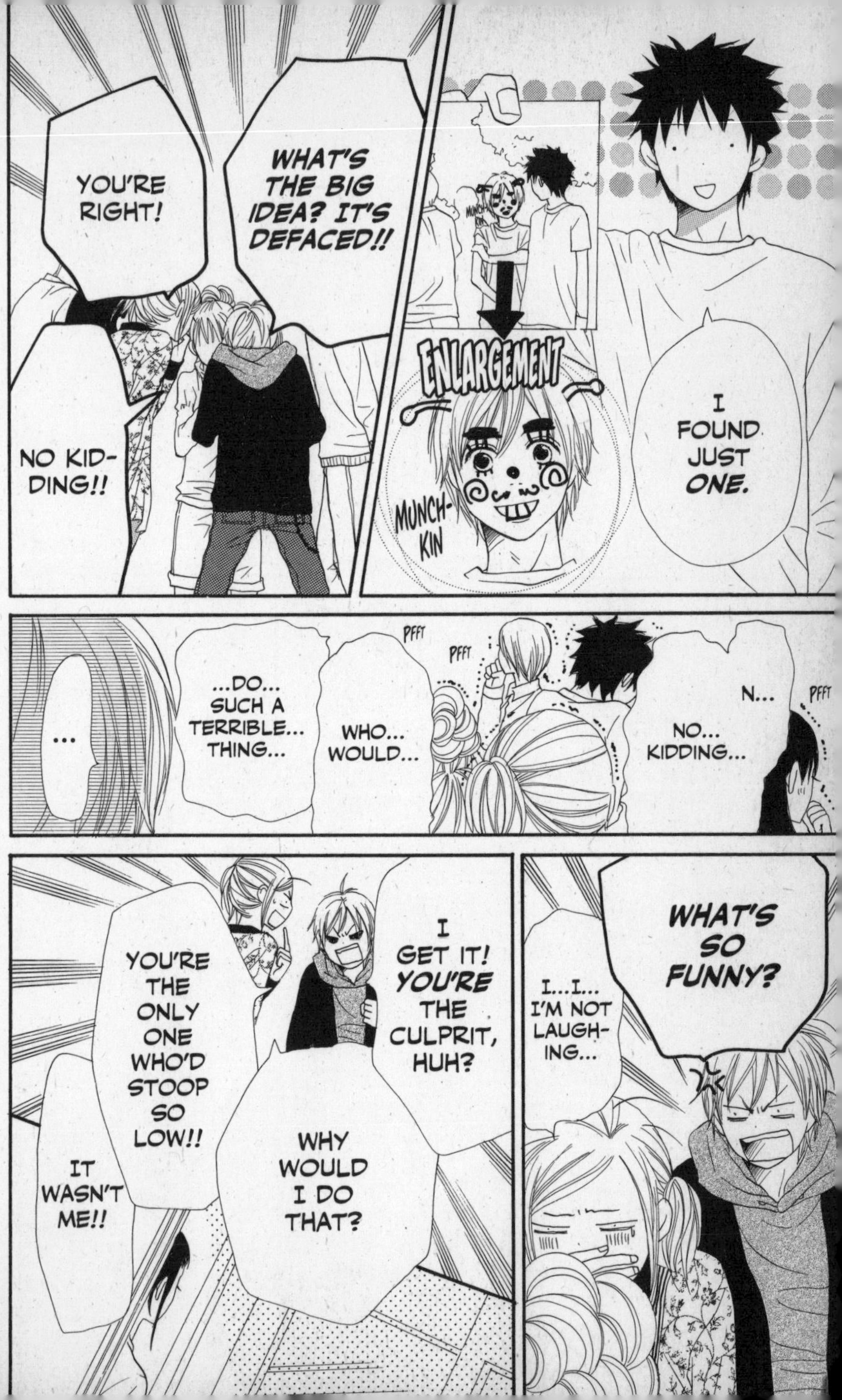
I FOUND JUST ONE.
ENLARGEMENT
MUNCH-KIN
WHAT'S THE BIG IDEA? IT'S DEFACED!!
YOU'RE RIGHT!
NO KID-DING!!
N...
PFFT
NO... KIDDING...
PFFT
PFFT
WHO... WOULD...
...DO... SUCH A TERRIBLE... THING...
...
WHAT'S SO FUNNY?
I...I... I'M NOT LAUGH-ING...
I GET IT! YOU'RE THE CULPRIT, HUH?
YOU'RE THE ONLY ONE WHO'D STOOP SO LOW!!
WHY WOULD I DO THAT?
IT WASN'T ME!!

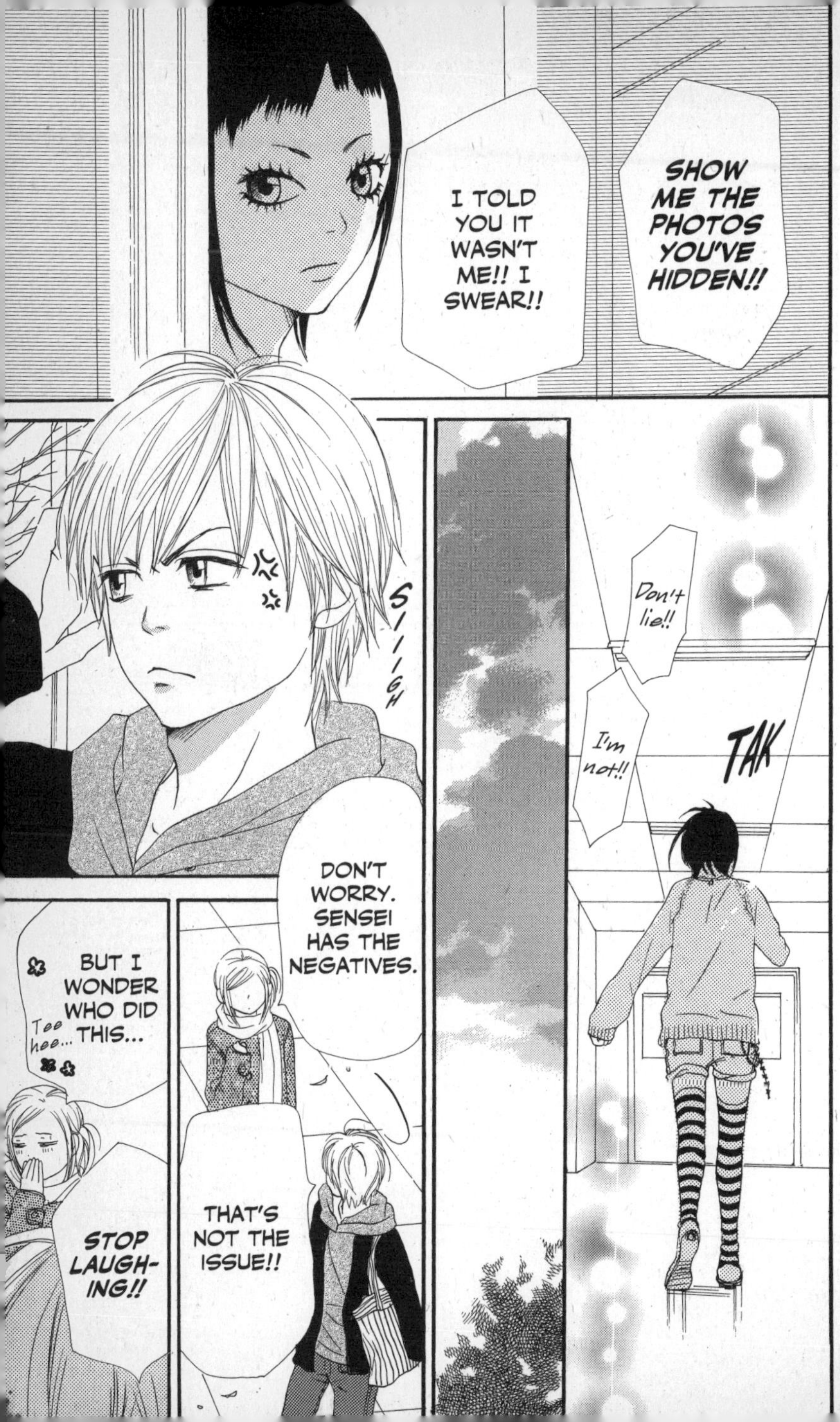
SHOW ME THE PHOTOS YOU'VE HIDDEN!!
I TOLD YOU IT WASN'T ME!! I SWEAR!!
Don't lie!!
I'm not!!
TAK
SIIIGH
DON'T WORRY. SENSEI HAS THE NEGATIVES.
THAT'S NOT THE ISSUE!!
BUT I WONDER WHO DID THIS...
Tee hee...
STOP LAUGHING!!

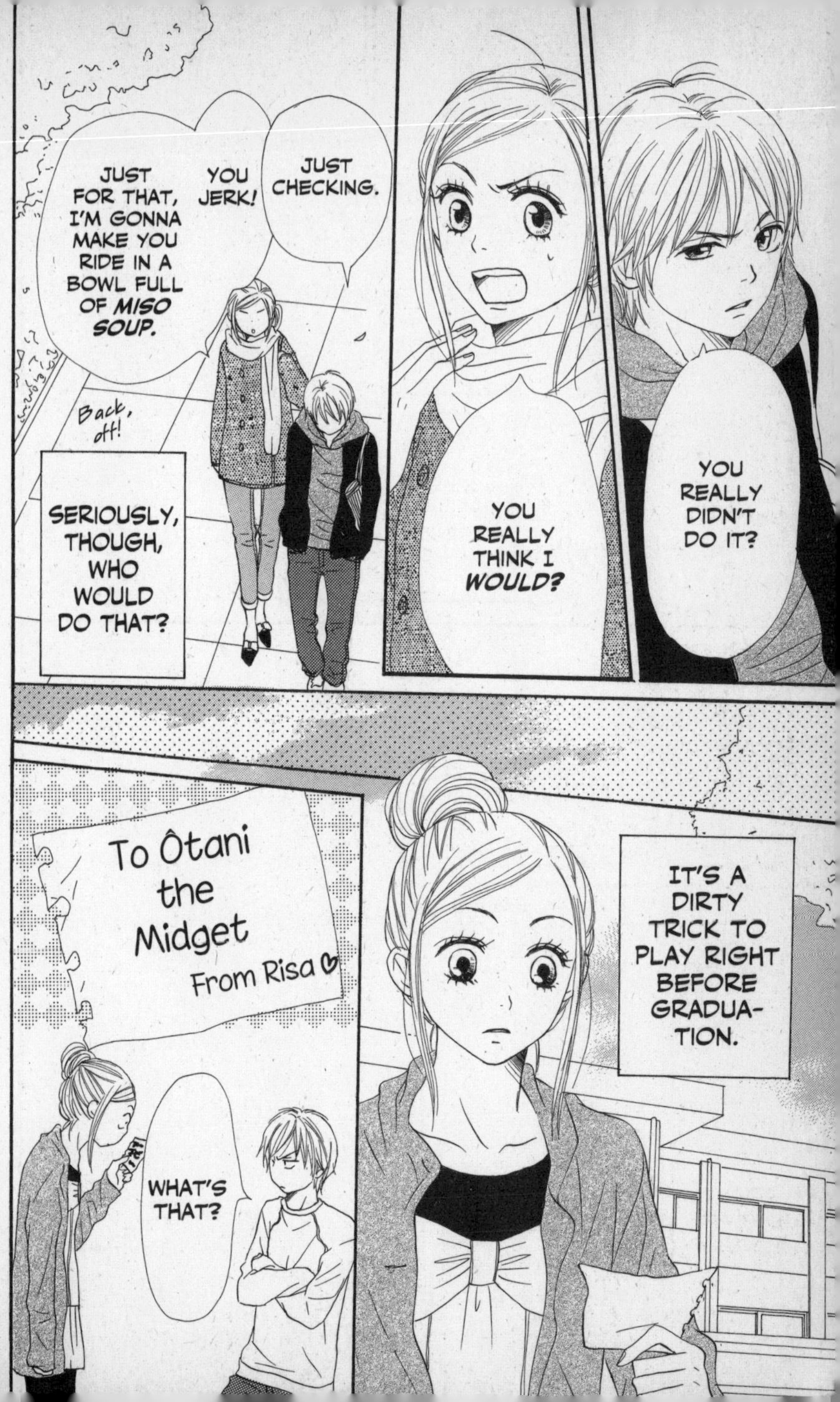
YOU REALLY DIDN'T DO IT?
YOU REALLY THINK I WOULD?
JUST CHECKING.
YOU JERK!
JUST FOR THAT, I'M GONNA MAKE YOU RIDE IN A BOWL FULL OF MISO SOUP.
Back, off!
SERIOUSLY, THOUGH, WHO WOULD DO THAT?
IT'S A DIRTY TRICK TO PLAY RIGHT BEFORE GRADUATION.
To Ôtani the Midget
From Risa ♡
WHAT'S THAT?

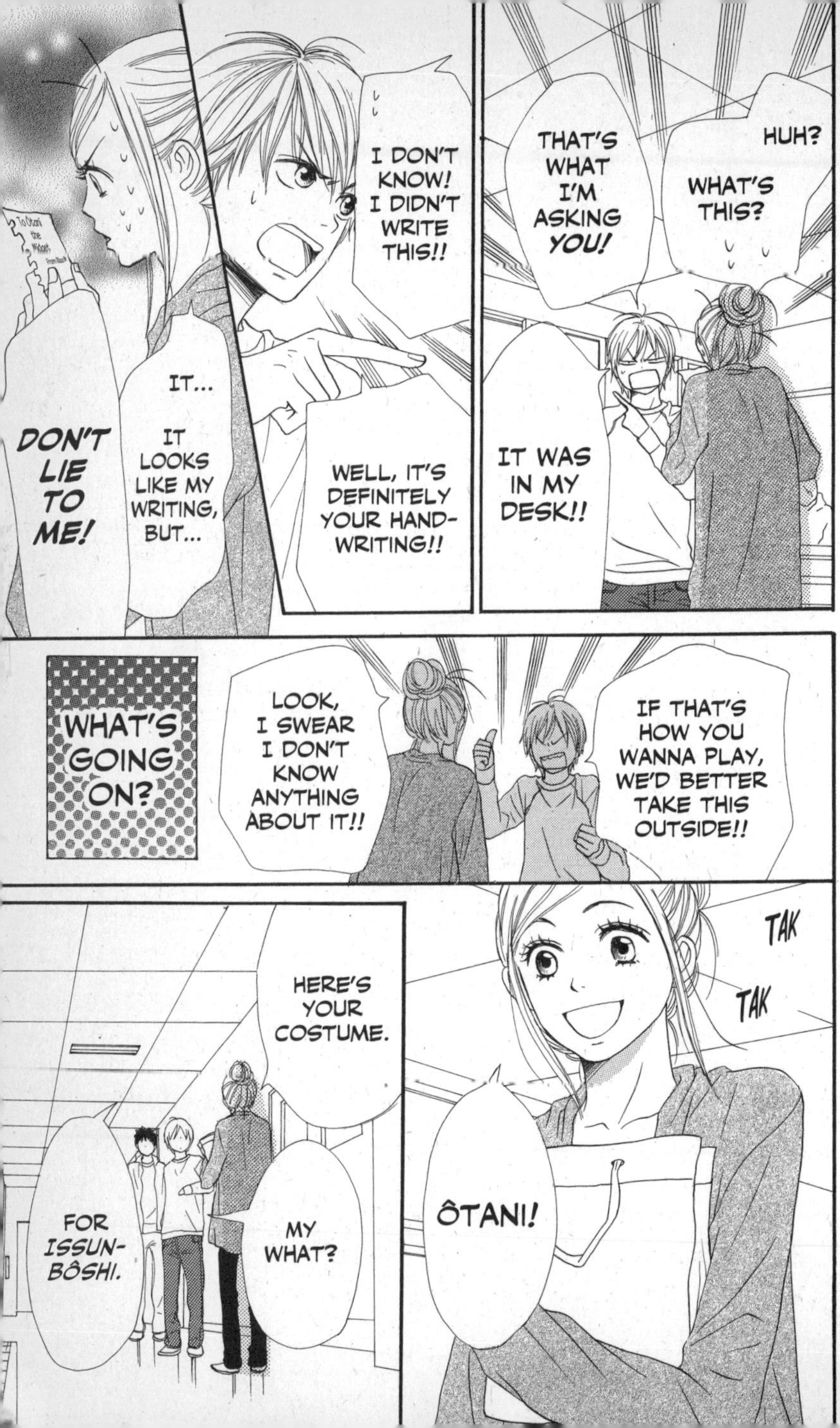
HUH? WHAT'S THIS?
THAT'S WHAT I'M ASKING YOU!
IT WAS IN MY DESK!!
I DON'T KNOW! I DIDN'T WRITE THIS!!
WELL, IT'S DEFINITELY YOUR HAND-WRITING!!
To Otani the Midget, From Risa
IT...
IT LOOKS LIKE MY WRITING, BUT...
DON'T LIE TO ME!
IF THAT'S HOW YOU WANNA PLAY, WE'D BETTER TAKE THIS OUTSIDE!!
LOOK, I SWEAR I DON'T KNOW ANYTHING ABOUT IT!!
WHAT'S GOING ON?
TAK
TAK
ÔTANI!
HERE'S YOUR COSTUME.
MY WHAT?
FOR ISSUN-BÔSHI.

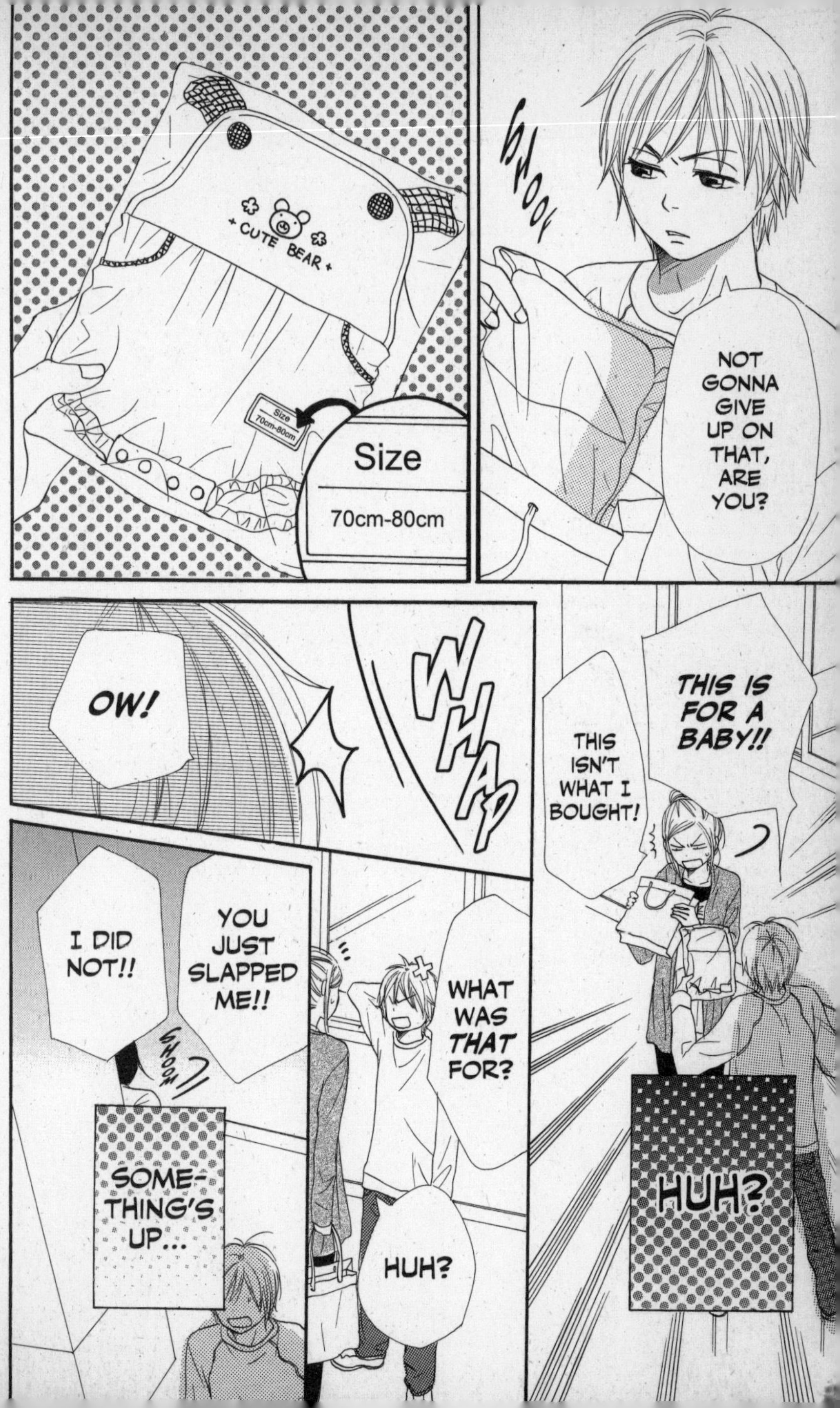
NOT GONNA GIVE UP ON THAT, ARE YOU?
+CUTE BEAR+
Size
70cm-80cm
THIS IS FOR A BABY!!
THIS ISN'T WHAT I BOUGHT!
HUH?
WHAP
OW!
WHAT WAS THAT FOR?
YOU JUST SLAPPED ME!!
I DID NOT!!
HUH?
SOME-THING'S UP...

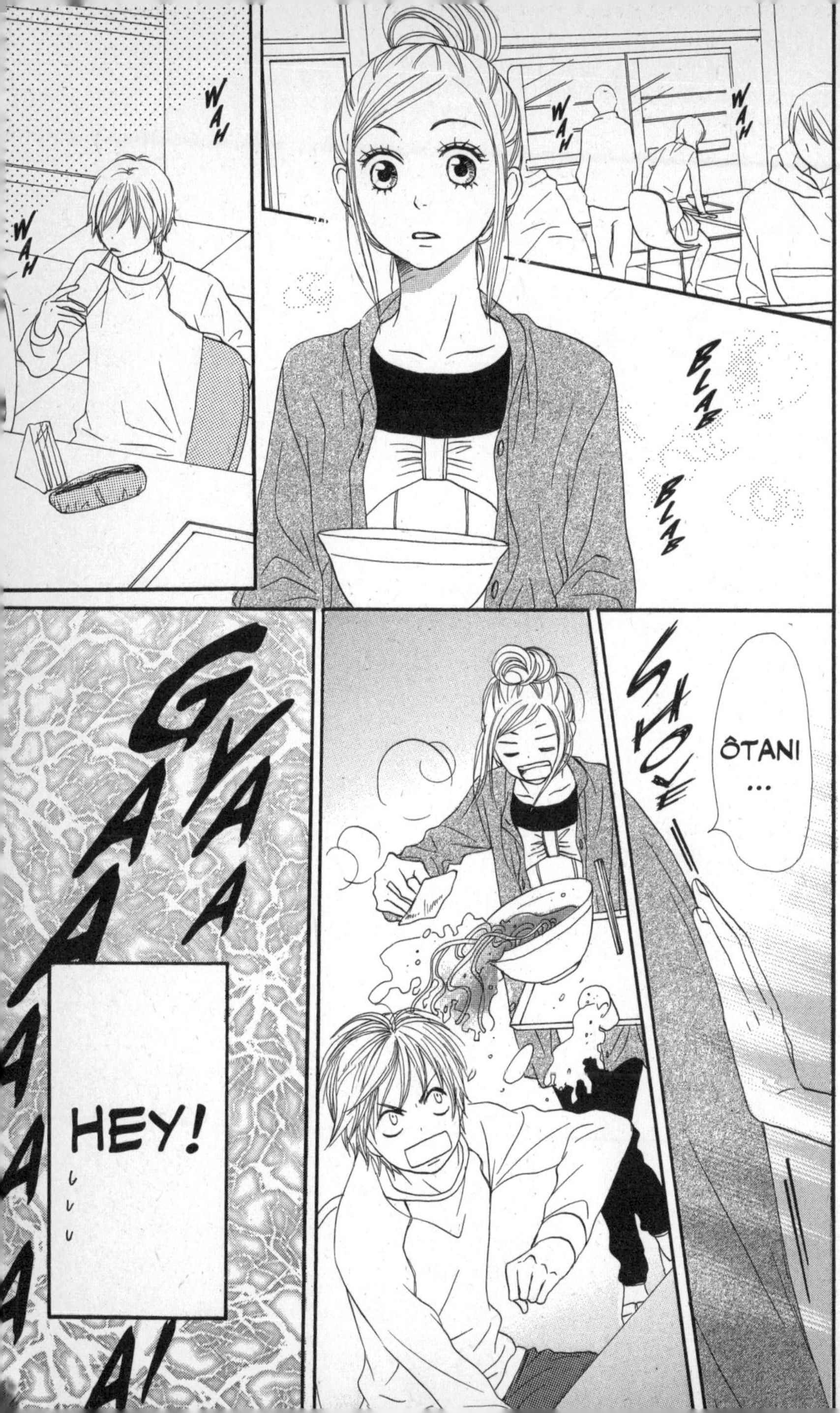
WAH
WAH
BLAB
BLAB
WAH
WAH
ÔTANI ...
SHOVE
GYAAAAAAAAAAA!
HEY!

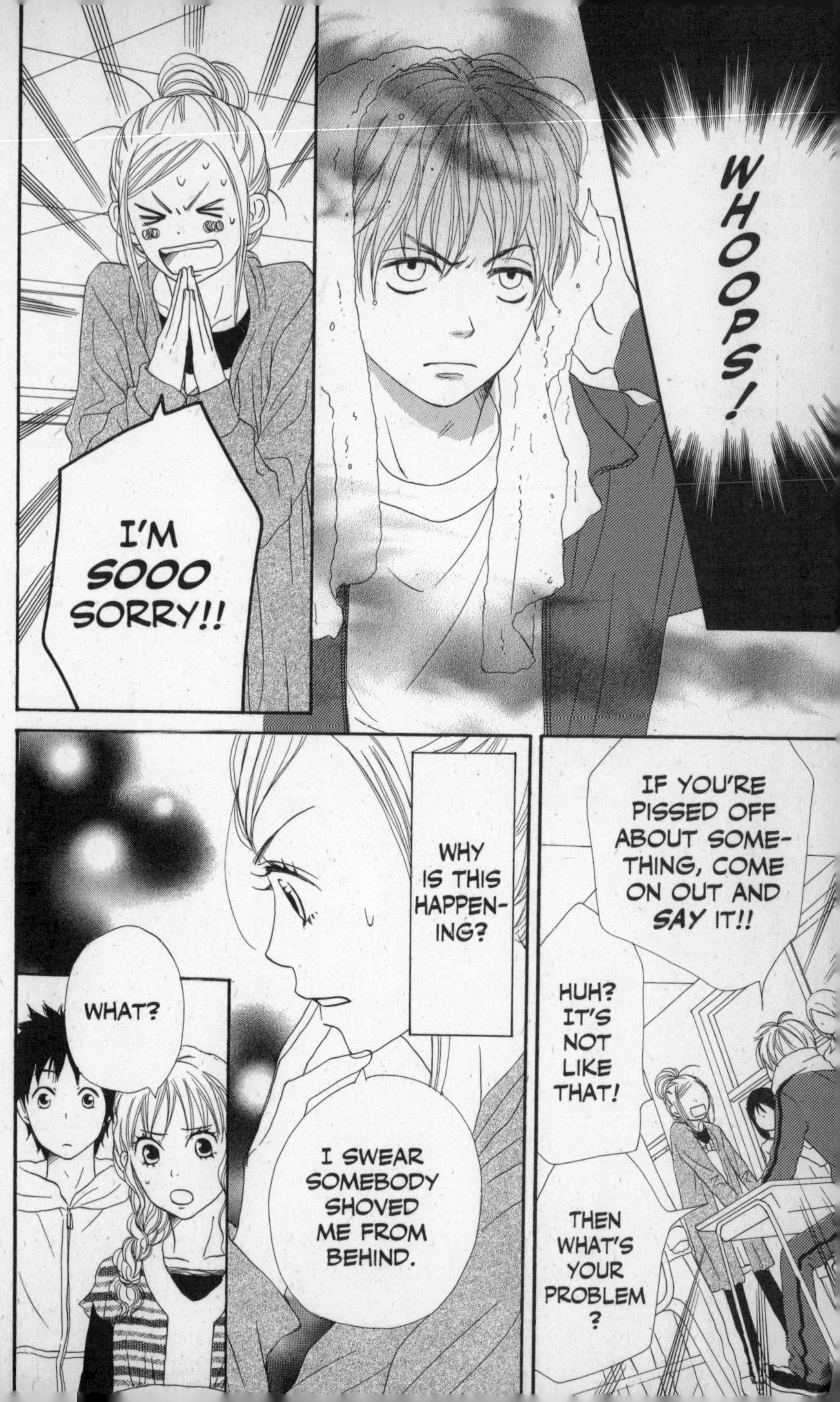
WHOOPS!
I'M SOOO SORRY!!
IF YOU'RE PISSED OFF ABOUT SOME-THING, COME ON OUT AND SAY IT!!
HUH? IT'S NOT LIKE THAT!
THEN WHAT'S YOUR PROBLEM?
WHY IS THIS HAPPEN-ING?
I SWEAR SOMEBODY SHOVED ME FROM BEHIND.
WHAT?

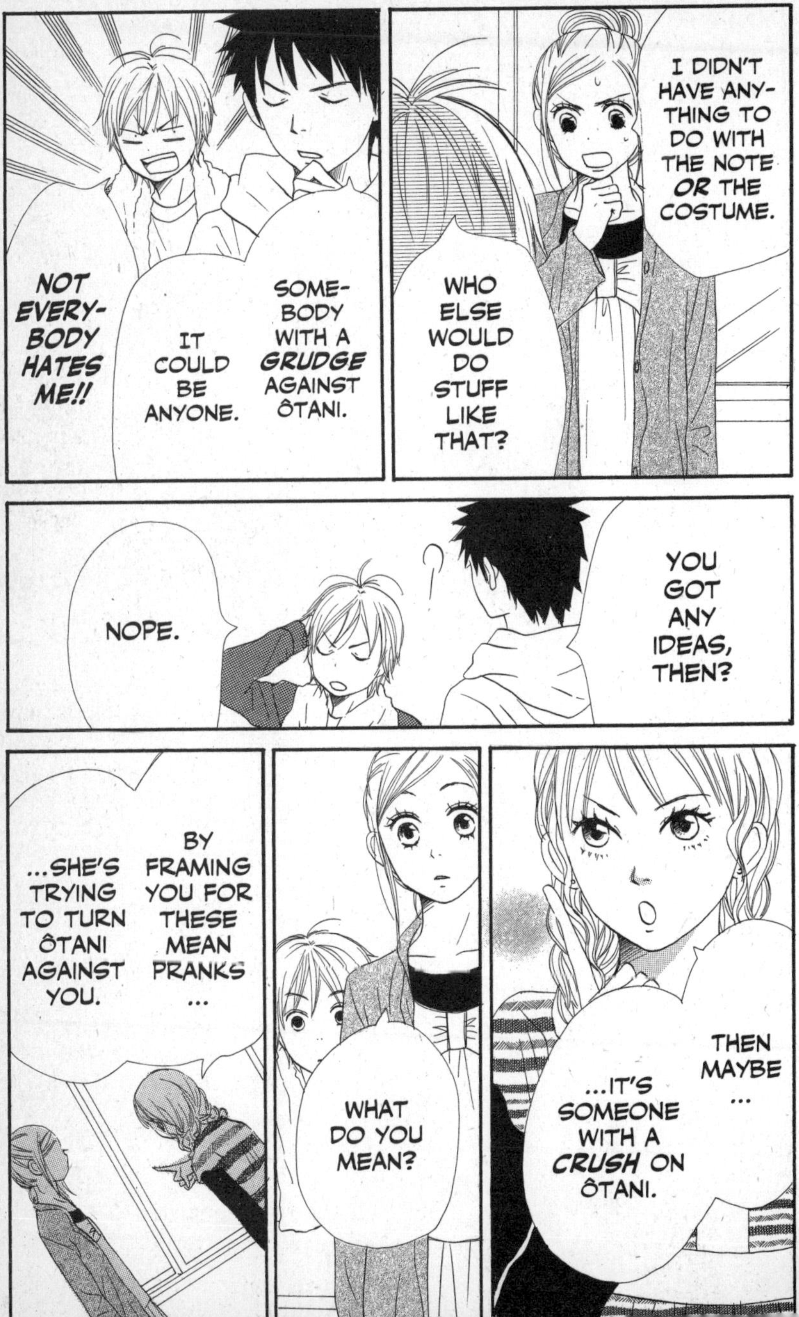
I DIDN'T HAVE ANYTHING TO DO WITH THE NOTE *OR* THE COSTUME.
WHO ELSE WOULD DO STUFF LIKE THAT?
SOMEBODY WITH A *GRUDGE* AGAINST ÔTANI.
IT COULD BE ANYONE.
NOT EVERYBODY HATES ME!!
YOU GOT ANY IDEAS, THEN?
NOPE.
THEN MAYBE...
...IT'S SOMEONE WITH A *CRUSH* ON ÔTANI.
WHAT DO YOU MEAN?
BY FRAMING YOU FOR THESE MEAN PRANKS...
...SHE'S TRYING TO TURN ÔTANI AGAINST YOU.

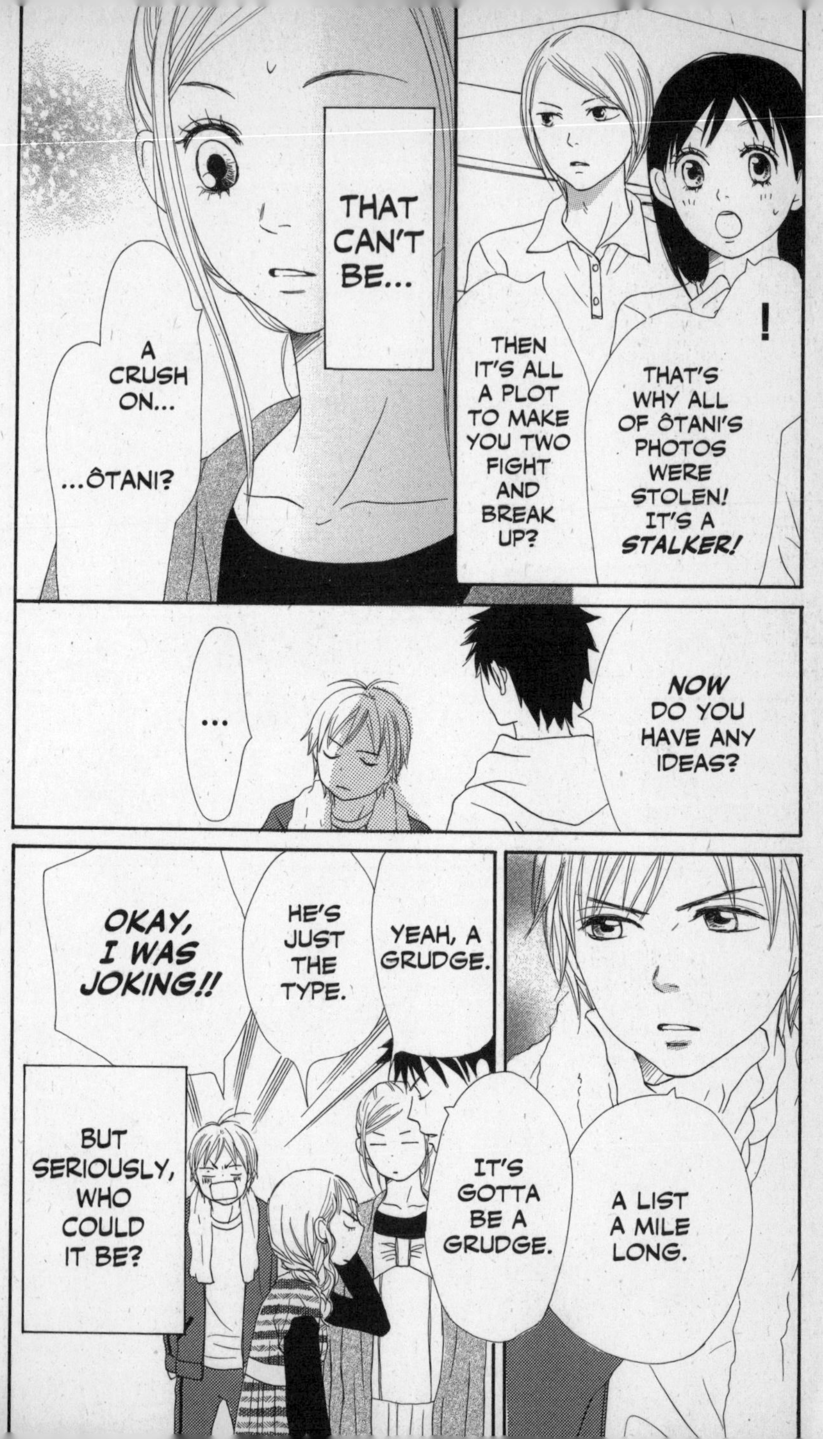
!
THAT'S WHY ALL OF ÔTANI'S PHOTOS WERE STOLEN! IT'S A *STALKER!*
THEN IT'S ALL A PLOT TO MAKE YOU TWO FIGHT AND BREAK UP?
THAT CAN'T BE...
A CRUSH ON...
...ÔTANI?
NOW DO YOU HAVE ANY IDEAS?
...
A LIST A MILE LONG.
IT'S GOTTA BE A GRUDGE.
YEAH, A GRUDGE.
HE'S JUST THE TYPE.
OKAY, I WAS JOKING!!
BUT SERIOUSLY, WHO COULD IT BE?

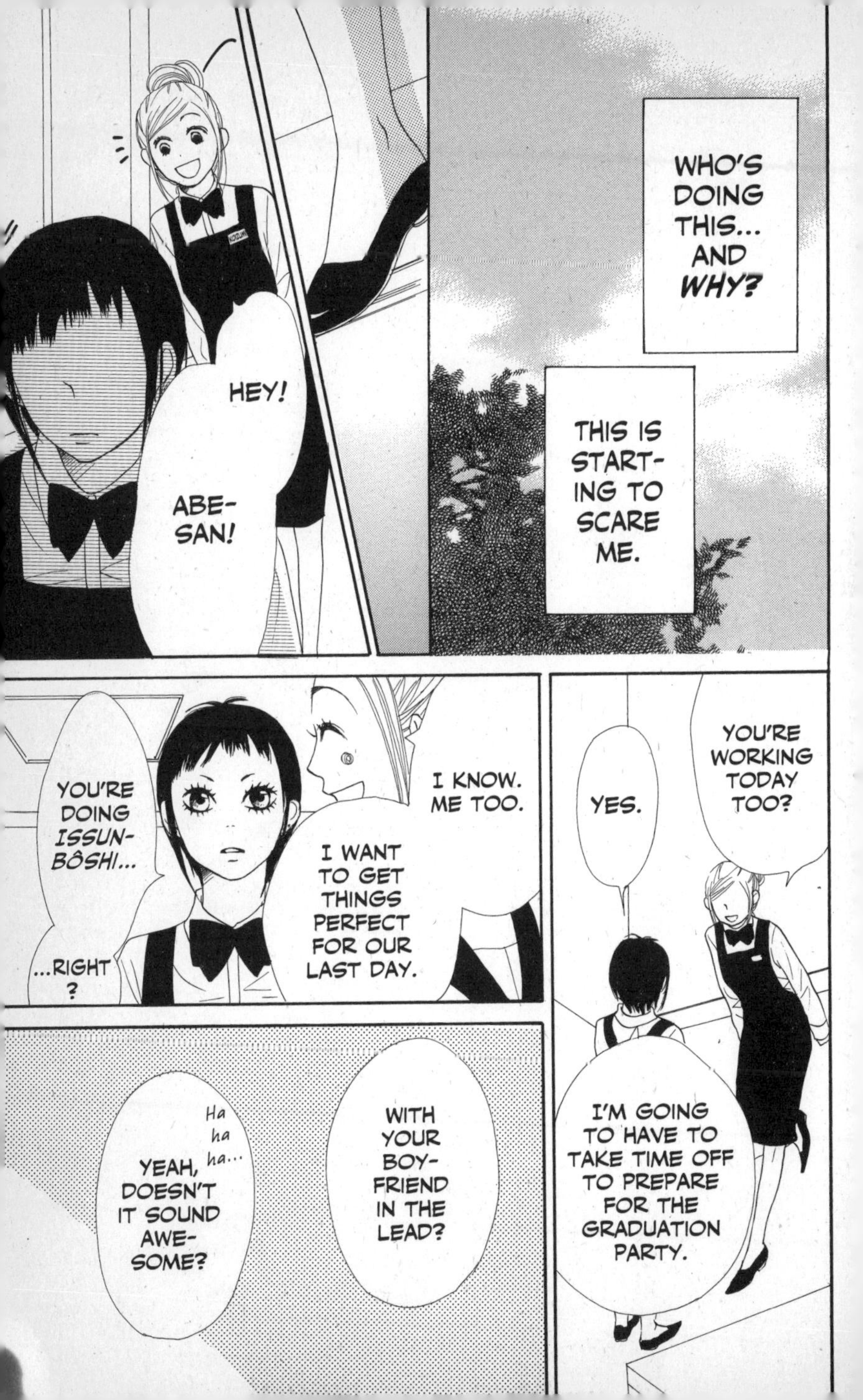
WHO'S DOING THIS... AND *WHY?*
THIS IS STARTING TO SCARE ME.
HEY!
ABE-SAN!
YOU'RE WORKING TODAY TOO?
YES.
I'M GOING TO HAVE TO TAKE TIME OFF TO PREPARE FOR THE GRADUATION PARTY.
I KNOW. ME TOO.
I WANT TO GET THINGS PERFECT FOR OUR LAST DAY.
YOU'RE DOING *ISSUN-BÔSHI*...
...RIGHT?
WITH YOUR BOYFRIEND IN THE LEAD?
YEAH, DOESN'T IT SOUND AWESOME?
Ha ha ha...

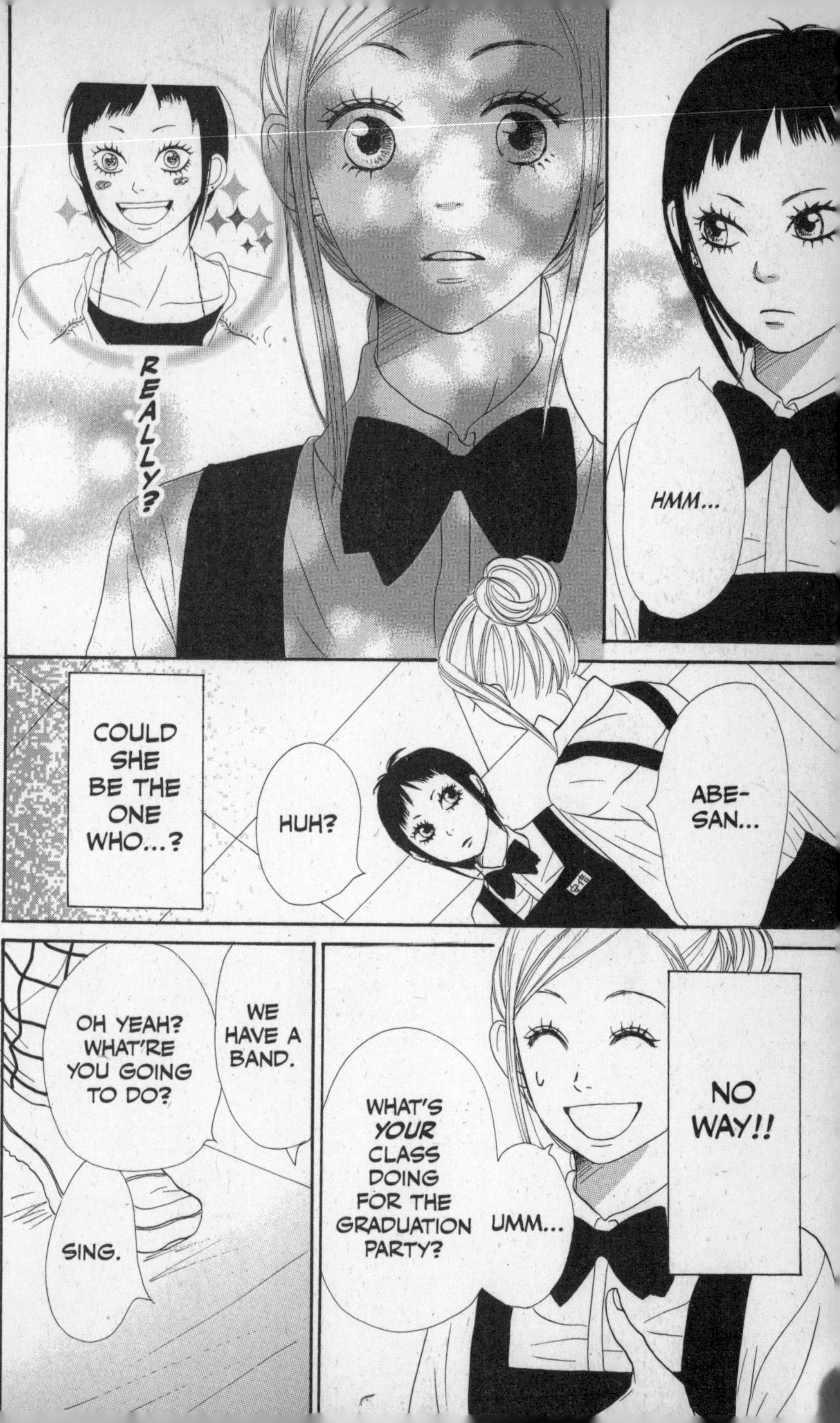
HMM...
REALLY?
ABE-SAN...
HUH?
COULD SHE BE THE ONE WHO...?
NO WAY!!
WHAT'S *YOUR* CLASS DOING FOR THE GRADUATION PARTY?
UMM...
WE HAVE A BAND.
OH YEAH? WHAT'RE YOU GOING TO DO?
SING.

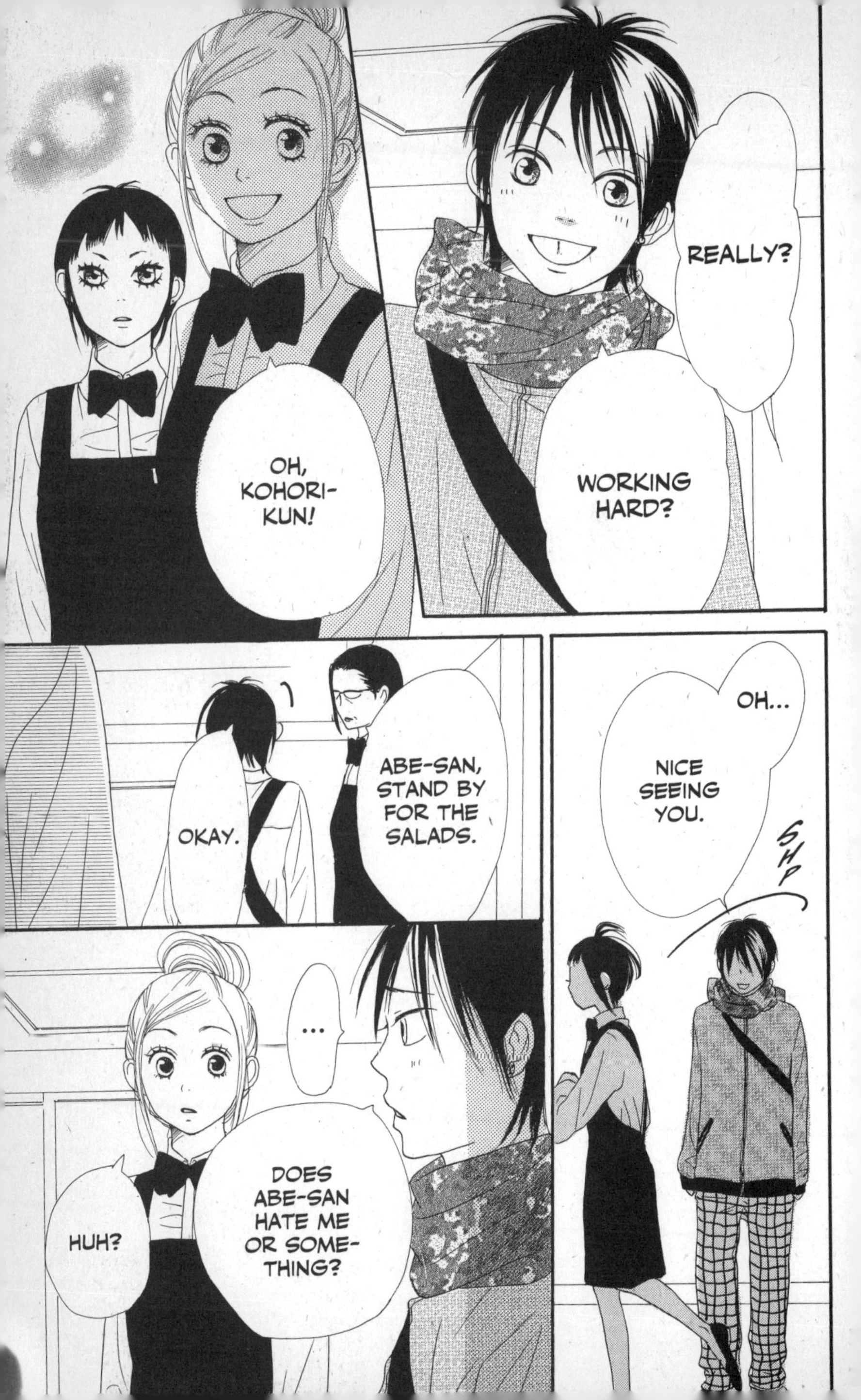
REALLY?
WORKING HARD?
OH, KOHORI-KUN!
OH...
NICE SEEING YOU.
SHP
ABE-SAN, STAND BY FOR THE SALADS.
OKAY.
...
DOES ABE-SAN HATE ME OR SOME-THING?
HUH?

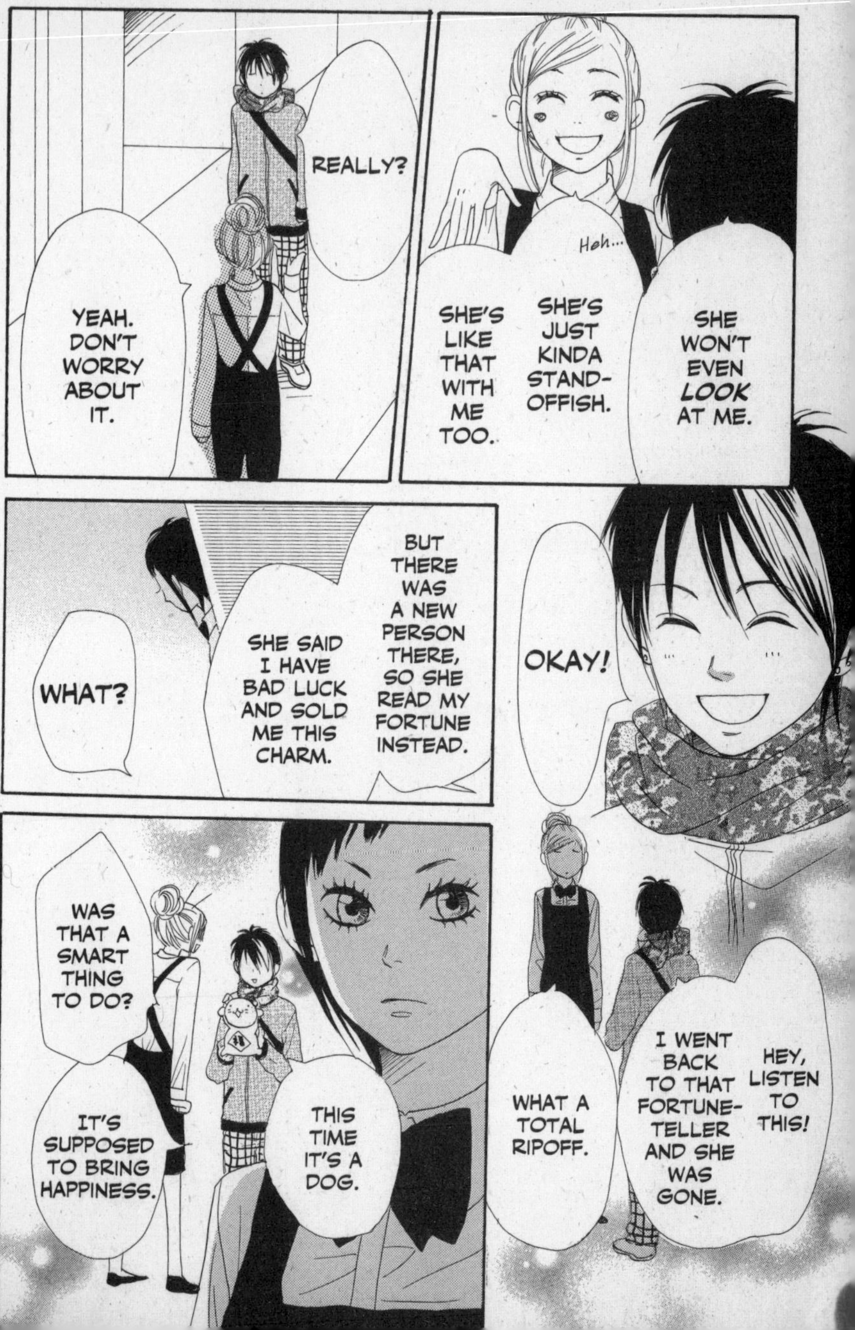

SHE WON'T EVEN LOOK AT ME.
SHE'S JUST KINDA STAND-OFFISH.
Heh...
SHE'S LIKE THAT WITH ME TOO.
REALLY?
YEAH. DON'T WORRY ABOUT IT.
OKAY!
HEY, LISTEN TO THIS!
I WENT BACK TO THAT FORTUNE-TELLER AND SHE WAS GONE.
WHAT A TOTAL RIPOFF.
BUT THERE WAS A NEW PERSON THERE, SO SHE READ MY FORTUNE INSTEAD.
SHE SAID I HAVE BAD LUCK AND SOLD ME THIS CHARM.
WHAT?
THIS TIME IT'S A DOG.
IT'S SUPPOSED TO BRING HAPPINESS.
WAS THAT A SMART THING TO DO?

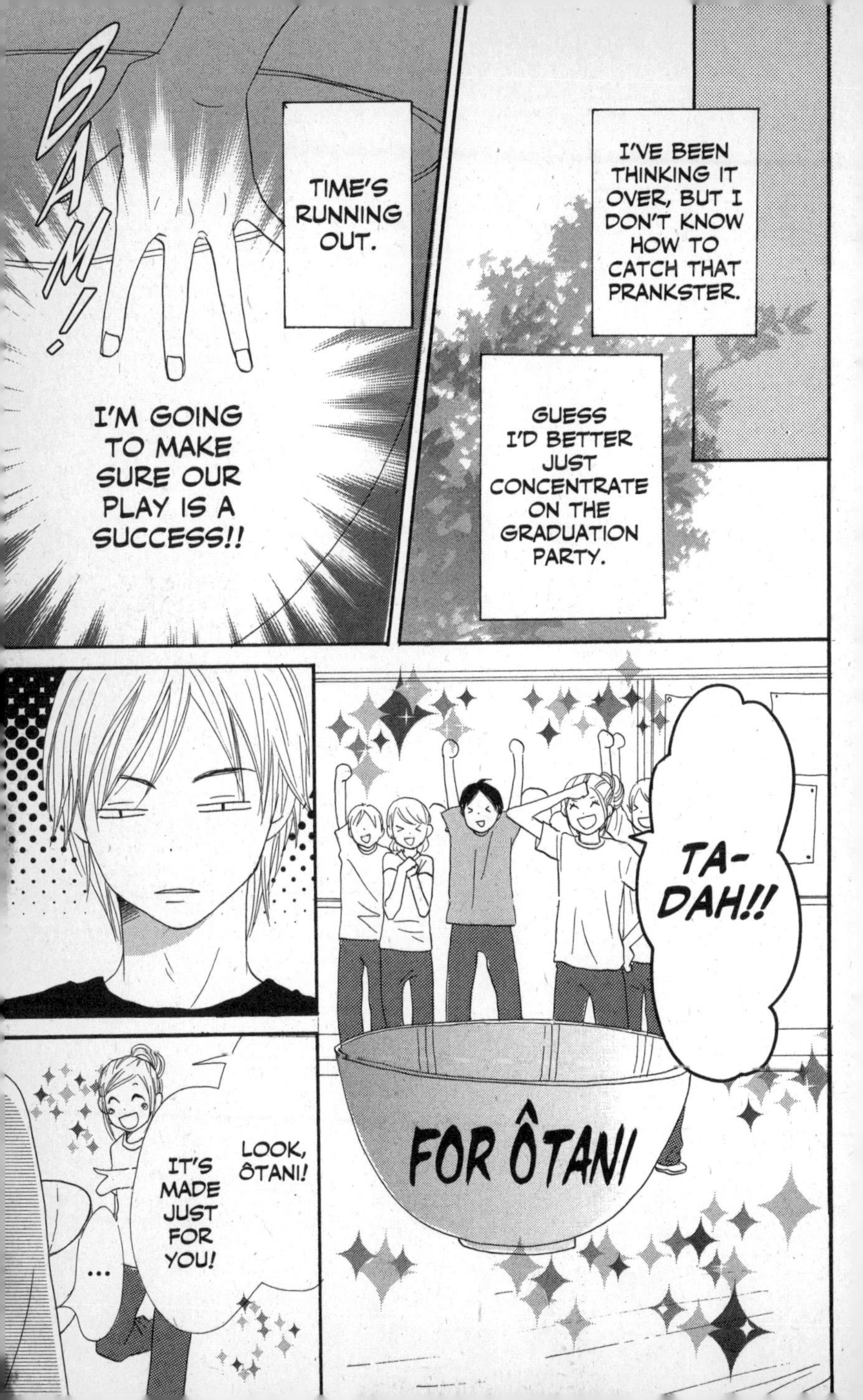
I'VE BEEN THINKING IT OVER, BUT I DON'T KNOW HOW TO CATCH THAT PRANKSTER.
GUESS I'D BETTER JUST CONCENTRATE ON THE GRADUATION PARTY.
TIME'S RUNNING OUT.
BAM!
I'M GOING TO MAKE SURE OUR PLAY IS A SUCCESS!!
TA-DAH!!
FOR ÔTANI
LOOK, ÔTANI!
IT'S MADE JUST FOR YOU!
...

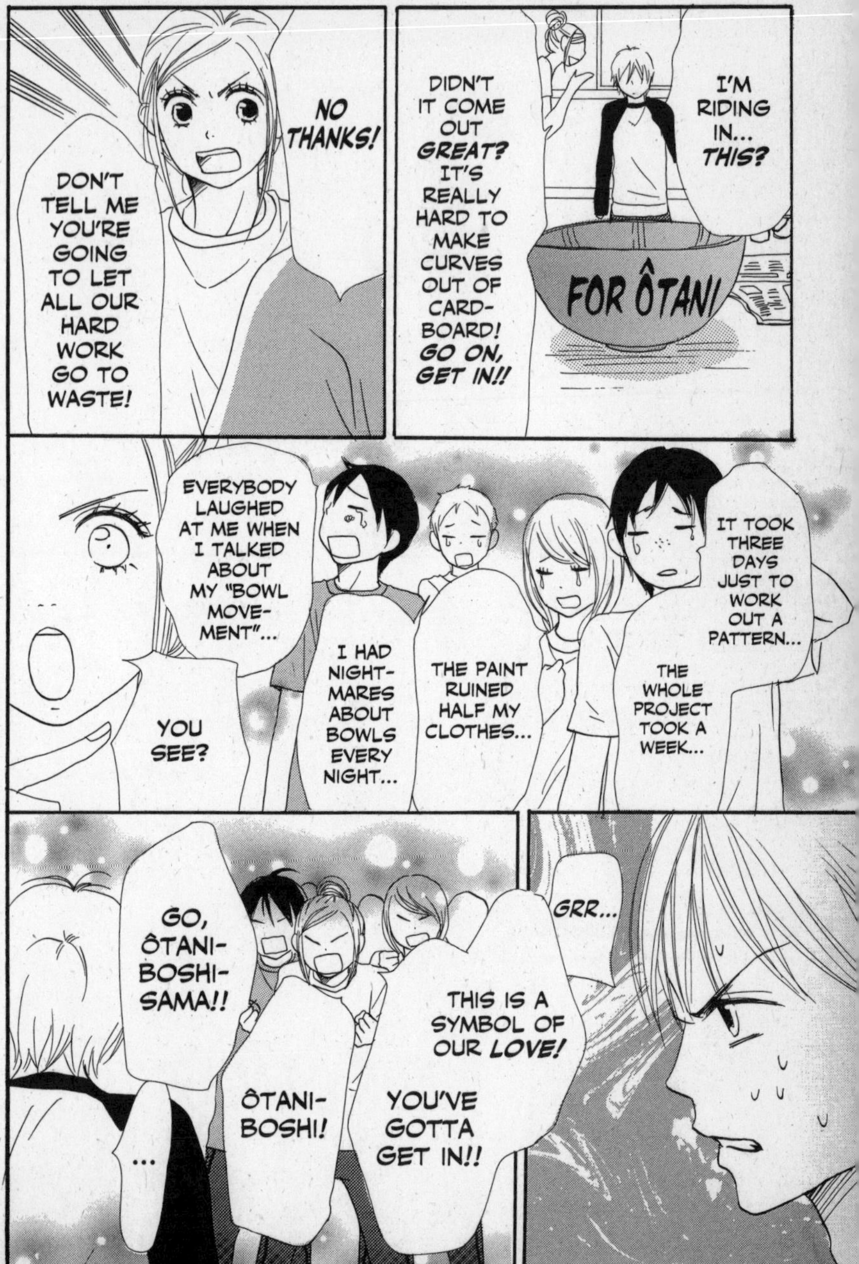
I'M RIDING IN... THIS?
FOR ÔTANI
DIDN'T IT COME OUT GREAT? IT'S REALLY HARD TO MAKE CURVES OUT OF CARD-BOARD! GO ON, GET IN!!
NO THANKS!
DON'T TELL ME YOU'RE GOING TO LET ALL OUR HARD WORK GO TO WASTE!
IT TOOK THREE DAYS JUST TO WORK OUT A PATTERN...
THE WHOLE PROJECT TOOK A WEEK...
THE PAINT RUINED HALF MY CLOTHES...
I HAD NIGHT-MARES ABOUT BOWLS EVERY NIGHT...
EVERYBODY LAUGHED AT ME WHEN I TALKED ABOUT MY "BOWL MOVE-MENT"...
YOU SEE?
GRR...
THIS IS A SYMBOL OF OUR LOVE!
GO, ÔTANI-BOSHI-SAMA!!
YOU'VE GOTTA GET IN!!
ÔTANI-BOSHI!
...

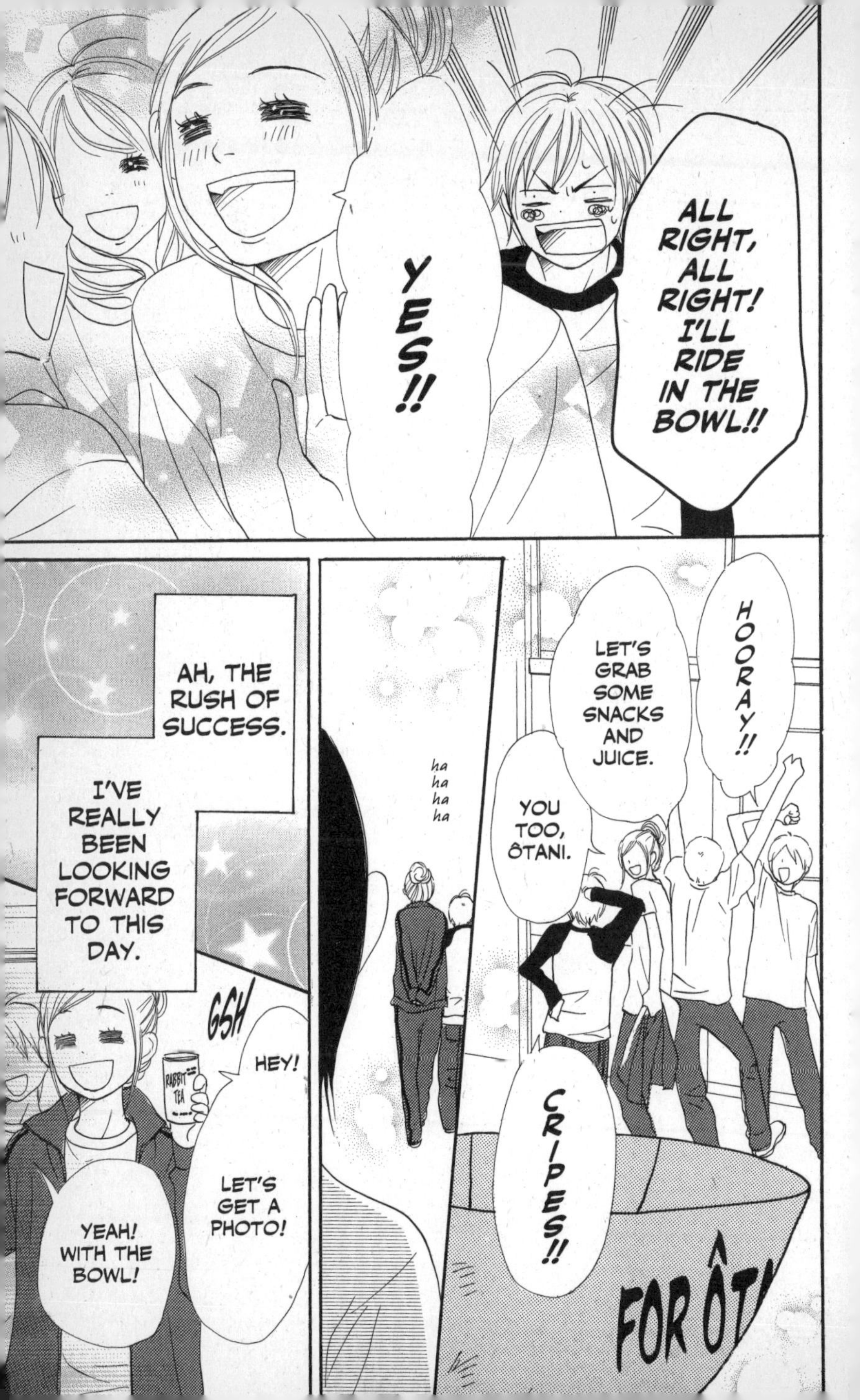
ALL RIGHT, ALL RIGHT! I'LL RIDE IN THE BOWL!!
YES!!
HOORAY!!
LET'S GRAB SOME SNACKS AND JUICE.
YOU TOO, ÔTANI.
ha ha ha ha
CRIPES!!
FOR ÔT
AH, THE RUSH OF SUCCESS.
I'VE REALLY BEEN LOOKING FORWARD TO THIS DAY.
GSH
HEY!
LET'S GET A PHOTO!
RABBIT TEA
YEAH! WITH THE BOWL!

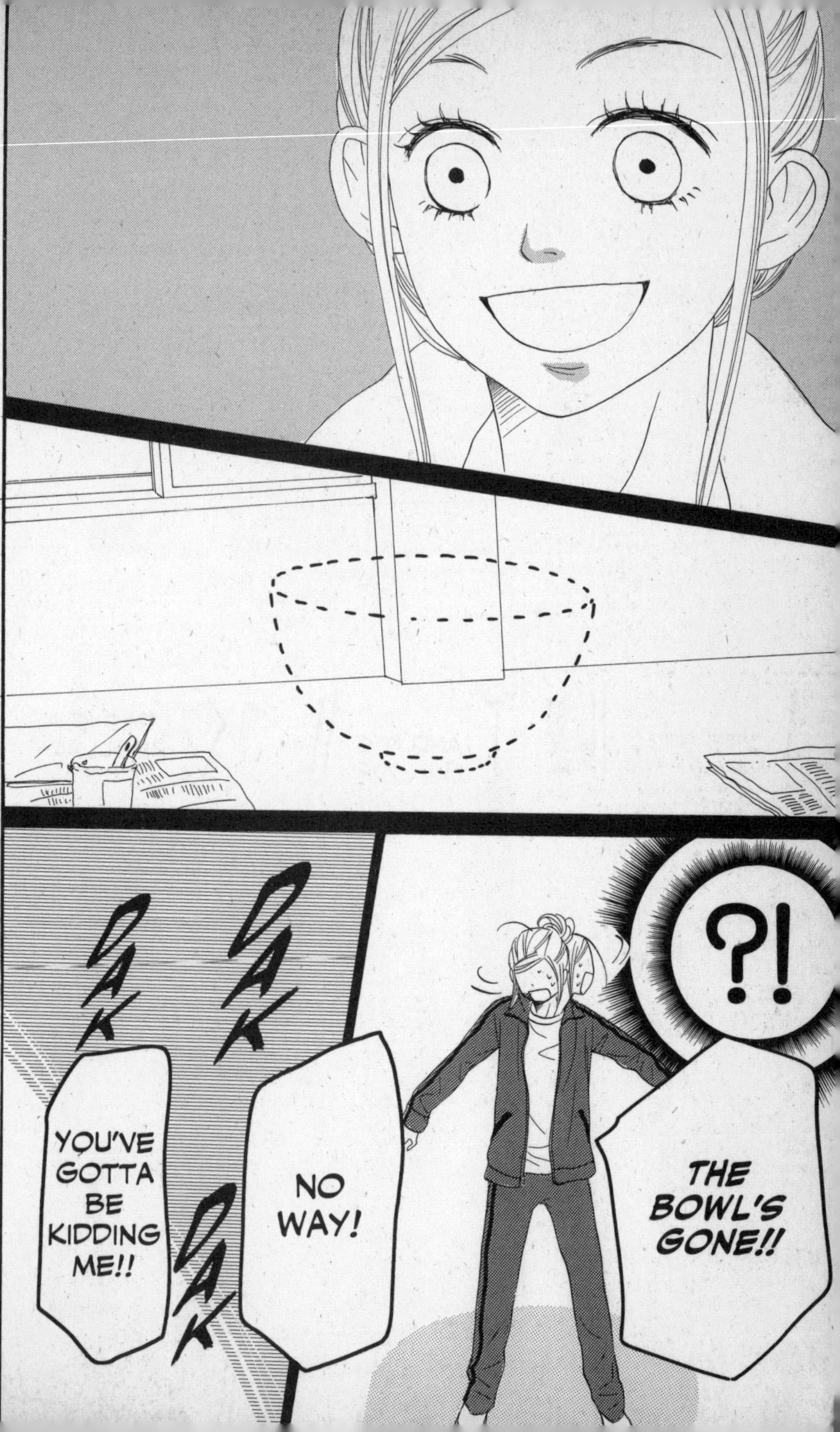
?!
THE BOWL'S GONE!!
NO WAY!
YOU'VE GOTTA BE KIDDING ME!!
DAK
DAK
DAK

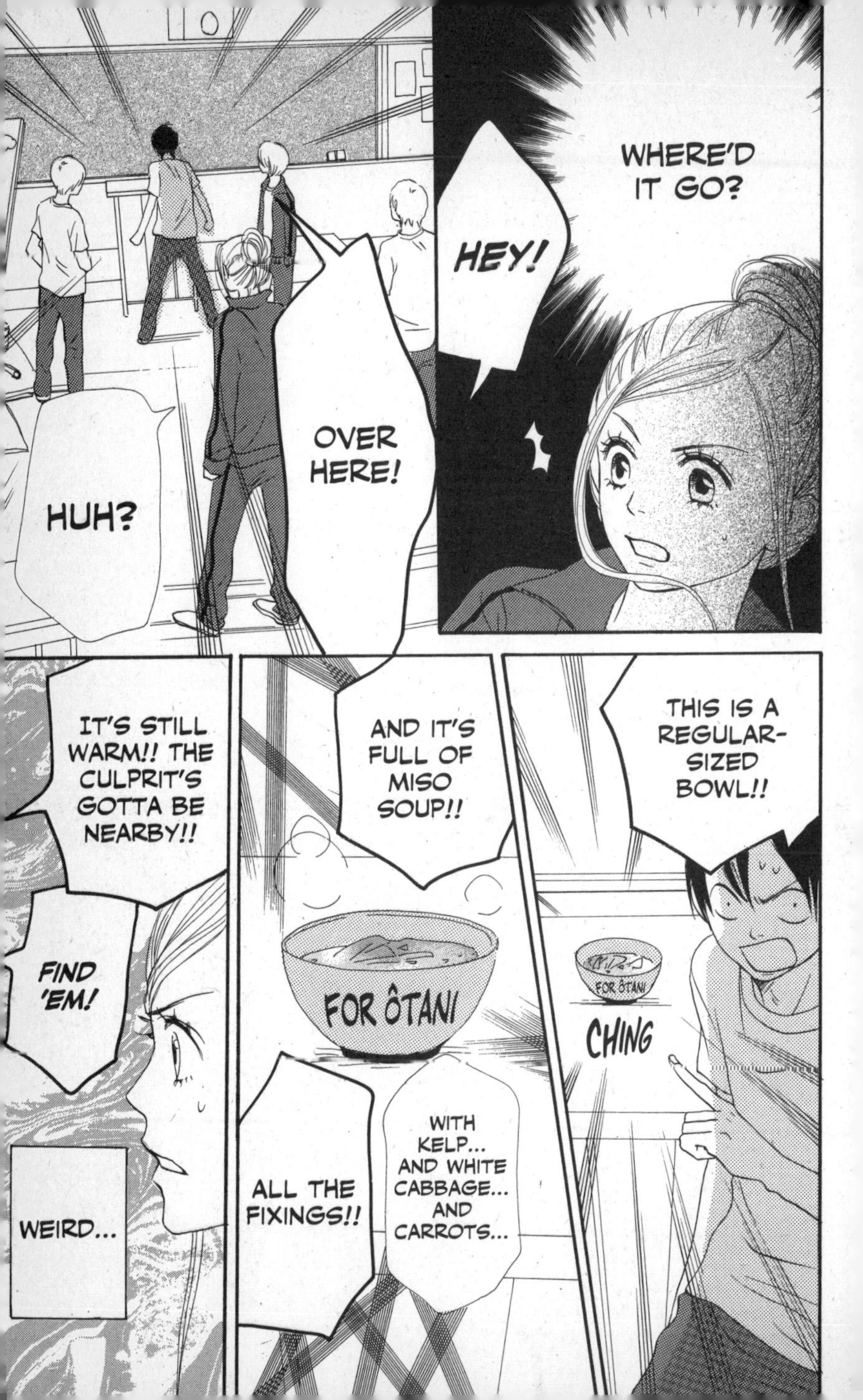
WHERE'D IT GO?
HEY!
OVER HERE!
HUH?
THIS IS A REGULAR-SIZED BOWL!!
FOR ÔTANI
CHING
AND IT'S FULL OF MISO SOUP!!
FOR ÔTANI
WITH KELP... AND WHITE CABBAGE... AND CARROTS...
ALL THE FIXINGS!!
IT'S STILL WARM!! THE CULPRIT'S GOTTA BE NEARBY!!
FIND 'EM!
WEIRD...

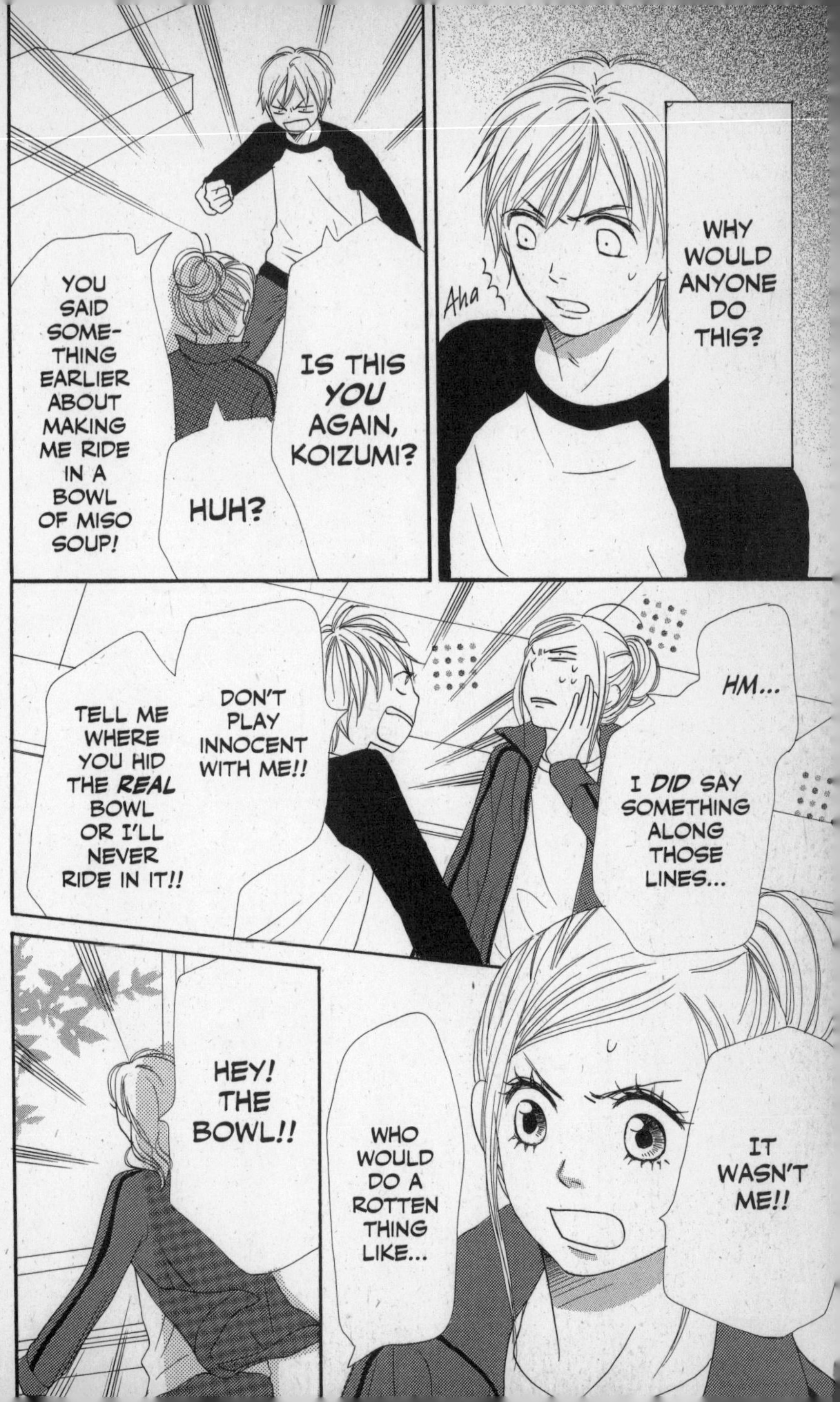
WHY WOULD ANYONE DO THIS?
Aha
IS THIS *YOU* AGAIN, KOIZUMI?
YOU SAID SOME-THING EARLIER ABOUT MAKING ME RIDE IN A BOWL OF MISO SOUP!
HUH?
HM...
I *DID* SAY SOMETHING ALONG THOSE LINES...
DON'T PLAY INNOCENT WITH ME!!
TELL ME WHERE YOU HID THE *REAL* BOWL OR I'LL NEVER RIDE IN IT!!
IT WASN'T ME!!
WHO WOULD DO A ROTTEN THING LIKE...
HEY! THE BOWL!!

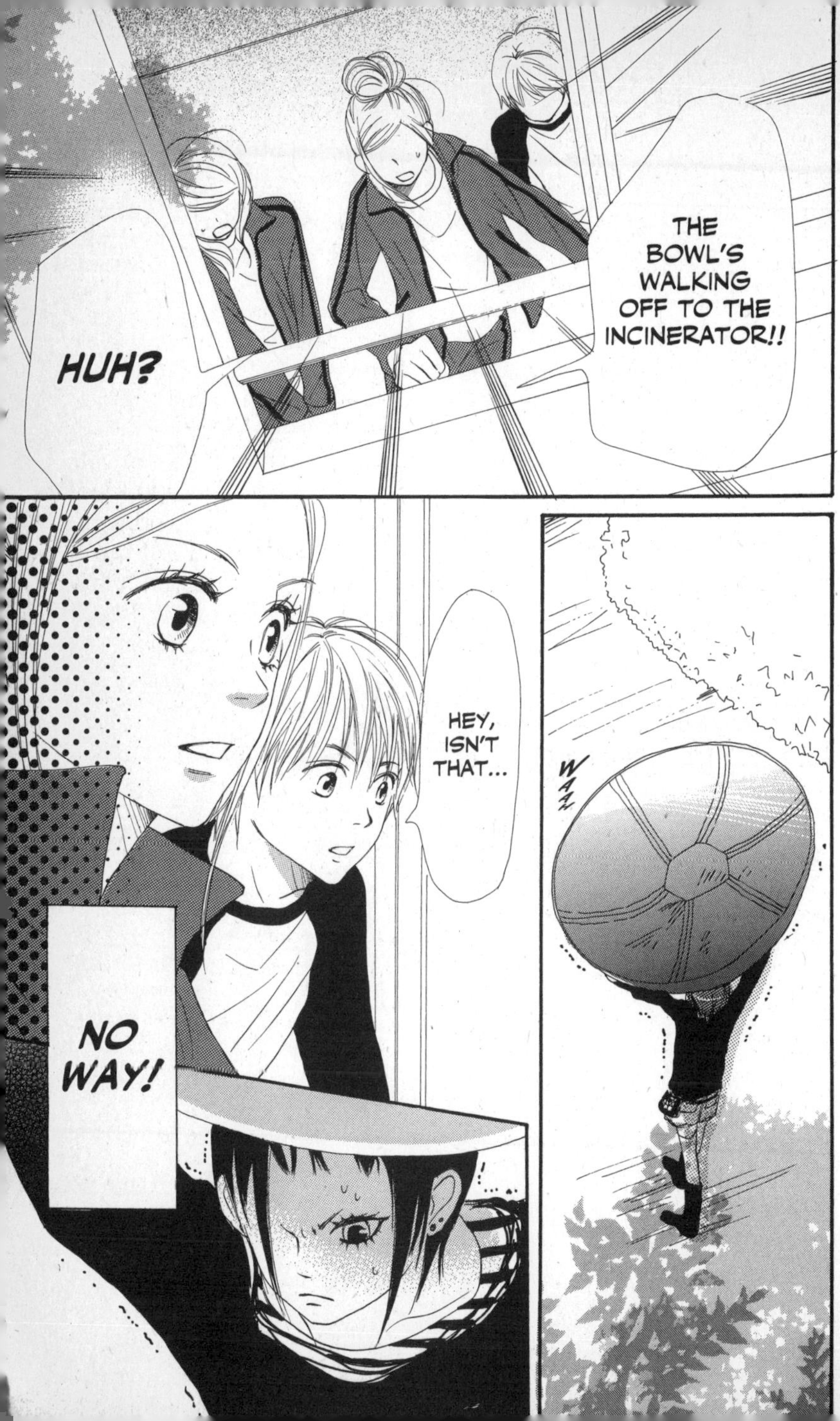
THE BOWL'S WALKING OFF TO THE INCINERATOR!!
HUH?
HEY, ISN'T THAT...
NO WAY!

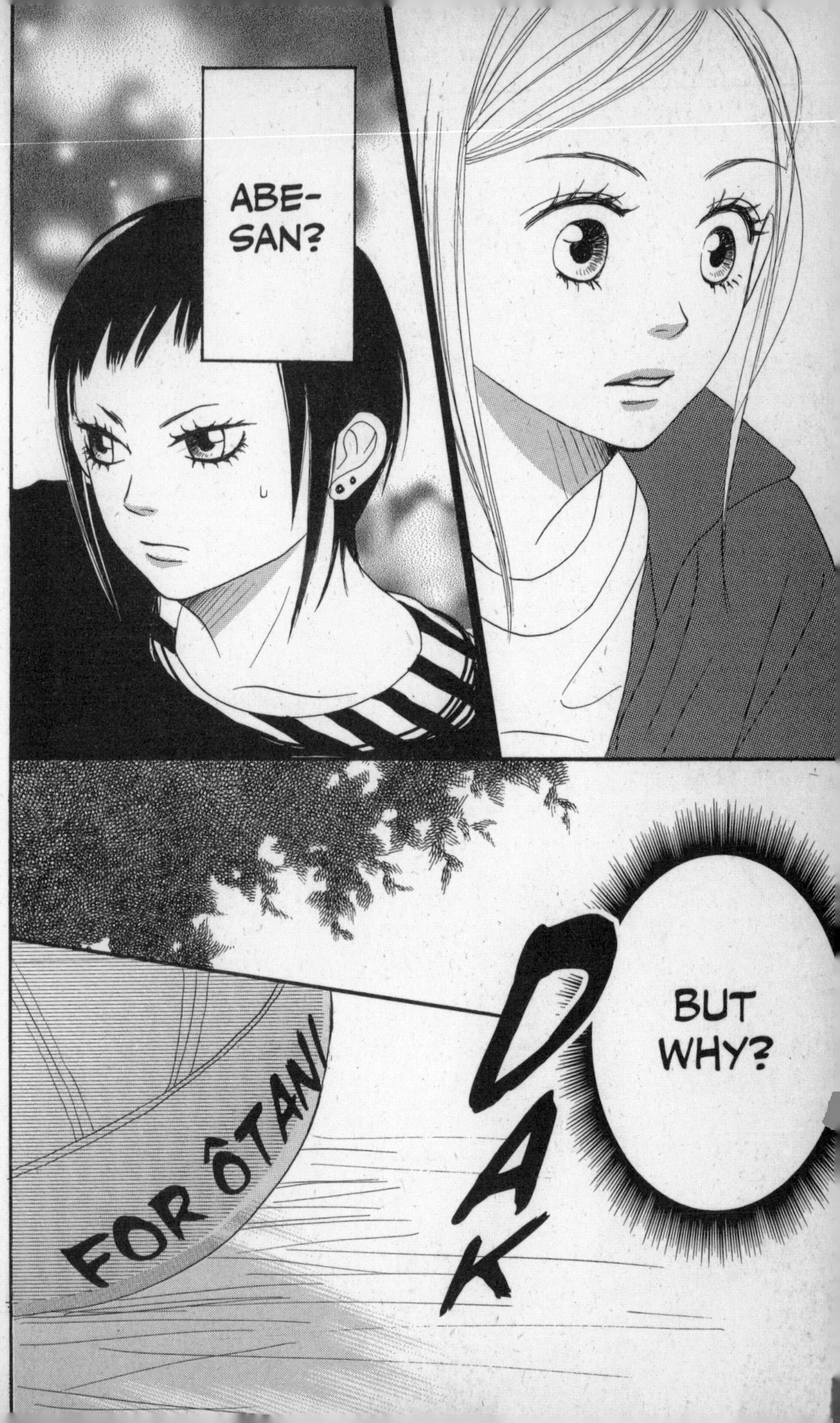
ABE-SAN?
BUT WHY?
DAK
FOR ÔTANI

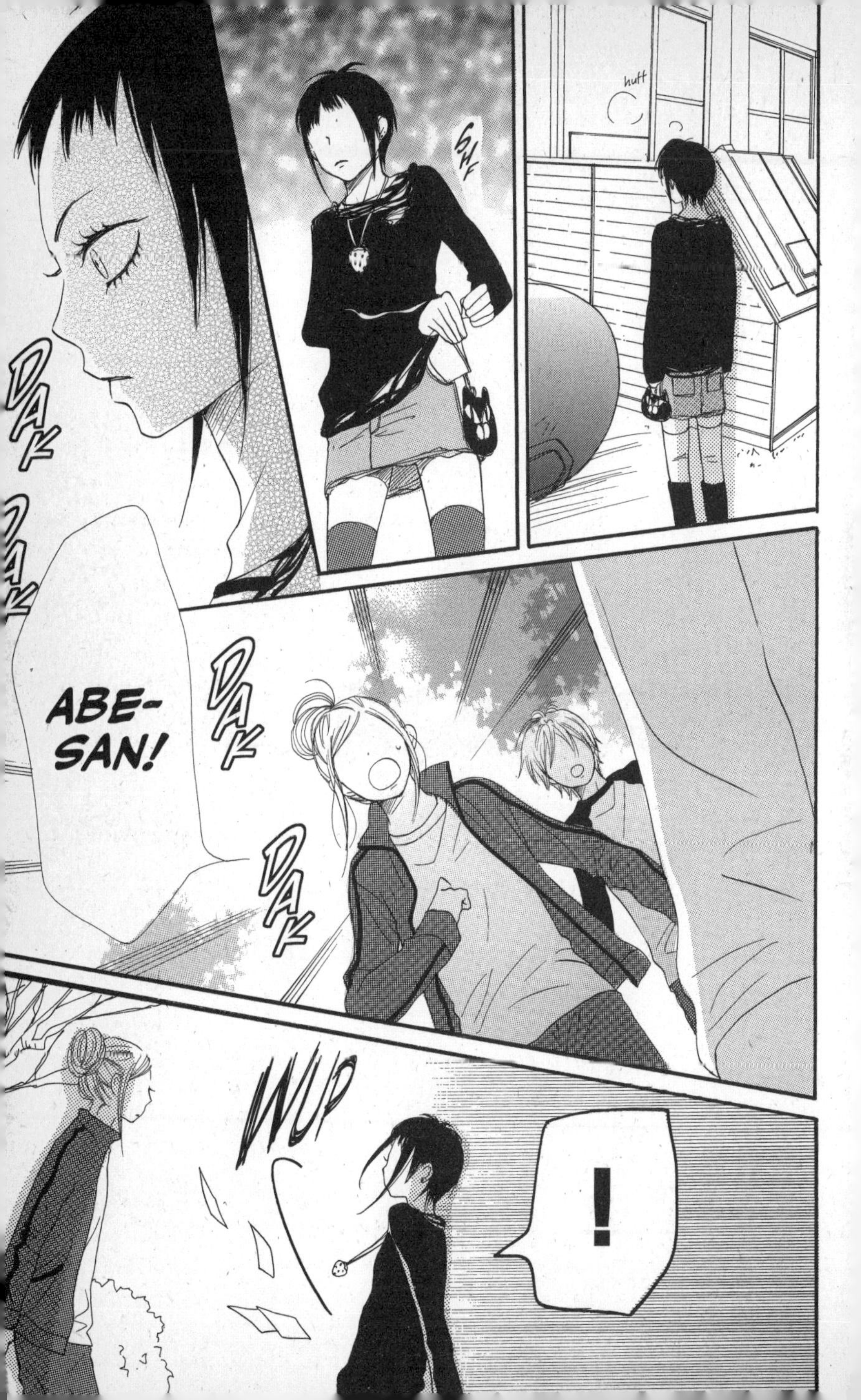
huff
SHF
DAK
DAK
DAK
ABE-SAN!
DAK
DAK
WUP
!

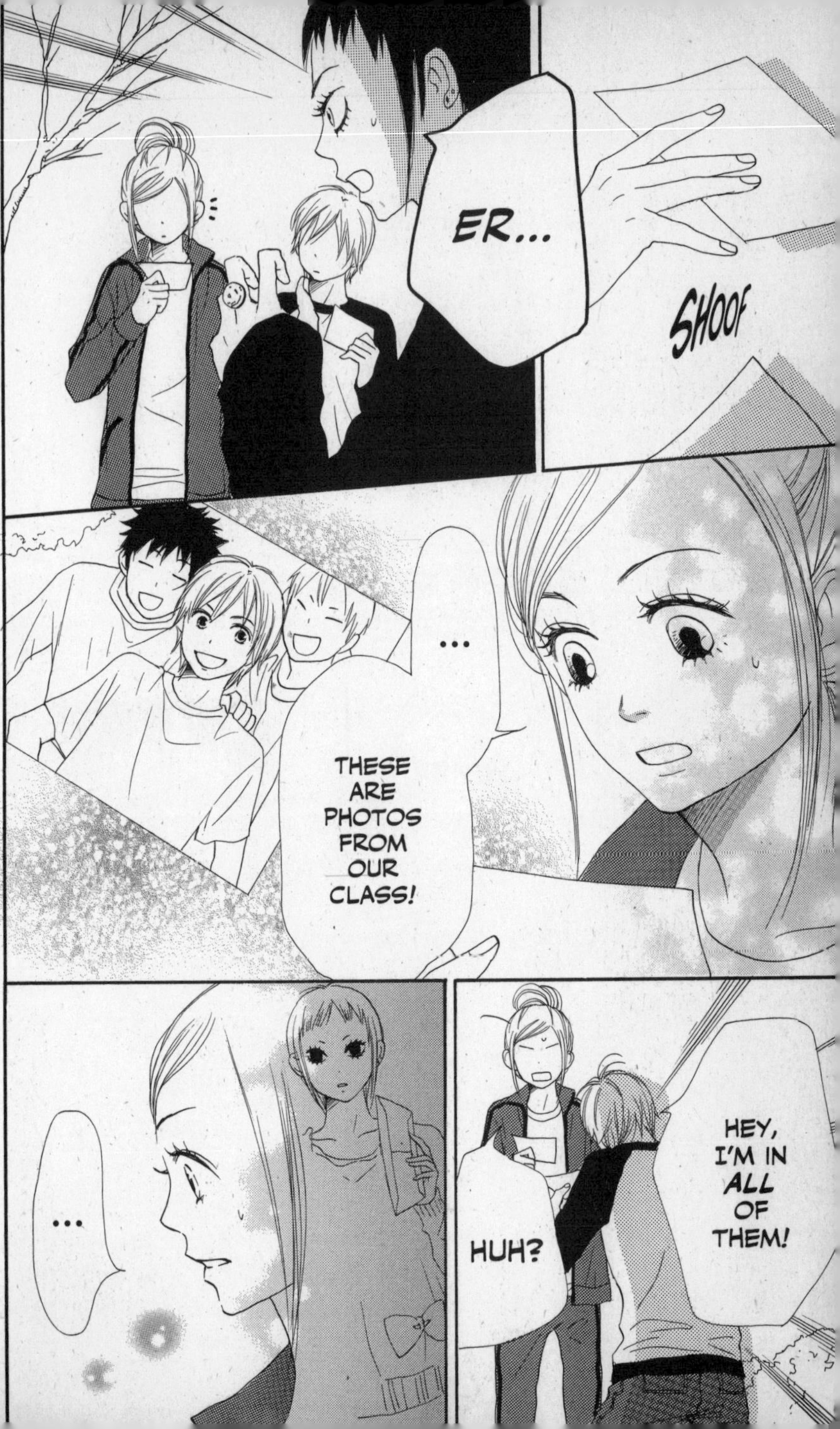
ER...
SHOOF
...
THESE ARE PHOTOS FROM OUR CLASS!
HEY, I'M IN *ALL* OF THEM!
HUH?
...

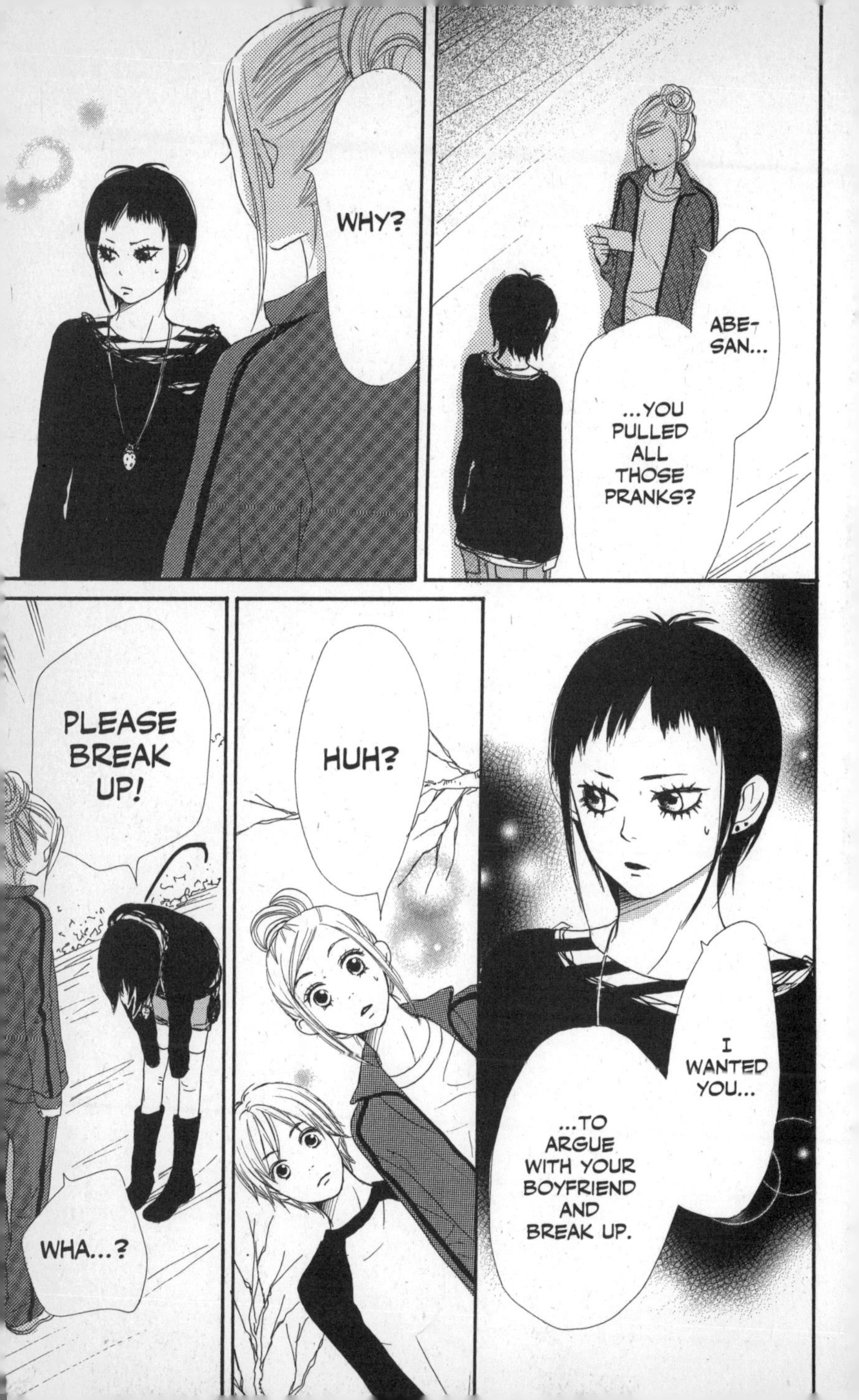
ABE-SAN...
...YOU PULLED ALL THOSE PRANKS?
WHY?
I WANTED YOU...
...TO ARGUE WITH YOUR BOYFRIEND AND BREAK UP.
HUH?
PLEASE BREAK UP!
WHA...?

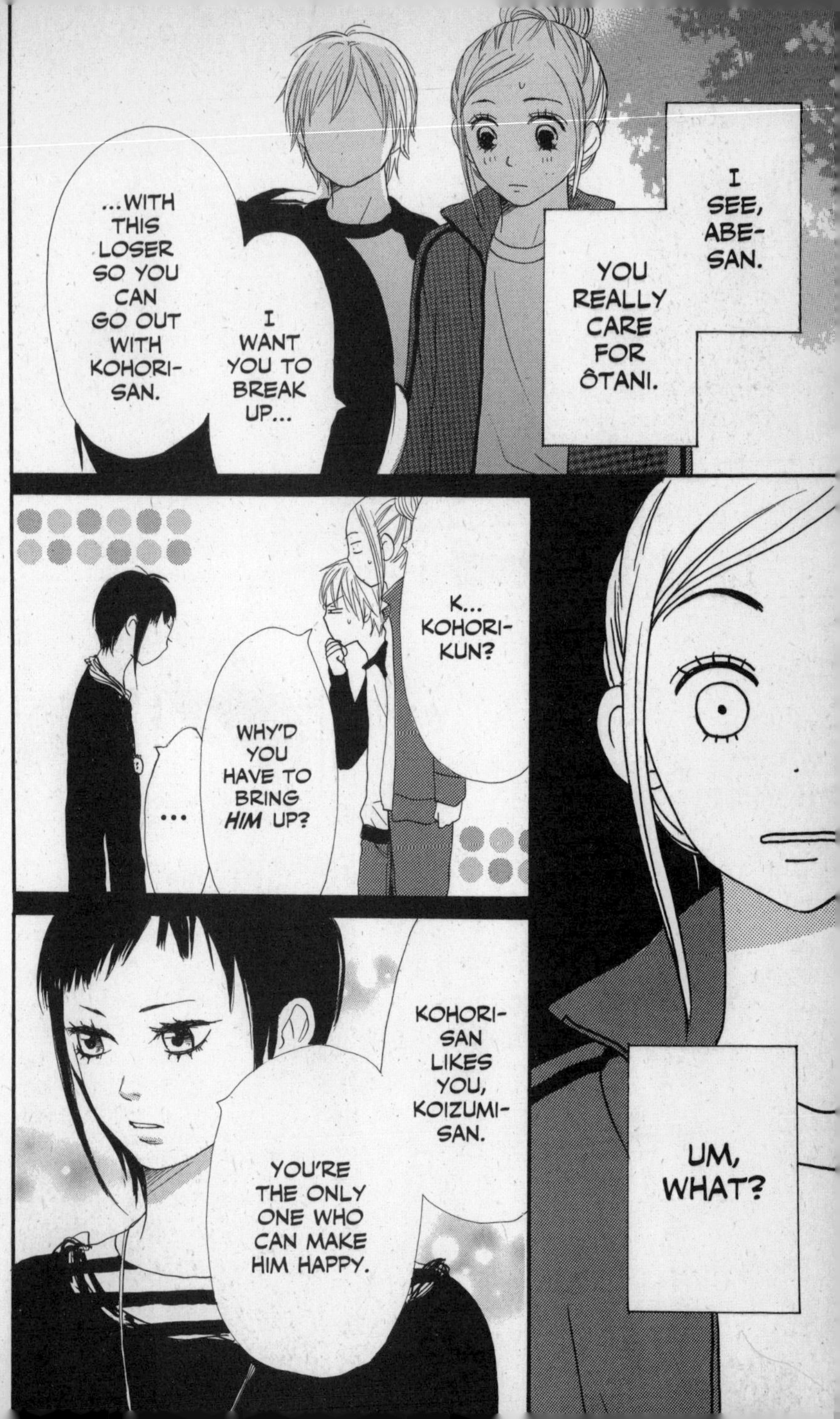
I SEE, ABE-SAN.
YOU REALLY CARE FOR ÔTANI.
I WANT YOU TO BREAK UP...
...WITH THIS LOSER SO YOU CAN GO OUT WITH KOHORI-SAN.
UM, WHAT?
K... KOHORI-KUN?
WHY'D YOU HAVE TO BRING *HIM* UP?
...
KOHORI-SAN LIKES YOU, KOIZUMI-SAN.
YOU'RE THE ONLY ONE WHO CAN MAKE HIM HAPPY.

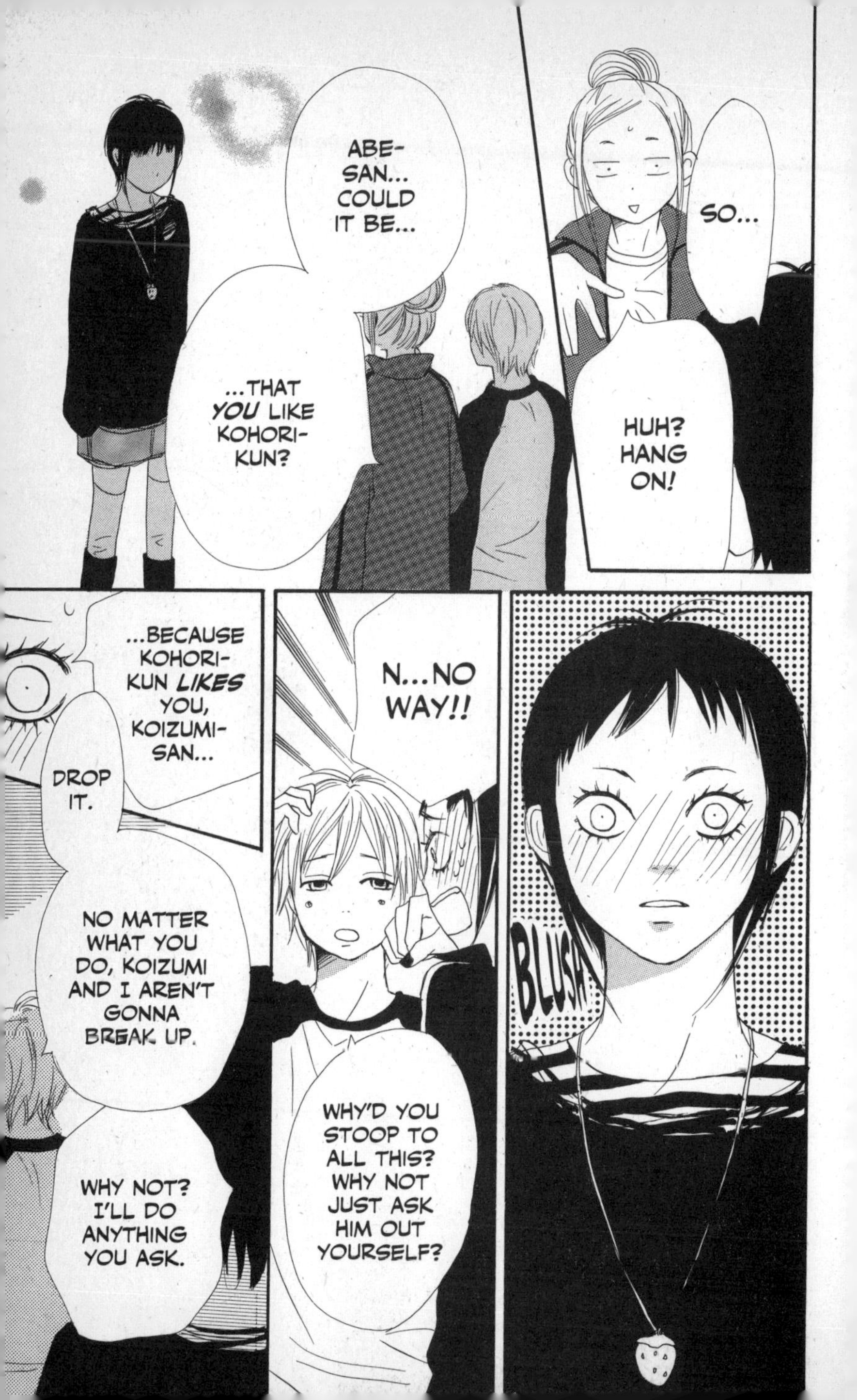
SO...
HUH? HANG ON!
ABE-SAN... COULD IT BE...
...THAT YOU LIKE KOHORI-KUN?
BLUSH
N...NO WAY!!
WHY'D YOU STOOP TO ALL THIS? WHY NOT JUST ASK HIM OUT YOURSELF?
...BECAUSE KOHORI-KUN LIKES YOU, KOIZUMI-SAN...
DROP IT.
NO MATTER WHAT YOU DO, KOIZUMI AND I AREN'T GONNA BREAK UP.
WHY NOT? I'LL DO ANYTHING YOU ASK.

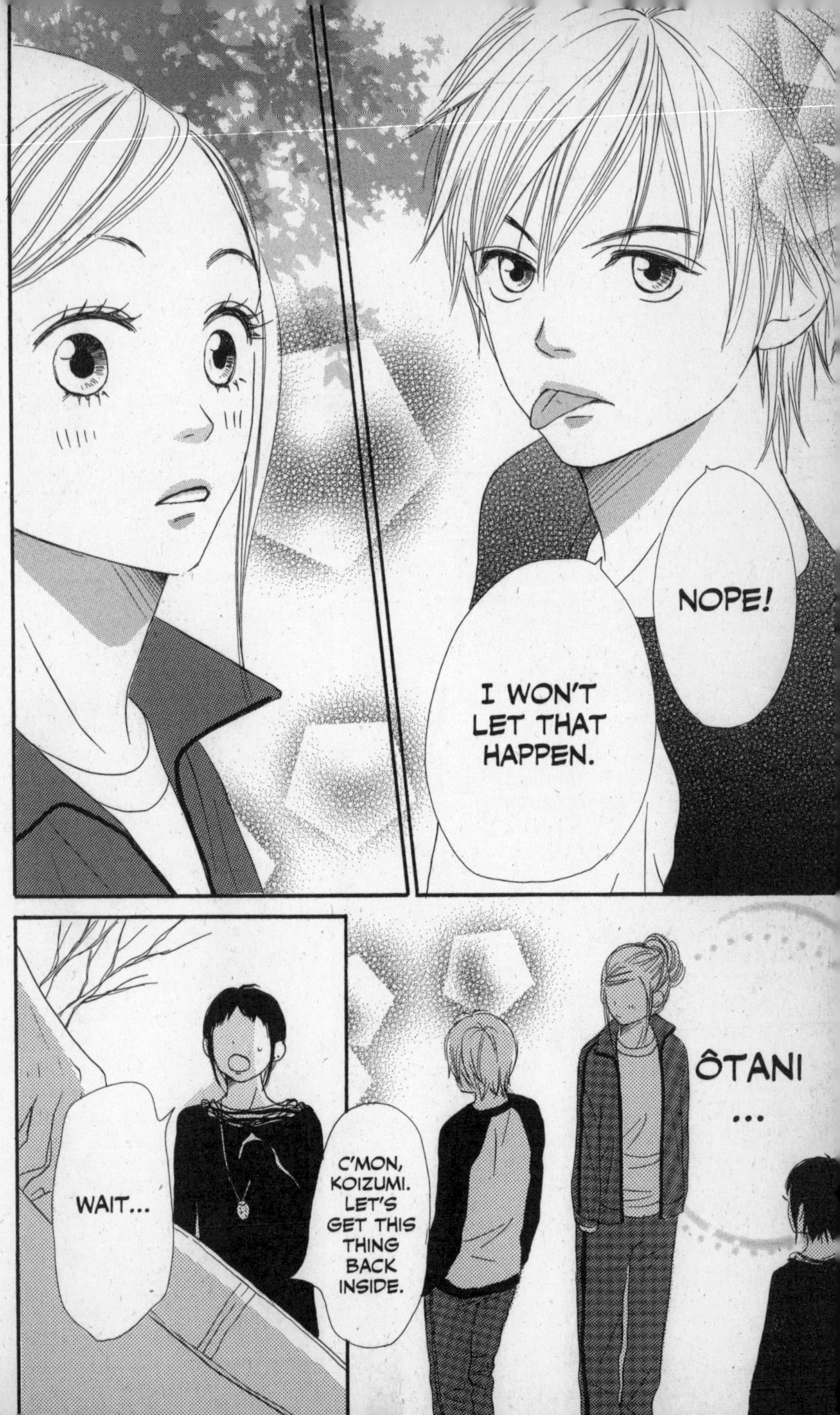
NOPE!
I WON'T LET THAT HAPPEN.
ÔTANI ...
C'MON, KOIZUMI. LET'S GET THIS THING BACK INSIDE.
WAIT...

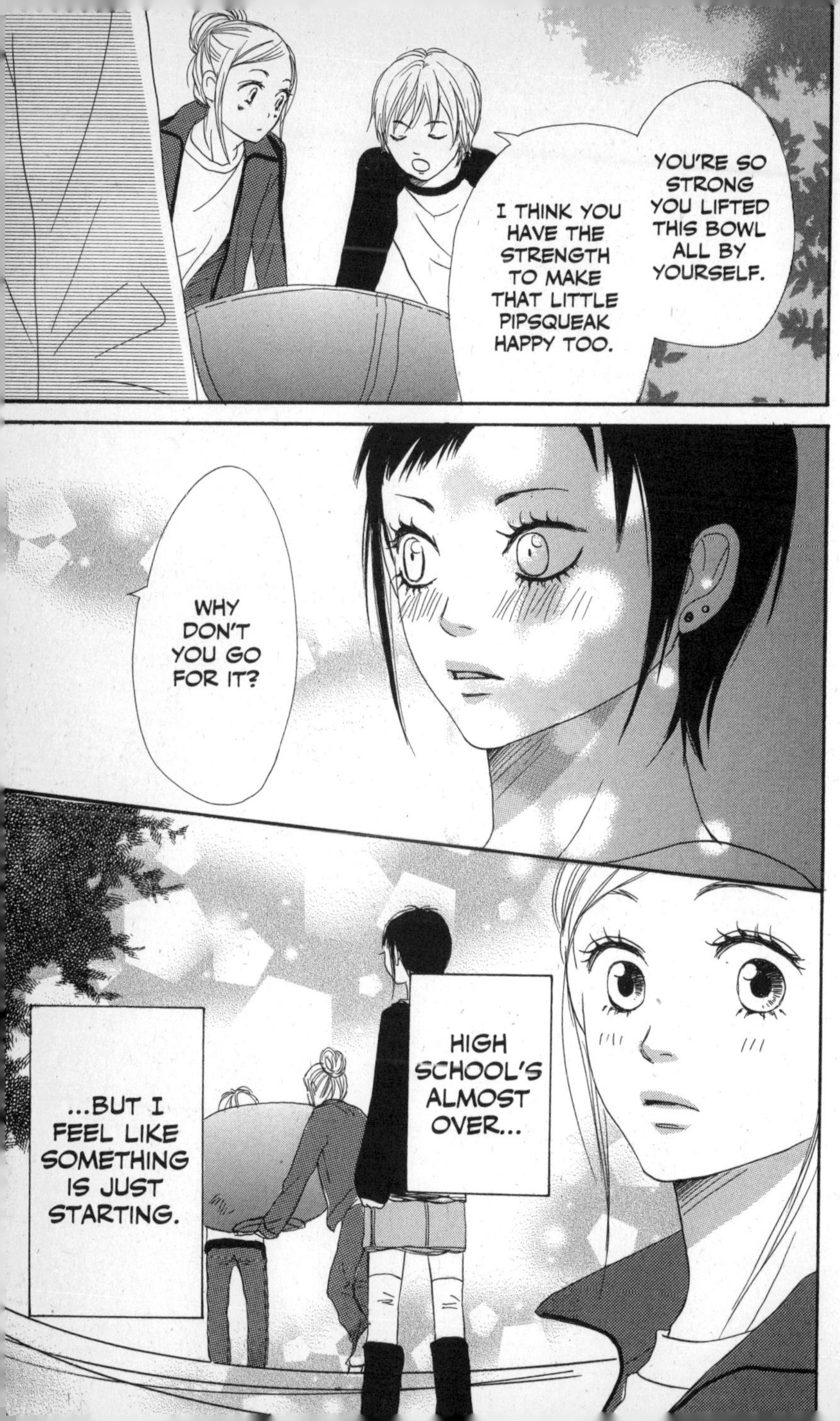
YOU'RE SO STRONG YOU LIFTED THIS BOWL ALL BY YOURSELF.
I THINK YOU HAVE THE STRENGTH TO MAKE THAT LITTLE PIPSQUEAK HAPPY TOO.
WHY DON'T YOU GO FOR IT?
HIGH SCHOOL'S ALMOST OVER...
...BUT I FEEL LIKE SOMETHING IS JUST STARTING.

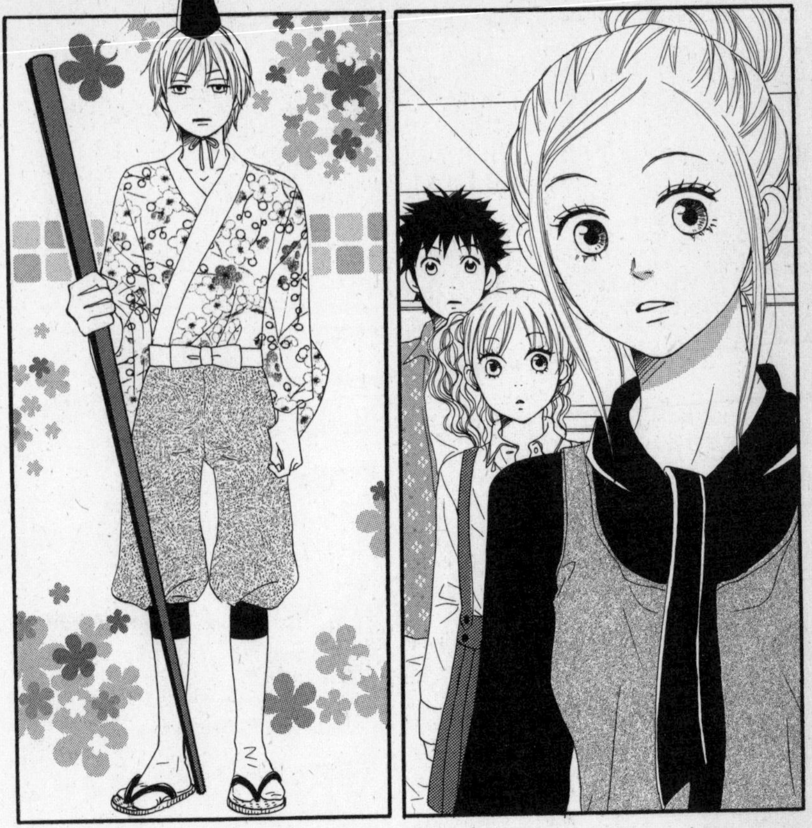

CHAPTER 61

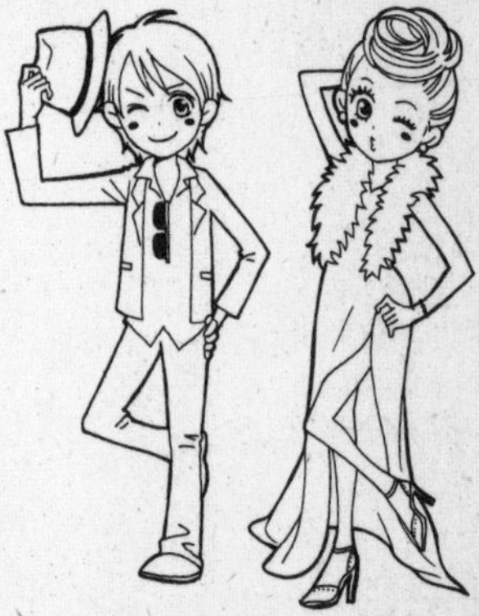

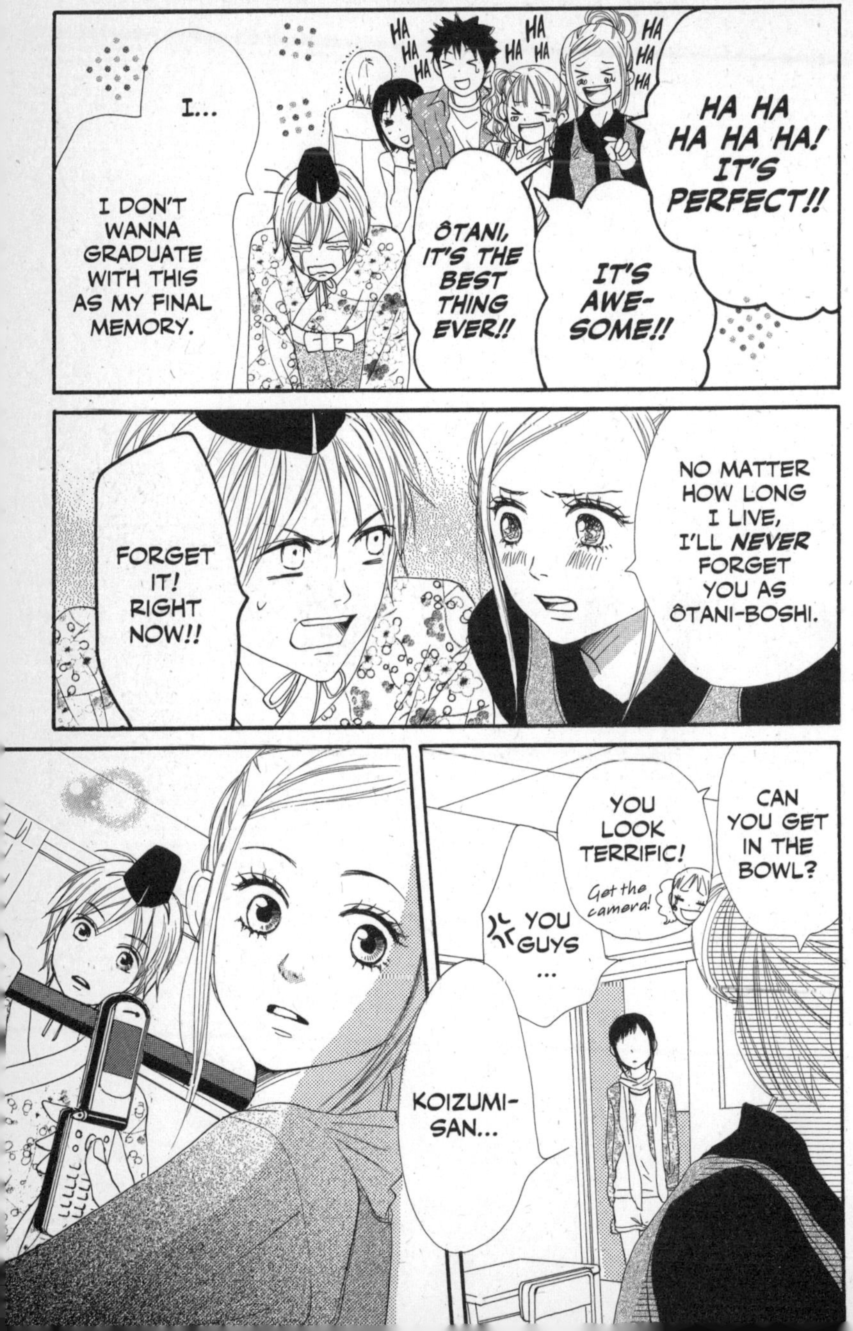
HA HA HA
HA HA HA HA HA! IT'S PERFECT!!
HA HA HA
HA HA HA
IT'S AWE-SOME!!
ŌTANI, IT'S THE BEST THING EVER!!
I...
I DON'T WANNA GRADUATE WITH THIS AS MY FINAL MEMORY.
NO MATTER HOW LONG I LIVE, I'LL *NEVER* FORGET YOU AS ŌTANI-BOSHI.
FORGET IT! RIGHT NOW!!
CAN YOU GET IN THE BOWL?
YOU LOOK TERRIFIC!
Get the camera!
YOU GUYS...
KOIZUMI-SAN...

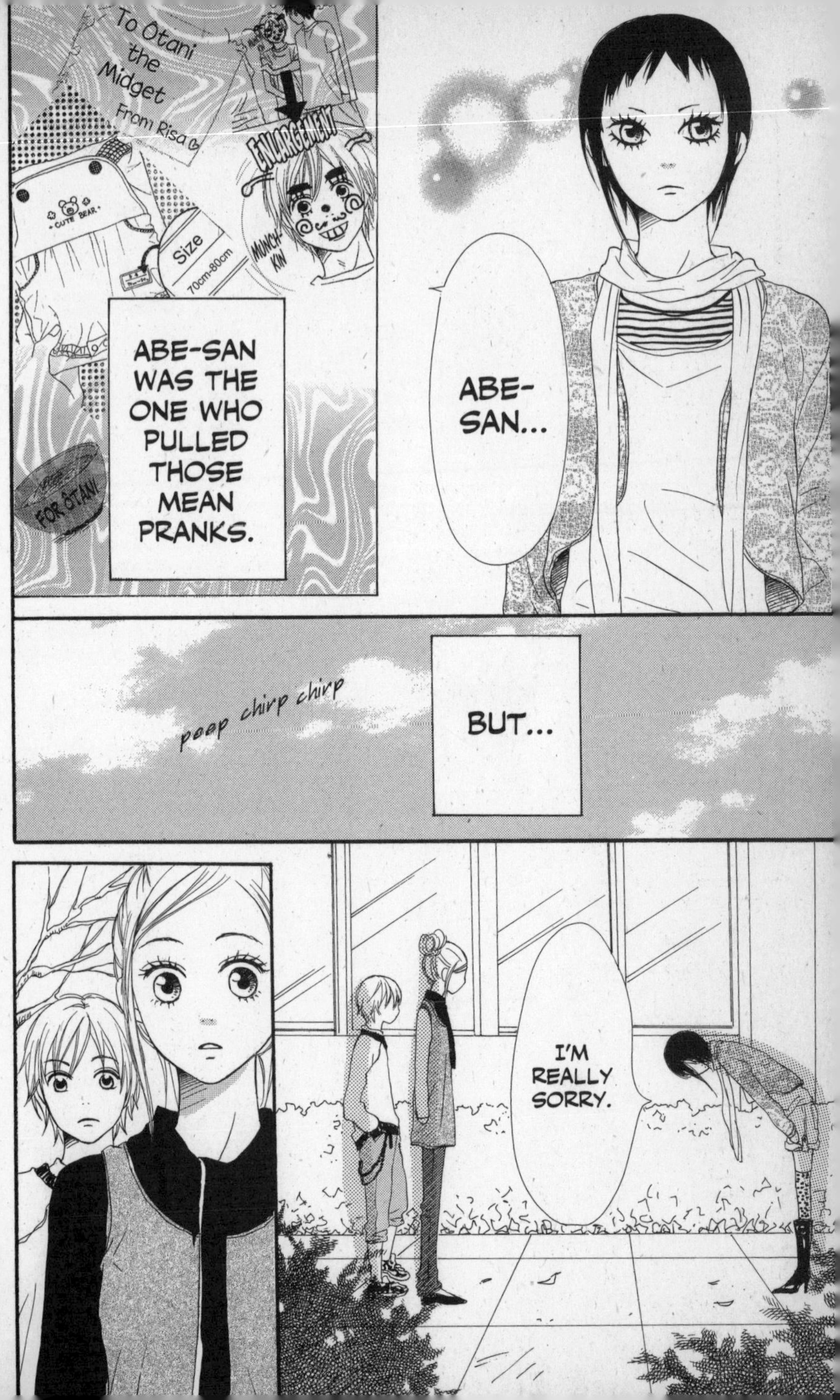
ABE-SAN...
To Ōtani the Midget
From Risa
ENLARGEMENT
MUNCH-KIN
CUTE BEAR
Size
70cm-80cm
FOR ŌTANI
ABE-SAN WAS THE ONE WHO PULLED THOSE MEAN PRANKS.
BUT...
peep chirp chirp
I'M REALLY SORRY.

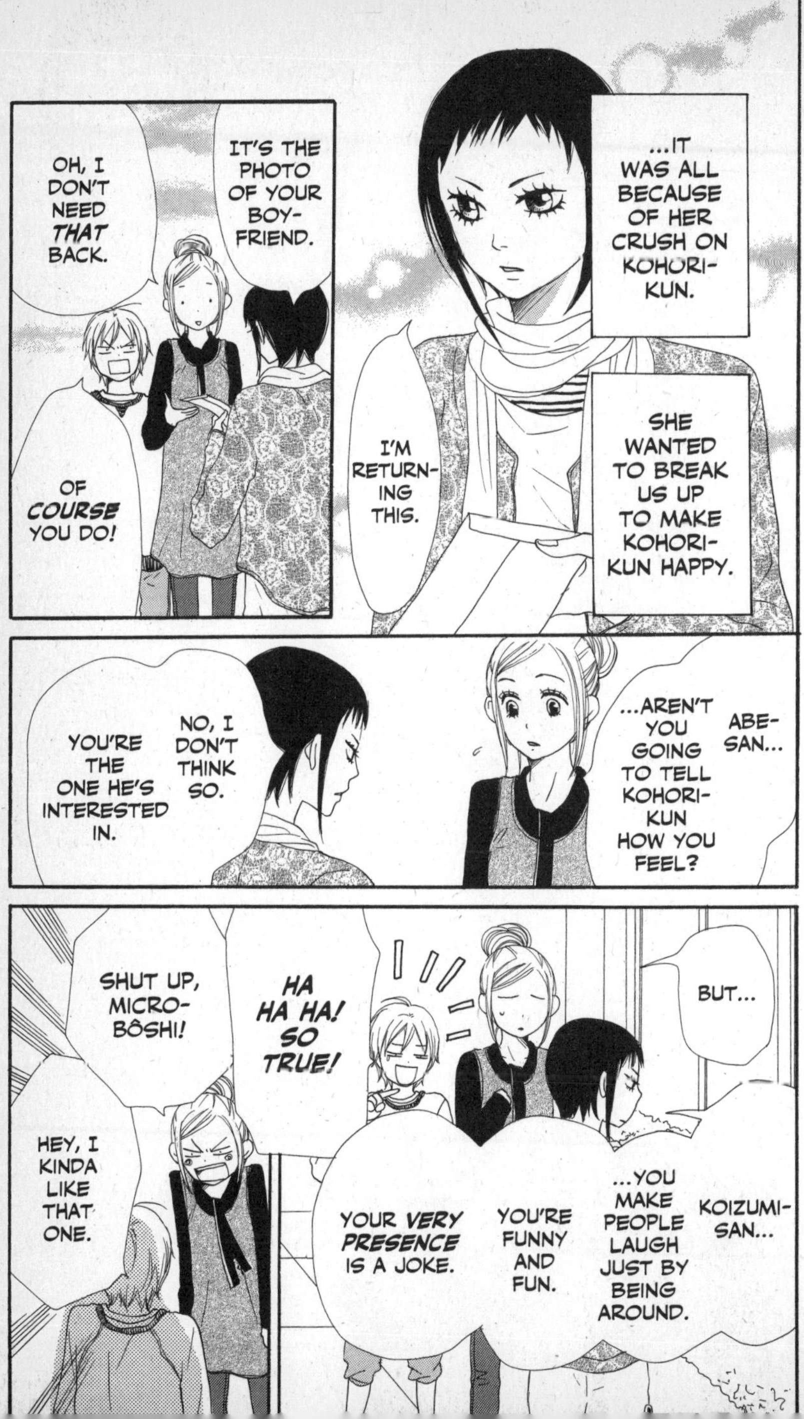

...IT WAS ALL BECAUSE OF HER CRUSH ON KOHORI-KUN.
SHE WANTED TO BREAK US UP TO MAKE KOHORI-KUN HAPPY.
I'M RETURNING THIS.
IT'S THE PHOTO OF YOUR BOY-FRIEND.
OH, I DON'T NEED *THAT* BACK.
OF *COURSE* YOU DO!
ABE-SAN...
...AREN'T YOU GOING TO TELL KOHORI-KUN HOW YOU FEEL?
NO, I DON'T THINK SO.
YOU'RE THE ONE HE'S INTERESTED IN.
BUT...
KOIZUMI-SAN...
...YOU MAKE PEOPLE LAUGH JUST BY BEING AROUND.
YOU'RE FUNNY AND FUN.
YOUR *VERY PRESENCE* IS A JOKE.
HA HA HA! SO TRUE!
SHUT UP, MICRO-BÔSHI!
HEY, I KINDA LIKE THAT ONE.

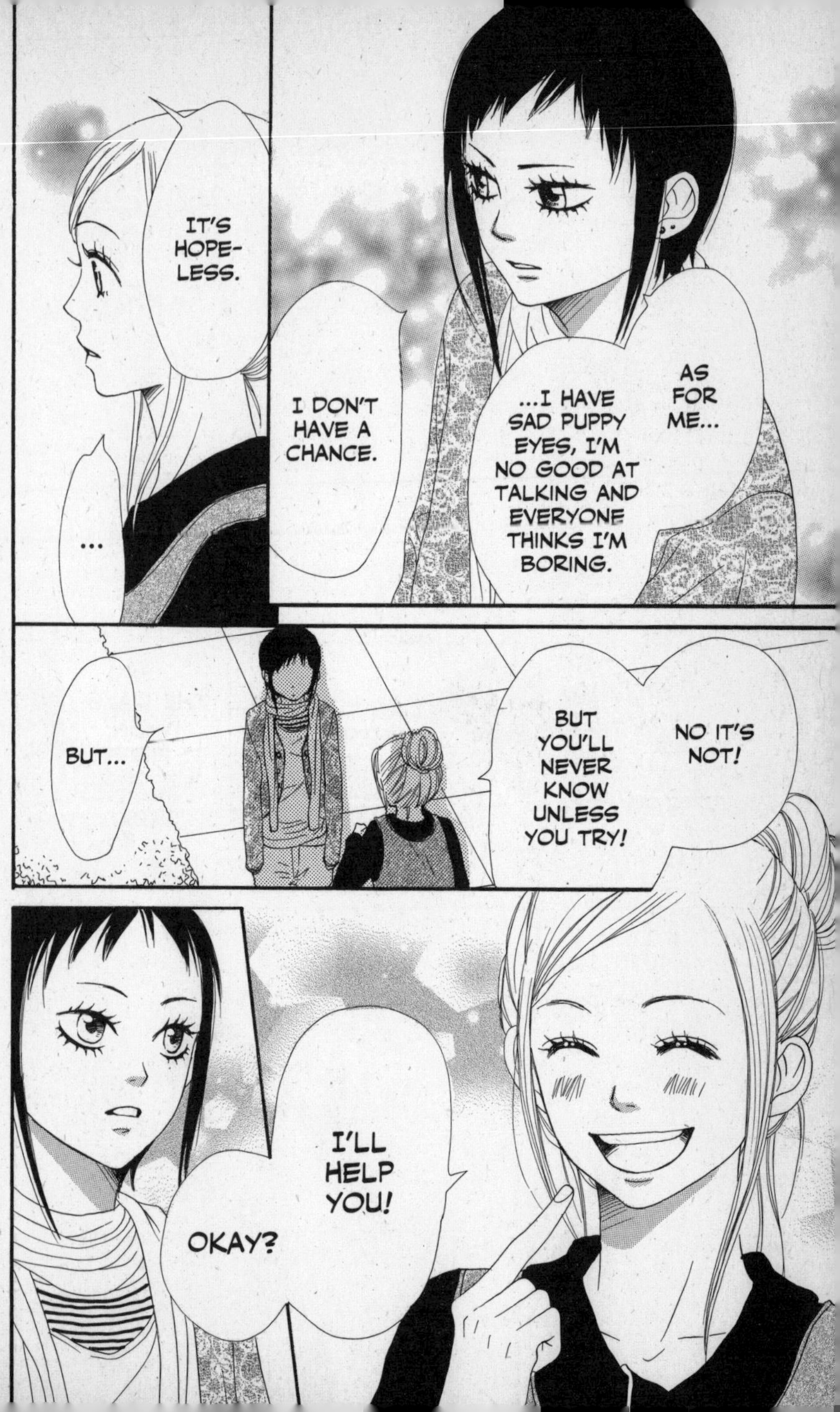
AS FOR ME...
...I HAVE SAD PUPPY EYES, I'M NO GOOD AT TALKING AND EVERYONE THINKS I'M BORING.
I DON'T HAVE A CHANCE.
IT'S HOPE-LESS.
...
NO IT'S NOT!
BUT YOU'LL NEVER KNOW UNLESS YOU TRY!
BUT...
I'LL HELP YOU!
OKAY?

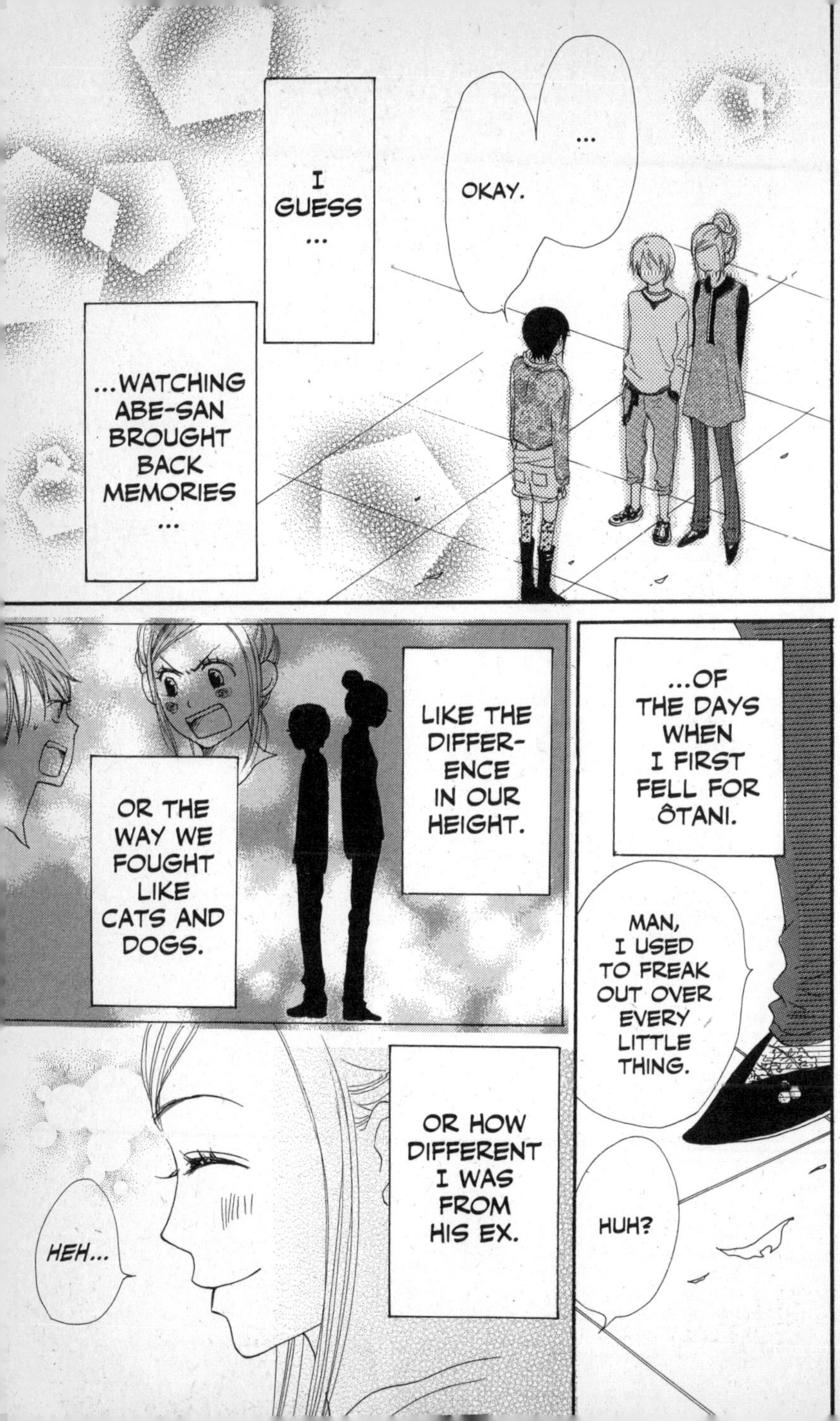
...
OKAY.
I GUESS ...
...WATCHING ABE-SAN BROUGHT BACK MEMORIES ...
...OF THE DAYS WHEN I FIRST FELL FOR ÔTANI.
MAN, I USED TO FREAK OUT OVER EVERY LITTLE THING.
HUH?
LIKE THE DIFFER-ENCE IN OUR HEIGHT.
OR THE WAY WE FOUGHT LIKE CATS AND DOGS.
OR HOW DIFFERENT I WAS FROM HIS EX.
HEH...

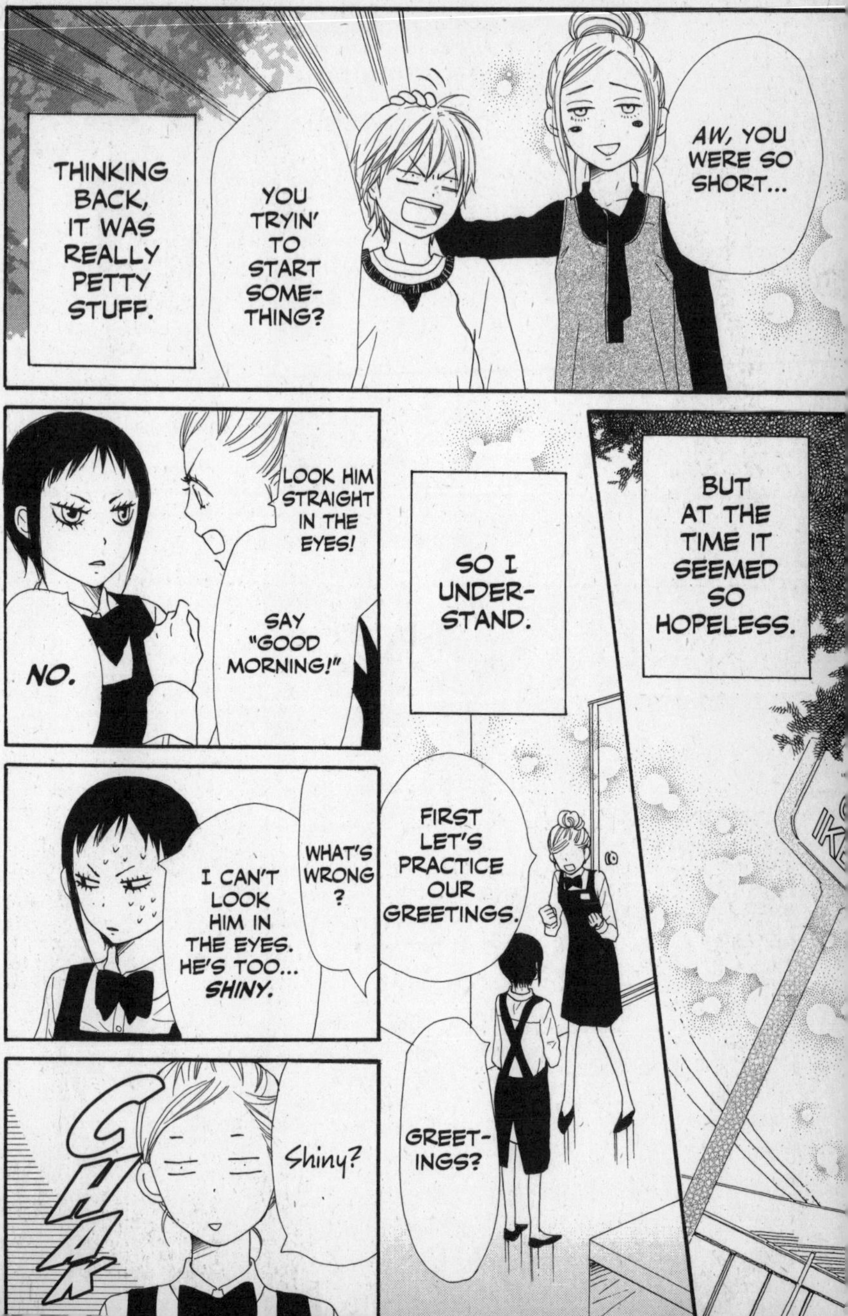
AW, YOU WERE SO SHORT...
YOU TRYIN' TO START SOMETHING?
THINKING BACK, IT WAS REALLY PETTY STUFF.
BUT AT THE TIME IT SEEMED SO HOPELESS.
SO I UNDERSTAND.
FIRST LET'S PRACTICE OUR GREETINGS.
GREETINGS?
LOOK HIM STRAIGHT IN THE EYES!
SAY "GOOD MORNING!"
NO.
WHAT'S WRONG?
I CAN'T LOOK HIM IN THE EYES. HE'S TOO... SHINY.
Shiny?
CHAK

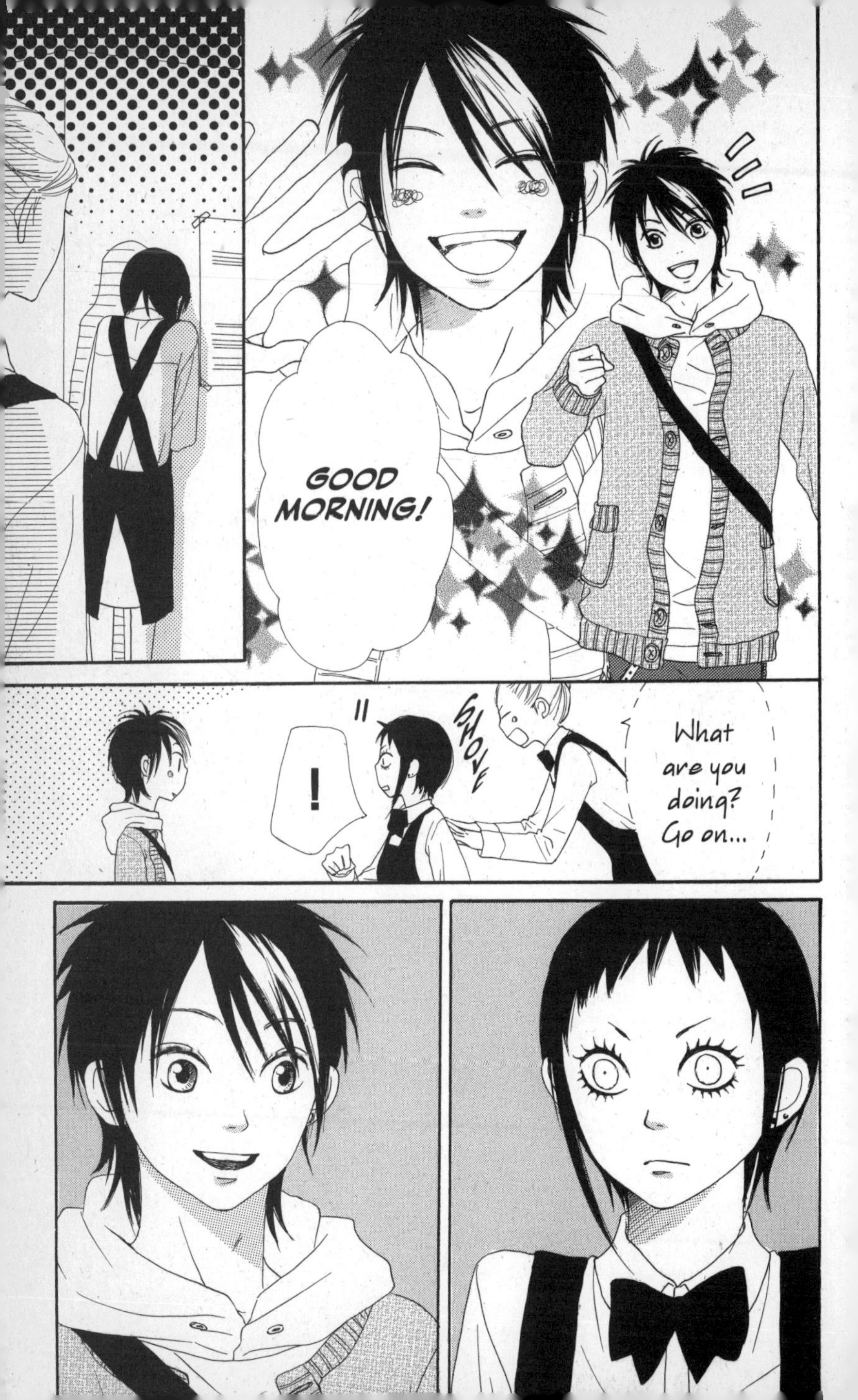
GOOD MORNING!
What are you doing? Go on...
SHOVE
!!
!

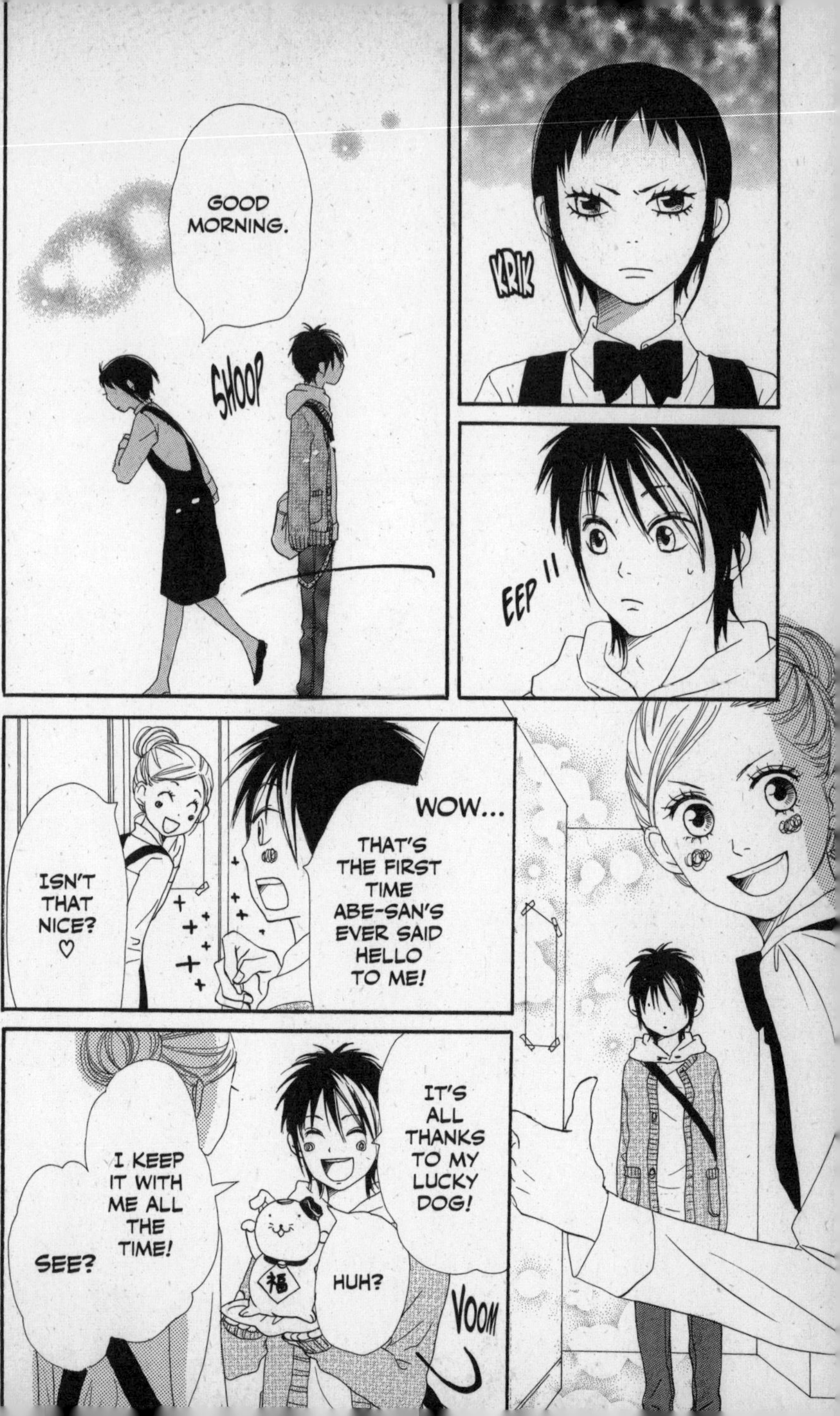
KRIK
EEP
GOOD MORNING.
SHOOP
WOW...
THAT'S THE FIRST TIME ABE-SAN'S EVER SAID HELLO TO ME!
ISN'T THAT NICE? ♡
IT'S ALL THANKS TO MY LUCKY DOG!
HUH?
VOOM
I KEEP IT WITH ME ALL THE TIME!
SEE?

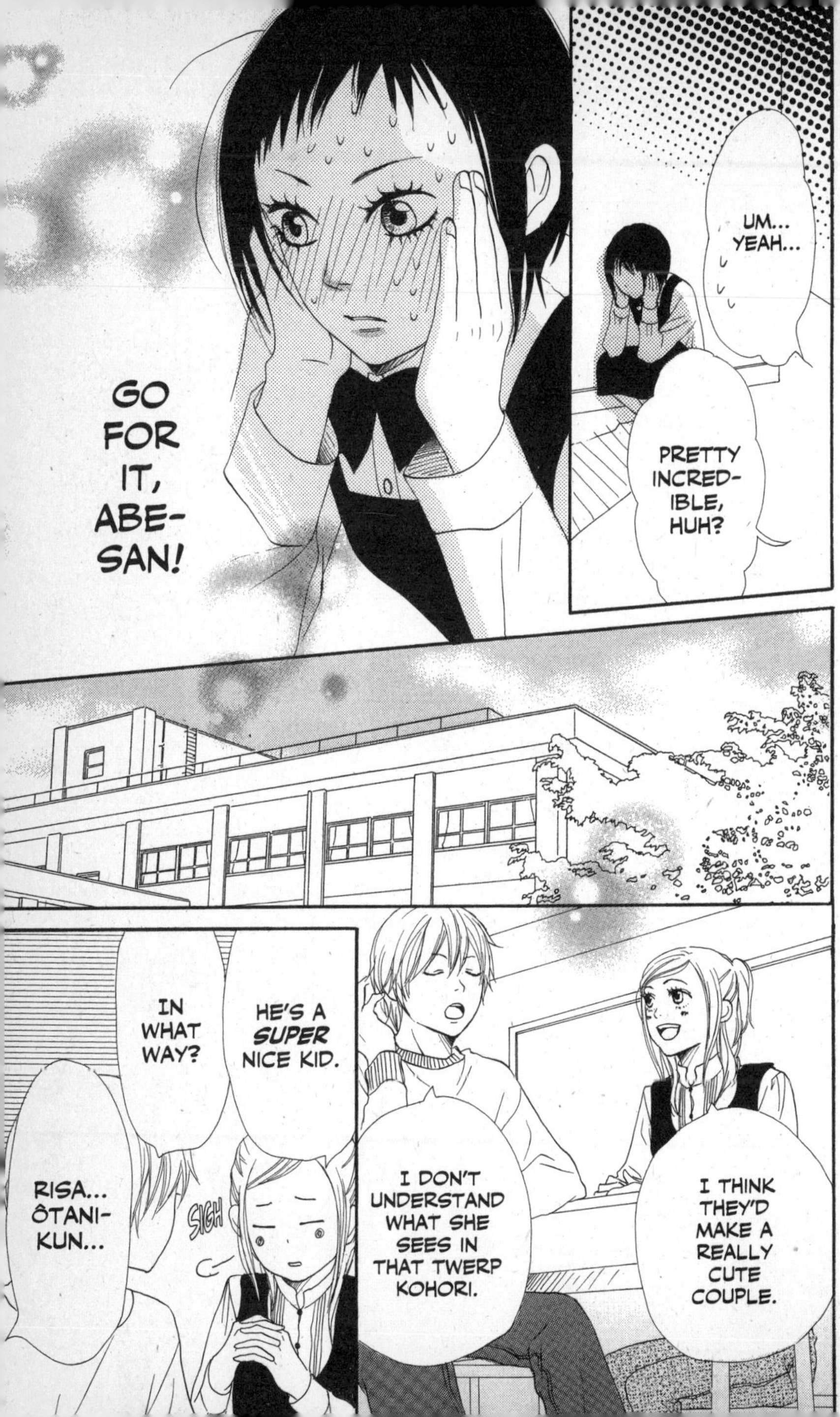
UM... YEAH...
PRETTY INCREDIBLE, HUH?
GO FOR IT, ABE-SAN!
I THINK THEY'D MAKE A REALLY CUTE COUPLE.
I DON'T UNDERSTAND WHAT SHE SEES IN THAT TWERP KOHORI.
HE'S A SUPER NICE KID.
IN WHAT WAY?
SIGH
RISA... ÔTANI-KUN...

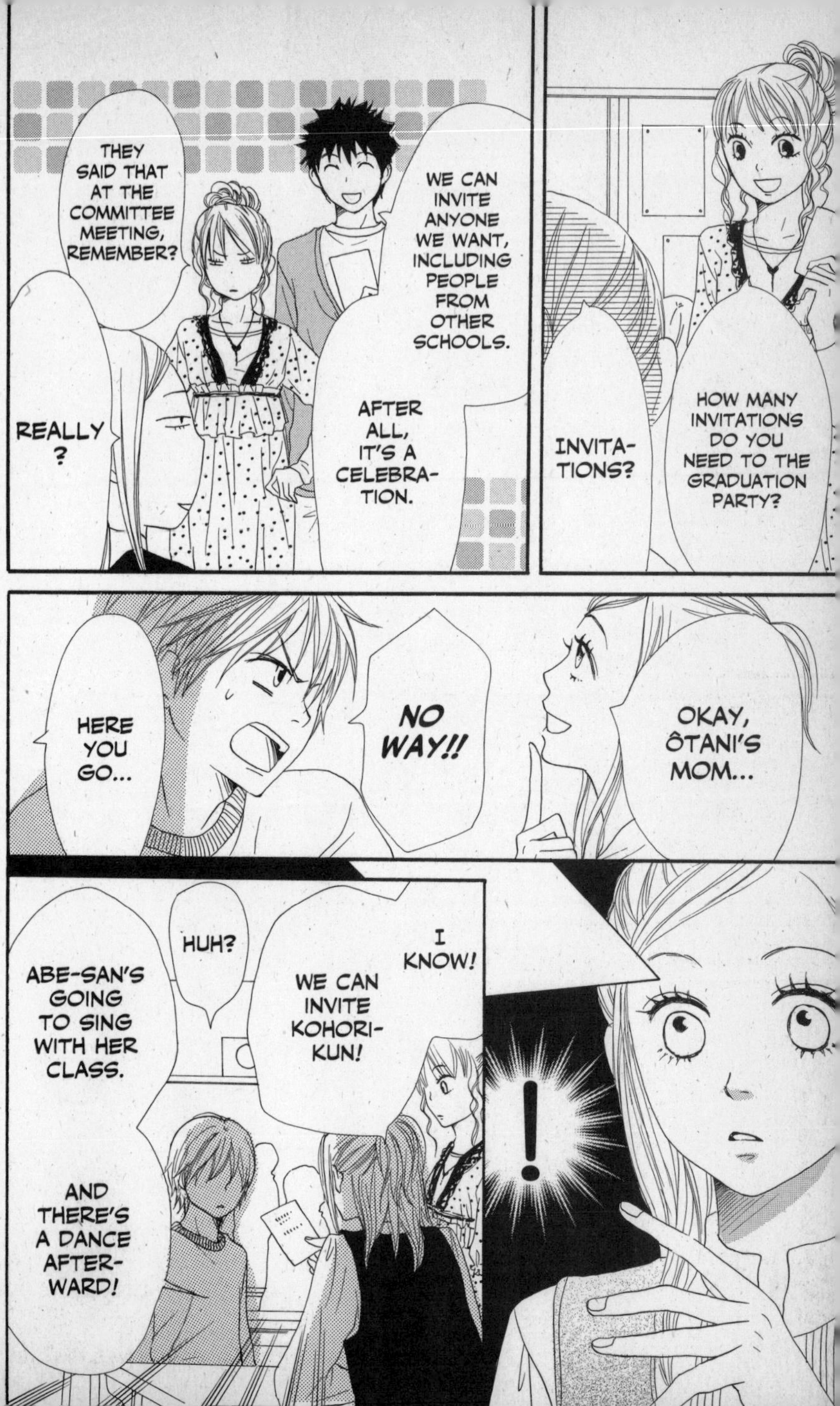
HOW MANY INVITATIONS DO YOU NEED TO THE GRADUATION PARTY?
INVITA-TIONS?
WE CAN INVITE ANYONE WE WANT, INCLUDING PEOPLE FROM OTHER SCHOOLS.
THEY SAID THAT AT THE COMMITTEE MEETING, REMEMBER?
AFTER ALL, IT'S A CELEBRA-TION.
REALLY?
OKAY, ÔTANI'S MOM...
NO WAY!!
HERE YOU GO...
!
I KNOW!
WE CAN INVITE KOHORI-KUN!
HUH?
ABE-SAN'S GOING TO SING WITH HER CLASS.
AND THERE'S A DANCE AFTER-WARD!

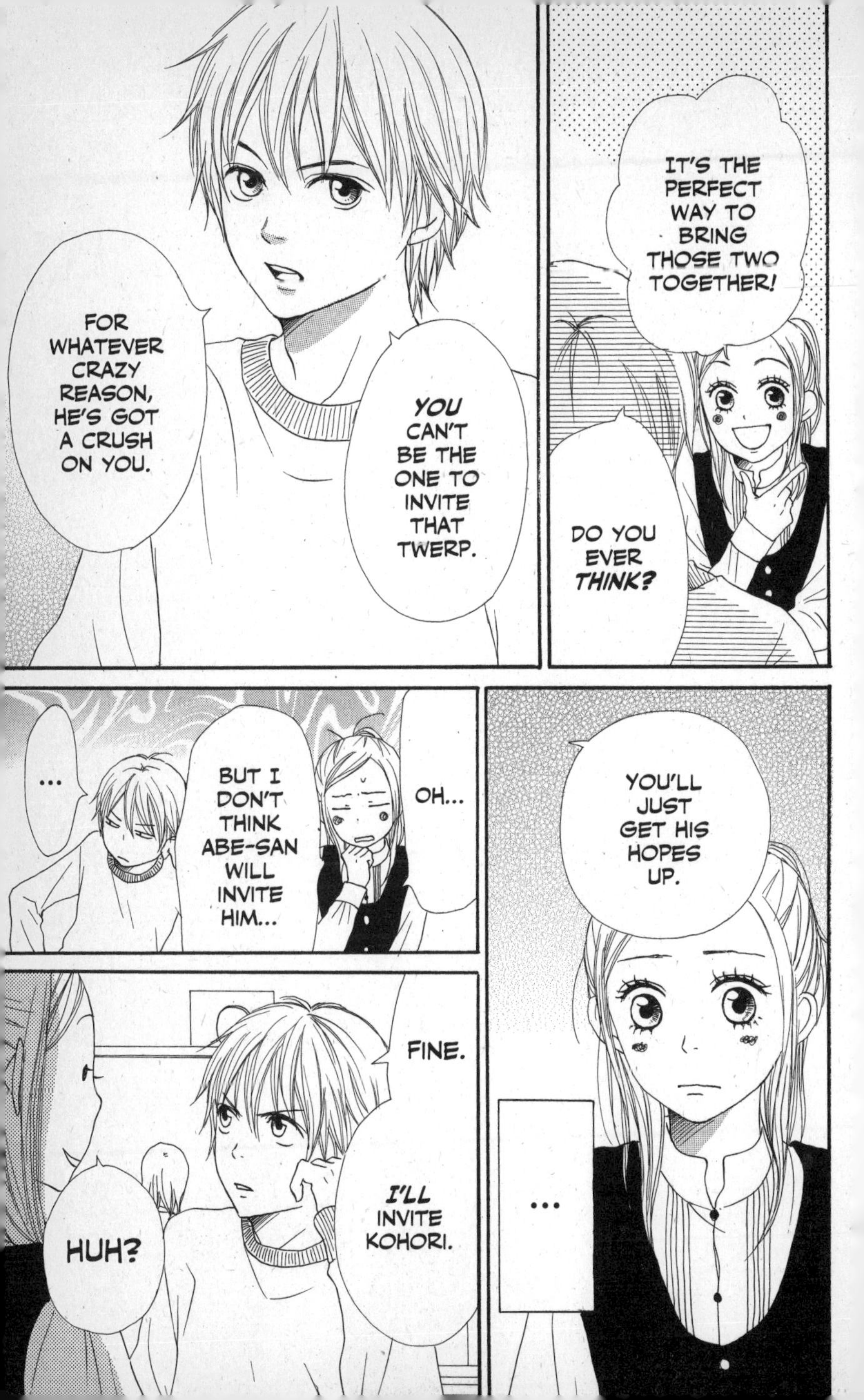
IT'S THE PERFECT WAY TO BRING THOSE TWO TOGETHER!
DO YOU EVER *THINK?*
YOU CAN'T BE THE ONE TO INVITE THAT TWERP.
FOR WHATEVER CRAZY REASON, HE'S GOT A CRUSH ON YOU.
YOU'LL JUST GET HIS HOPES UP.
...
OH...
BUT I DON'T THINK ABE-SAN WILL INVITE HIM...
...
FINE.
I'LL INVITE KOHORI.
HUH?

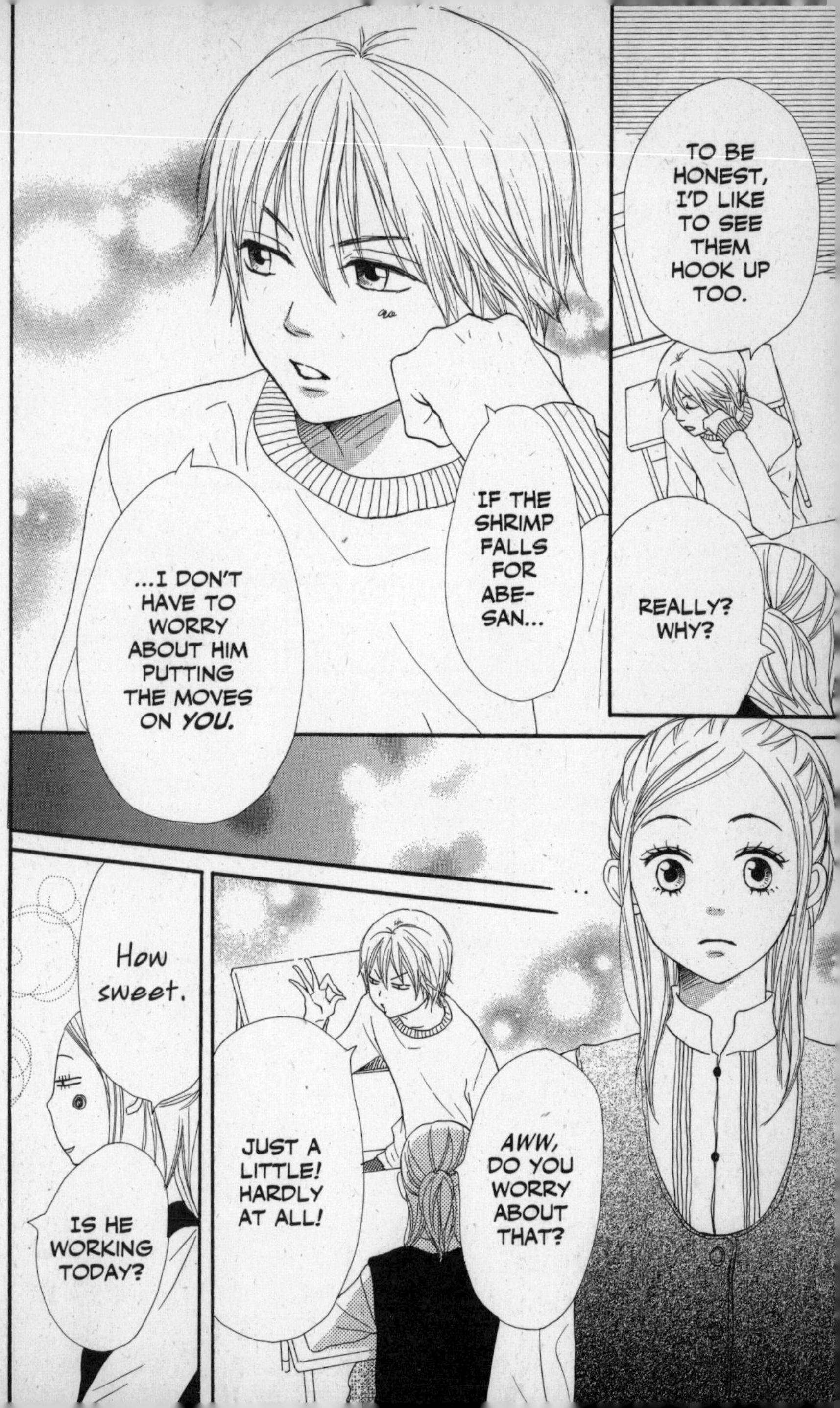
TO BE HONEST, I'D LIKE TO SEE THEM HOOK UP TOO.
REALLY? WHY?
IF THE SHRIMP FALLS FOR ABE-SAN...
...I DON'T HAVE TO WORRY ABOUT HIM PUTTING THE MOVES ON *YOU*.
..
AWW, DO YOU WORRY ABOUT THAT?
JUST A LITTLE! HARDLY AT ALL!
How sweet.
IS HE WORKING TODAY?

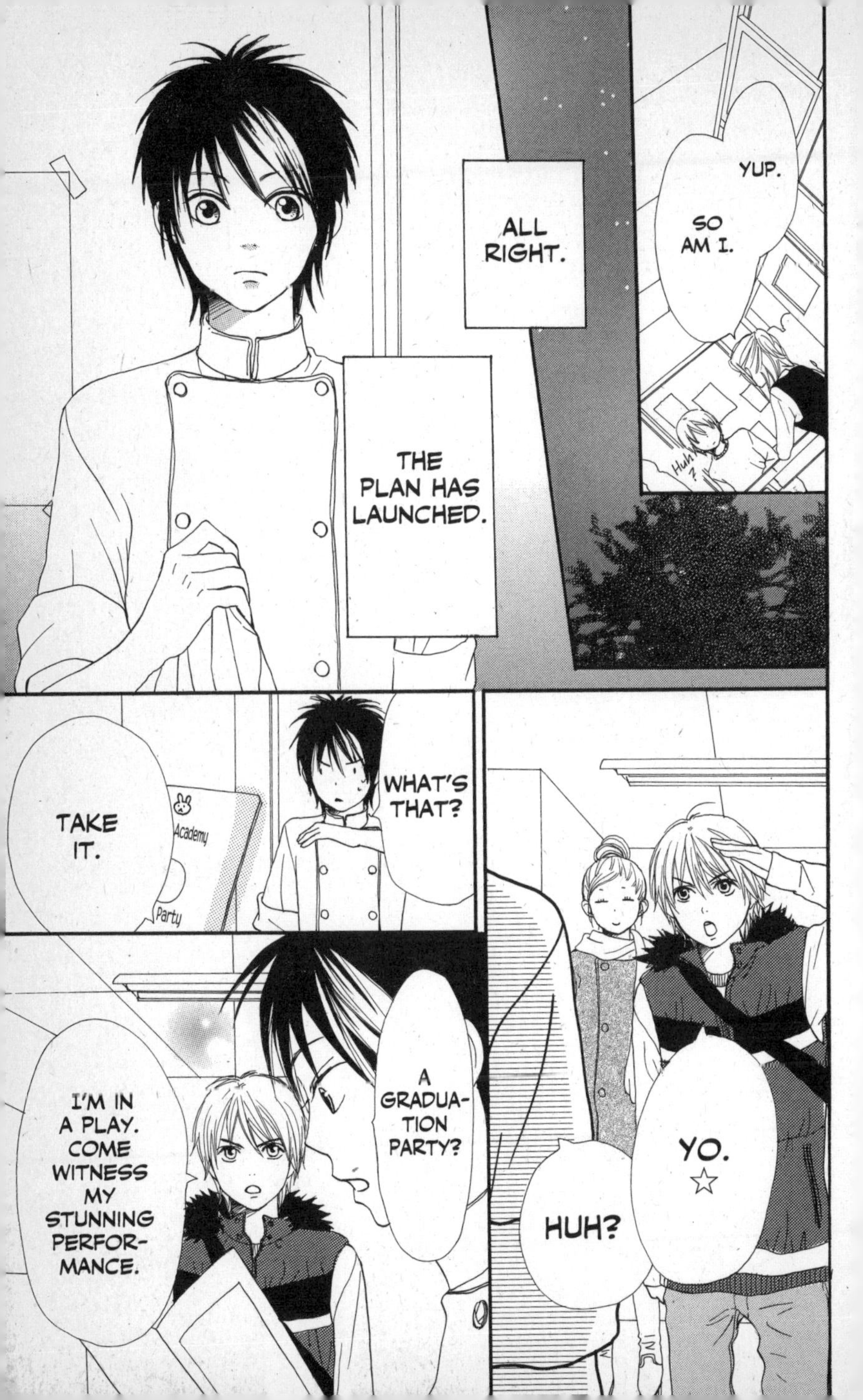
YUP.
SO AM I.
Huh!?
ALL RIGHT.
THE PLAN HAS LAUNCHED.
YO. ☆
HUH?
WHAT'S THAT?
TAKE IT.
Academy
Party
A GRADUATION PARTY?
I'M IN A PLAY. COME WITNESS MY STUNNING PERFORMANCE.

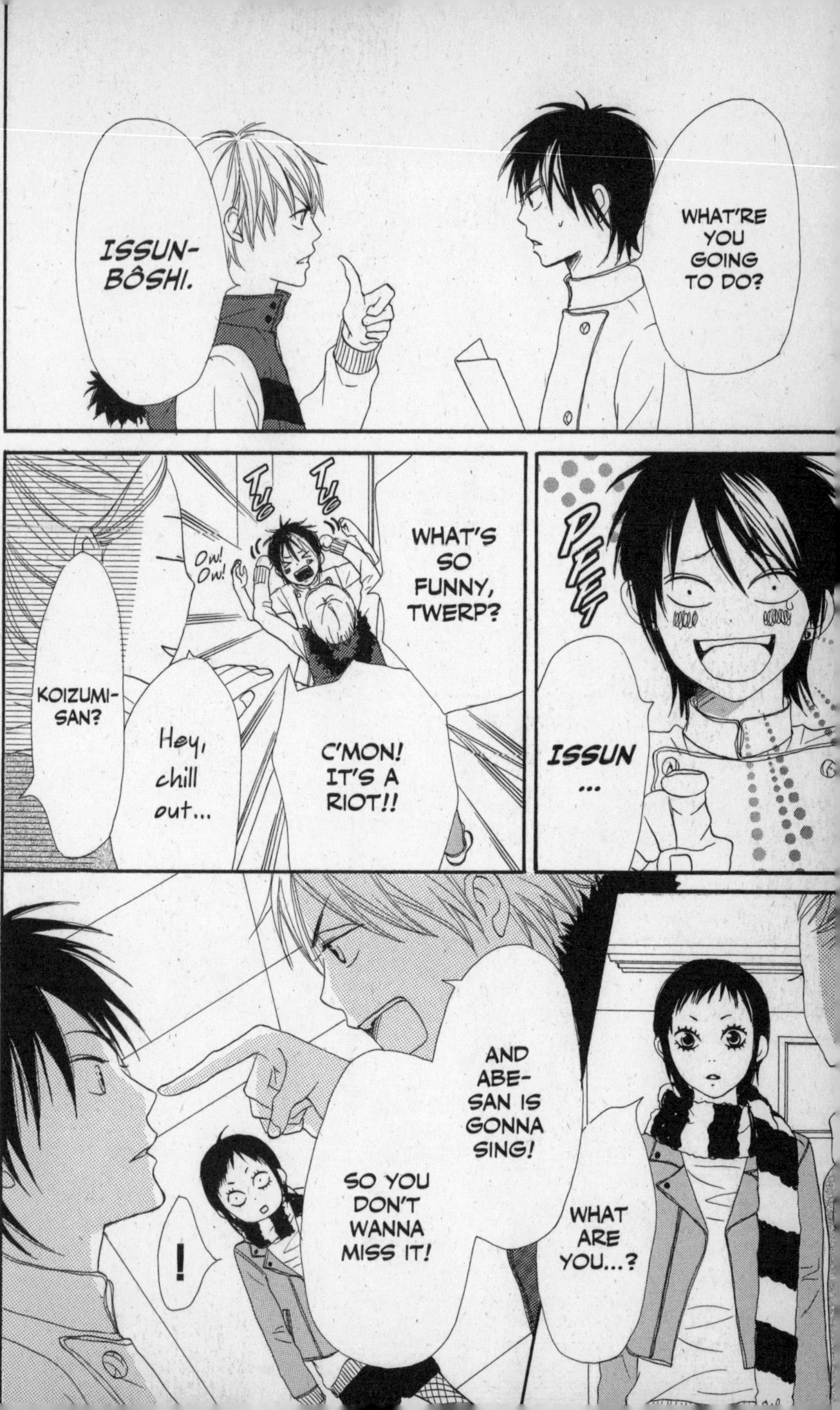
WHAT'RE YOU GOING TO DO?
ISSUN-BÔSHI.
ISSUN ...
WHAT'S SO FUNNY, TWERP?
Ow! Ow!
C'MON! IT'S A RIOT!!
Hey, chill out...
KOIZUMI-SAN?
WHAT ARE YOU...?
AND ABE-SAN IS GONNA SING!
SO YOU DON'T WANNA MISS IT!
!

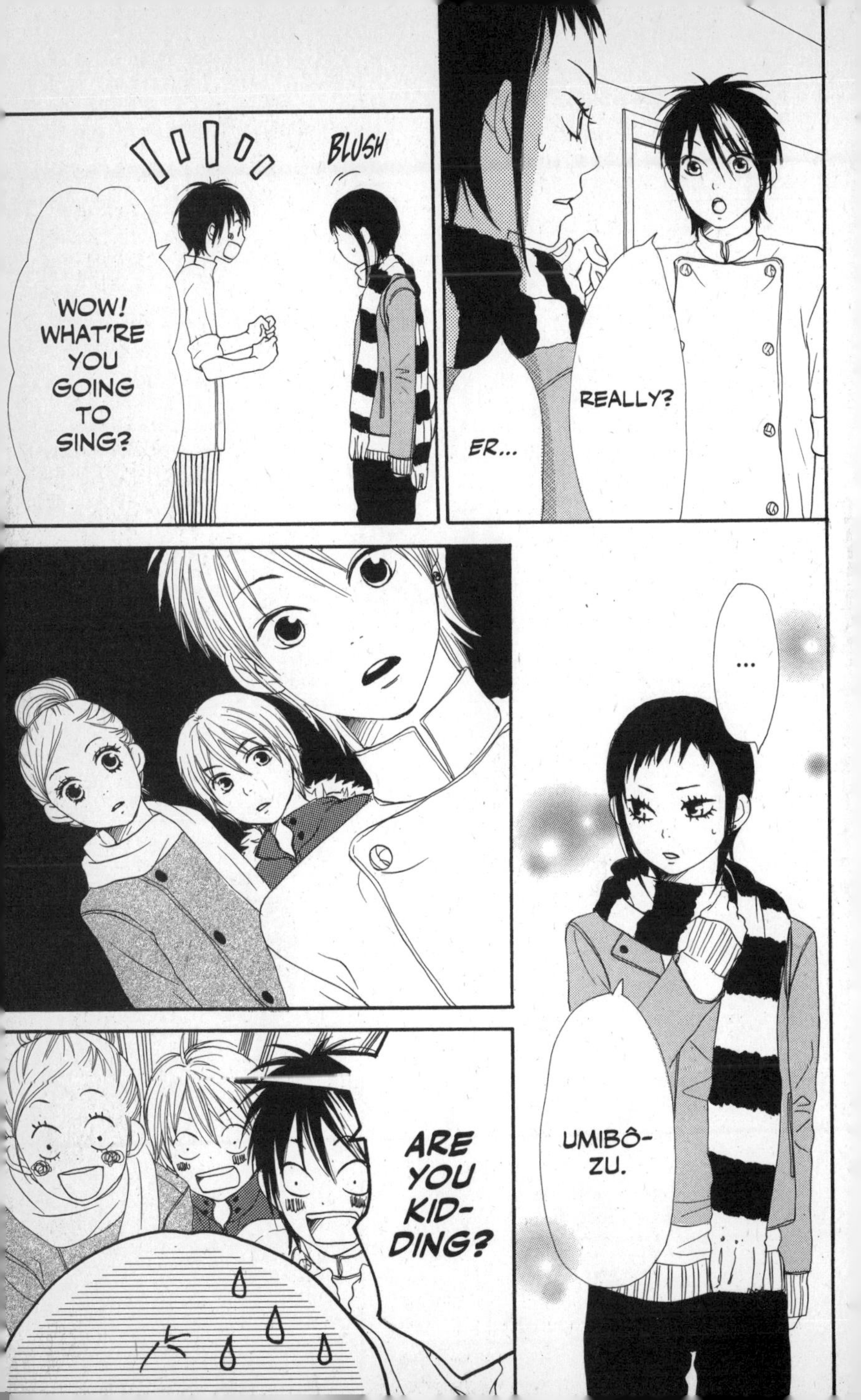
REALLY?
ER...
BLUSH
WOW! WHAT'RE YOU GOING TO SING?
...
UMIBÔ-ZU.
ARE YOU KID-DING?

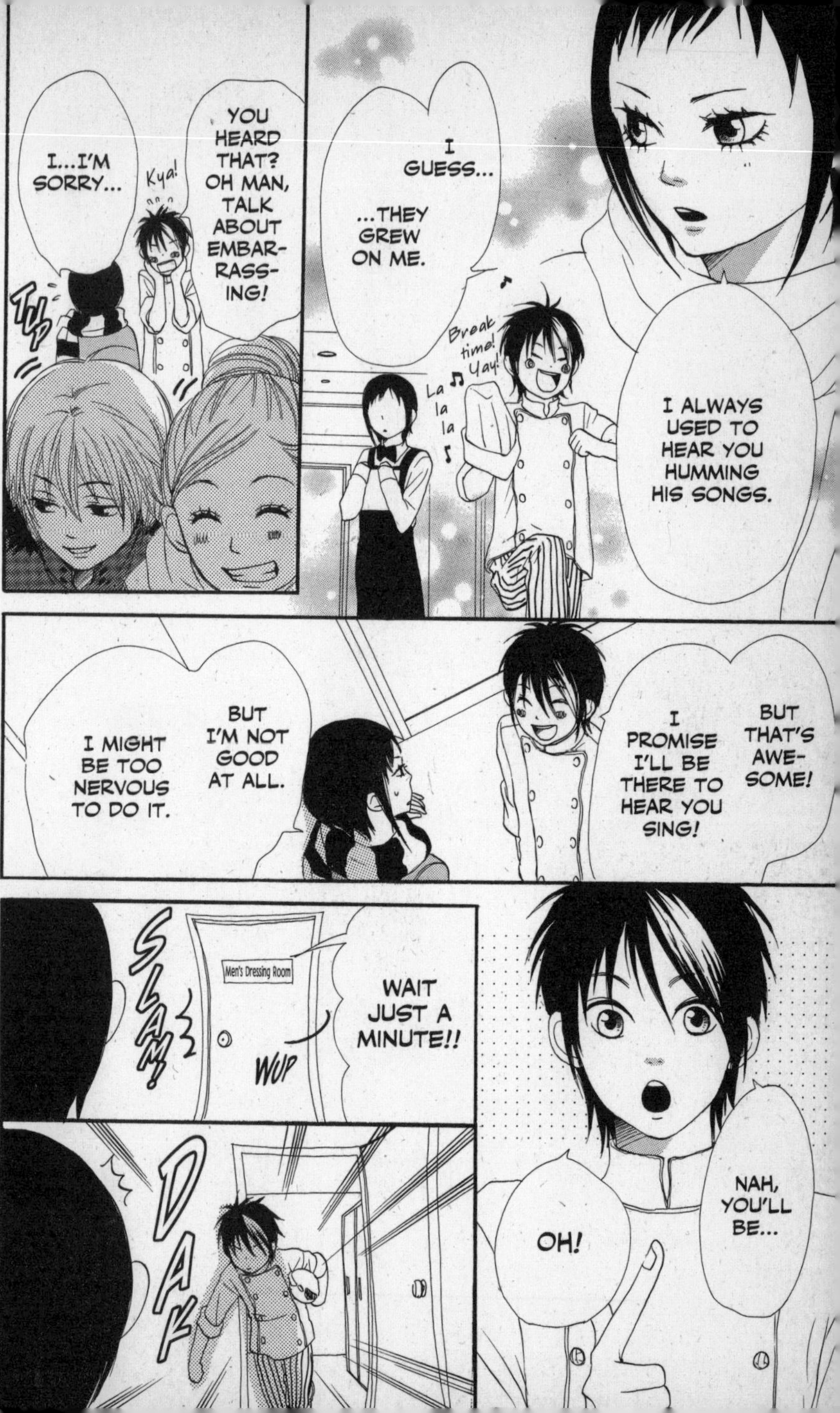
I ALWAYS USED TO HEAR YOU HUMMING HIS SONGS.
Break time! Yay!
La la la
I GUESS...
...THEY GREW ON ME.
YOU HEARD THAT? OH MAN, TALK ABOUT EMBARRASSING!
Kya!
I...I'M SORRY...
TUP
BUT THAT'S AWESOME!
I PROMISE I'LL BE THERE TO HEAR YOU SING!
BUT I'M NOT GOOD AT ALL.
I MIGHT BE TOO NERVOUS TO DO IT.
NAH, YOU'LL BE...
OH!
WAIT JUST A MINUTE!!
Men's Dressing Room
WUP
SLAM!
DAAK

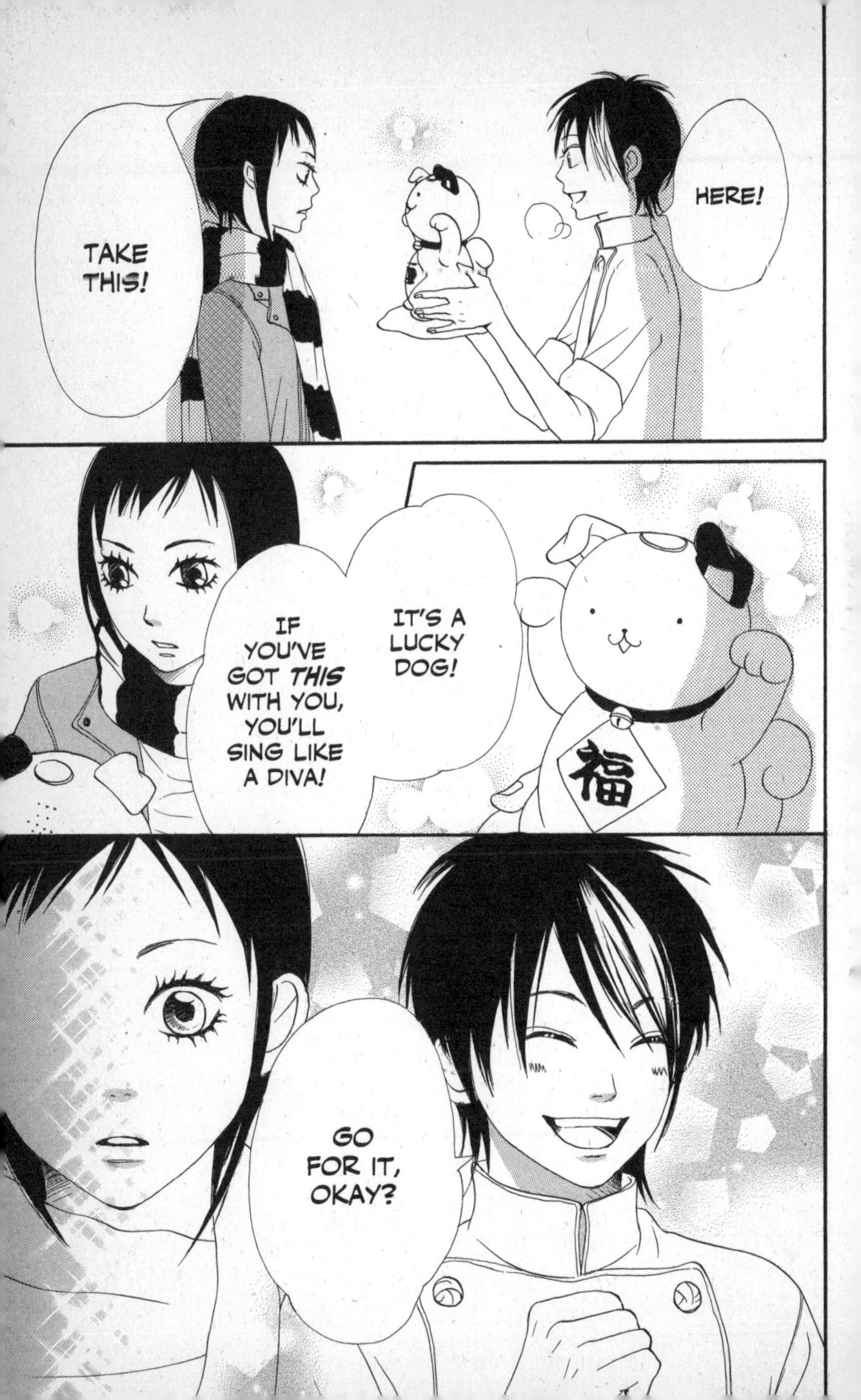
HERE!
TAKE THIS!
IT'S A LUCKY DOG!
IF YOU'VE GOT *THIS* WITH YOU, YOU'LL SING LIKE A DIVA!
福
GO FOR IT, OKAY?

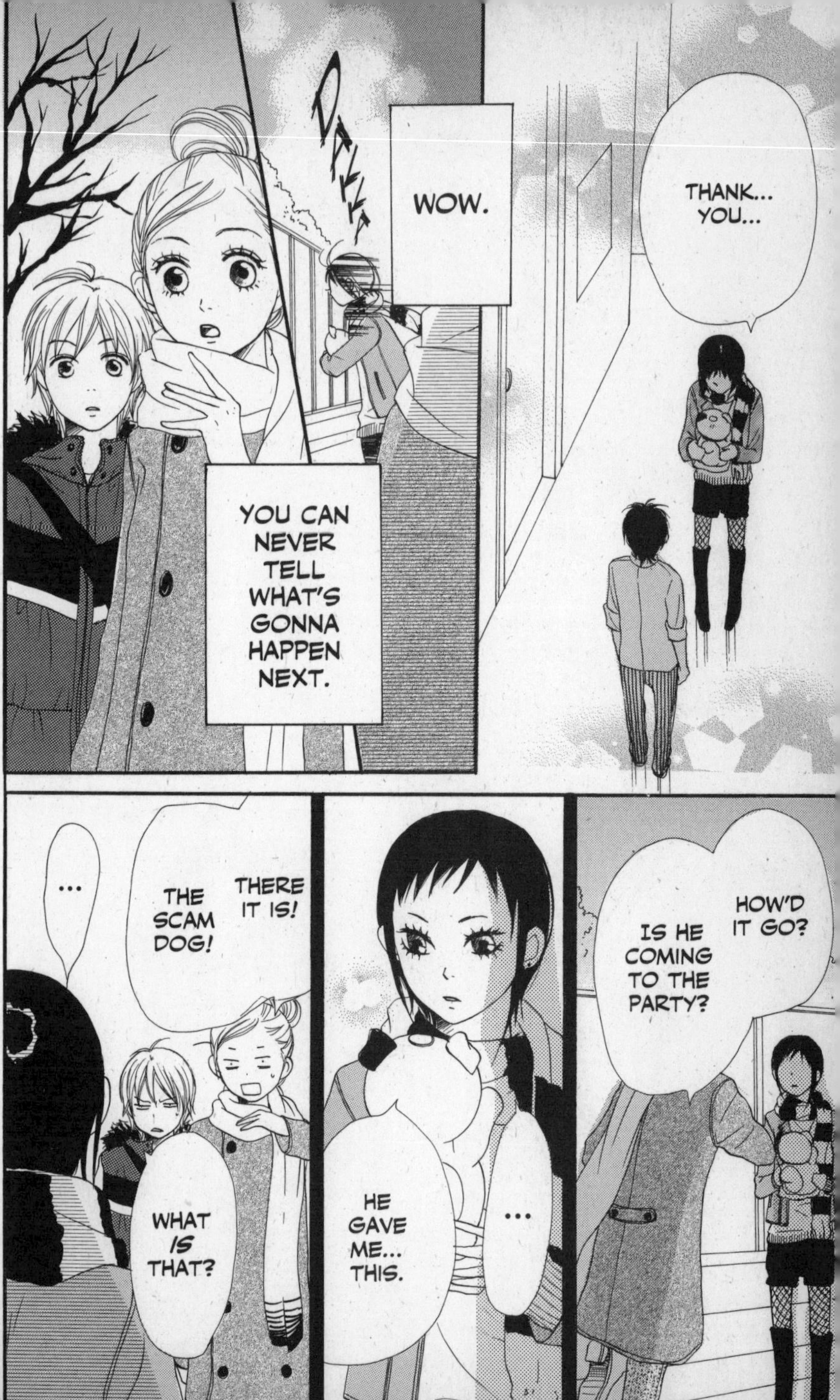
THANK... YOU...
WOW.
YOU CAN NEVER TELL WHAT'S GONNA HAPPEN NEXT.
HOW'D IT GO?
IS HE COMING TO THE PARTY?
...
HE GAVE ME... THIS.
THERE IT IS!
THE SCAM DOG!
...
WHAT *IS* THAT?

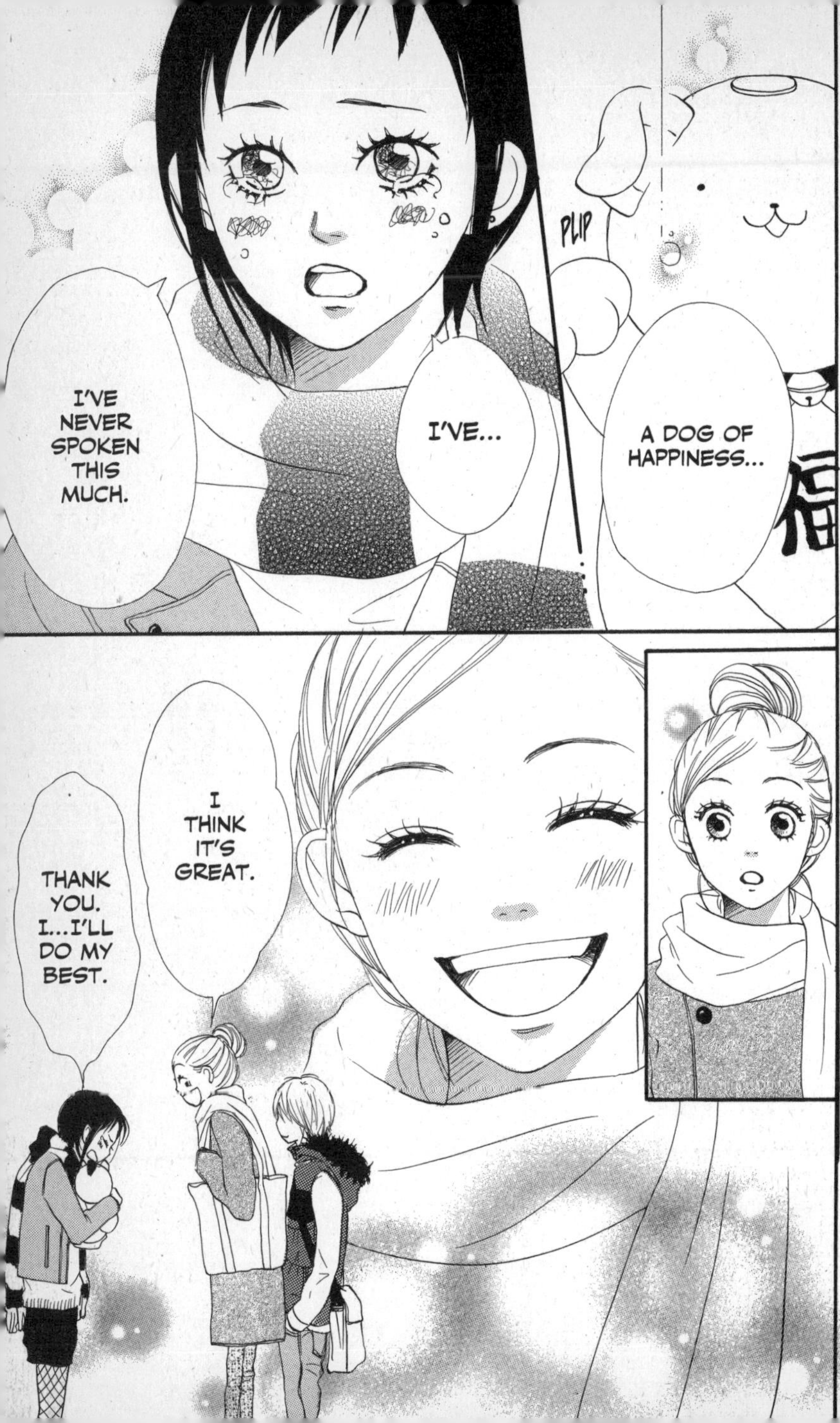
PLIP
A DOG OF HAPPINESS...
福
I'VE...
I'VE NEVER SPOKEN THIS MUCH.
I THINK IT'S GREAT.
THANK YOU. I...I'LL DO MY BEST.

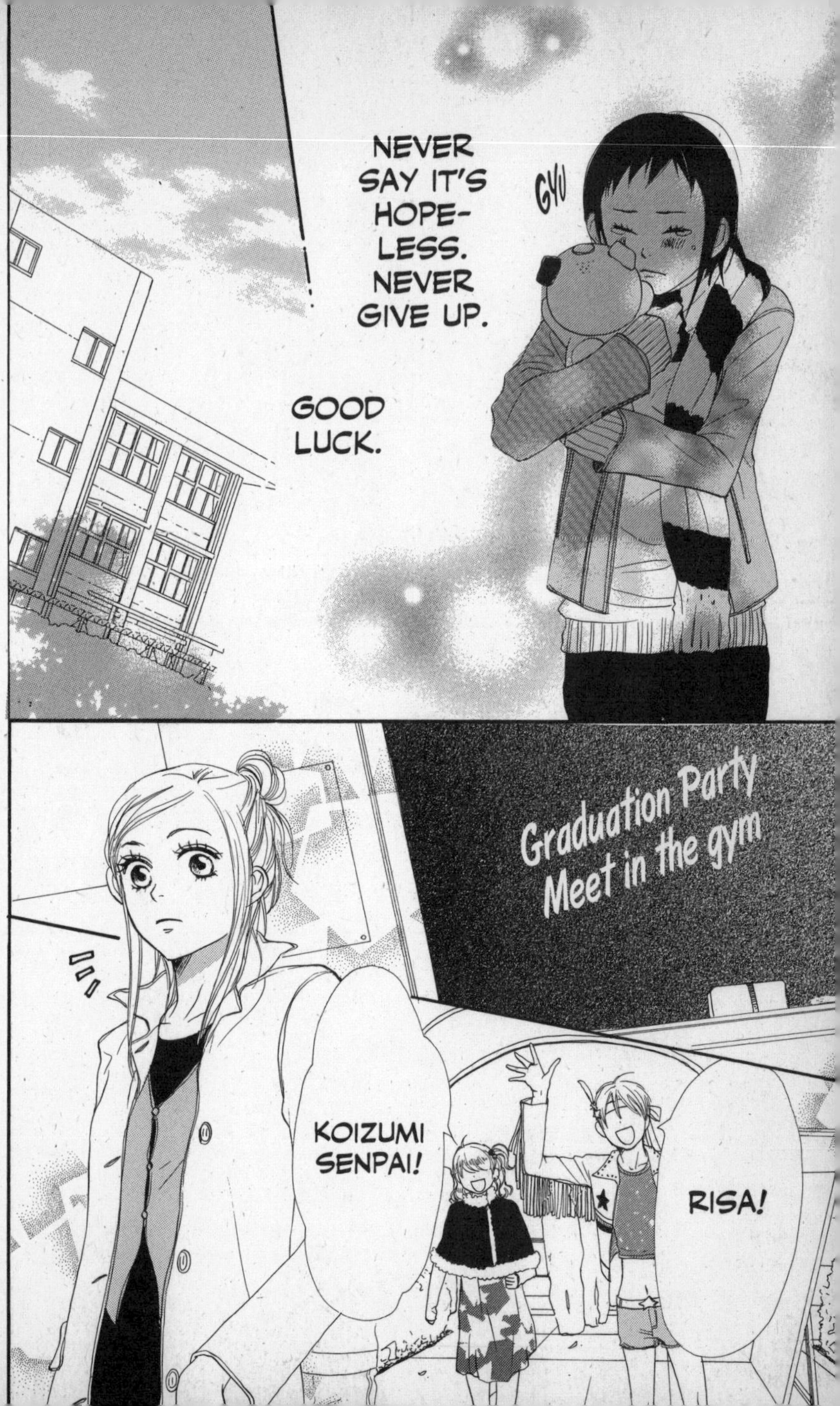
GYU
NEVER SAY IT'S HOPE-LESS. NEVER GIVE UP.
GOOD LUCK.
Graduation Party
Meet in the gym
RISA!
KOIZUMI SENPAI!

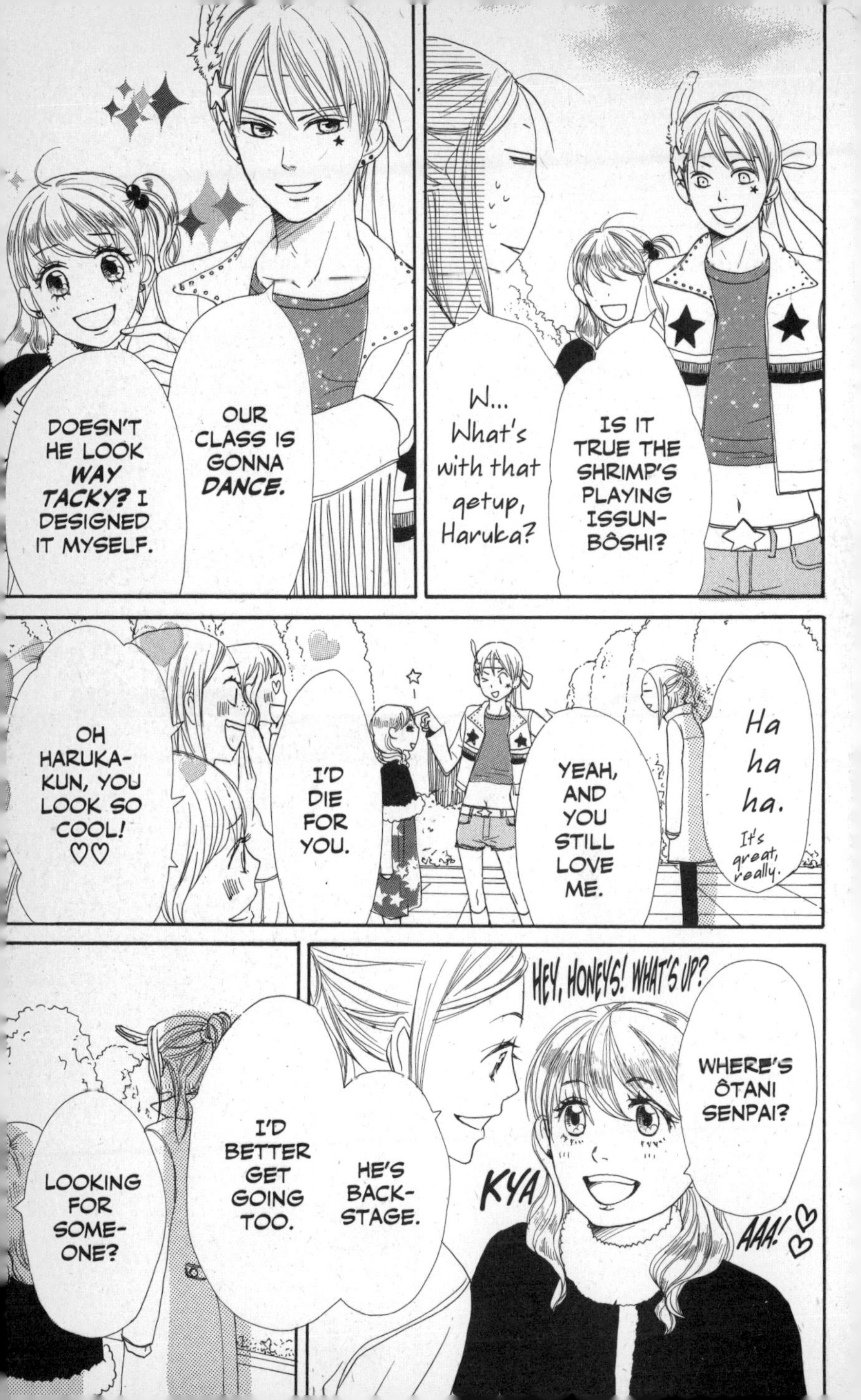
IS IT TRUE THE SHRIMP'S PLAYING ISSUN-BÔSHI?
W... What's with that getup, Haruka?
OUR CLASS IS GONNA *DANCE.*
DOESN'T HE LOOK *WAY TACKY?* I DESIGNED IT MYSELF.
Ha ha ha.
It's great, really.
YEAH, AND YOU STILL LOVE ME.
I'D DIE FOR YOU.
OH HARUKA-KUN, YOU LOOK SO COOL! ♡♡
HEY, HONEYS! WHAT'S UP?
WHERE'S ÔTANI SENPAI?
KYA
AAA! ♡♡
HE'S BACKSTAGE.
I'D BETTER GET GOING TOO.
LOOKING FOR SOME-ONE?

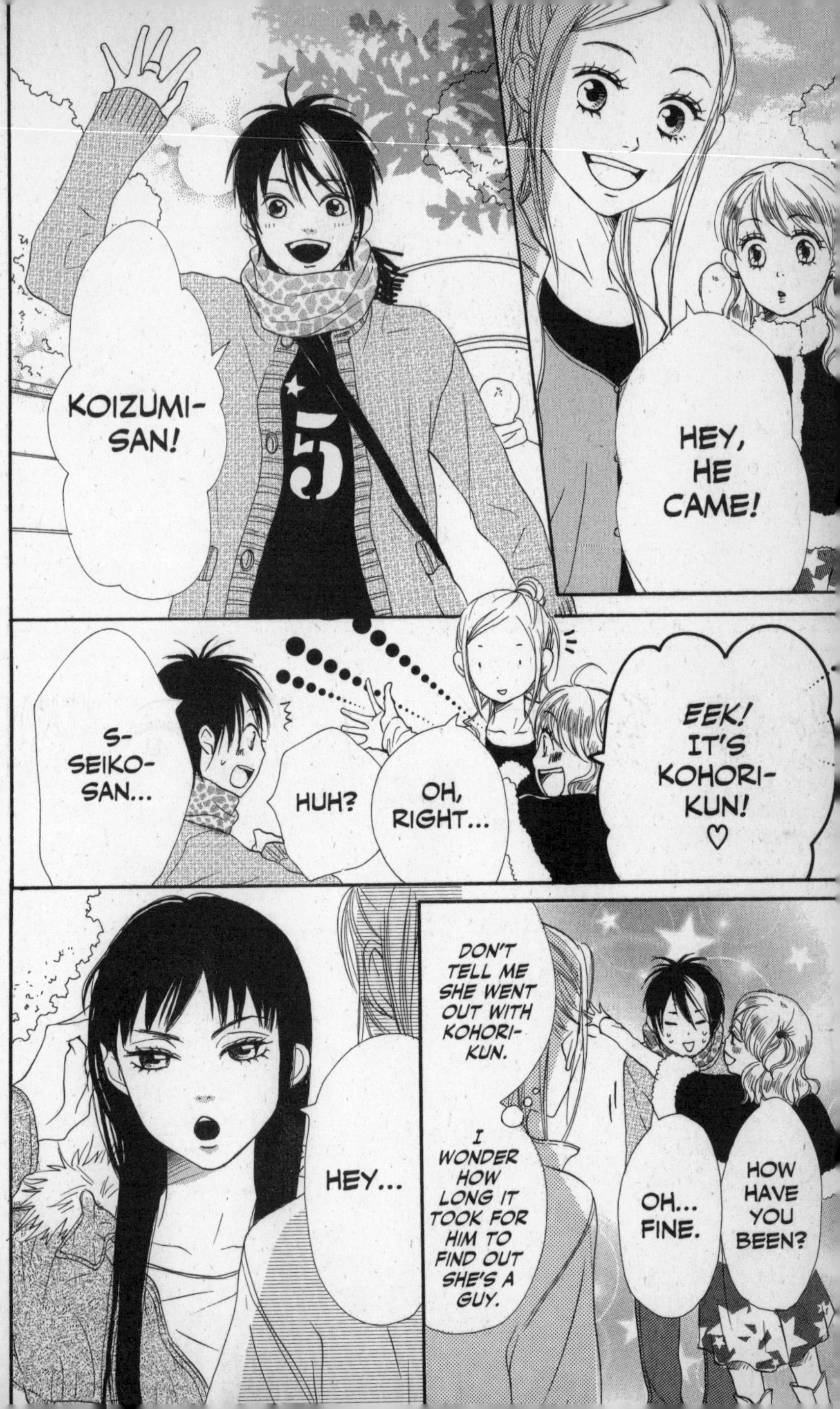
HEY, HE CAME!
KOIZUMI-SAN!
EEK! IT'S KOHORI-KUN! ♡
OH, RIGHT...
HUH?
S-SEIKO-SAN...
HOW HAVE YOU BEEN?
OH... FINE.
DON'T TELL ME SHE WENT OUT WITH KOHORI-KUN.
I WONDER HOW LONG IT TOOK FOR HIM TO FIND OUT SHE'S A GUY.
HEY...

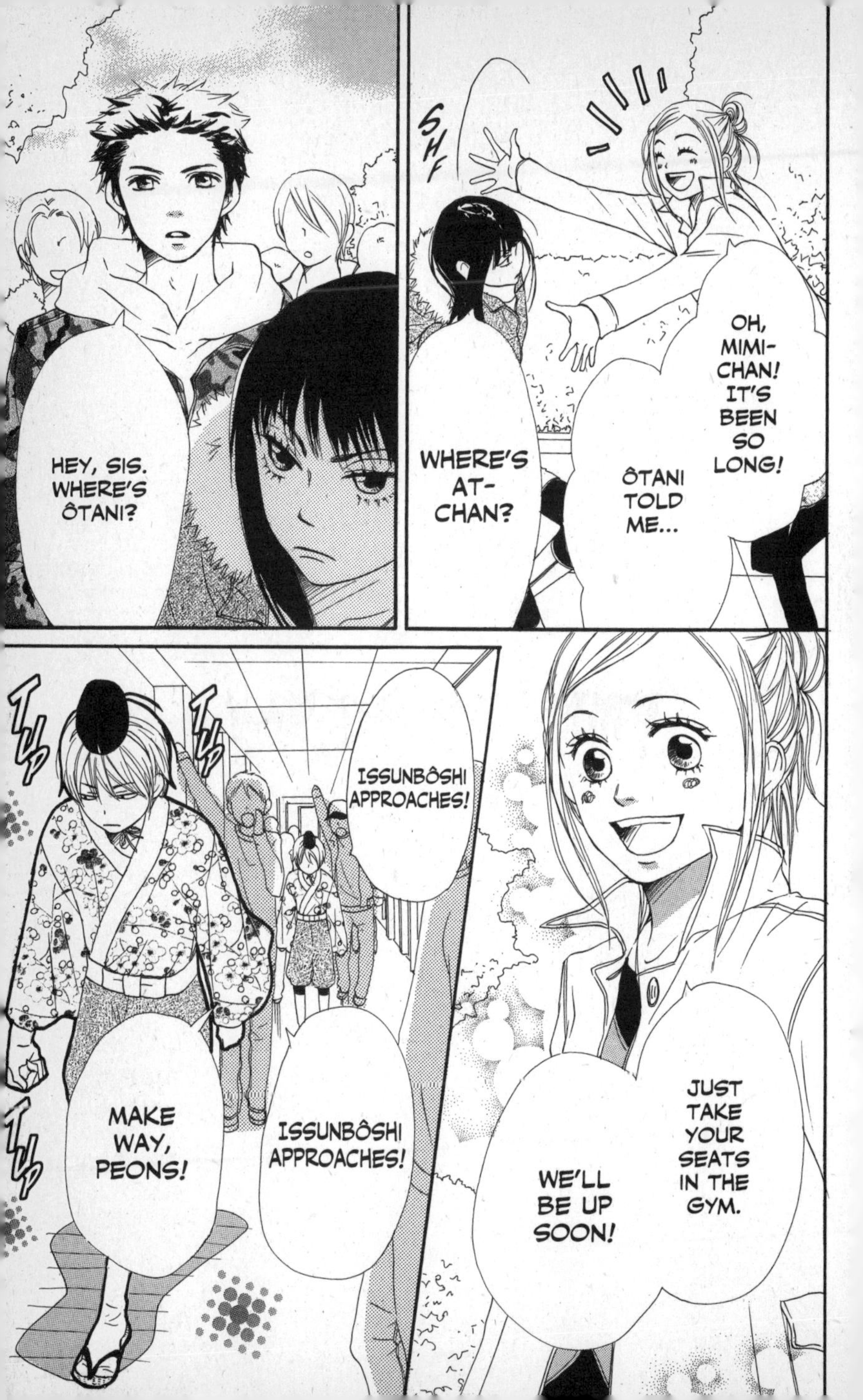
SHF
OH, MIMI-CHAN! IT'S BEEN SO LONG!
ÔTANI TOLD ME...
WHERE'S AT-CHAN?
HEY, SIS. WHERE'S ÔTANI?
JUST TAKE YOUR SEATS IN THE GYM.
WE'LL BE UP SOON!
TUP
TUP
ISSUNBÔSHI APPROACHES!
ISSUNBÔSHI APPROACHES!
MAKE WAY, PEONS!
TUP

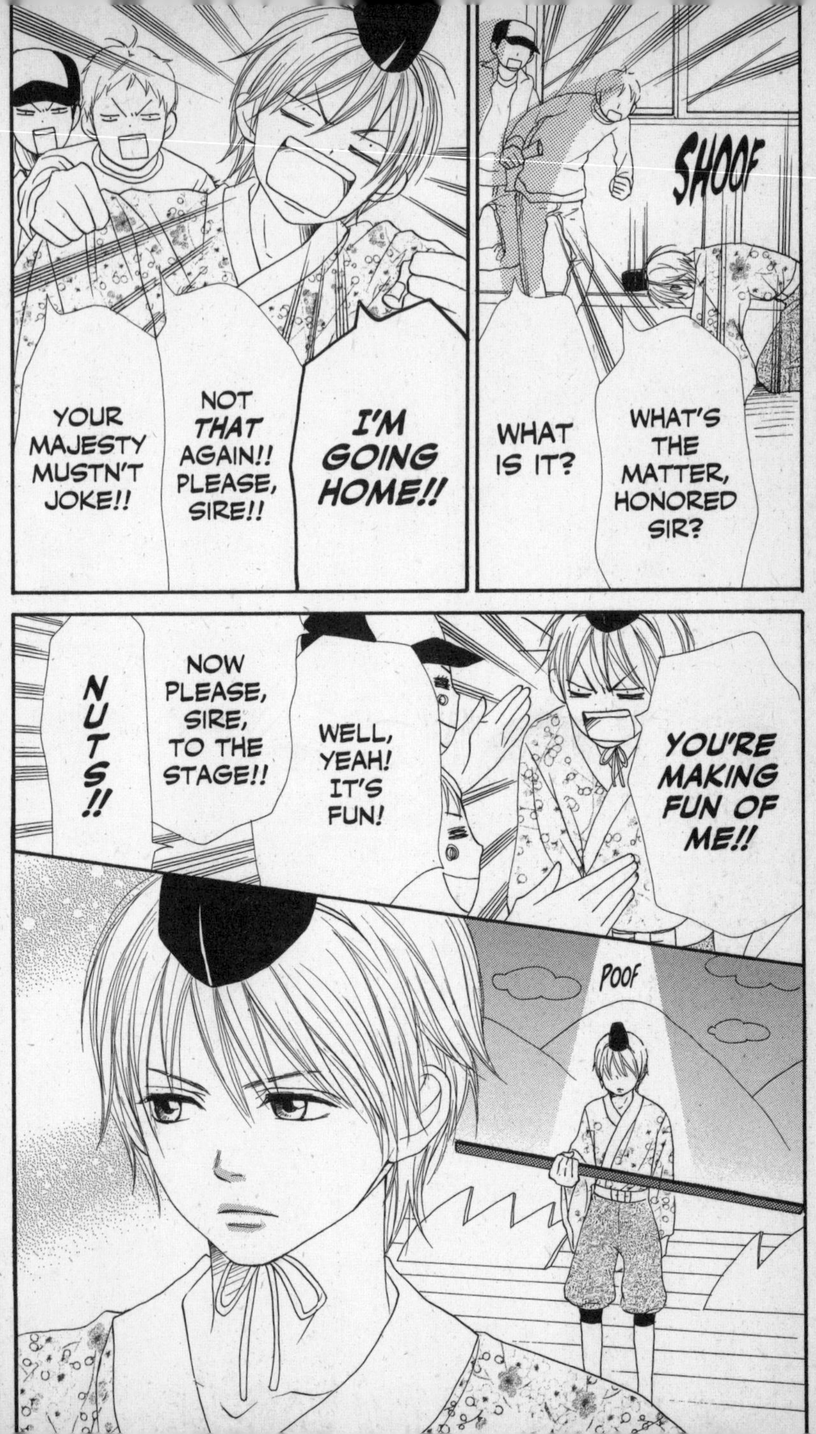
SHOOF
WHAT'S THE MATTER, HONORED SIR?
WHAT IS IT?
I'M GOING HOME!!
NOT *THAT* AGAIN!! PLEASE, SIRE!!
YOUR MAJESTY MUSTN'T JOKE!!
YOU'RE MAKING FUN OF ME!!
WELL, YEAH! IT'S FUN!
NOW PLEASE, SIRE, TO THE STAGE!!
NUTS!!
POOF

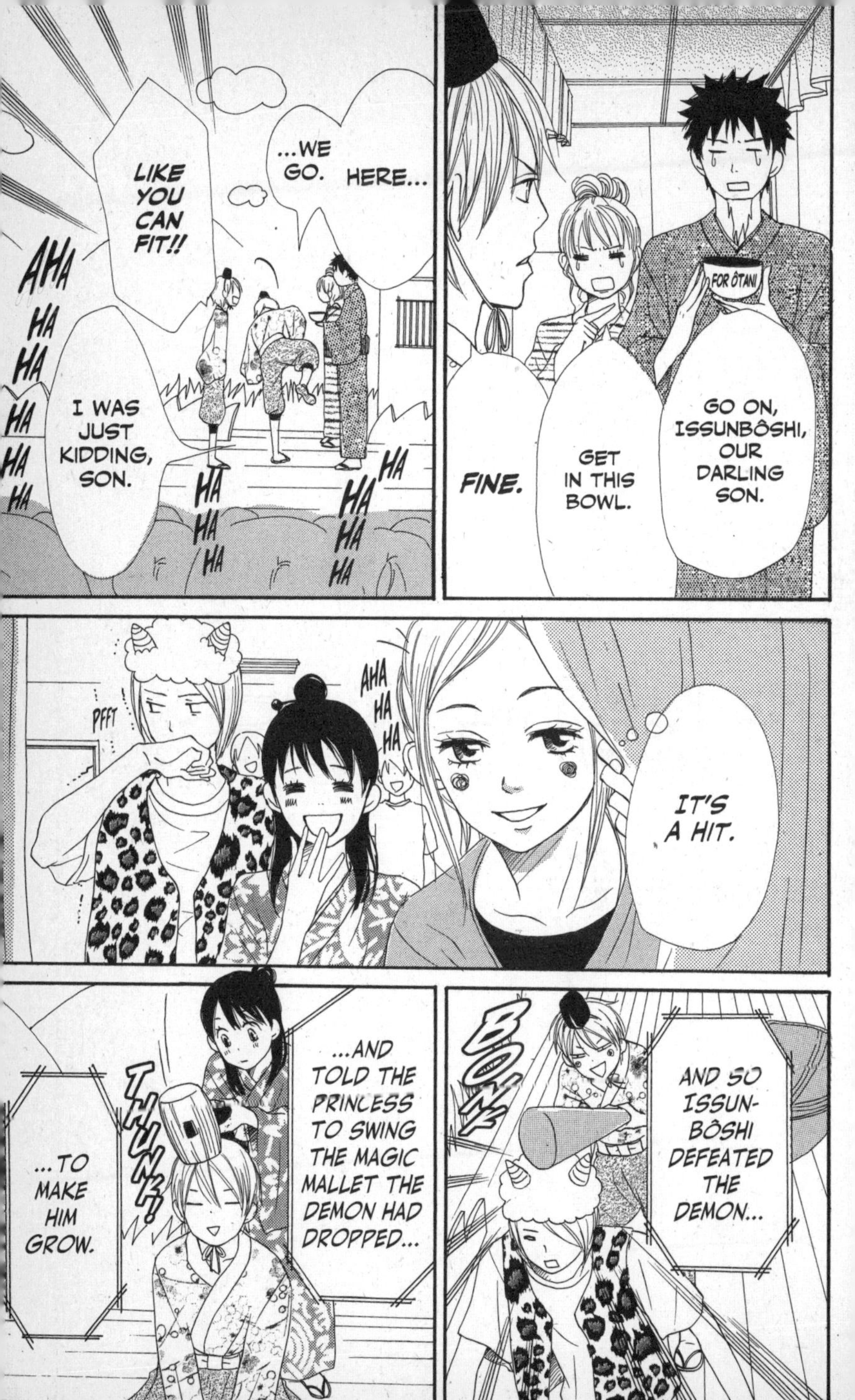
FOR ÔTANI
GO ON, ISSUNBÔSHI, OUR DARLING SON.
GET IN THIS BOWL.
FINE.
HERE...
...WE GO.
LIKE YOU CAN FIT!!
AHA HA HA HA HA HA
I WAS JUST KIDDING, SON.
HA HA HA HA
HA HA HA HA HA
IT'S A HIT.
AHA HA HA
PFFT
AND SO ISSUN-BÔSHI DEFEATED THE DEMON...
BONK
...AND TOLD THE PRINCESS TO SWING THE MAGIC MALLET THE DEMON HAD DROPPED...
THUNK!
...TO MAKE HIM GROW.

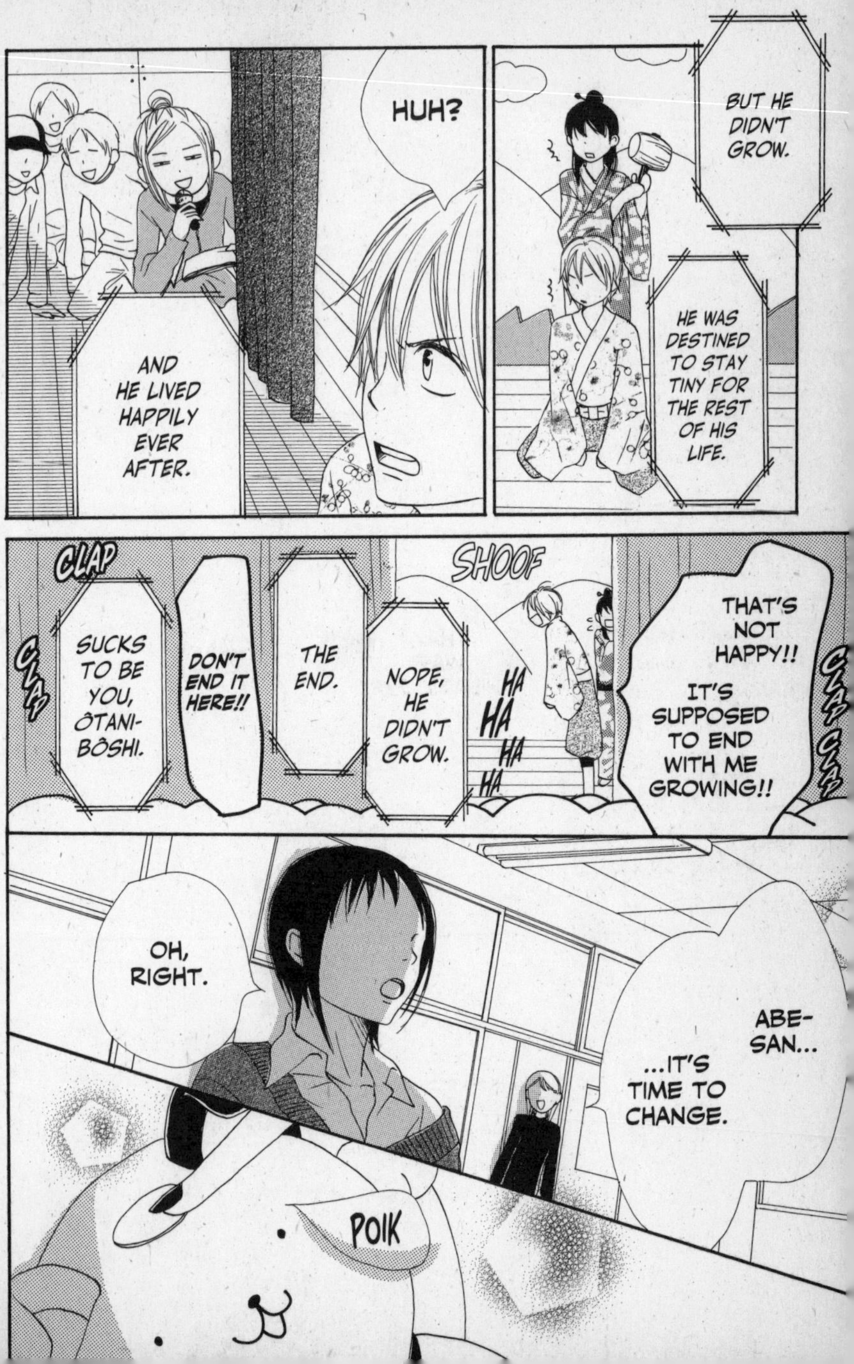
BUT HE DIDN'T GROW.
HE WAS DESTINED TO STAY TINY FOR THE REST OF HIS LIFE.
HUH?
AND HE LIVED HAPPILY EVER AFTER.
CLAP CLAP CLAP
THAT'S NOT HAPPY!!
IT'S SUPPOSED TO END WITH ME GROWING!!
HA HA HA HA
SHOOF
NOPE, HE DIDN'T GROW.
THE END.
DON'T END IT HERE!!
SUCKS TO BE YOU, ÔTANI-BÔSHI.
CLAP
CLAP
ABE-SAN...
...IT'S TIME TO CHANGE.
OH, RIGHT.
POIK

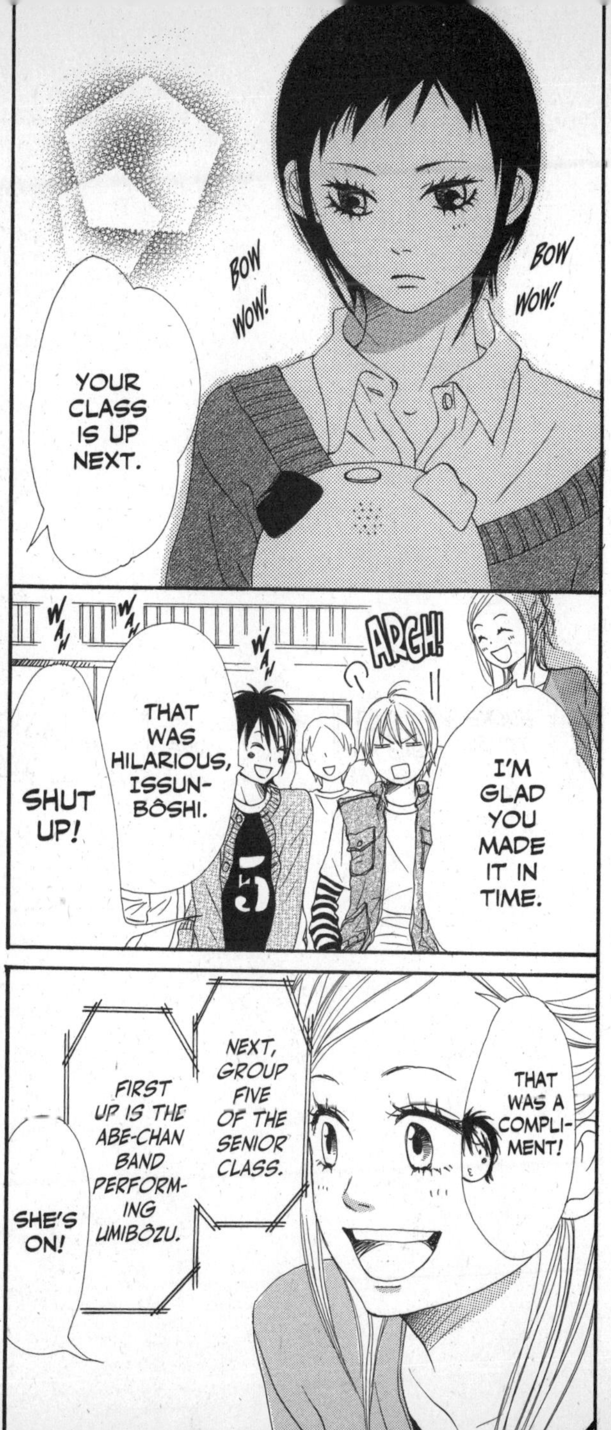
BOW WOW!
BOW WOW!
YOUR CLASS IS UP NEXT.
I'M GLAD YOU MADE IT IN TIME.
ARGH!
WAH
WAH
WAH
THAT WAS HILARIOUS, ISSUN-BÔSHI.
SHUT UP!
THAT WAS A COMPLIMENT!
NEXT, GROUP FIVE OF THE SENIOR CLASS.
FIRST UP IS THE ABE-CHAN BAND PERFORMING UMIBÔZU.
SHE'S ON!

1

Hi, it's me, Nakahara. Hey...volume 16! If you've got this one, you've got the ending! But they're letting me do another volume with bonus stories, so please check that out too. I'm drawing the bonus stuff now. This long series is finally nearing its end! I guess I should be reminiscing about everything that happened to me... But nothing comes to mind. Okay, I'll do it in volume 17!

So...Love★Com ran for five years. For the first time in five years, I don't have a deadline coming up. I'm not feeling well. I look so gaunt. When I was drawing manga, I was never sick!

To be continued...

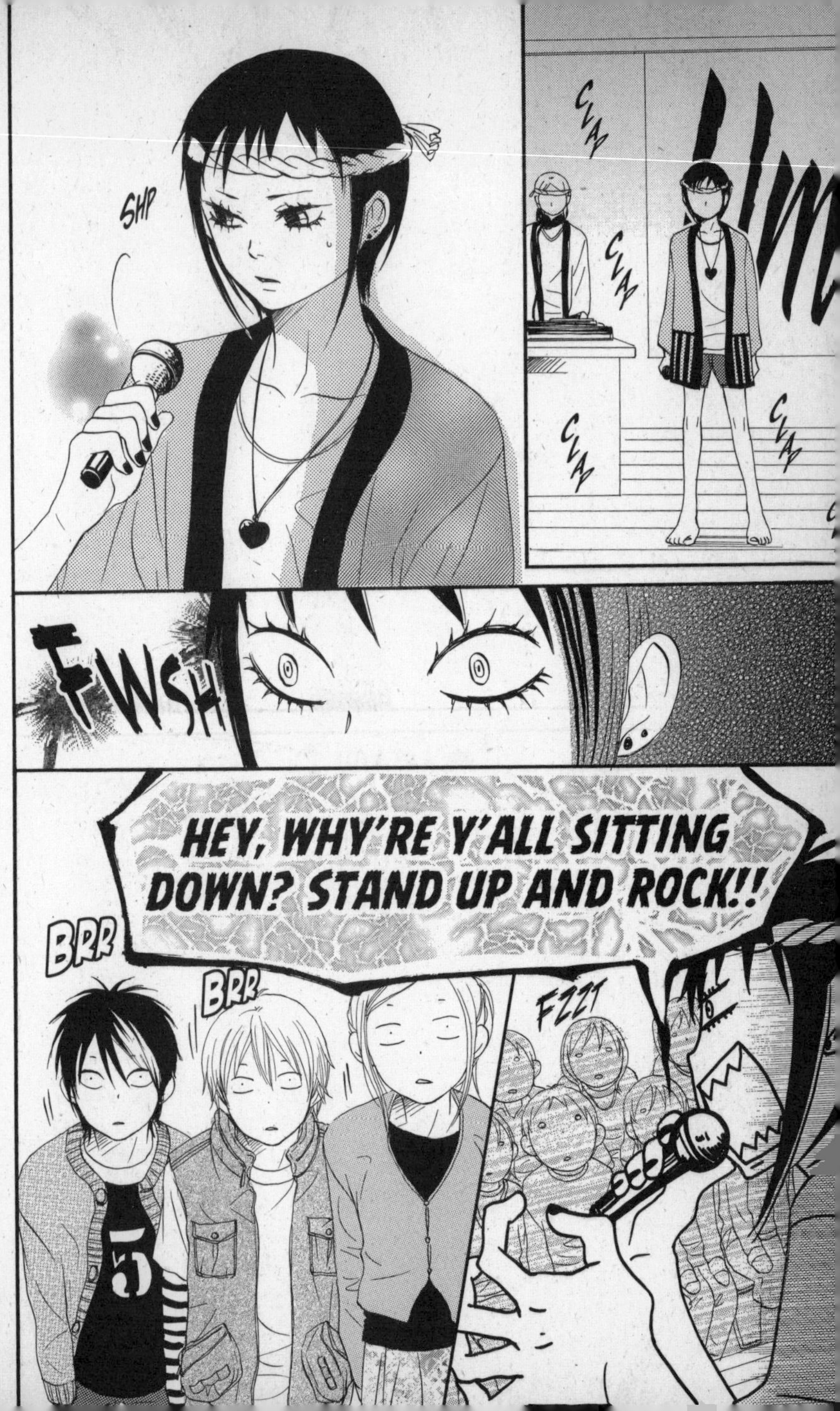
CLAP
CLAP
CLAP
CLAP
SHP
FWSH
HEY, WHY'RE Y'ALL SITTING DOWN? STAND UP AND ROCK!!
BRR
BRR
FZZT

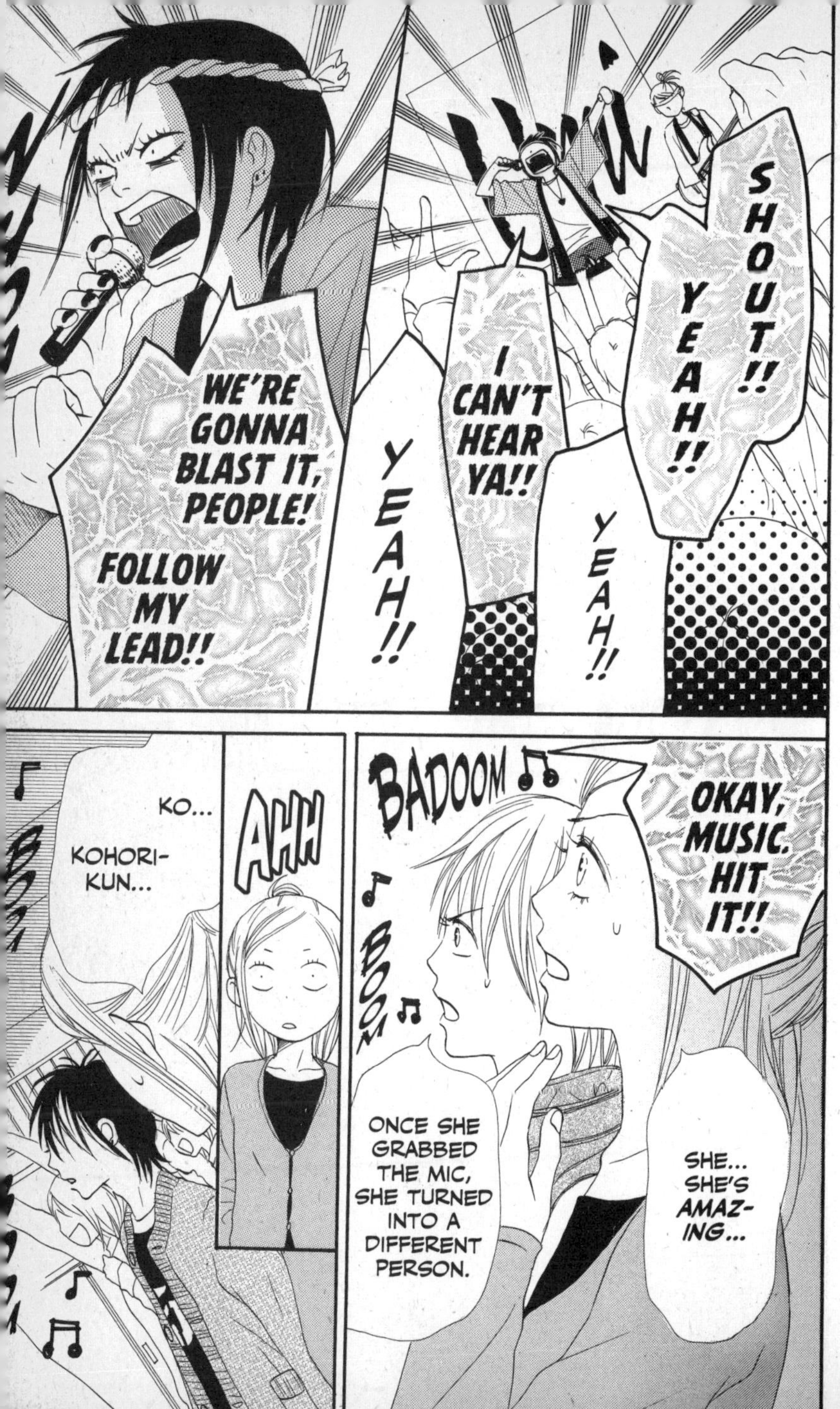
SHOUT!!
YEAH!!
YEAH!!
I CAN'T HEAR YA!!
YEAH!!
WE'RE GONNA BLAST IT, PEOPLE!
FOLLOW MY LEAD!!
OKAY, MUSIC. HIT IT!!
BADOOM
BOOM
SHE... SHE'S AMAZ-ING...
ONCE SHE GRABBED THE MIC, SHE TURNED INTO A DIFFERENT PERSON.
AHH
KO...
KOHORI-KUN...

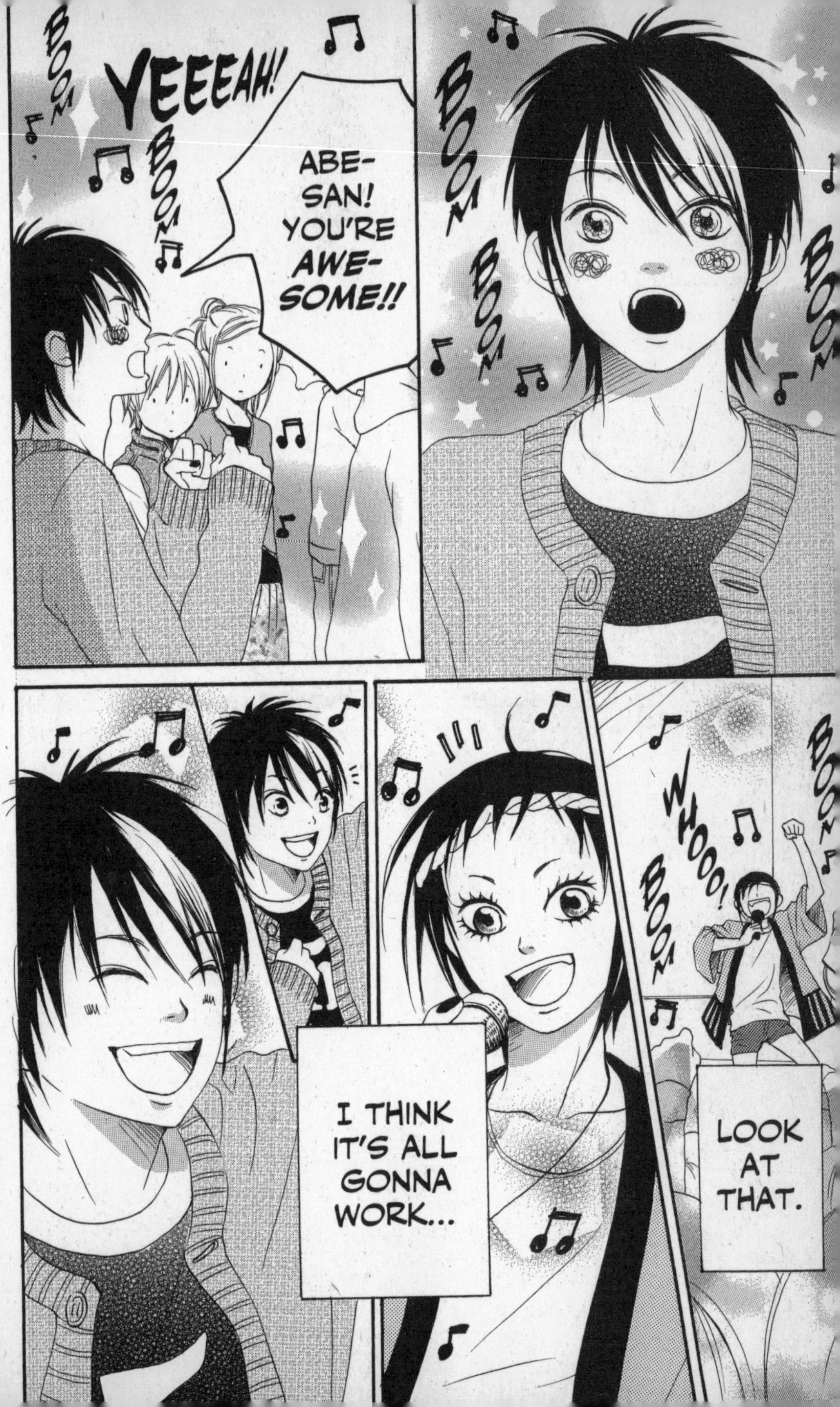
BOOM
BOOM
BOOM
YEEEAH!
BOOM
BOOM
ABE-SAN! YOU'RE AWESOME!!
BOOM
WHOOO!
BOOM
LOOK AT THAT.
I THINK IT'S ALL GONNA WORK...

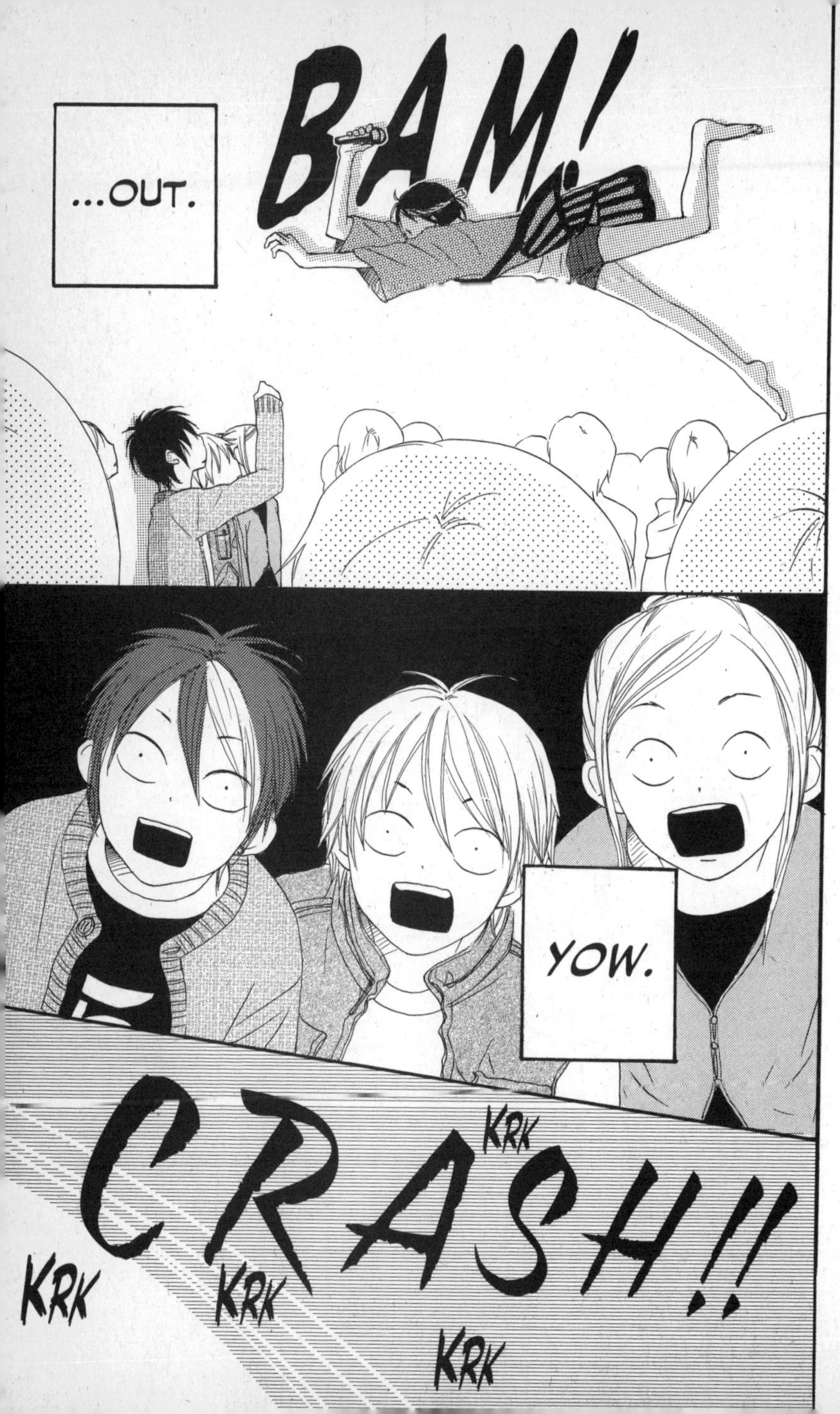
BAM!
...OUT.
YOW.
KRK
CRASH!!
KRK
KRK
KRK

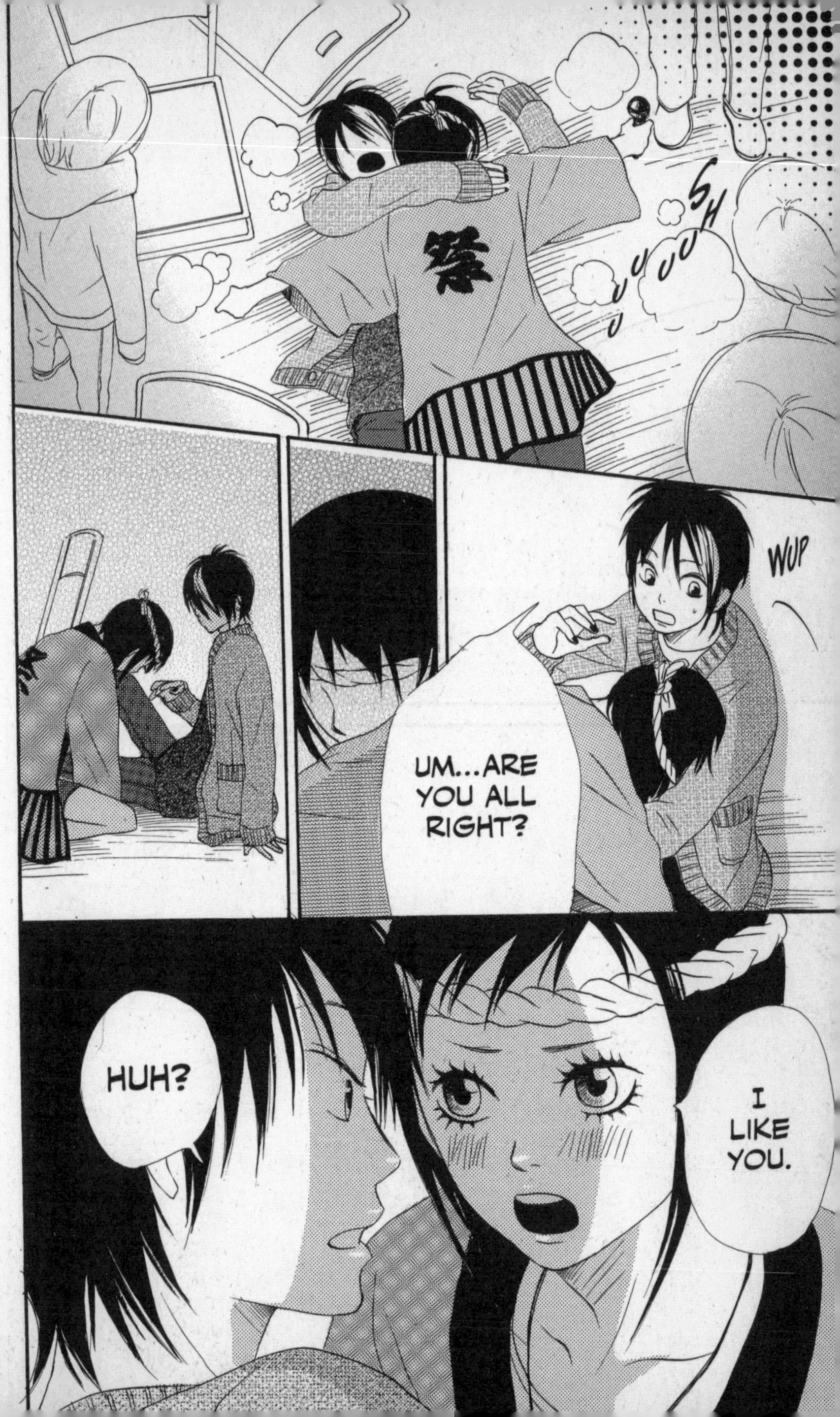
SHUUUUU
WUP
UM...ARE YOU ALL RIGHT?
I LIKE YOU.
HUH?

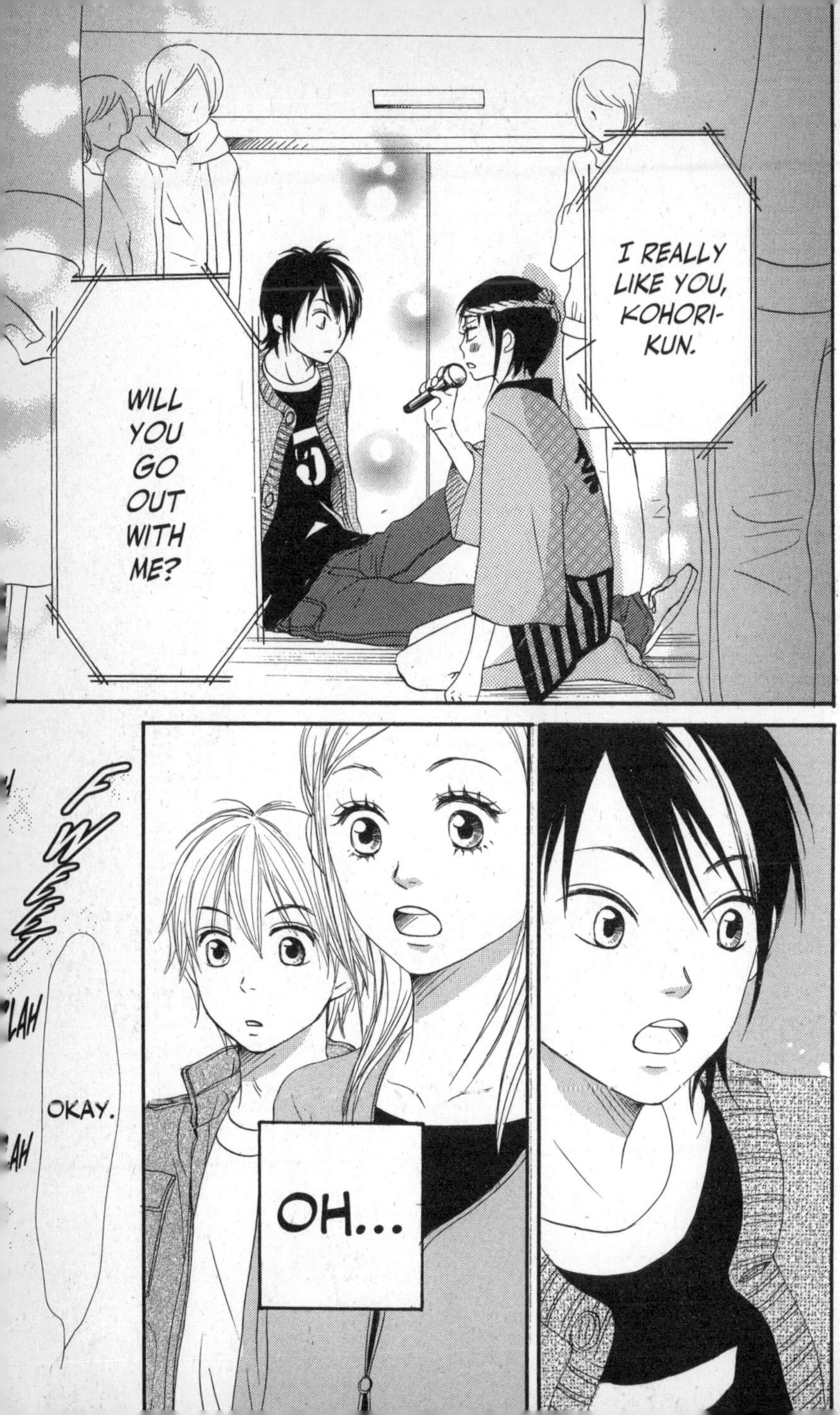
I REALLY LIKE YOU, KOHORI-KUN.
WILL YOU GO OUT WITH ME?
OH...
OKAY.

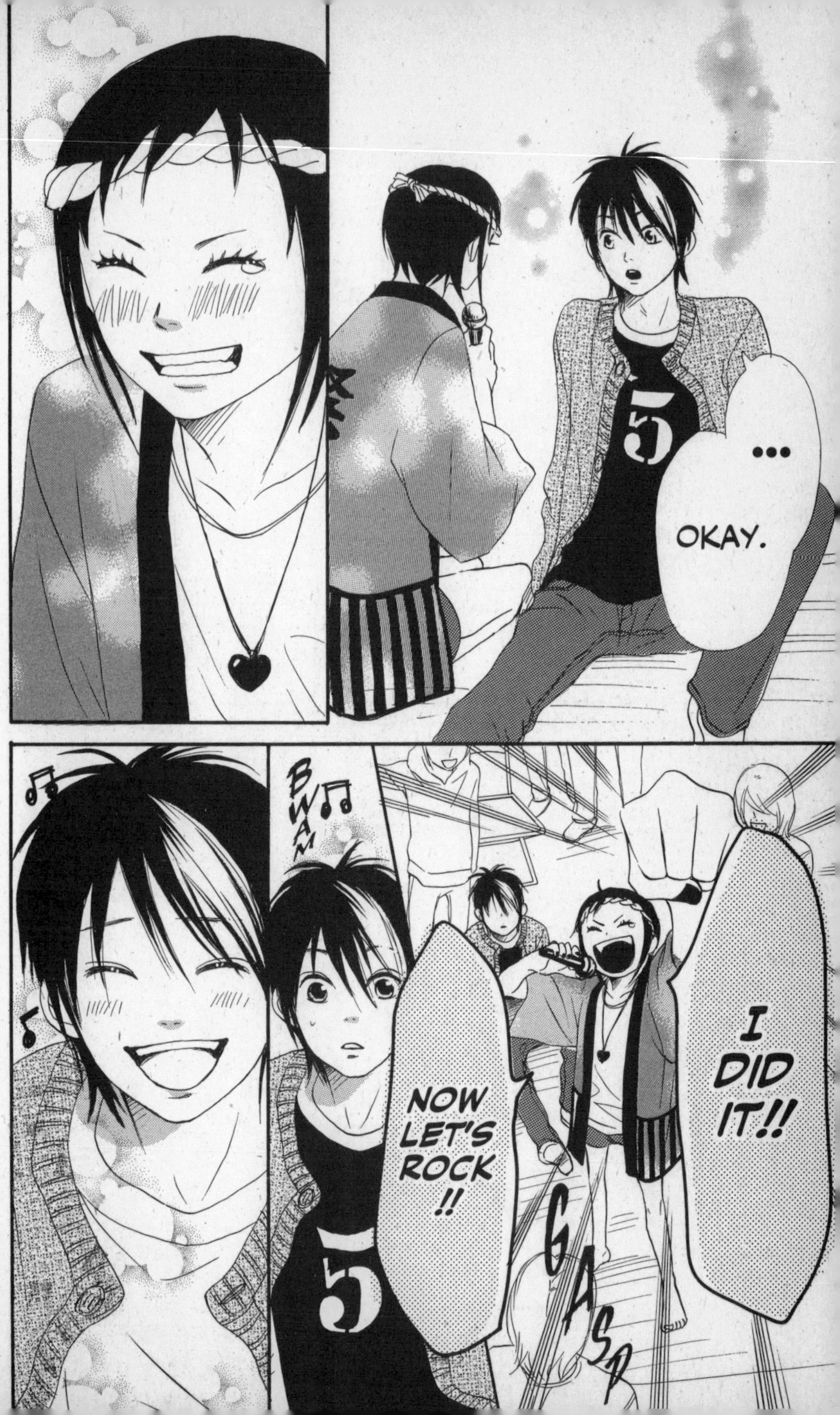
...
OKAY.
I DID IT!!
GASP
NOW LET'S ROCK!!
BWAM

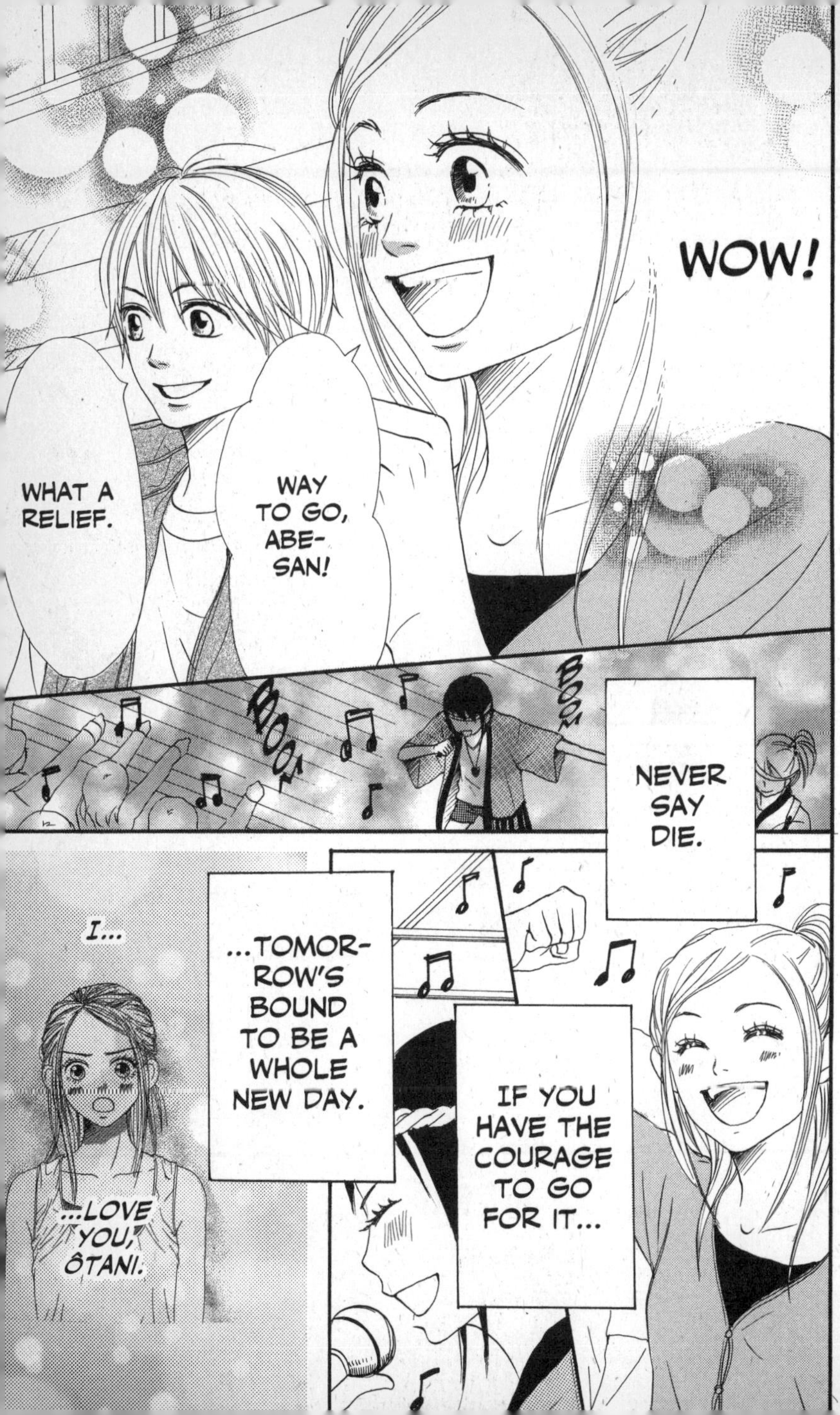
WOW!
WAY TO GO, ABE-SAN!
WHAT A RELIEF.
BOOM
BOOM
NEVER SAY DIE.
IF YOU HAVE THE COURAGE TO GO FOR IT...
...TOMORROW'S BOUND TO BE A WHOLE NEW DAY.
I...
...LOVE YOU, ÔTANI.

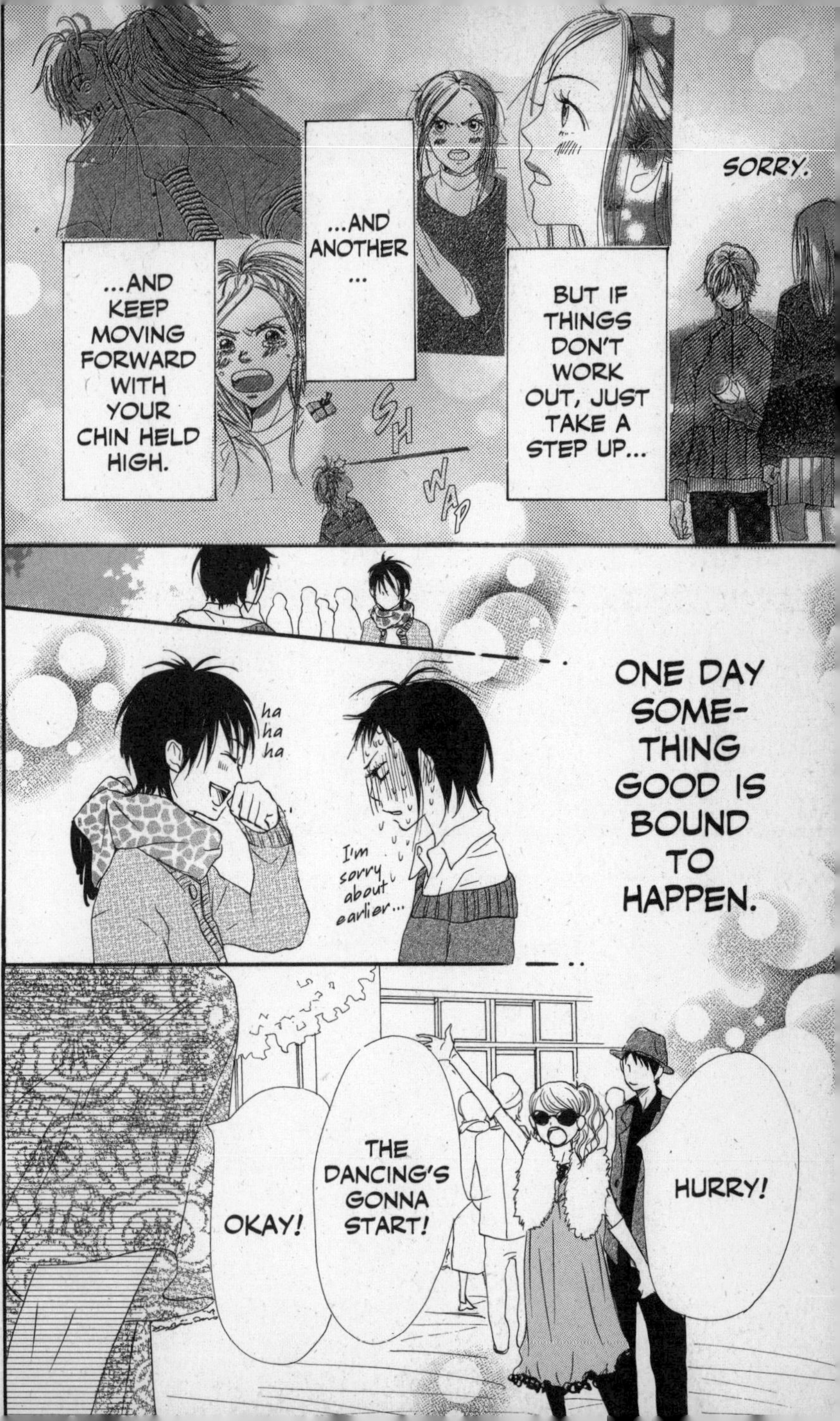
SORRY.
BUT IF THINGS DON'T WORK OUT, JUST TAKE A STEP UP...
...AND ANOTHER ...
...AND KEEP MOVING FORWARD WITH YOUR CHIN HELD HIGH.
SH
WAP
ONE DAY SOME-THING GOOD IS BOUND TO HAPPEN.
I'm sorry about earlier...
ha ha ha
HURRY!
THE DANCING'S GONNA START!
OKAY!

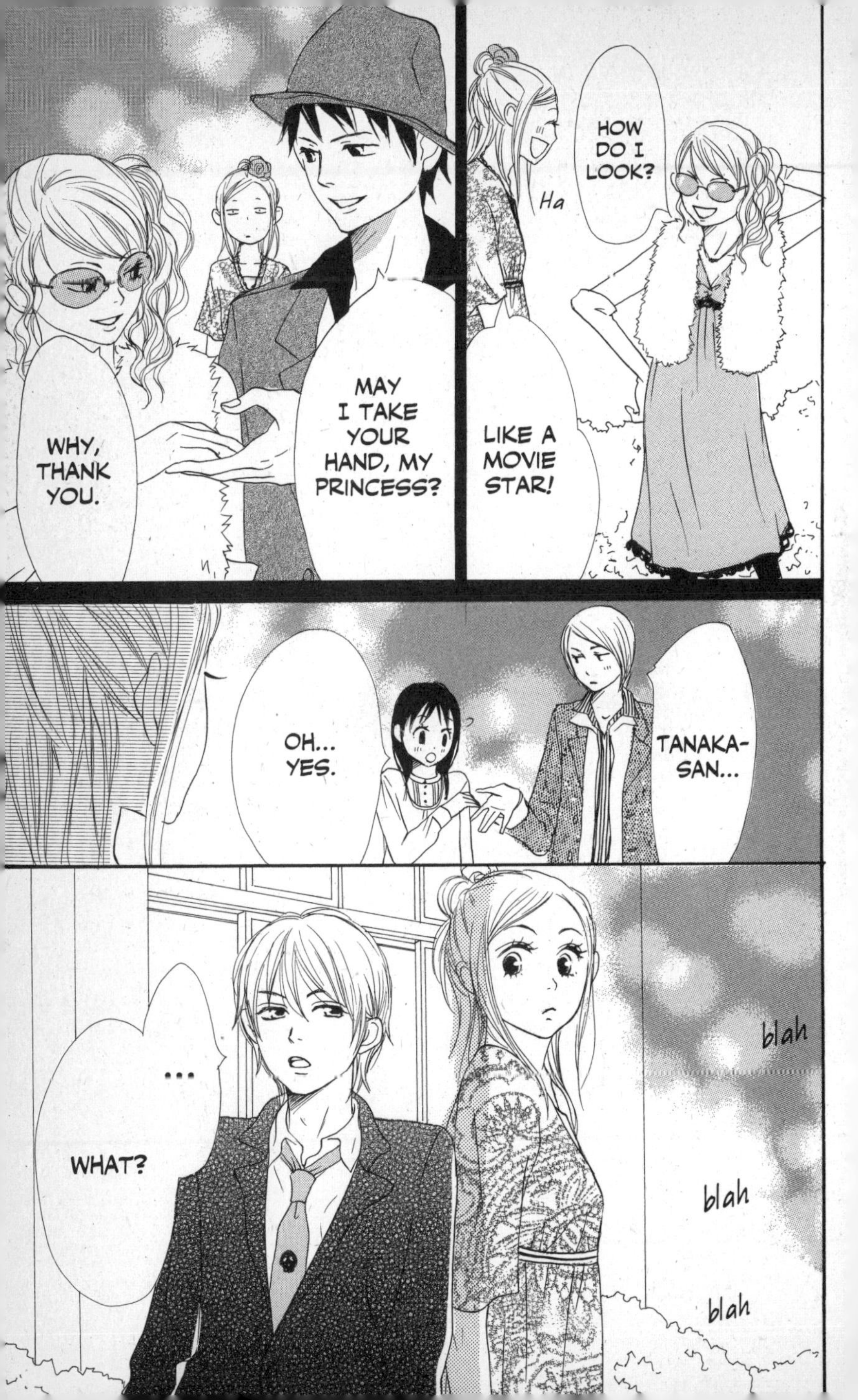
HOW DO I LOOK?
Ha
LIKE A MOVIE STAR!
MAY I TAKE YOUR HAND, MY PRINCESS?
WHY, THANK YOU.
TANAKA-SAN...
OH... YES.
blah
blah
blah
...
WHAT?

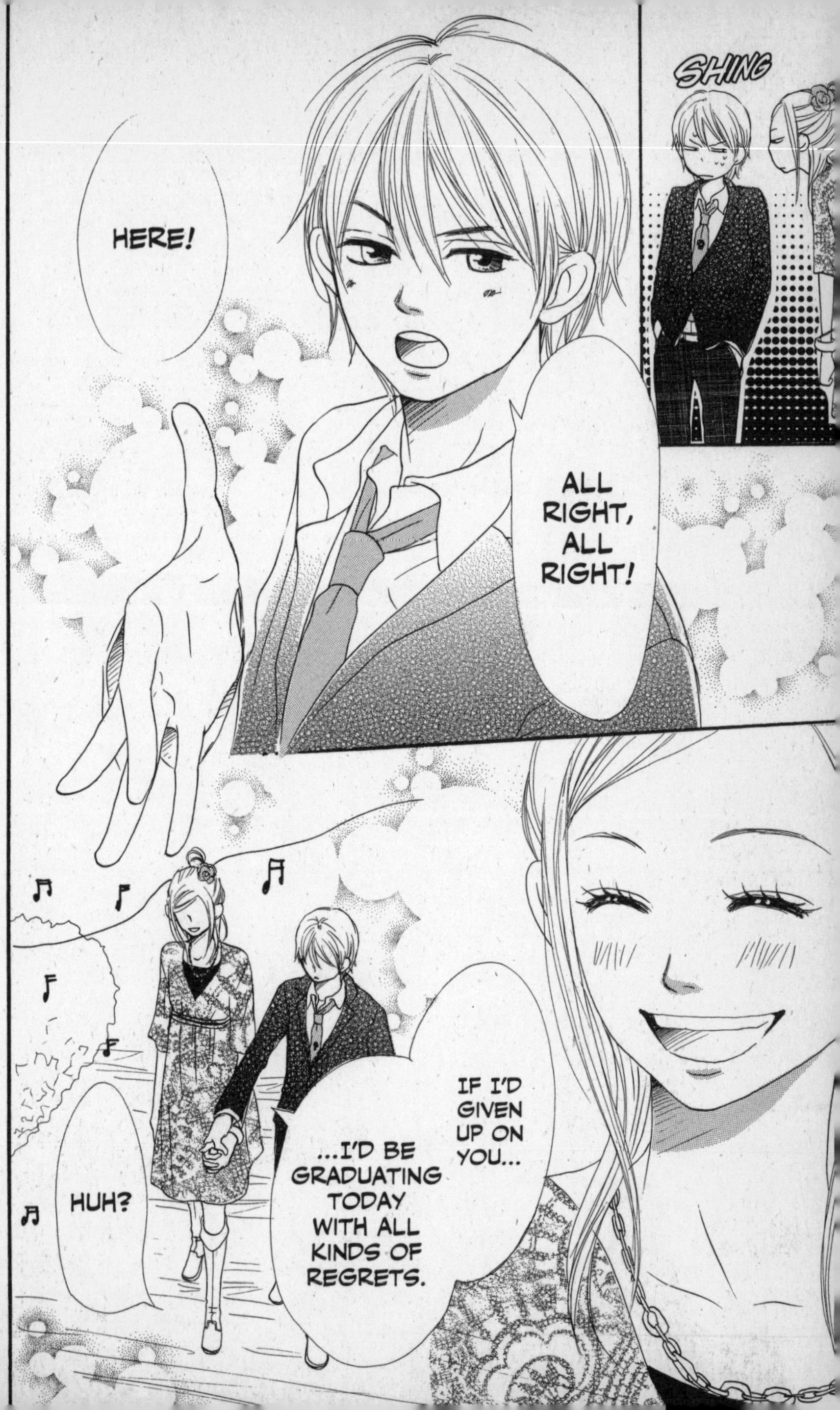
SHING
ALL RIGHT, ALL RIGHT!
HERE!
IF I'D GIVEN UP ON YOU...
...I'D BE GRADUATING TODAY WITH ALL KINDS OF REGRETS.
HUH?

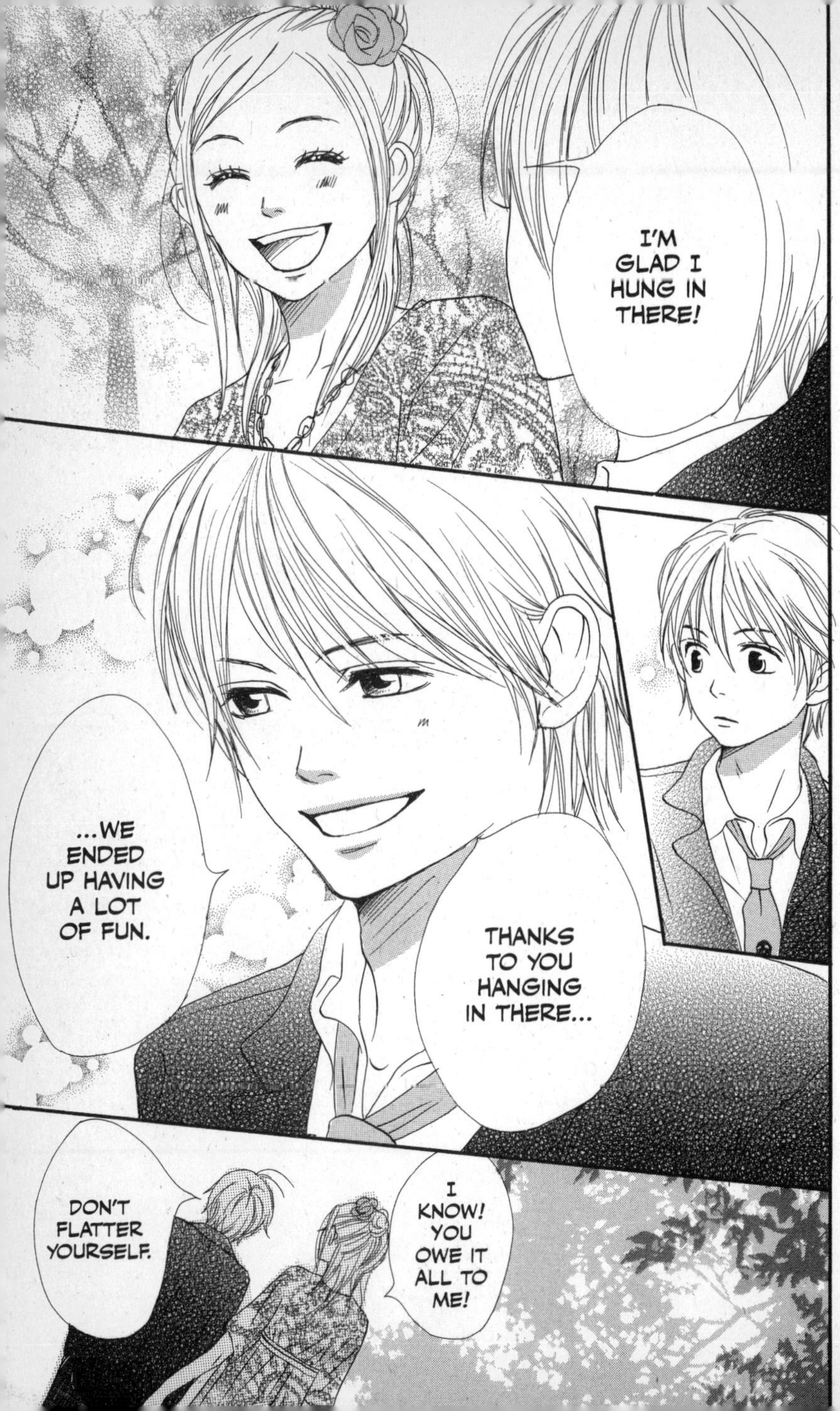
I'M GLAD I HUNG IN THERE!
THANKS TO YOU HANGING IN THERE...
...WE ENDED UP HAVING A LOT OF FUN.
I KNOW! YOU OWE IT ALL TO ME!
DON'T FLATTER YOURSELF.

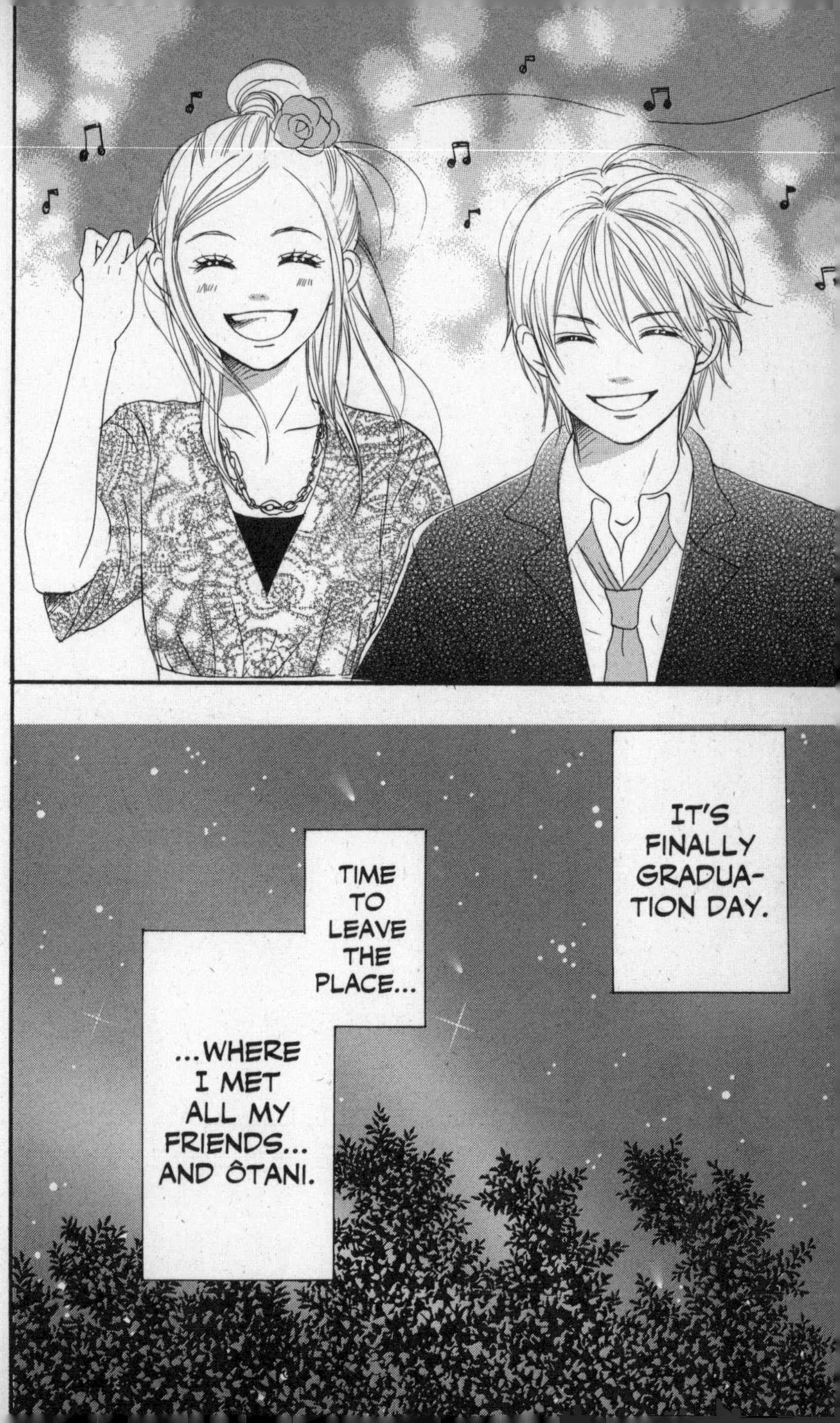
IT'S FINALLY GRADUA-TION DAY.
TIME TO LEAVE THE PLACE...
...WHERE I MET ALL MY FRIENDS... AND ÔTANI.

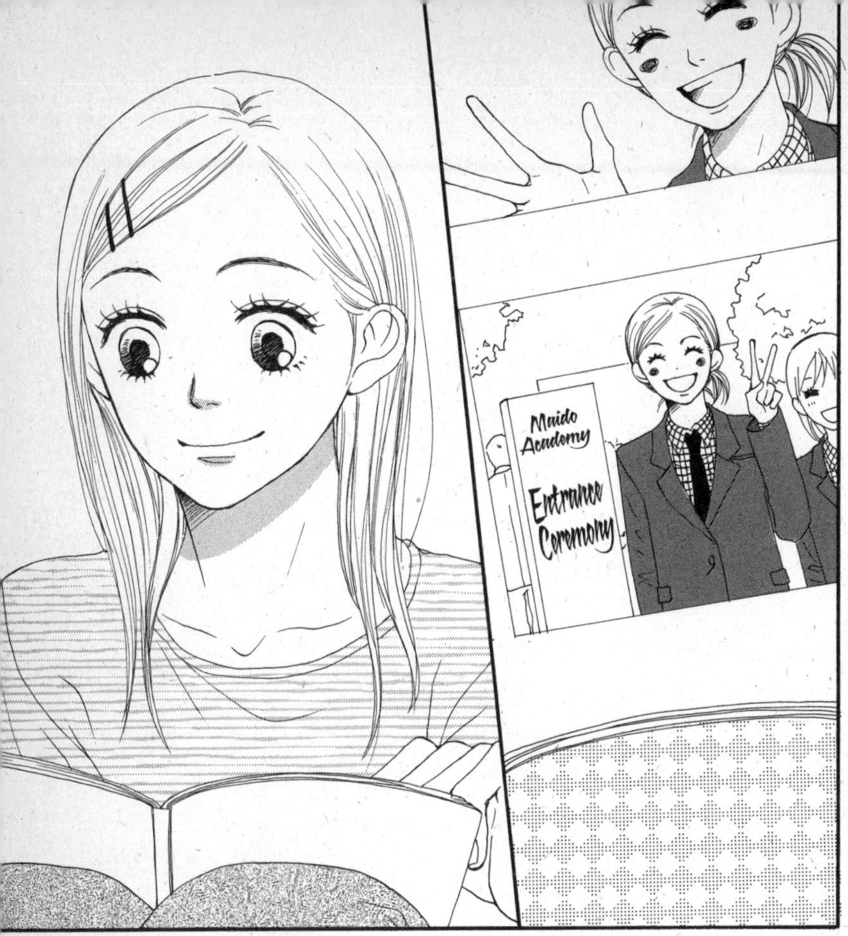
Maido Academy
Entrance Ceremony

CHAPTER 62

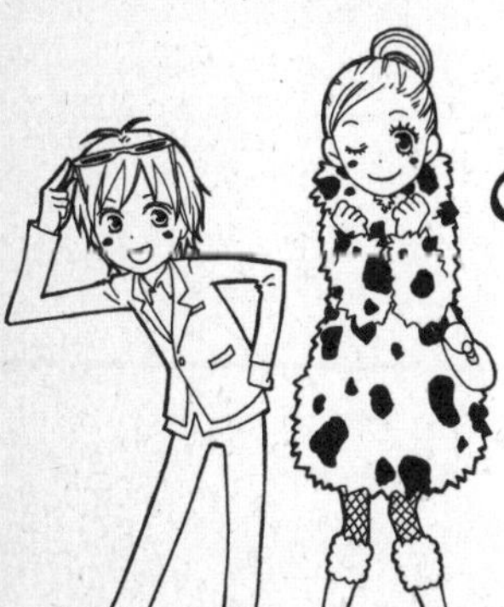

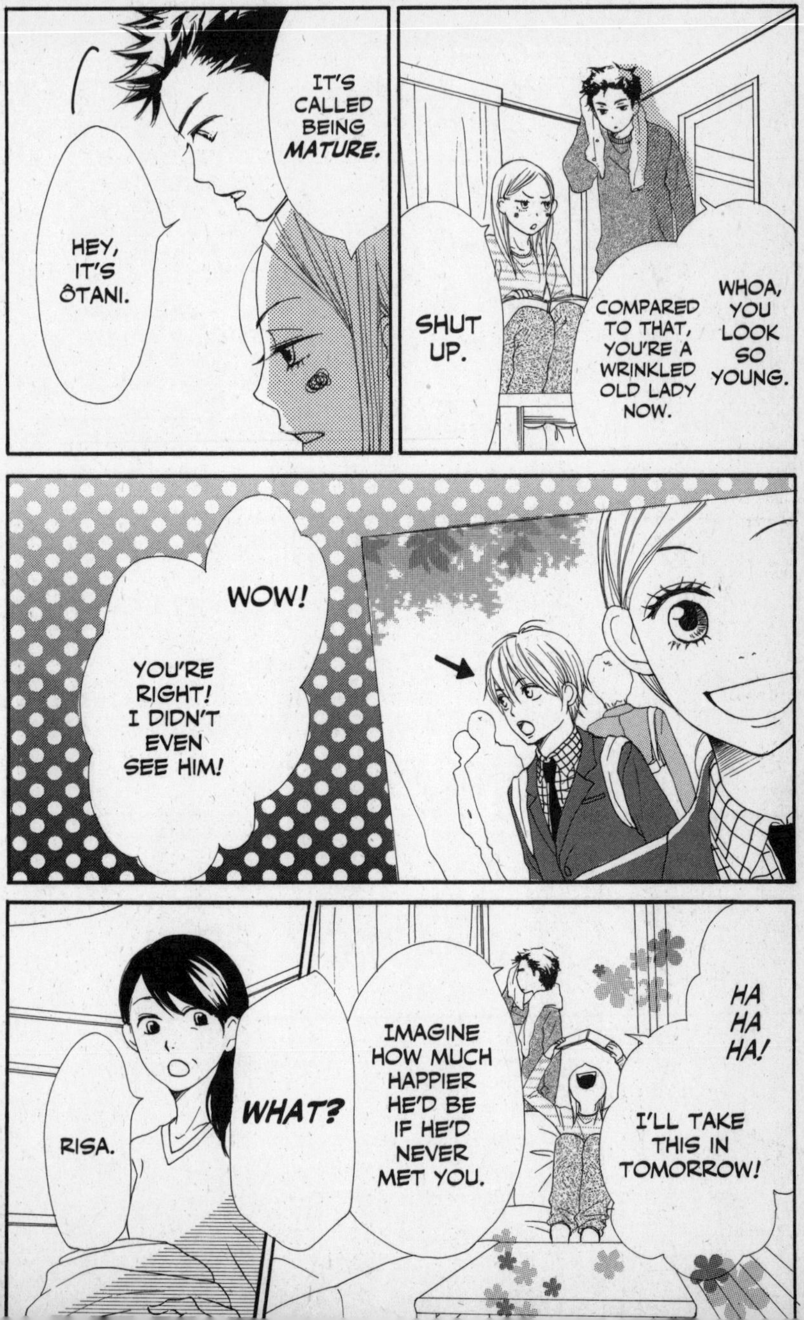
WHOA, YOU LOOK SO YOUNG.
COMPARED TO THAT, YOU'RE A WRINKLED OLD LADY NOW.
SHUT UP.
IT'S CALLED BEING *MATURE.*
HEY, IT'S ŌTANI.
WOW!
YOU'RE RIGHT! I DIDN'T EVEN SEE HIM!
HA HA HA!
I'LL TAKE THIS IN TOMORROW!
IMAGINE HOW MUCH HAPPIER HE'D BE IF HE'D NEVER MET YOU.
WHAT?
RISA.

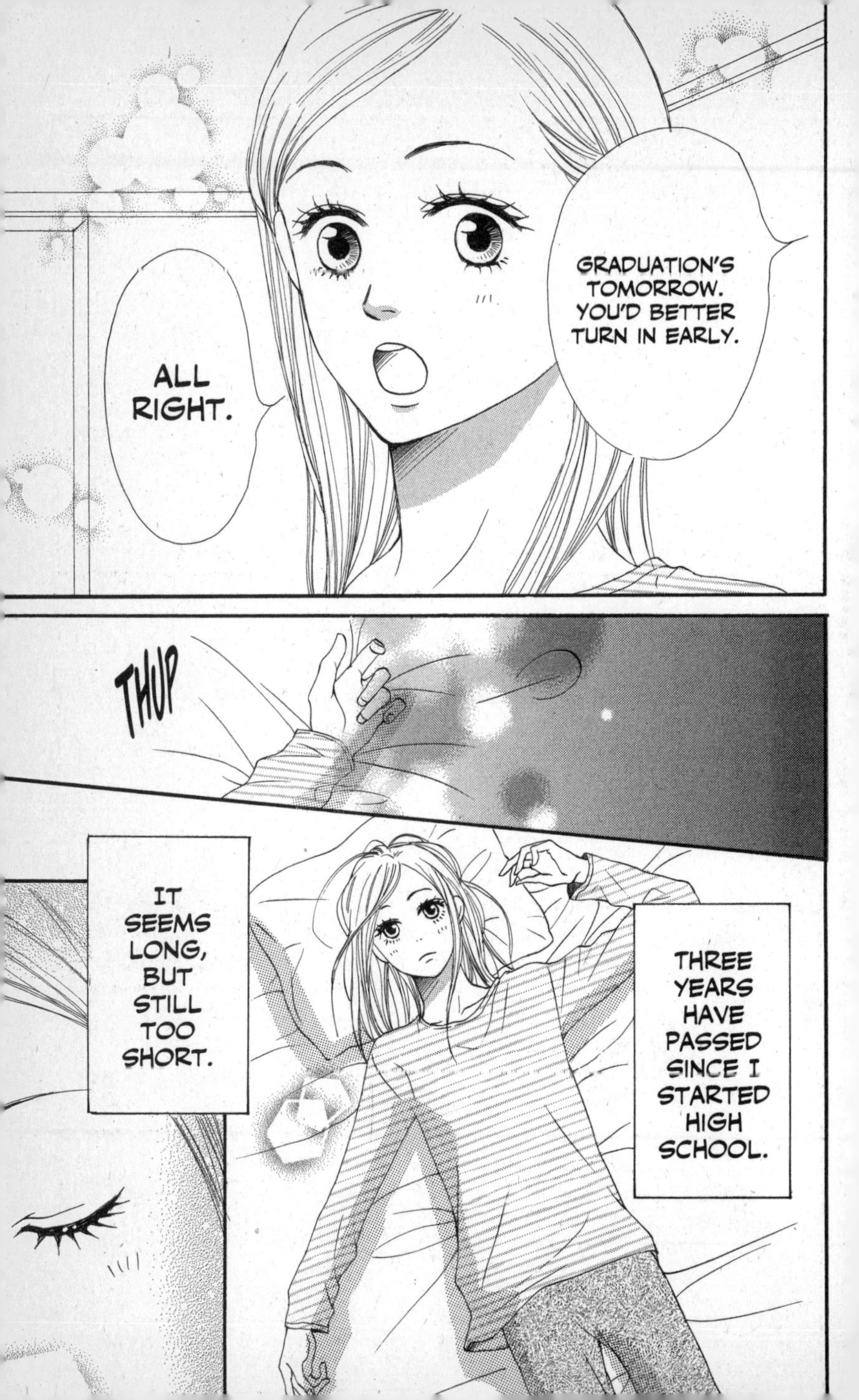
GRADUATION'S TOMORROW. YOU'D BETTER TURN IN EARLY.
ALL RIGHT.
THUP
THREE YEARS HAVE PASSED SINCE I STARTED HIGH SCHOOL.
IT SEEMS LONG, BUT STILL TOO SHORT.

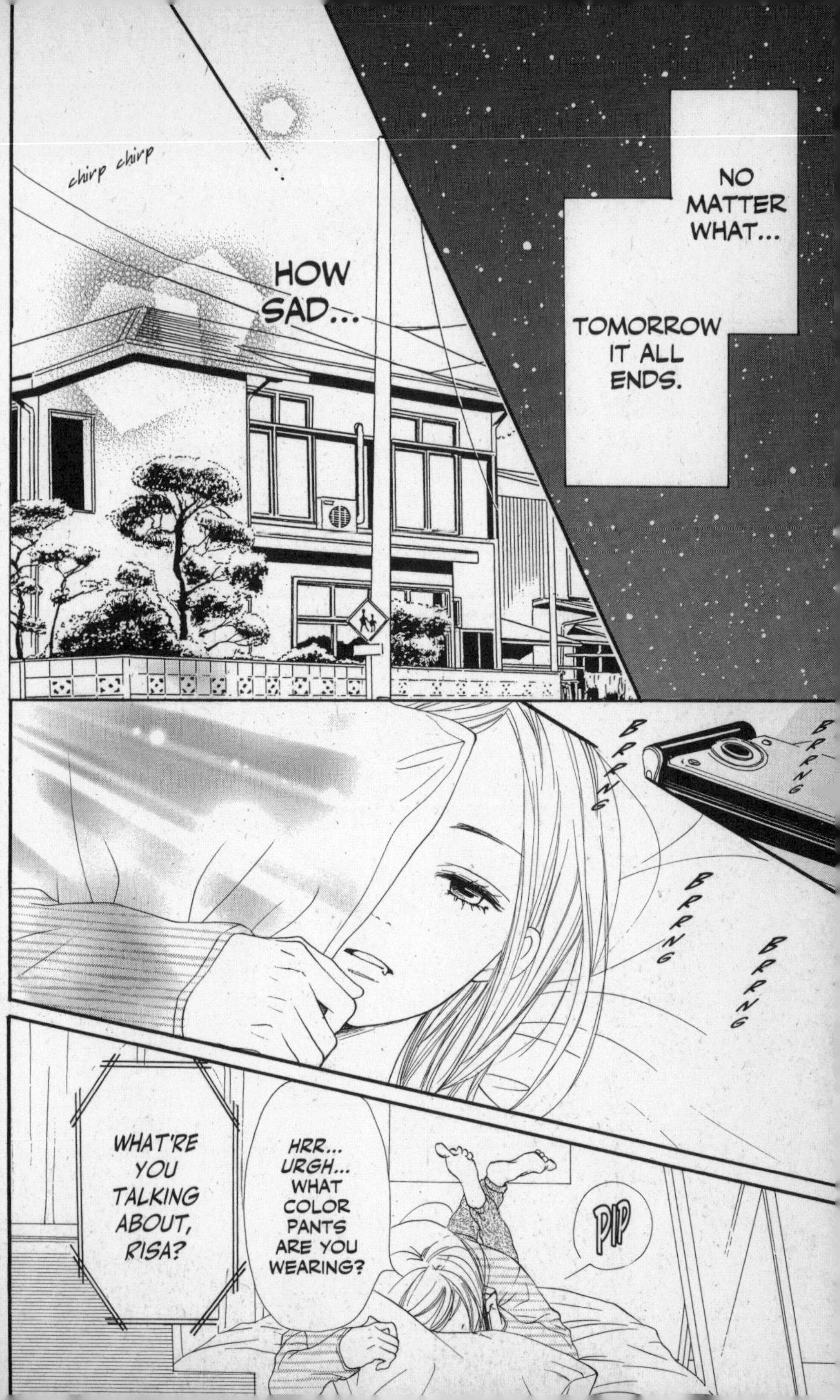
NO MATTER WHAT...
TOMORROW IT ALL ENDS.
HOW SAD...
chirp chirp
BRRNG
BRRNG
BRRNG
BRRNG
PIP
HRR... URGH... WHAT COLOR PANTS ARE YOU WEARING?
WHAT'RE YOU TALKING ABOUT, RISA?

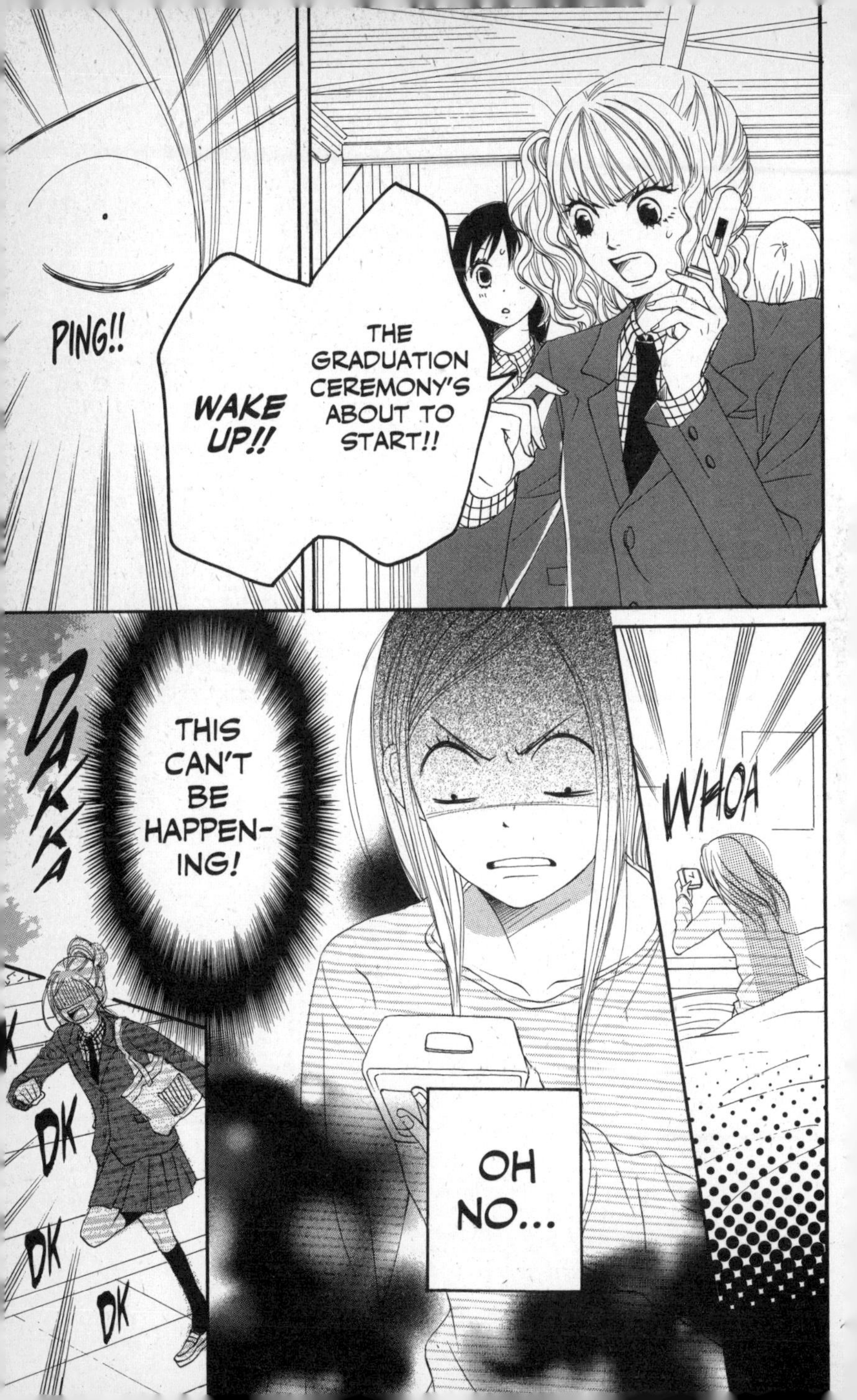
THE GRADUATION CEREMONY'S ABOUT TO START!!
WAKE UP!!
PING!!
WHOA
OH NO...
THIS CAN'T BE HAPPEN-ING!
DAKKA
DK
DK
DK

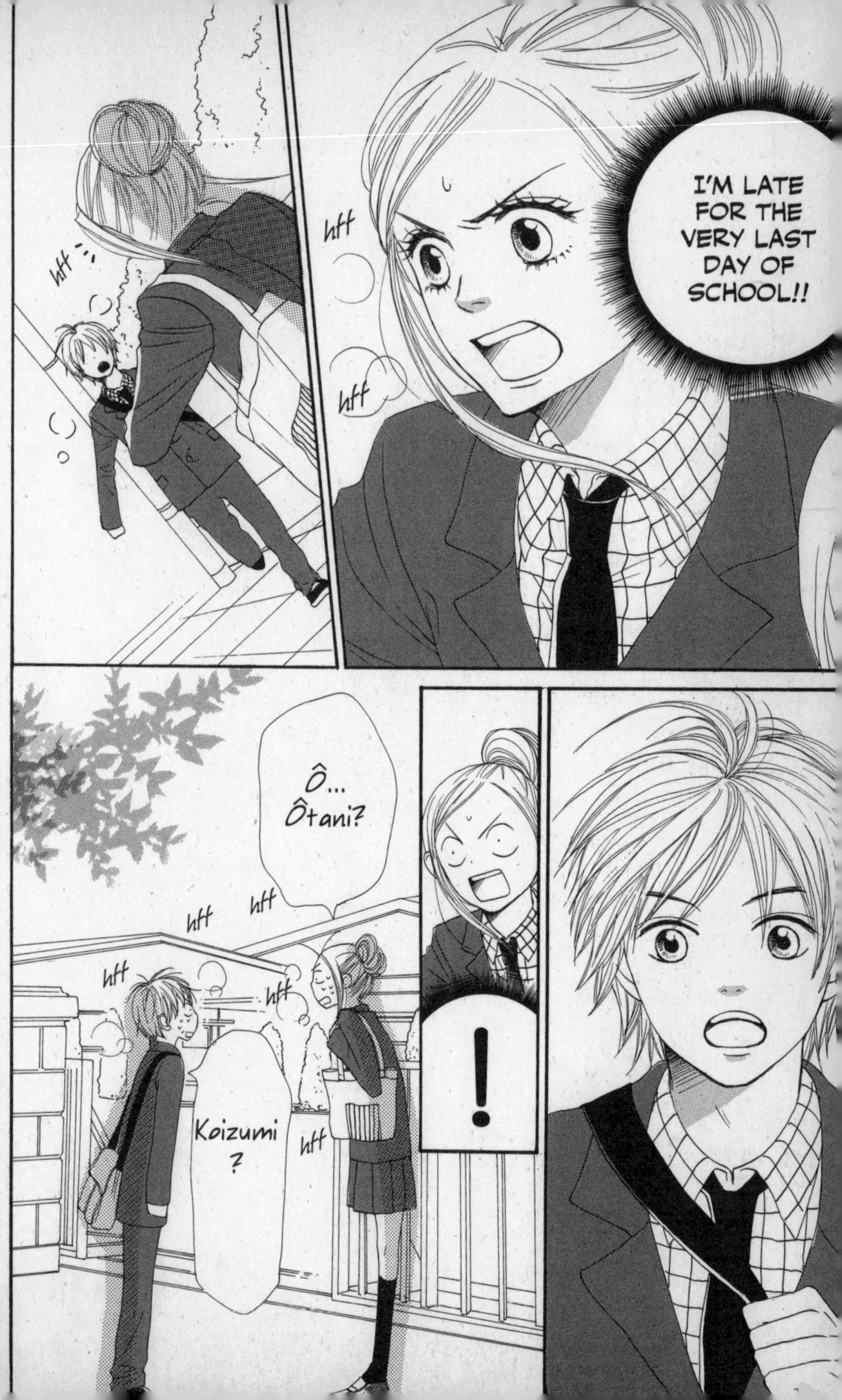
I'M LATE FOR THE VERY LAST DAY OF SCHOOL!!
hff
hff
hff ...
!
Ô... Ôtani?
hff
hff
hff
hff
Koizumi ?
hff

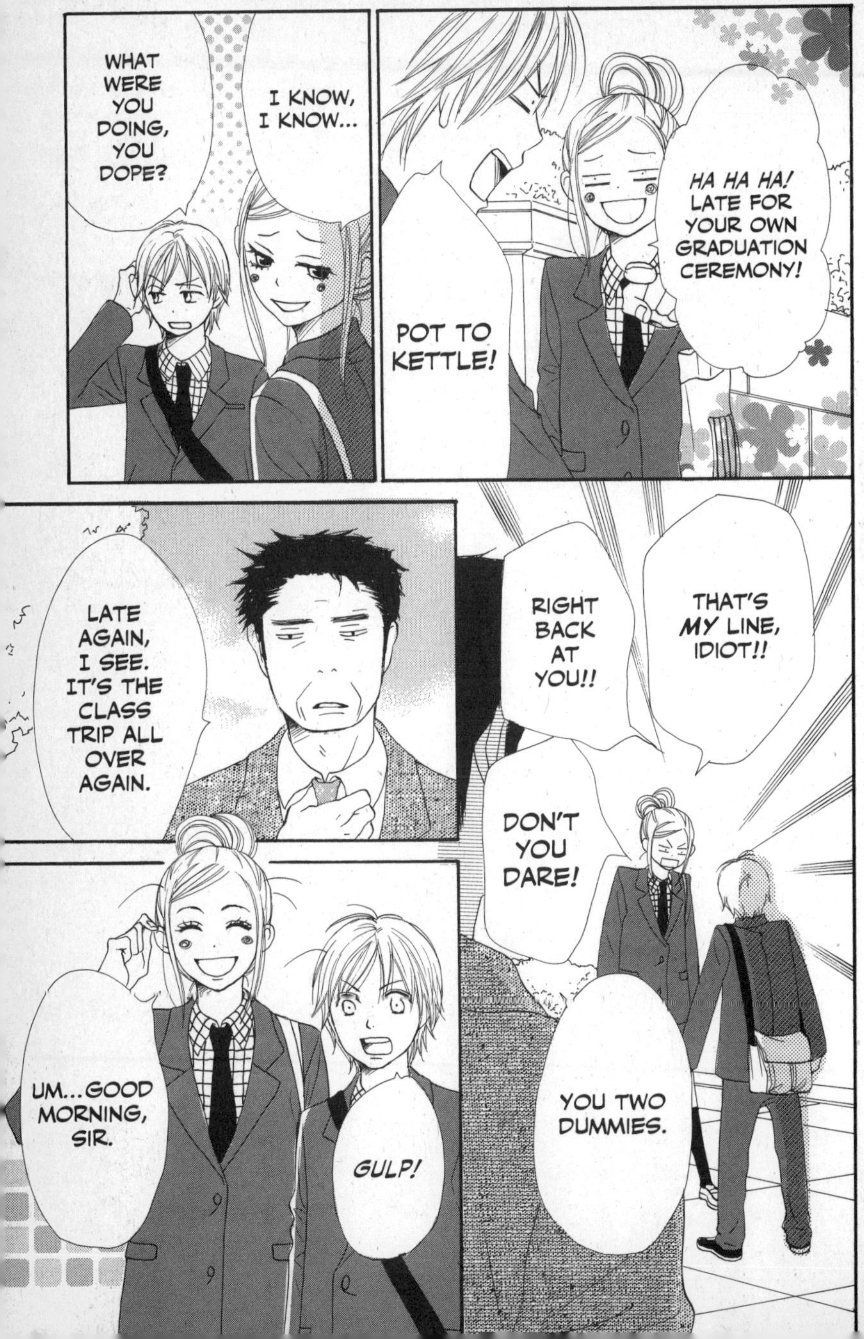
HA HA HA! LATE FOR YOUR OWN GRADUATION CEREMONY!
POT TO KETTLE!
I KNOW, I KNOW...
WHAT WERE YOU DOING, YOU DOPE?
THAT'S *MY* LINE, IDIOT!!
RIGHT BACK AT YOU!!
DON'T YOU DARE!
YOU TWO DUMMIES.
LATE AGAIN, I SEE. IT'S THE CLASS TRIP ALL OVER AGAIN.
GULP!
UM...GOOD MORNING, SIR.

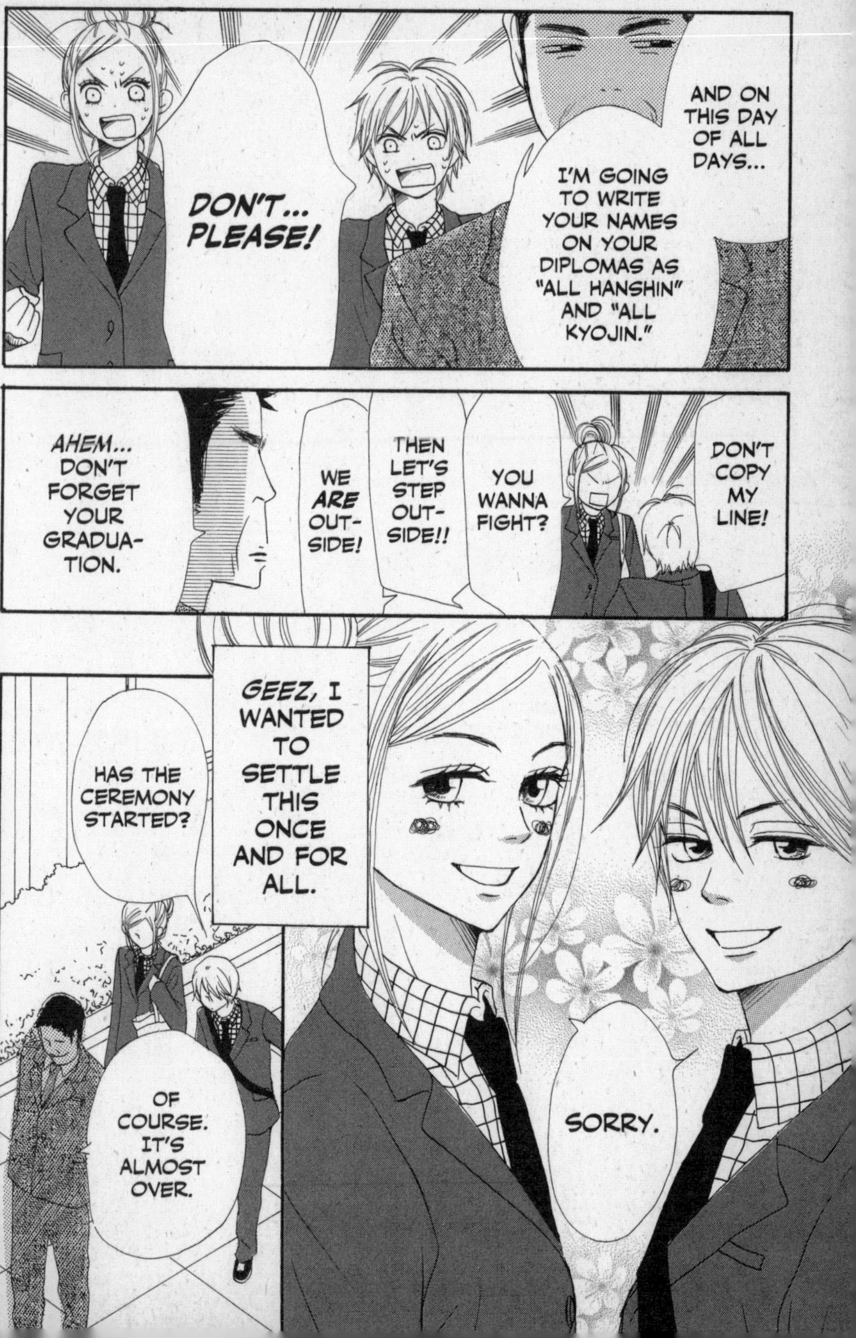
AND ON THIS DAY OF ALL DAYS...
I'M GOING TO WRITE YOUR NAMES ON YOUR DIPLOMAS AS "ALL HANSHIN" AND "ALL KYOJIN."
DON'T... PLEASE!
DON'T COPY MY LINE!
YOU WANNA FIGHT?
THEN LET'S STEP OUT-SIDE!!
WE *ARE* OUT-SIDE!
AHEM... DON'T FORGET YOUR GRADUA-TION.
GEEZ, I WANTED TO SETTLE THIS ONCE AND FOR ALL.
SORRY.
HAS THE CEREMONY STARTED?
OF COURSE. IT'S ALMOST OVER.

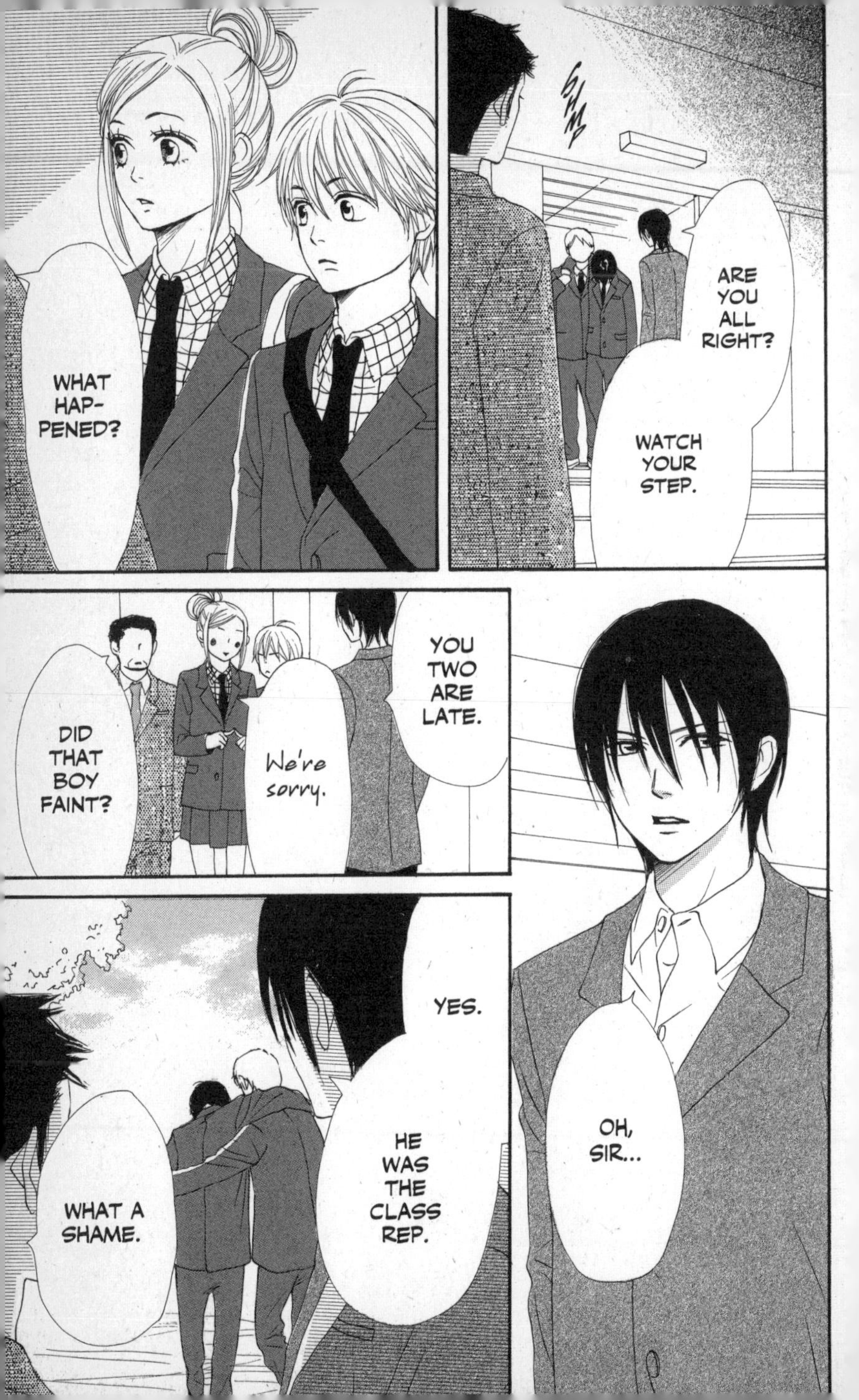
SHMP
ARE YOU ALL RIGHT?
WATCH YOUR STEP.
WHAT HAP-PENED?
OH, SIR...
YOU TWO ARE LATE.
We're sorry.
DID THAT BOY FAINT?
YES.
HE WAS THE CLASS REP.
WHAT A SHAME.

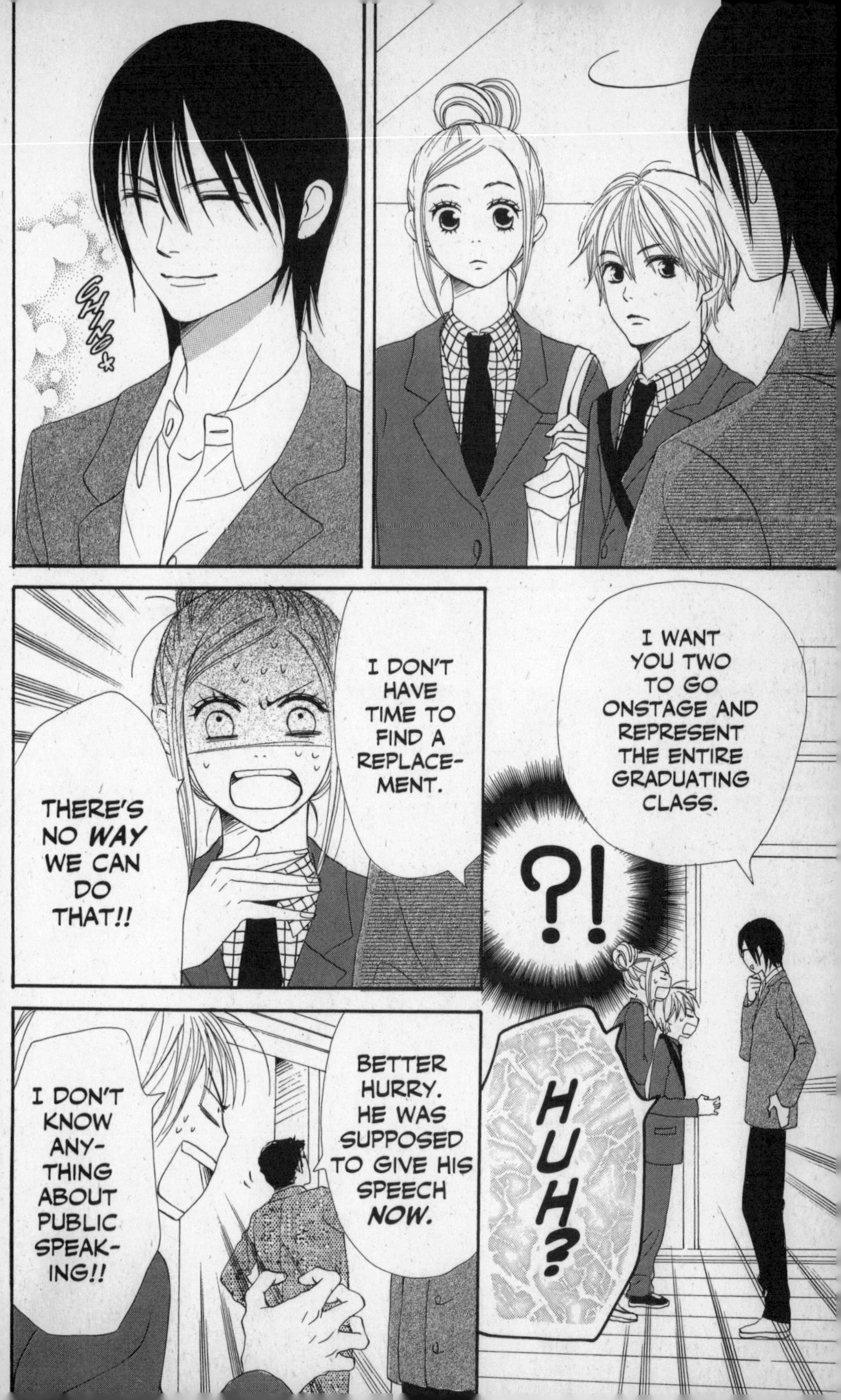
I WANT YOU TWO TO GO ONSTAGE AND REPRESENT THE ENTIRE GRADUATING CLASS.
?!
I DON'T HAVE TIME TO FIND A REPLACE-MENT.
THERE'S NO *WAY* WE CAN DO THAT!!
HUH?
BETTER HURRY. HE WAS SUPPOSED TO GIVE HIS SPEECH *NOW.*
I DON'T KNOW ANY-THING ABOUT PUBLIC SPEAK-ING!!

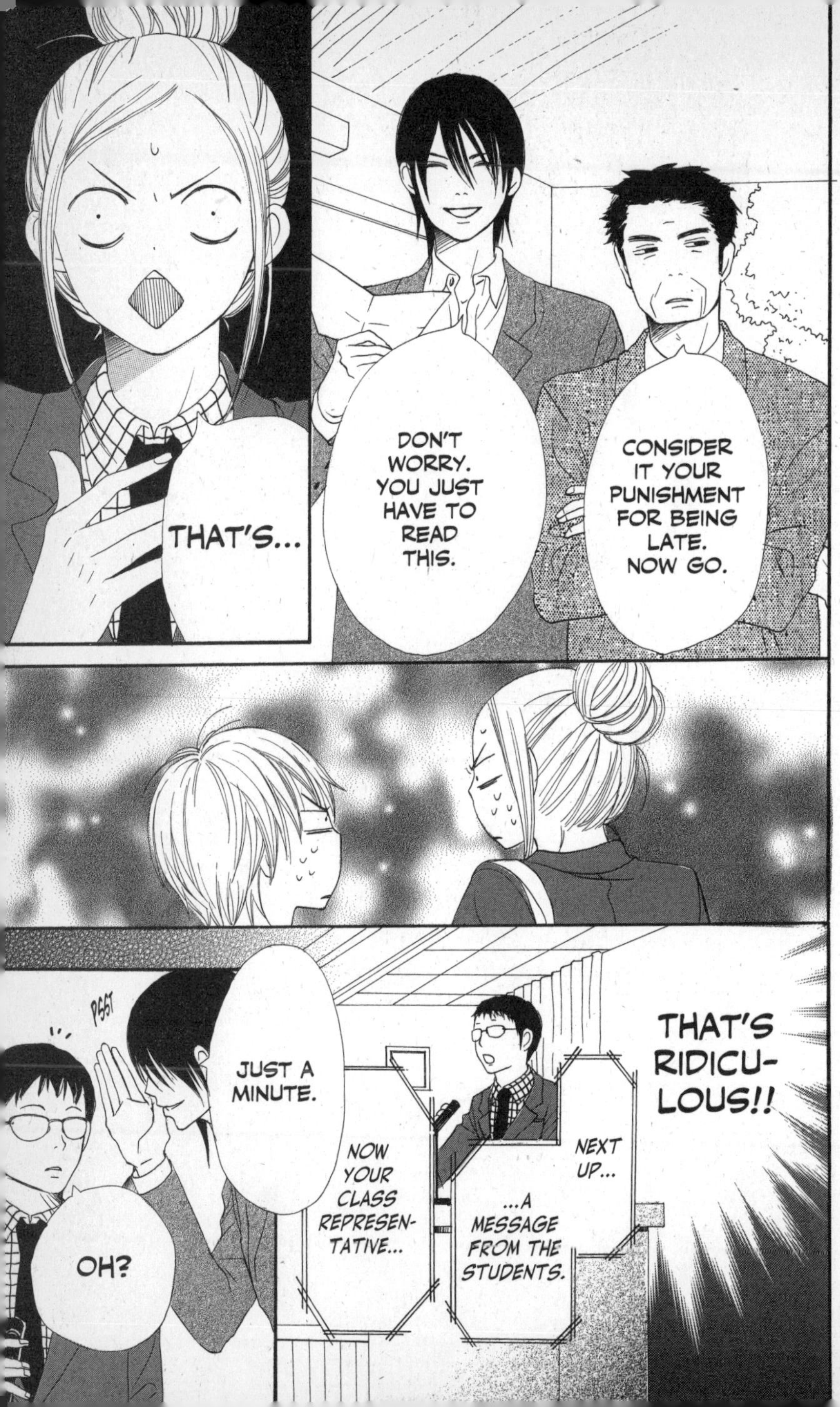
CONSIDER IT YOUR PUNISHMENT FOR BEING LATE. NOW GO.
DON'T WORRY. YOU JUST HAVE TO READ THIS.
THAT'S...
THAT'S RIDICULOUS!!
NEXT UP...
...A MESSAGE FROM THE STUDENTS.
NOW YOUR CLASS REPRESENTATIVE...
JUST A MINUTE.
PSST
OH?

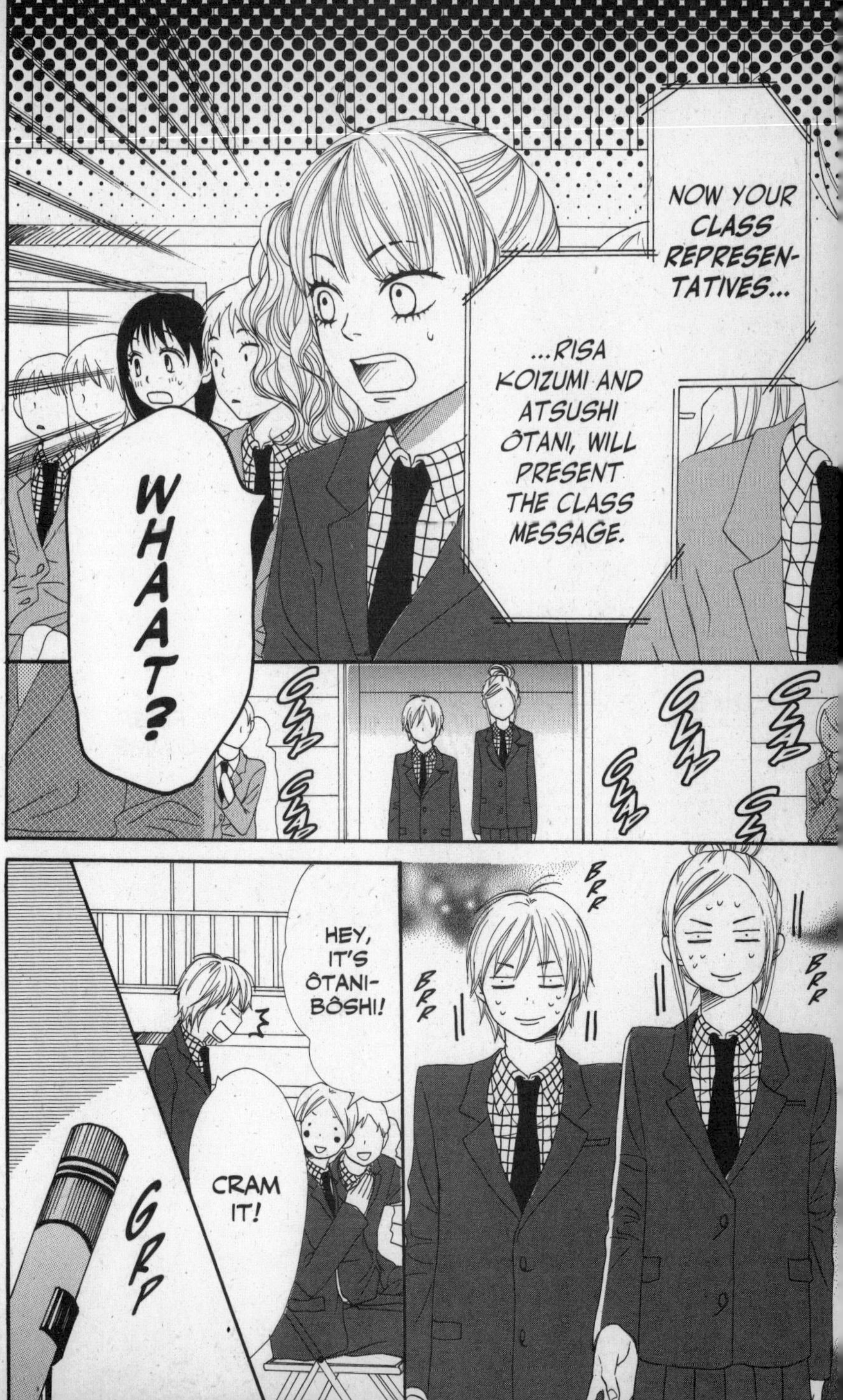
NOW YOUR CLASS REPRESEN-TATIVES...
...RISA KOIZUMI AND ATSUSHI ÔTANI, WILL PRESENT THE CLASS MESSAGE.
WHAAAT?
BRR
BRR
BRR
HEY, IT'S ÔTANI-BÔSHI!
CRAM IT!
GRP

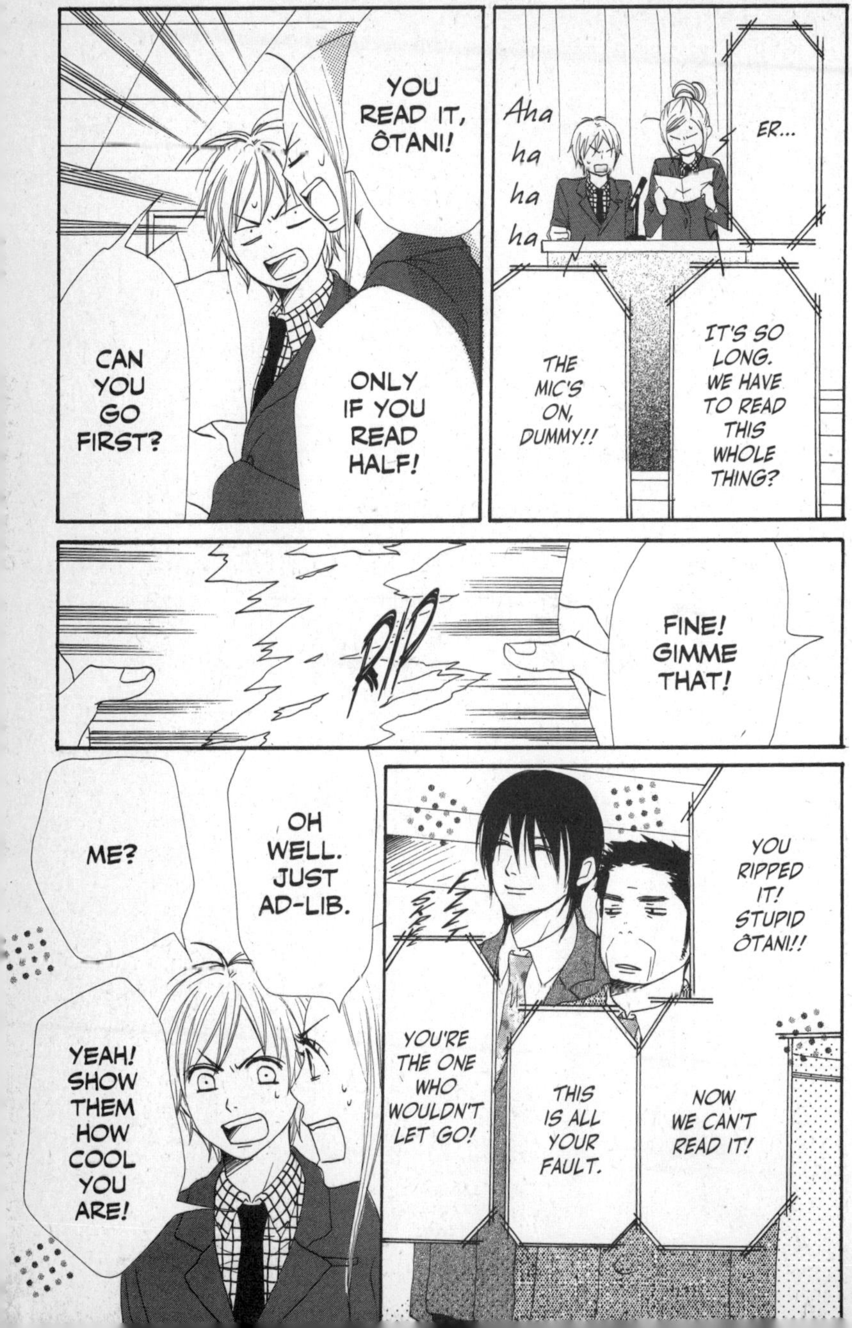
ER...
Aha ha ha ha
IT'S SO LONG. WE HAVE TO READ THIS WHOLE THING?
THE MIC'S ON, DUMMY!!
YOU READ IT, ÔTANI!
ONLY IF YOU READ HALF!
CAN YOU GO FIRST?
FINE! GIMME THAT!
RIP
YOU RIPPED IT! STUPID ÔTANI!!
NOW WE CAN'T READ IT!
THIS IS ALL YOUR FAULT.
YOU'RE THE ONE WHO WOULDN'T LET GO!
OH WELL. JUST AD-LIB.
ME?
YEAH! SHOW THEM HOW COOL YOU ARE!

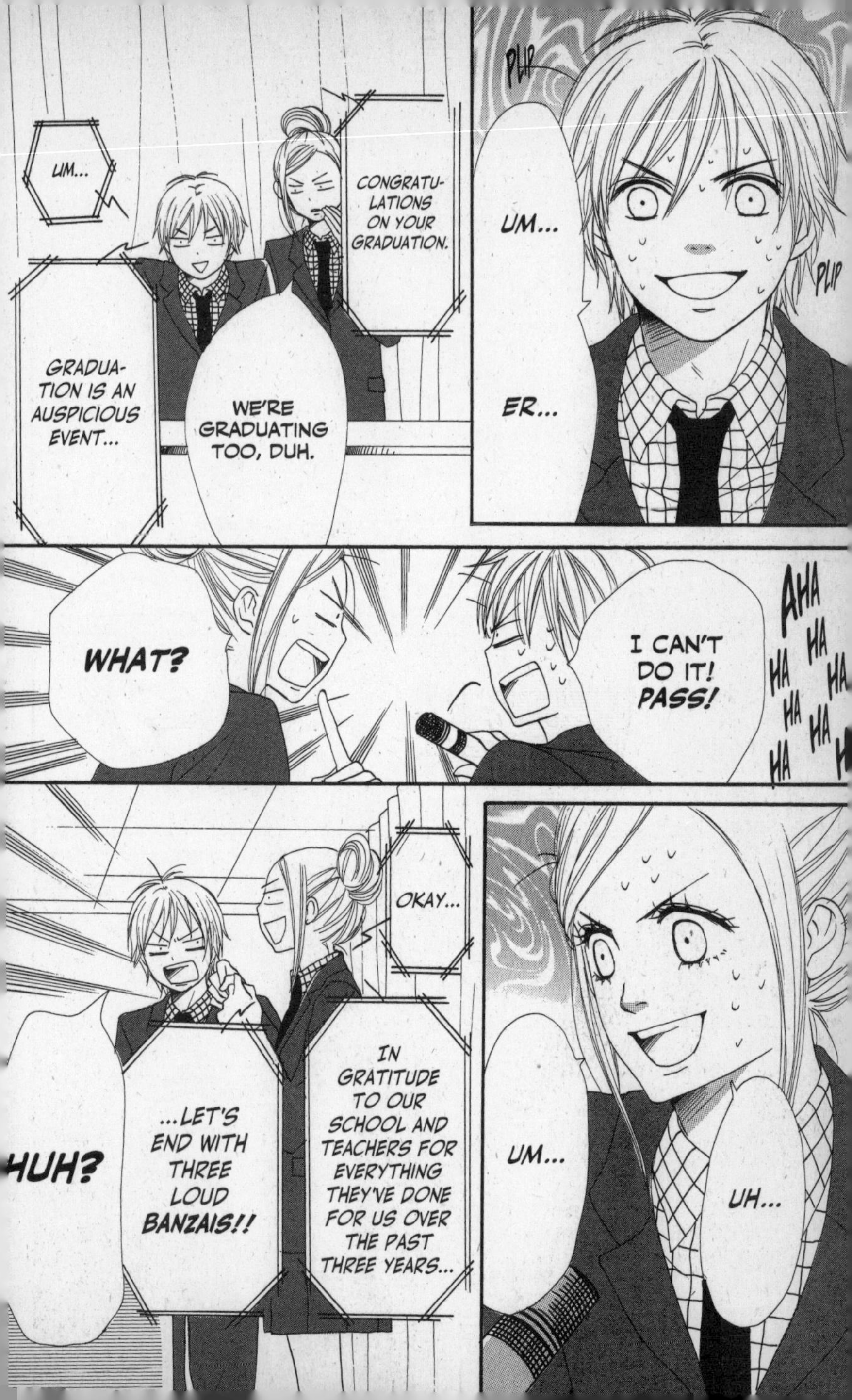
PLIP
UM...
PLIP
ER...
CONGRATULATIONS ON YOUR GRADUATION.
UM...
GRADUATION IS AN AUSPICIOUS EVENT...
WE'RE GRADUATING TOO, DUH.
AHA HA HA HA HA HA HA
I CAN'T DO IT! PASS!
WHAT?
UM...
UH...
OKAY...
IN GRATITUDE TO OUR SCHOOL AND TEACHERS FOR EVERYTHING THEY'VE DONE FOR US OVER THE PAST THREE YEARS...
...LET'S END WITH THREE LOUD BANZAIS!!
HUH?

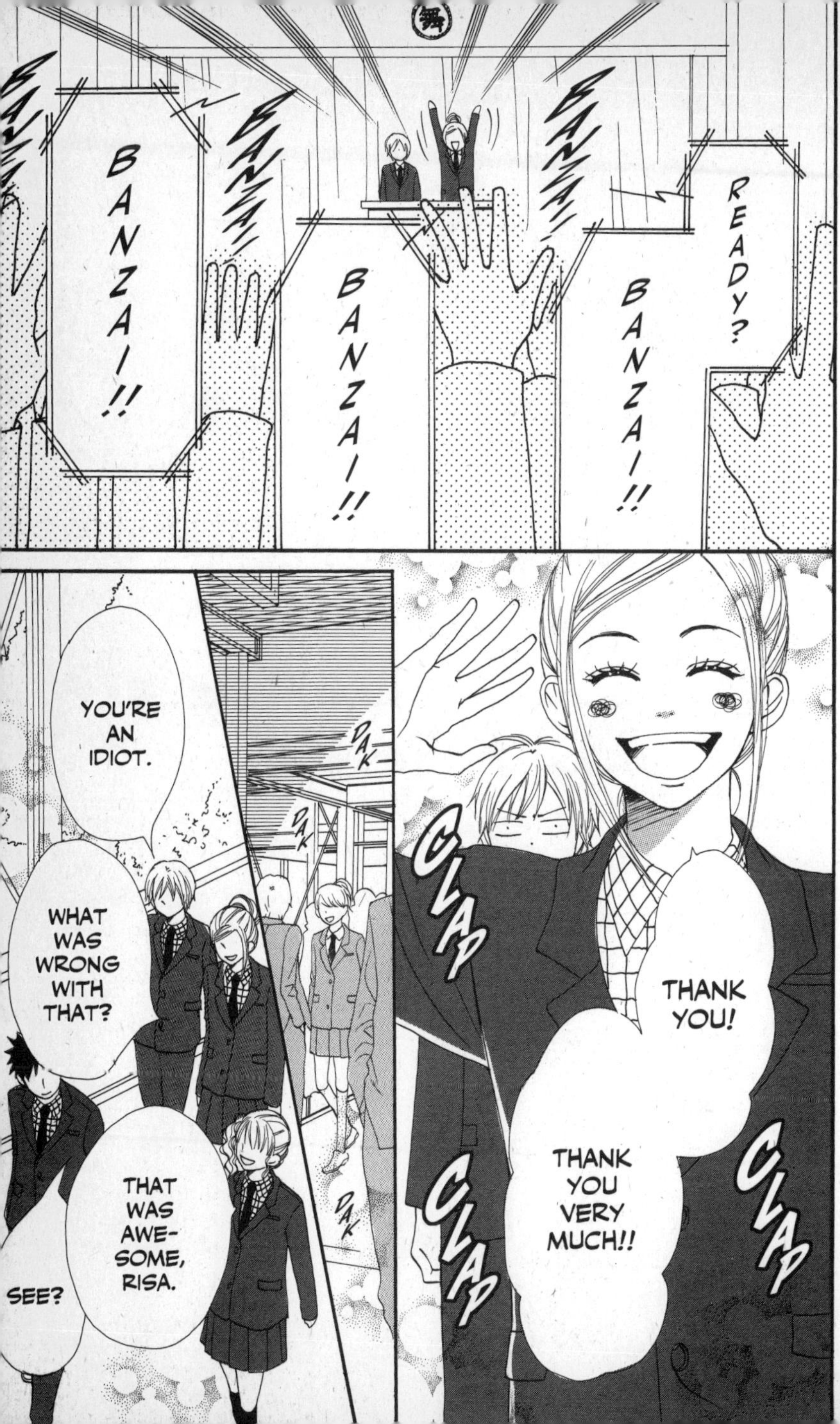
READY?
BANZAI!!
BANZAI!!
BANZAI!!
BANZAI!!
BANZAI!!
THANK YOU!
CLAP
THANK YOU VERY MUCH!!
CLAP
CLAP
DAK
DAK
DAK
YOU'RE AN IDIOT.
WHAT WAS WRONG WITH THAT?
THAT WAS AWE-SOME, RISA.
SEE?

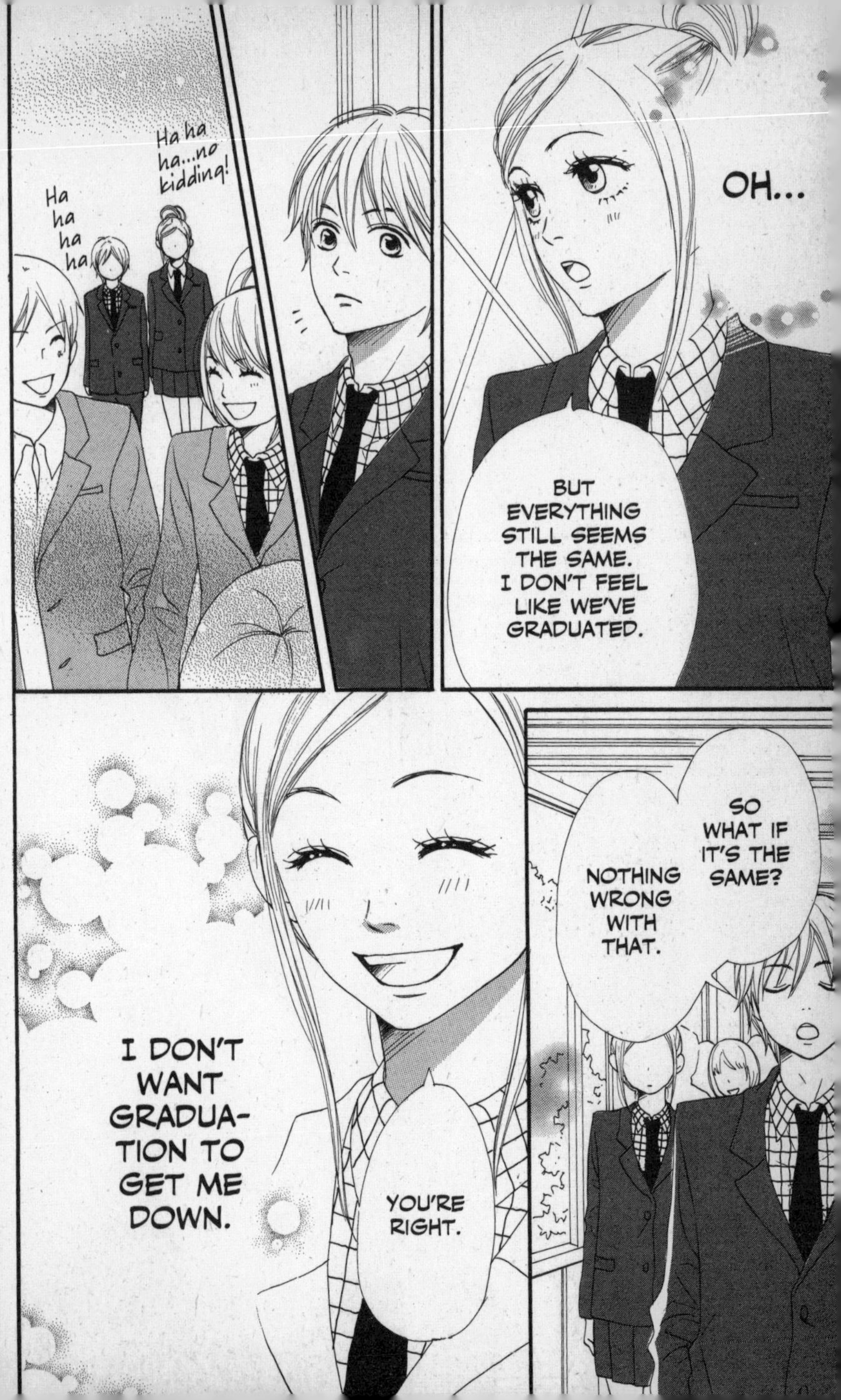
OH...
BUT EVERYTHING STILL SEEMS THE SAME. I DON'T FEEL LIKE WE'VE GRADUATED.
Ha ha ha...no kidding!
Ha ha ha ha
SO WHAT IF IT'S THE SAME?
NOTHING WRONG WITH THAT.
YOU'RE RIGHT.
I DON'T WANT GRADUA-TION TO GET ME DOWN.

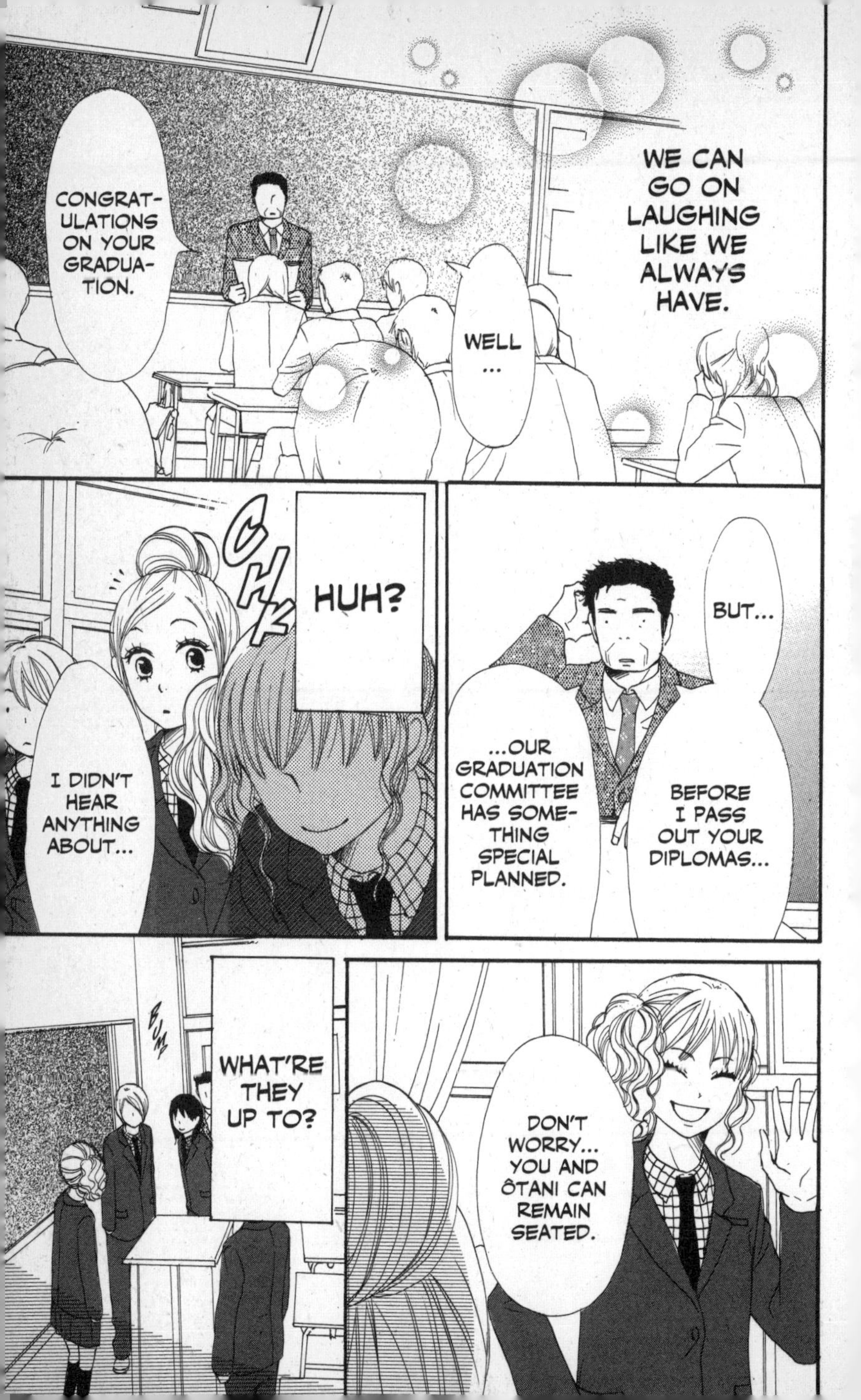
WE CAN GO ON LAUGHING LIKE WE ALWAYS HAVE.
CONGRATULATIONS ON YOUR GRADUATION.
WELL ...
BUT...
BEFORE I PASS OUT YOUR DIPLOMAS...
...OUR GRADUATION COMMITTEE HAS SOMETHING SPECIAL PLANNED.
CHK
HUH?
I DIDN'T HEAR ANYTHING ABOUT...
DON'T WORRY... YOU AND ŌTANI CAN REMAIN SEATED.
WHAT'RE THEY UP TO?

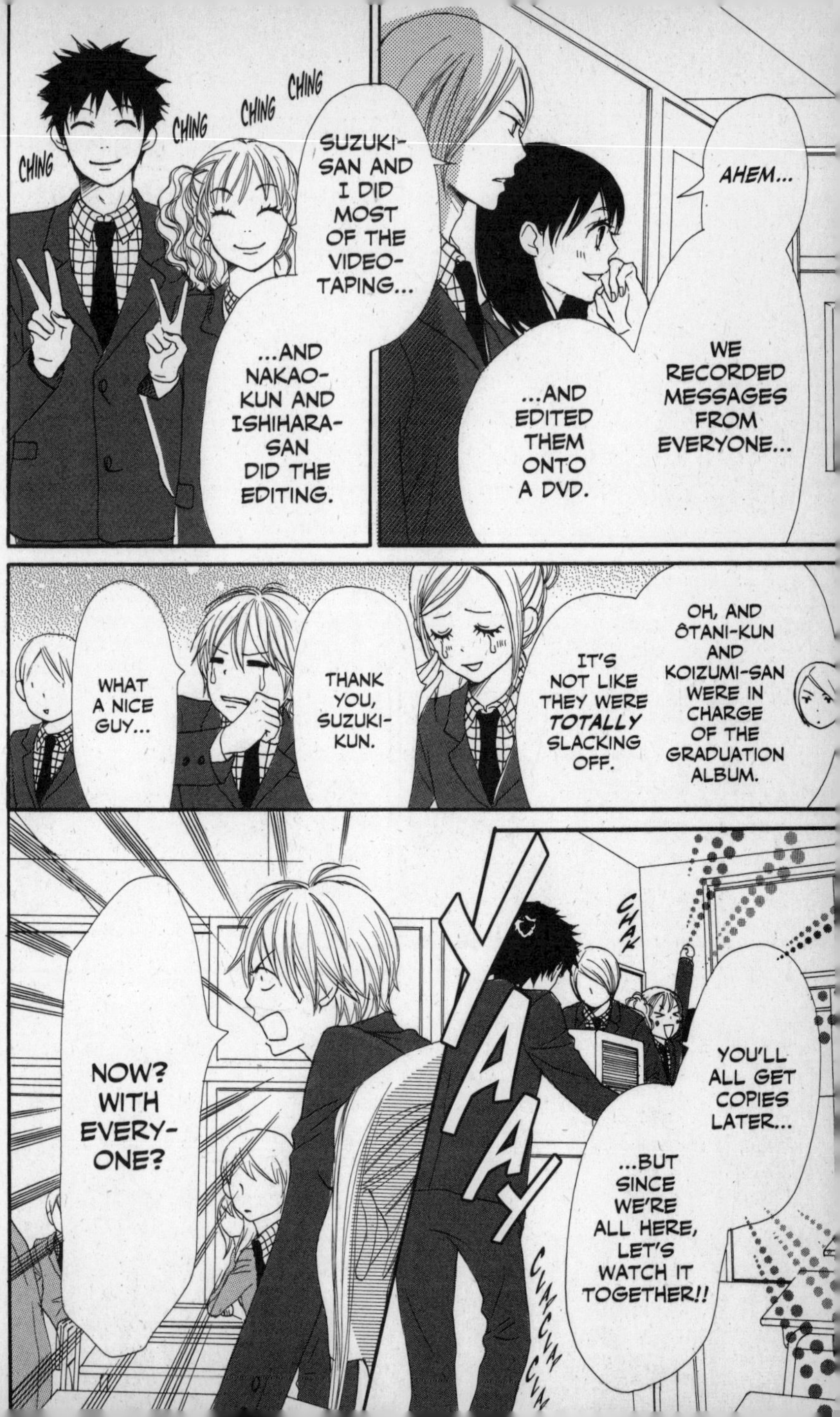
AHEM...
WE RECORDED MESSAGES FROM EVERYONE...
...AND EDITED THEM ONTO A DVD.
SUZUKI-SAN AND I DID MOST OF THE VIDEO-TAPING...
...AND NAKAO-KUN AND ISHIHARA-SAN DID THE EDITING.
CHING CHING CHING CHING
OH, AND ŌTANI-KUN AND KOIZUMI-SAN WERE IN CHARGE OF THE GRADUATION ALBUM.
IT'S NOT LIKE THEY WERE *TOTALLY* SLACKING OFF.
THANK YOU, SUZUKI-KUN.
WHAT A NICE GUY...
CHAK
YOU'LL ALL GET COPIES LATER...
...BUT SINCE WE'RE ALL HERE, LET'S WATCH IT TOGETHER!!
YAAAY
NOW? WITH EVERY-ONE?

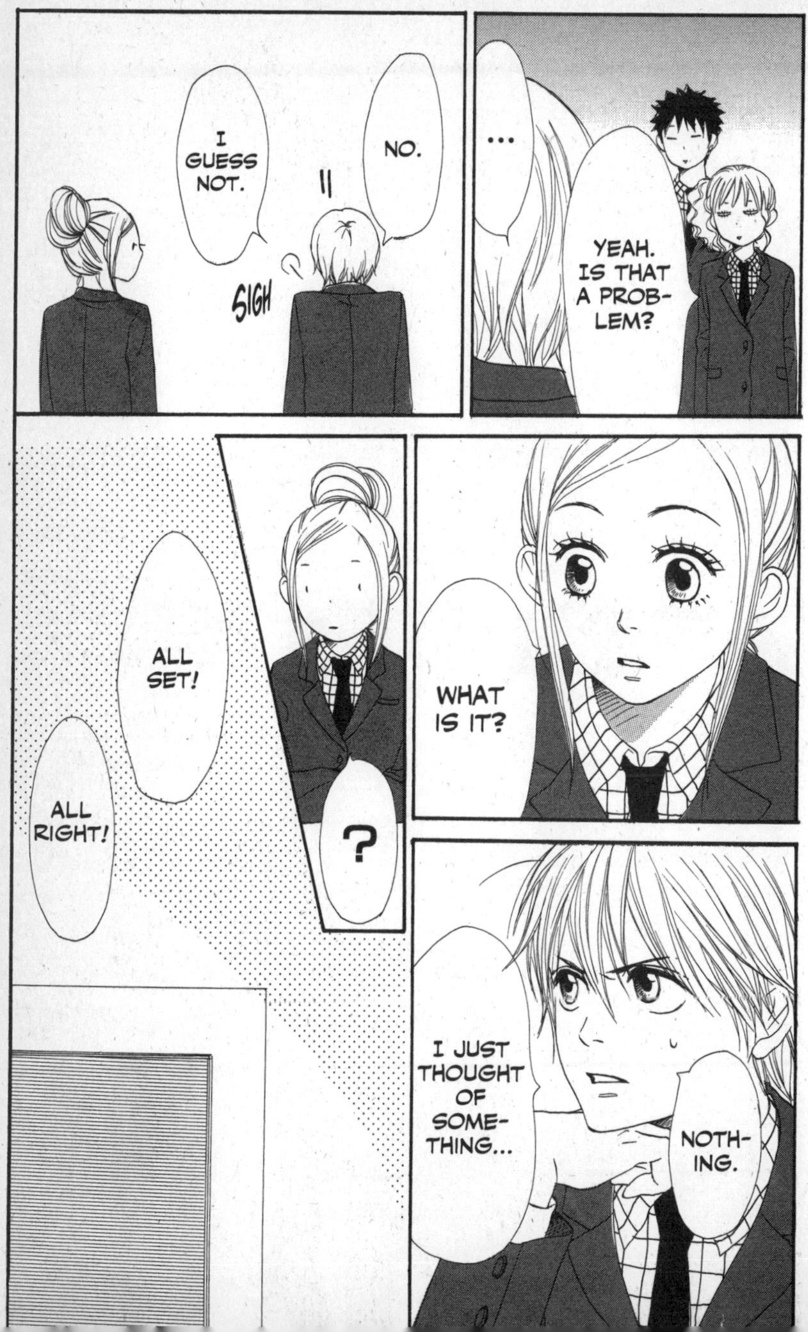
YEAH. IS THAT A PROBLEM?
...
NO.
I GUESS NOT.
SIGH
WHAT IS IT?
?
NOTHING.
I JUST THOUGHT OF SOMETHING...
ALL SET!
ALL RIGHT!

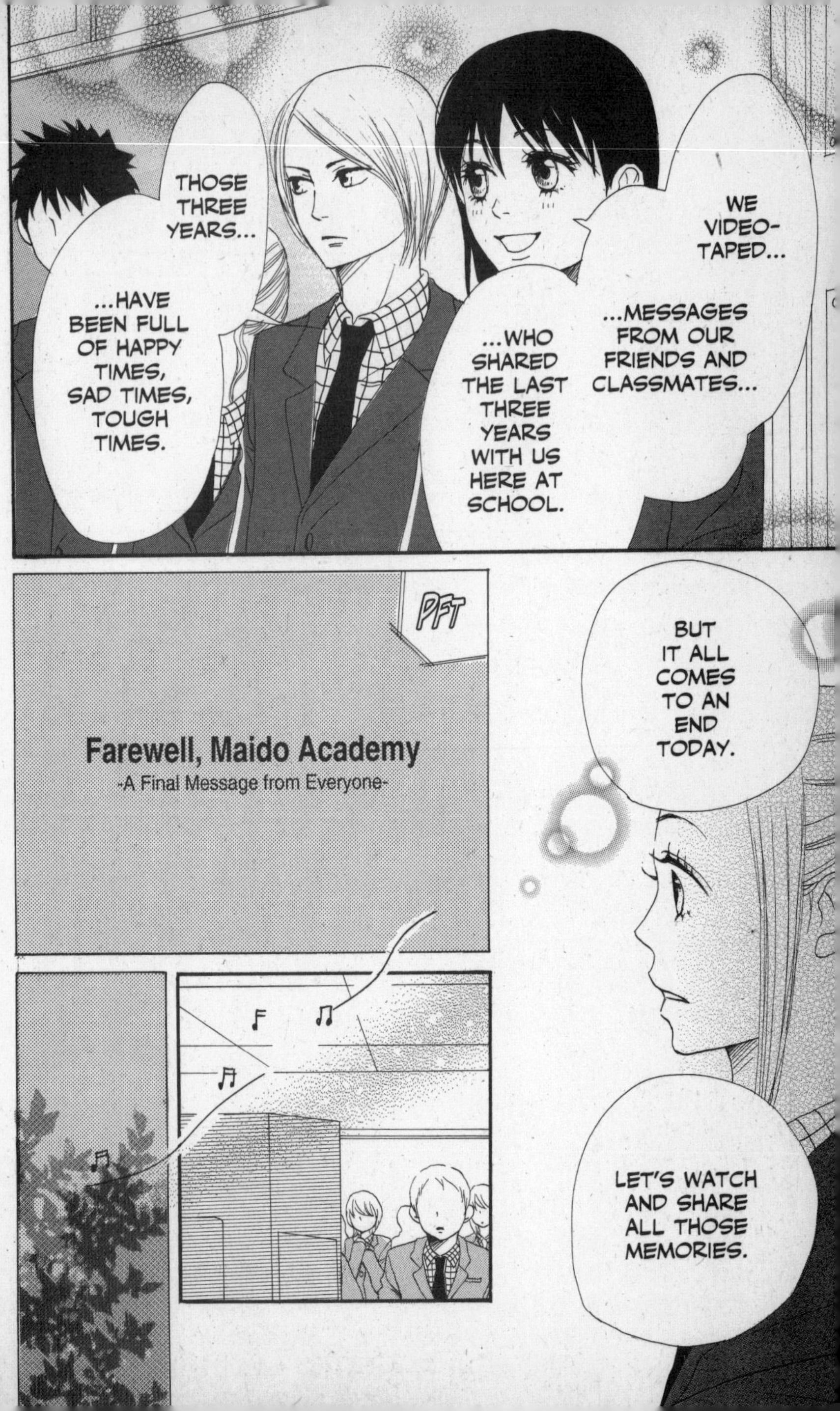
WE VIDEO-TAPED...
...MESSAGES FROM OUR FRIENDS AND CLASSMATES...
...WHO SHARED THE LAST THREE YEARS WITH US HERE AT SCHOOL.
THOSE THREE YEARS...
...HAVE BEEN FULL OF HAPPY TIMES, SAD TIMES, TOUGH TIMES.
BUT IT ALL COMES TO AN END TODAY.
LET'S WATCH AND SHARE ALL THOSE MEMORIES.
PFT
Farewell, Maido Academy
-A Final Message from Everyone-

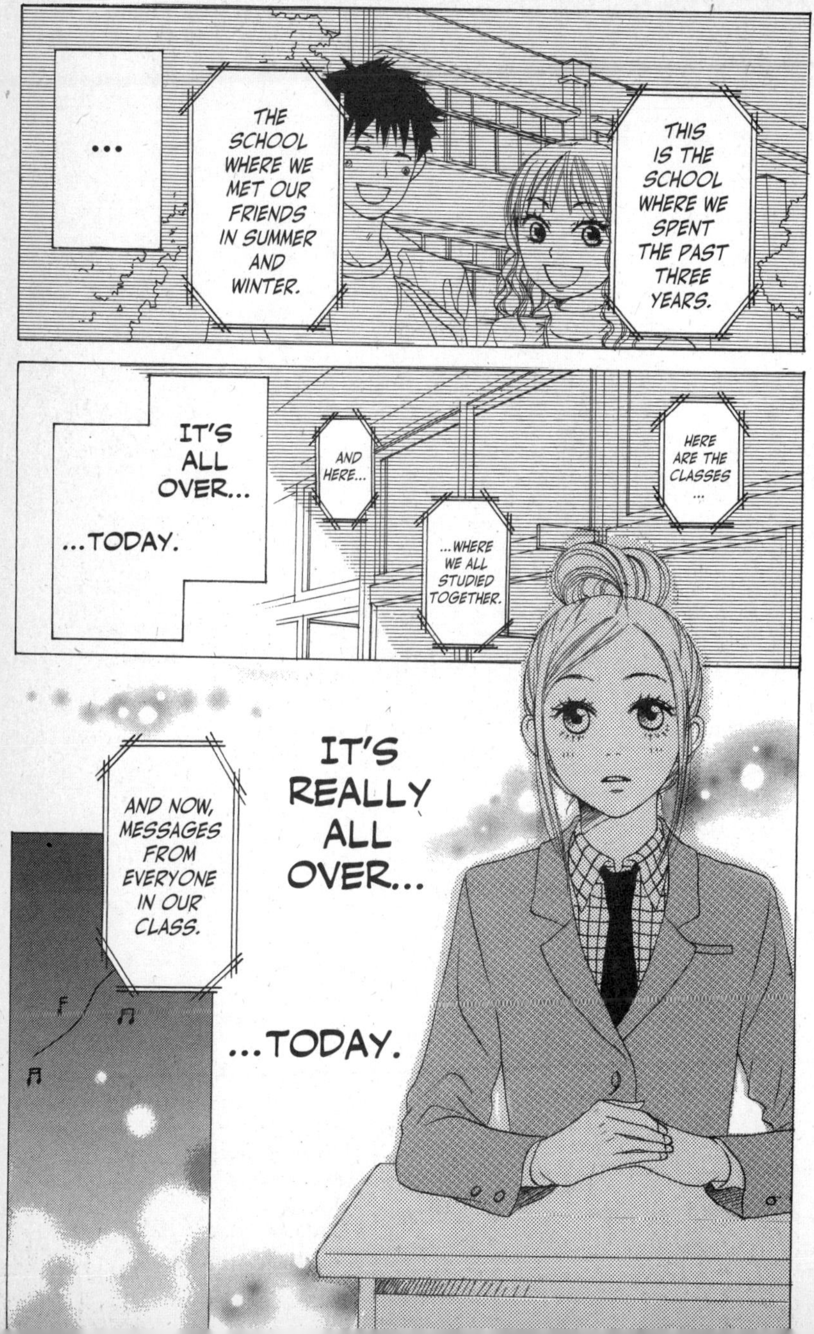
THIS IS THE SCHOOL WHERE WE SPENT THE PAST THREE YEARS.
THE SCHOOL WHERE WE MET OUR FRIENDS IN SUMMER AND WINTER.
...
HERE ARE THE CLASSES ...
...WHERE WE ALL STUDIED TOGETHER.
AND HERE...
IT'S ALL OVER...
...TODAY.
IT'S REALLY ALL OVER...
...TODAY.
AND NOW, MESSAGES FROM EVERYONE IN OUR CLASS.

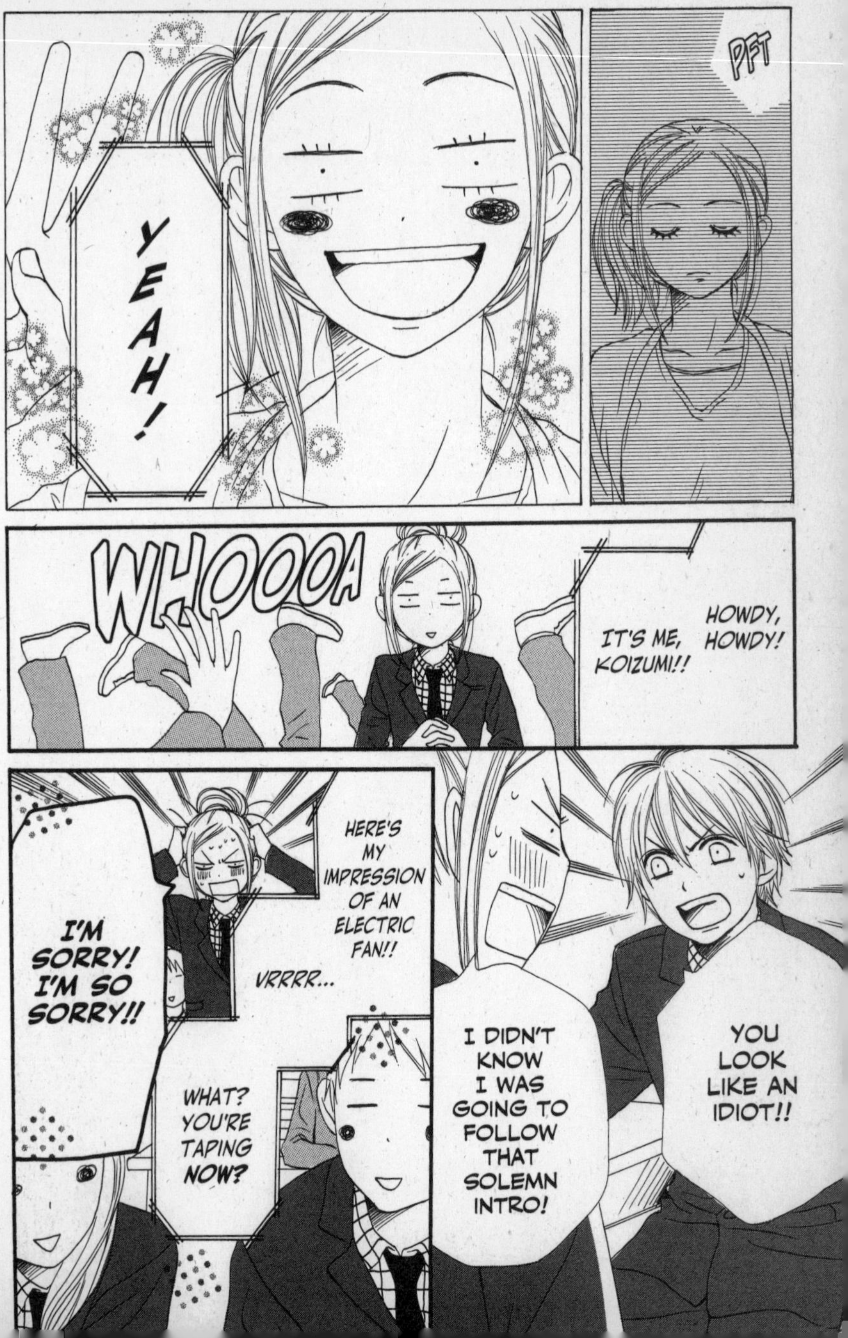
PFT
YEAH!
HOWDY, HOWDY!
IT'S ME, KOIZUMI!!
WHOOOA
YOU LOOK LIKE AN IDIOT!!
I DIDN'T KNOW I WAS GOING TO FOLLOW THAT SOLEMN INTRO!
HERE'S MY IMPRESSION OF AN ELECTRIC FAN!!
VRRRR...
WHAT? YOU'RE TAPING NOW?
I'M SORRY! I'M SO SORRY!!

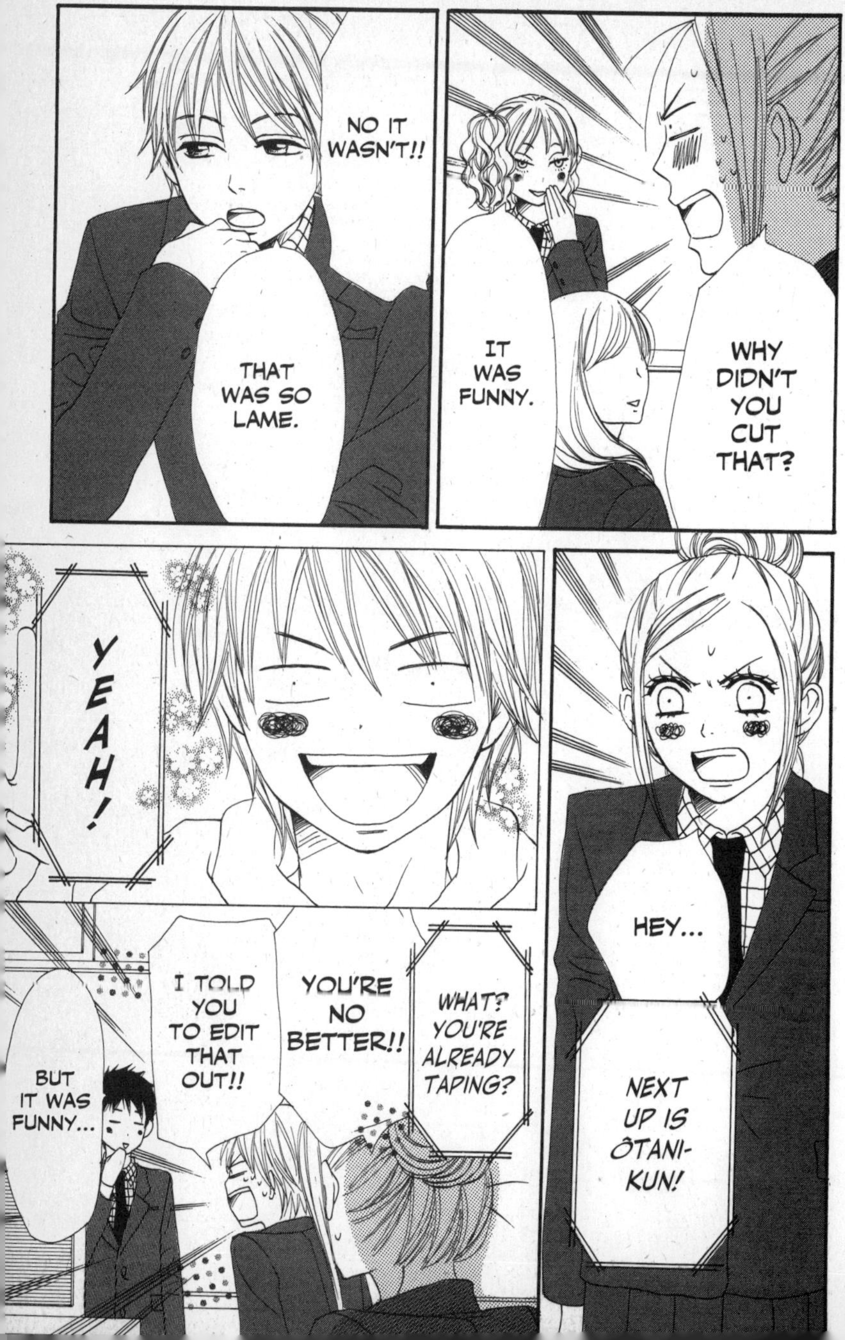
WHY DIDN'T YOU CUT THAT?
IT WAS FUNNY.
NO IT WASN'T!!
THAT WAS SO LAME.
HEY...
NEXT UP IS ÔTANI-KUN!
YEAH!
WHAT? YOU'RE ALREADY TAPING?
YOU'RE NO BETTER!!
I TOLD YOU TO EDIT THAT OUT!!
BUT IT WAS FUNNY...

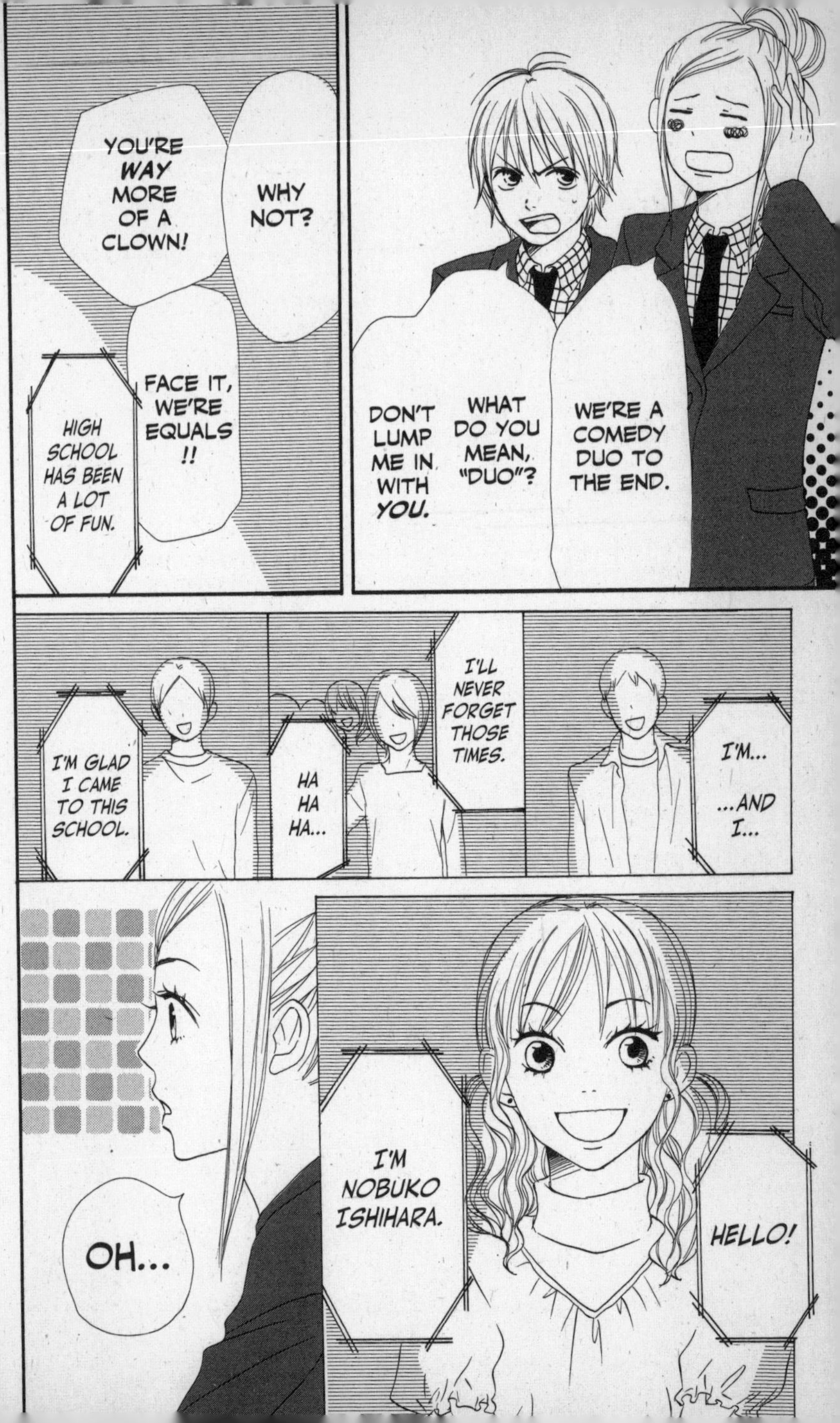
WE'RE A COMEDY DUO TO THE END.
WHAT DO YOU MEAN, "DUO"?
DON'T LUMP ME IN WITH YOU.
WHY NOT?
YOU'RE WAY MORE OF A CLOWN!
FACE IT, WE'RE EQUALS!!
HIGH SCHOOL HAS BEEN A LOT OF FUN.
I'M... ...AND I...
I'LL NEVER FORGET THOSE TIMES.
HA HA HA...
I'M GLAD I CAME TO THIS SCHOOL.
HELLO!
I'M NOBUKO ISHIHARA.
OH...

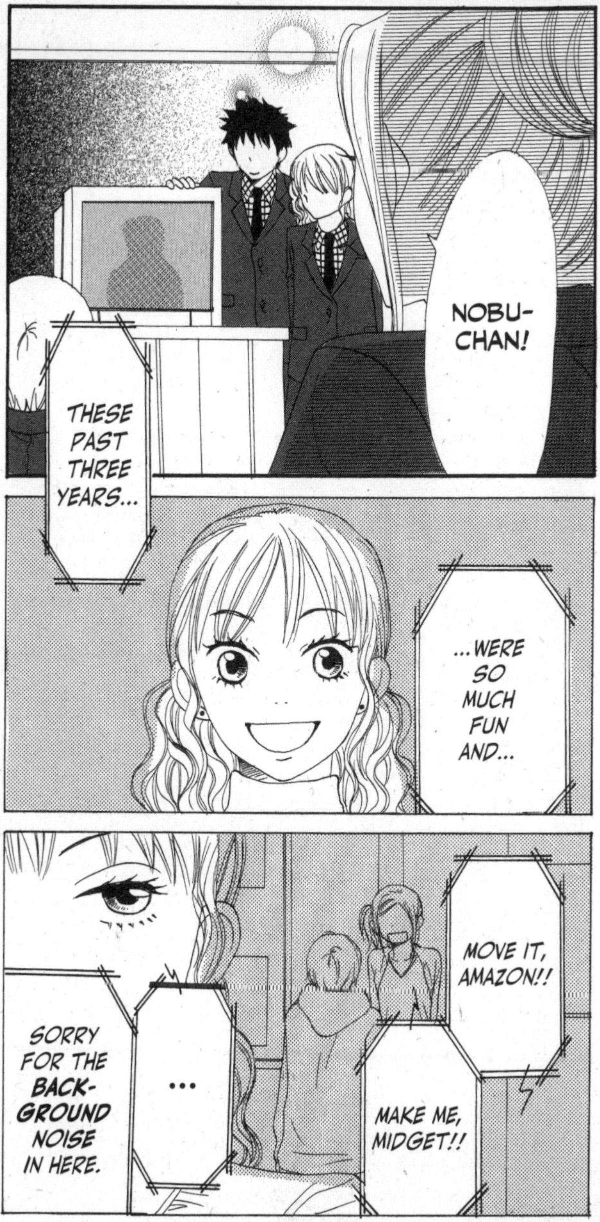
NOBU-CHAN!
THESE PAST THREE YEARS...
...WERE SO MUCH FUN AND...
MOVE IT, AMAZON!!
MAKE ME, MIDGET!!
...
SORRY FOR THE BACK-GROUND NOISE IN HERE.

②

I came down with food poisoning. I couldn't do a thing for a whole week. I guess during the five years I drew this comic, I developed a kind of rhythm in my life. Without a deadline hanging over my head, somehow things went out of whack.

I never let myself rest. And I won't rest now. I'll keep drawing manga, so please keep believing in me!

This will be the last note in this volume. I never write anything worthwhile, so I guess this is a good place to stop. Sorry! Am I depress-ing or what? Hee hee! Anyway...

I hope we can meet again in Love★Com volume 17.

Aya

January 2007

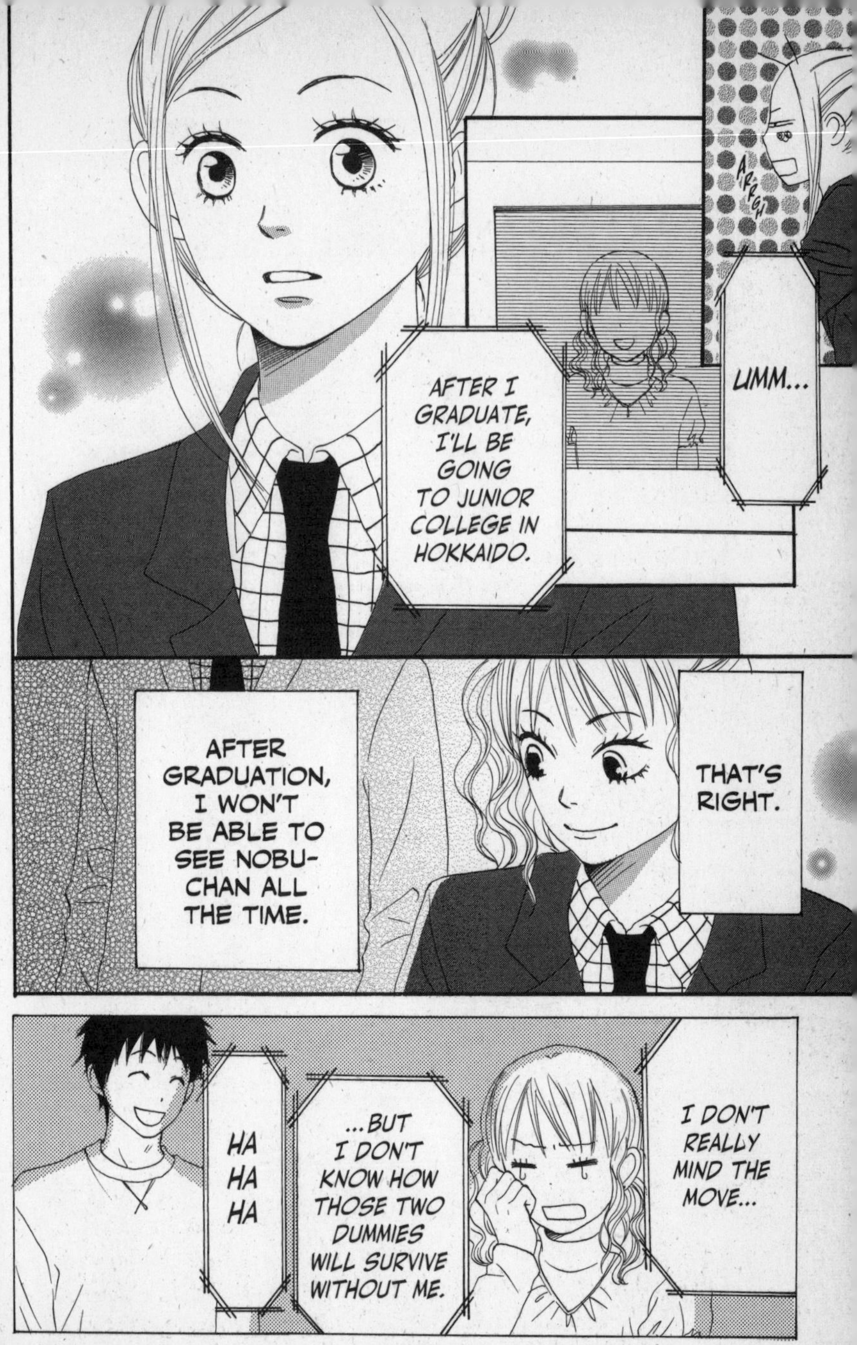
ARRGH
UMM...
AFTER I GRADUATE, I'LL BE GOING TO JUNIOR COLLEGE IN HOKKAIDO.
THAT'S RIGHT.
AFTER GRADUATION, I WON'T BE ABLE TO SEE NOBU-CHAN ALL THE TIME.
I DON'T REALLY MIND THE MOVE...
...BUT I DON'T KNOW HOW THOSE TWO DUMMIES WILL SURVIVE WITHOUT ME.
HA HA HA

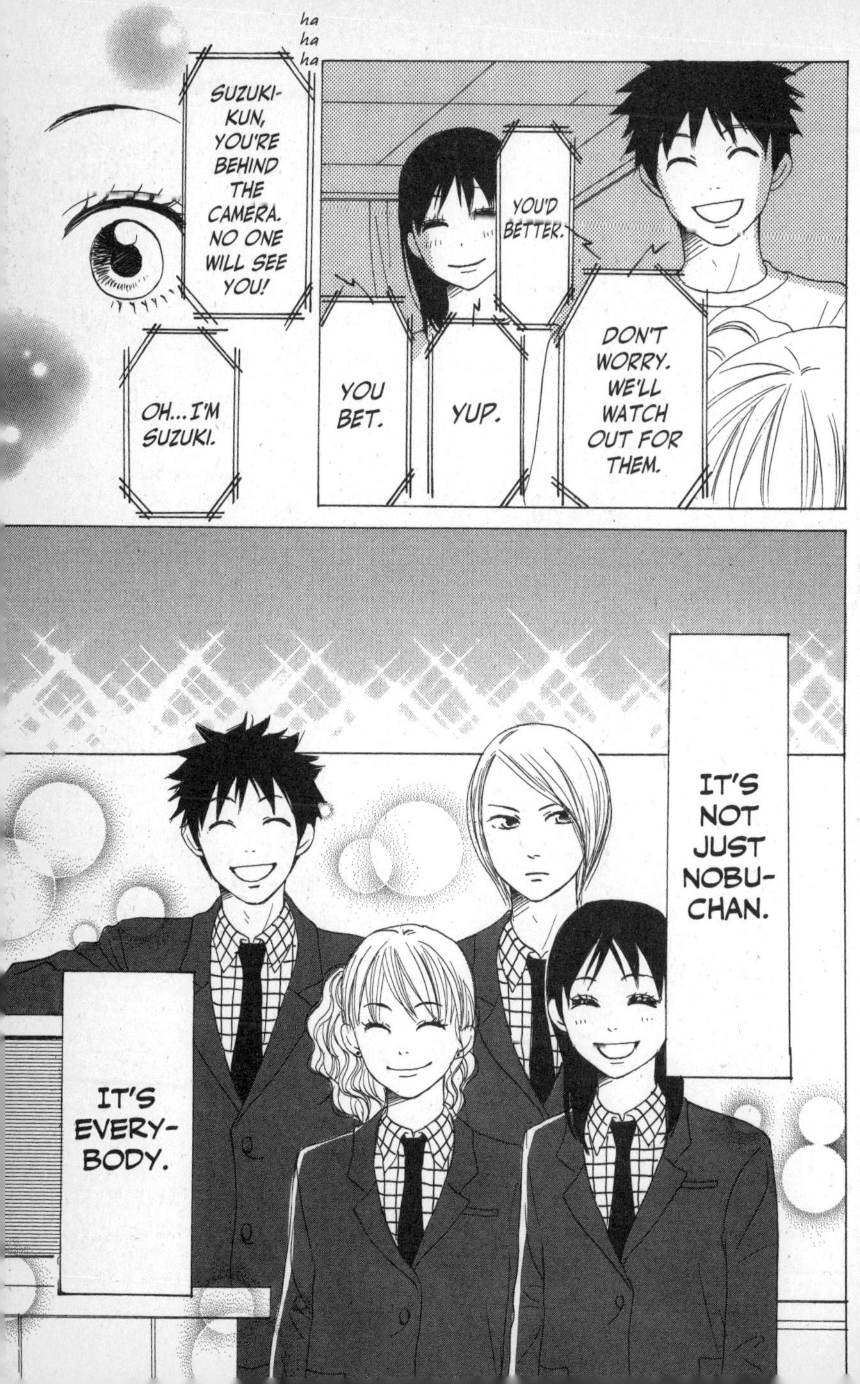

DON'T WORRY. WE'LL WATCH OUT FOR THEM.
YOU'D BETTER.
YUP.
YOU BET.
ha ha ha
SUZUKI-KUN, YOU'RE BEHIND THE CAMERA. NO ONE WILL SEE YOU!
OH...I'M SUZUKI.
IT'S NOT JUST NOBU-CHAN.
IT'S EVERY-BODY.

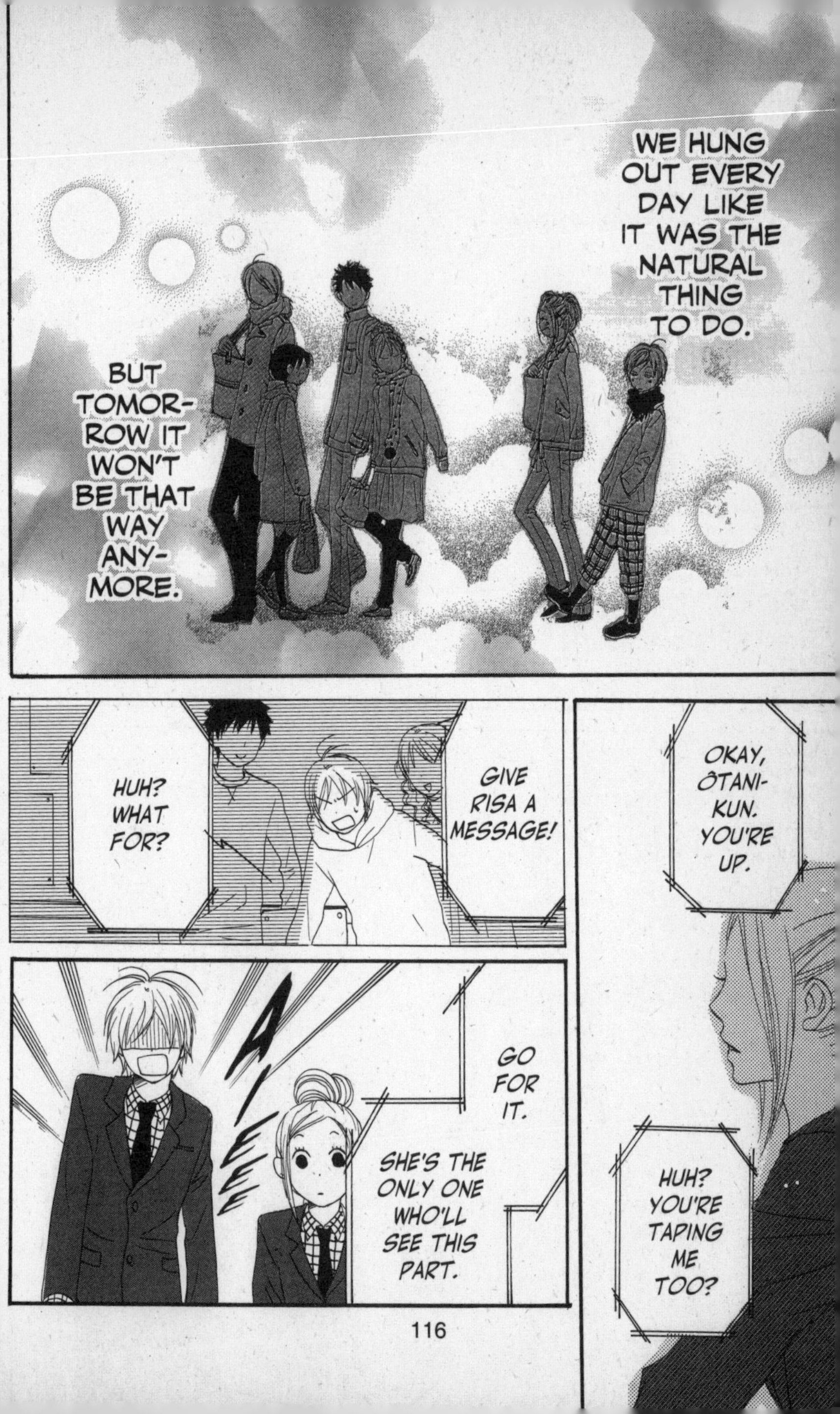
WE HUNG OUT EVERY DAY LIKE IT WAS THE NATURAL THING TO DO.
BUT TOMOR-ROW IT WON'T BE THAT WAY ANY-MORE.
OKAY, ŌTANI-KUN. YOU'RE UP.
HUH? YOU'RE TAPING ME TOO?
GIVE RISA A MESSAGE!
HUH? WHAT FOR?
GO FOR IT.
SHE'S THE ONLY ONE WHO'LL SEE THIS PART.
AIEEEE

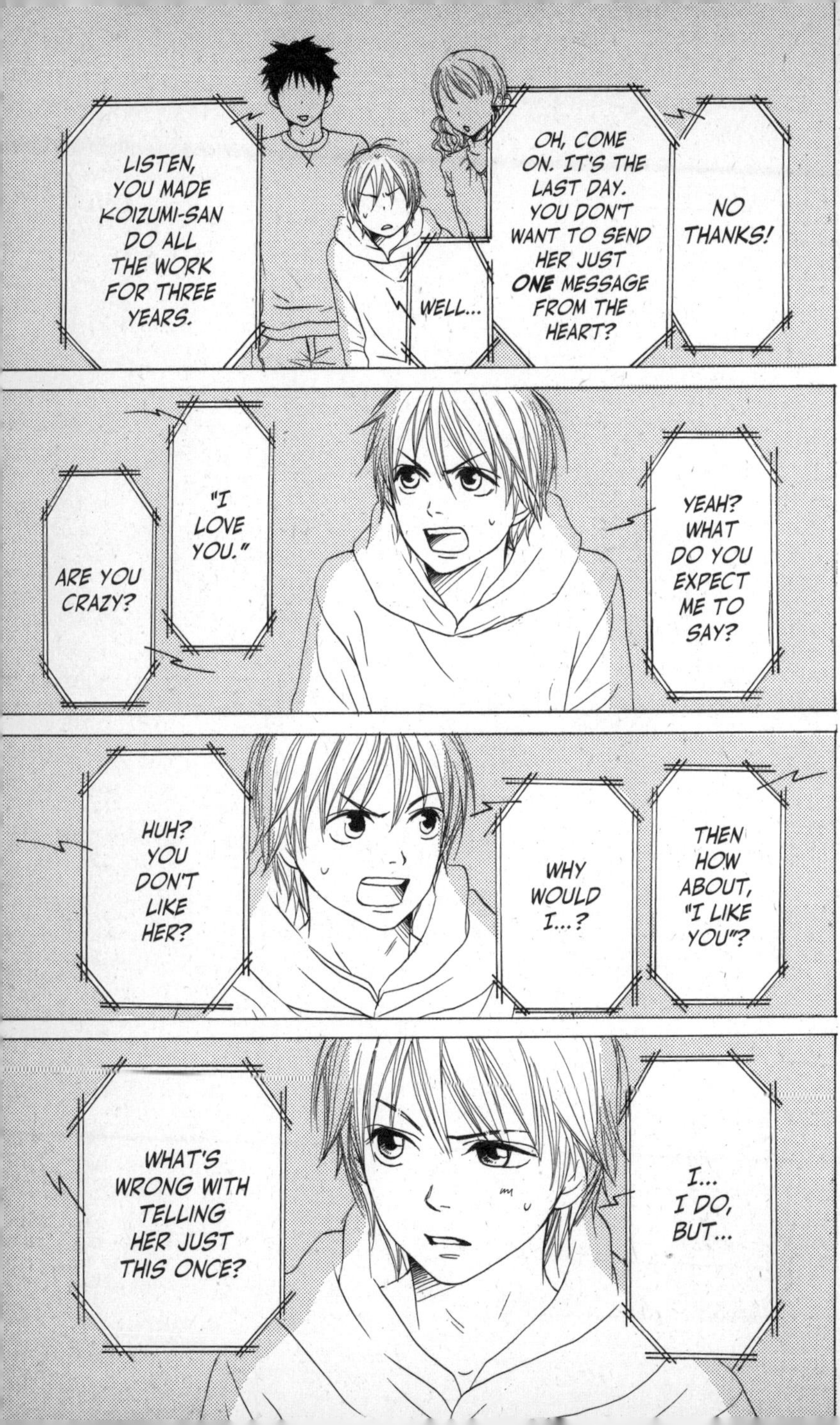
NO THANKS!
OH, COME ON. IT'S THE LAST DAY. YOU DON'T WANT TO SEND HER JUST **ONE** MESSAGE FROM THE HEART?
WELL...
LISTEN, YOU MADE KOIZUMI-SAN DO ALL THE WORK FOR THREE YEARS.
YEAH? WHAT DO YOU EXPECT ME TO SAY?
"I LOVE YOU."
ARE YOU CRAZY?
THEN HOW ABOUT, "I LIKE YOU"?
WHY WOULD I...?
HUH? YOU DON'T LIKE HER?
I... I DO, BUT...
WHAT'S WRONG WITH TELLING HER JUST THIS ONCE?

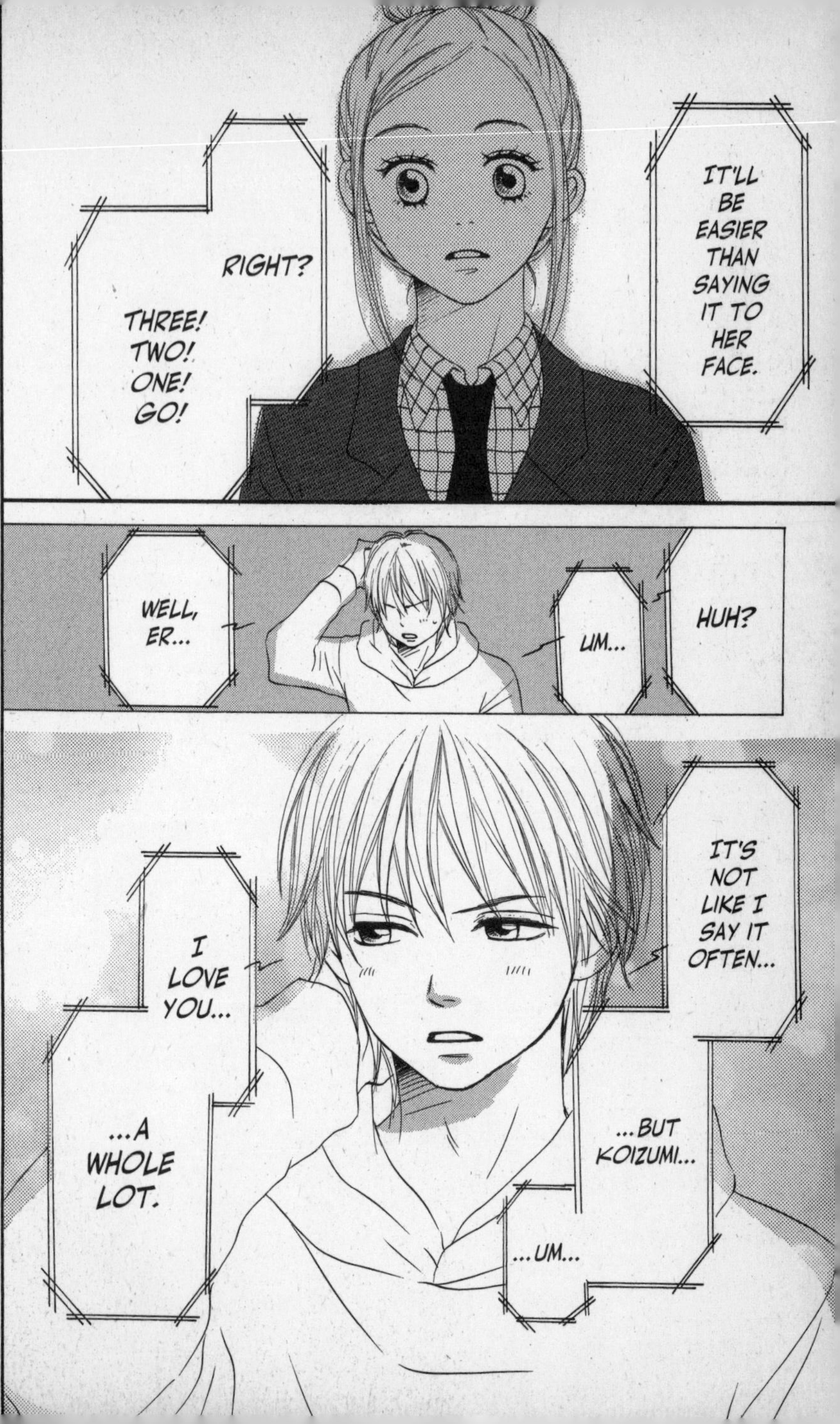

IT'LL BE EASIER THAN SAYING IT TO HER FACE.
RIGHT?
THREE! TWO! ONE! GO!
HUH?
UM...
WELL, ER...
IT'S NOT LIKE I SAY IT OFTEN...
...BUT KOIZUMI...
...UM...
I LOVE YOU...
...A WHOLE LOT.

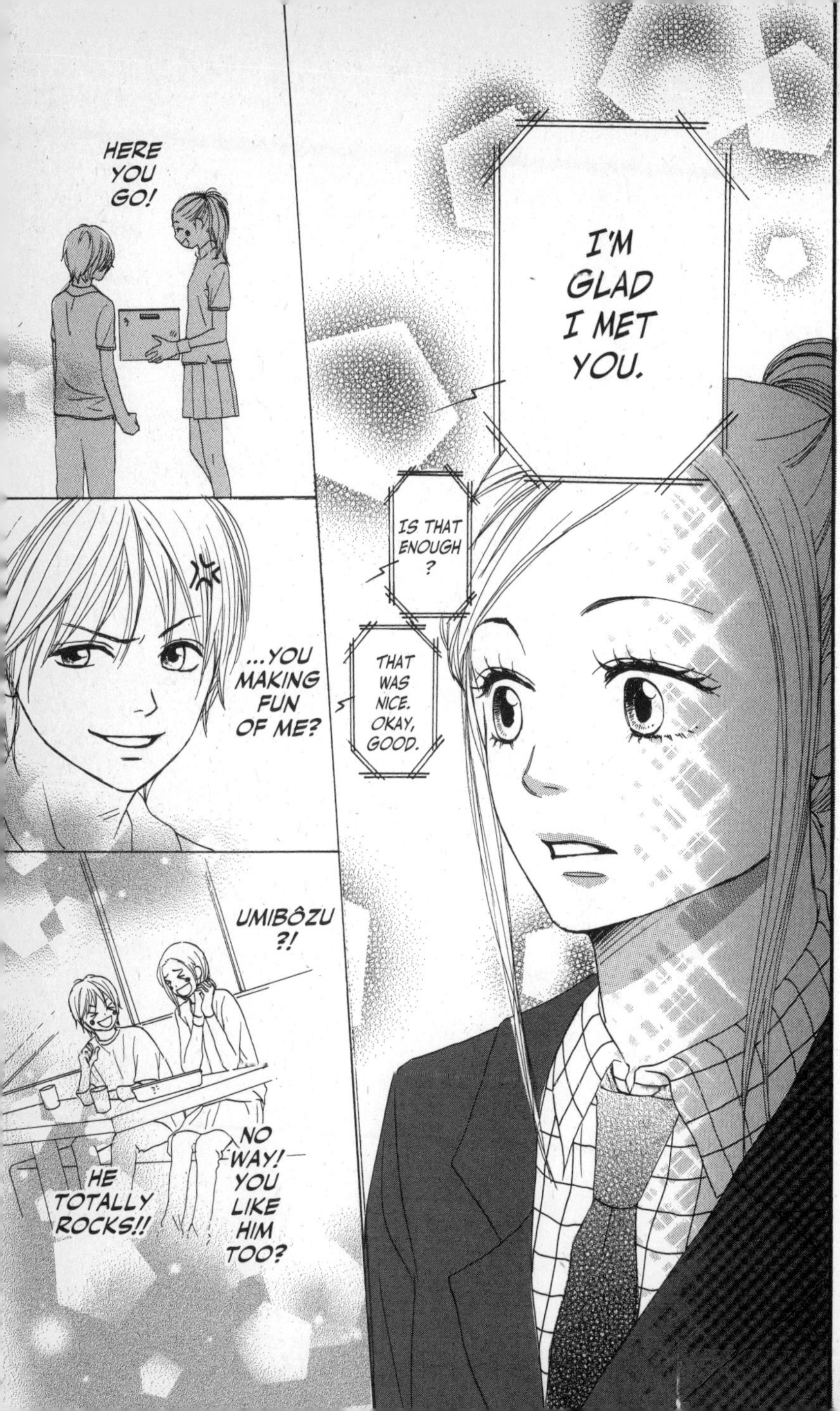
I'M GLAD I MET YOU.
IS THAT ENOUGH?
THAT WAS NICE. OKAY, GOOD.
HERE YOU GO!
...YOU MAKING FUN OF ME?
UMIBÔZU?!
NO WAY! YOU LIKE HIM TOO?
HE TOTALLY ROCKS!!

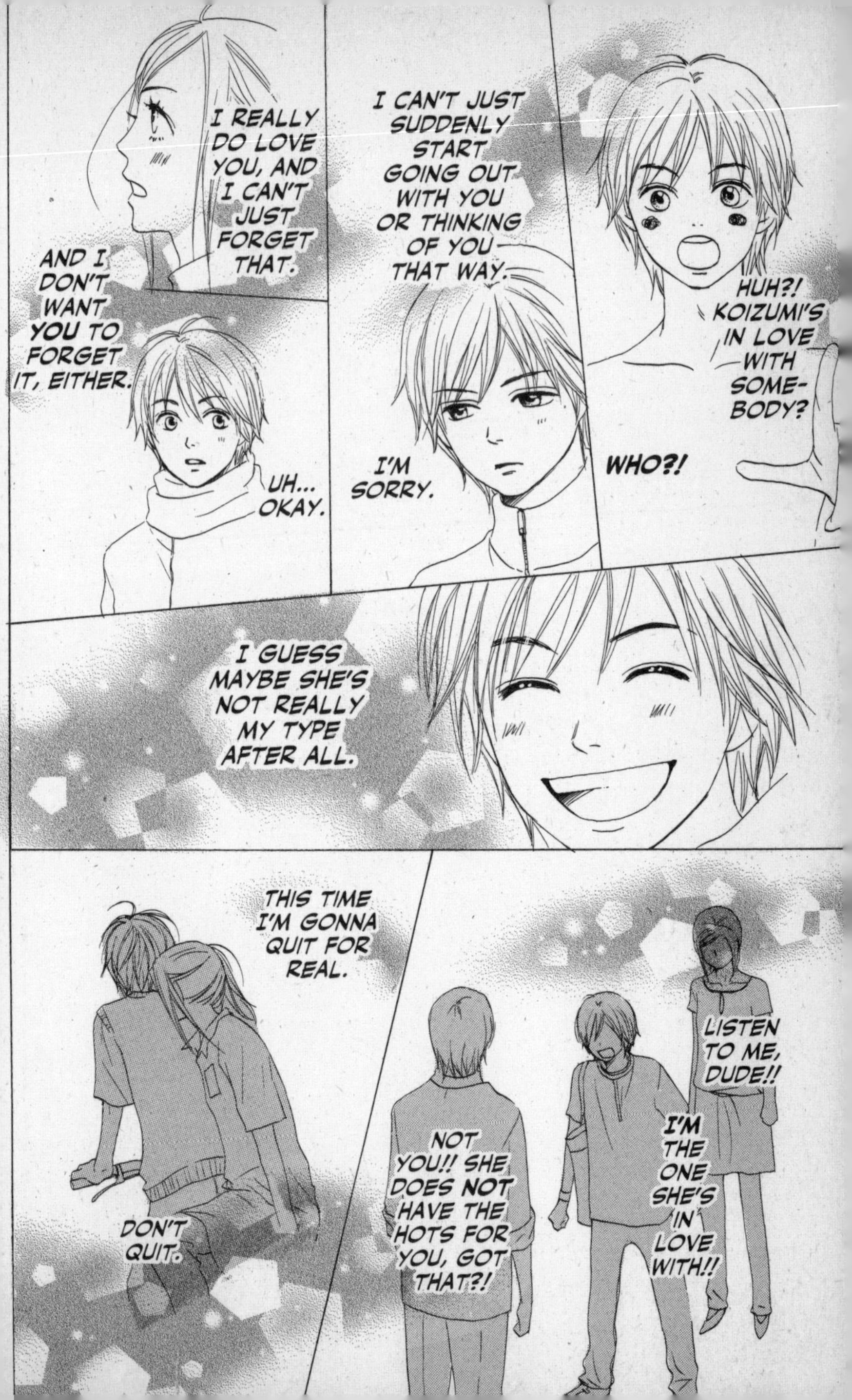
HUH?! KOIZUMI'S IN LOVE WITH SOME-BODY?
WHO?!
I CAN'T JUST SUDDENLY START GOING OUT WITH YOU OR THINKING OF YOU THAT WAY.
I'M SORRY.
I REALLY DO LOVE YOU, AND I CAN'T JUST FORGET THAT.
AND I DON'T WANT YOU TO FORGET IT, EITHER.
UH... OKAY.
I GUESS MAYBE SHE'S NOT REALLY MY TYPE AFTER ALL.
LISTEN TO ME, DUDE!!
I'M THE ONE SHE'S IN LOVE WITH!!
NOT YOU!! SHE DOES NOT HAVE THE HOTS FOR YOU, GOT THAT?!
THIS TIME I'M GONNA QUIT FOR REAL.
DON'T QUIT.

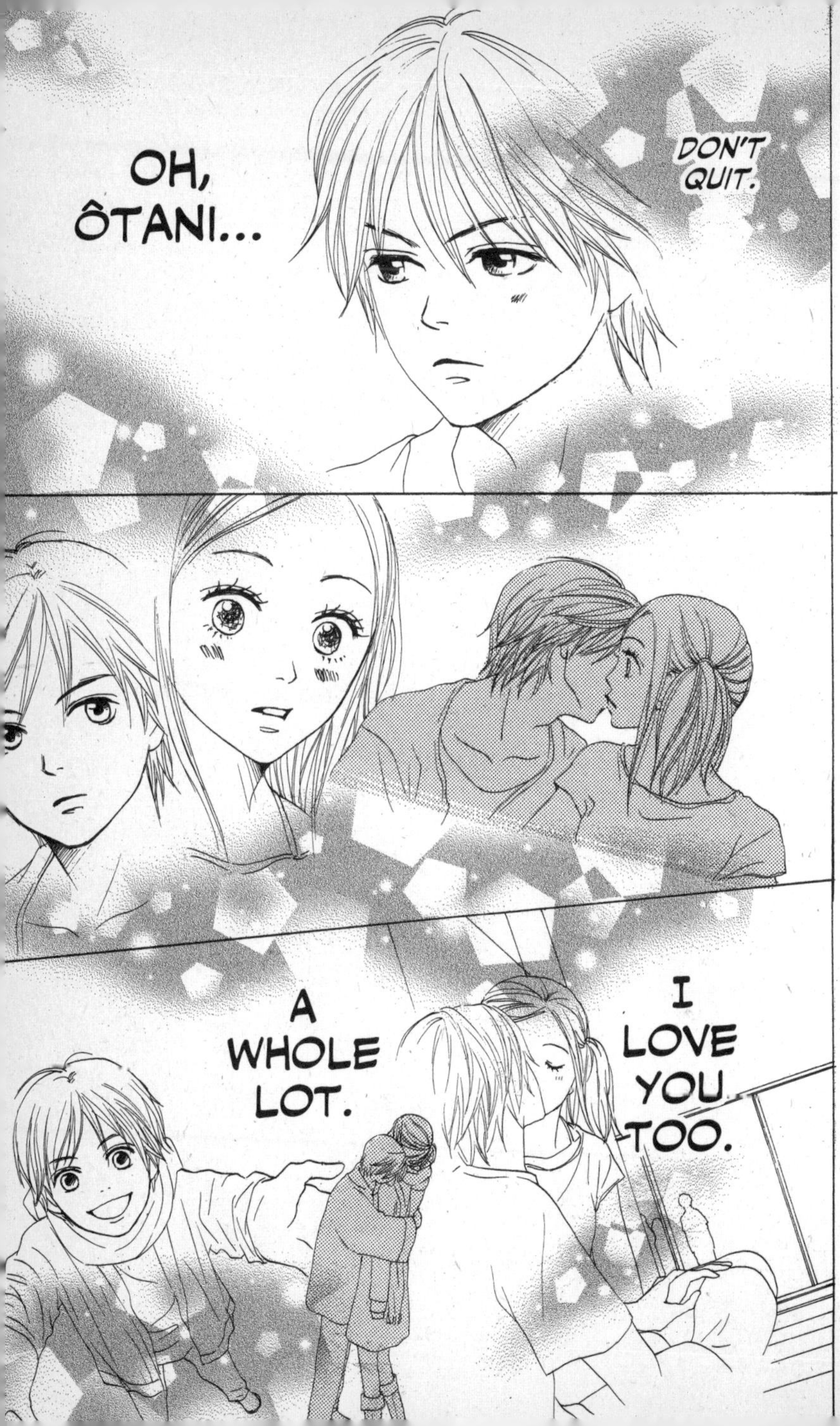
DON'T QUIT.
OH, ÔTANI...
I LOVE YOU TOO.
A WHOLE LOT.

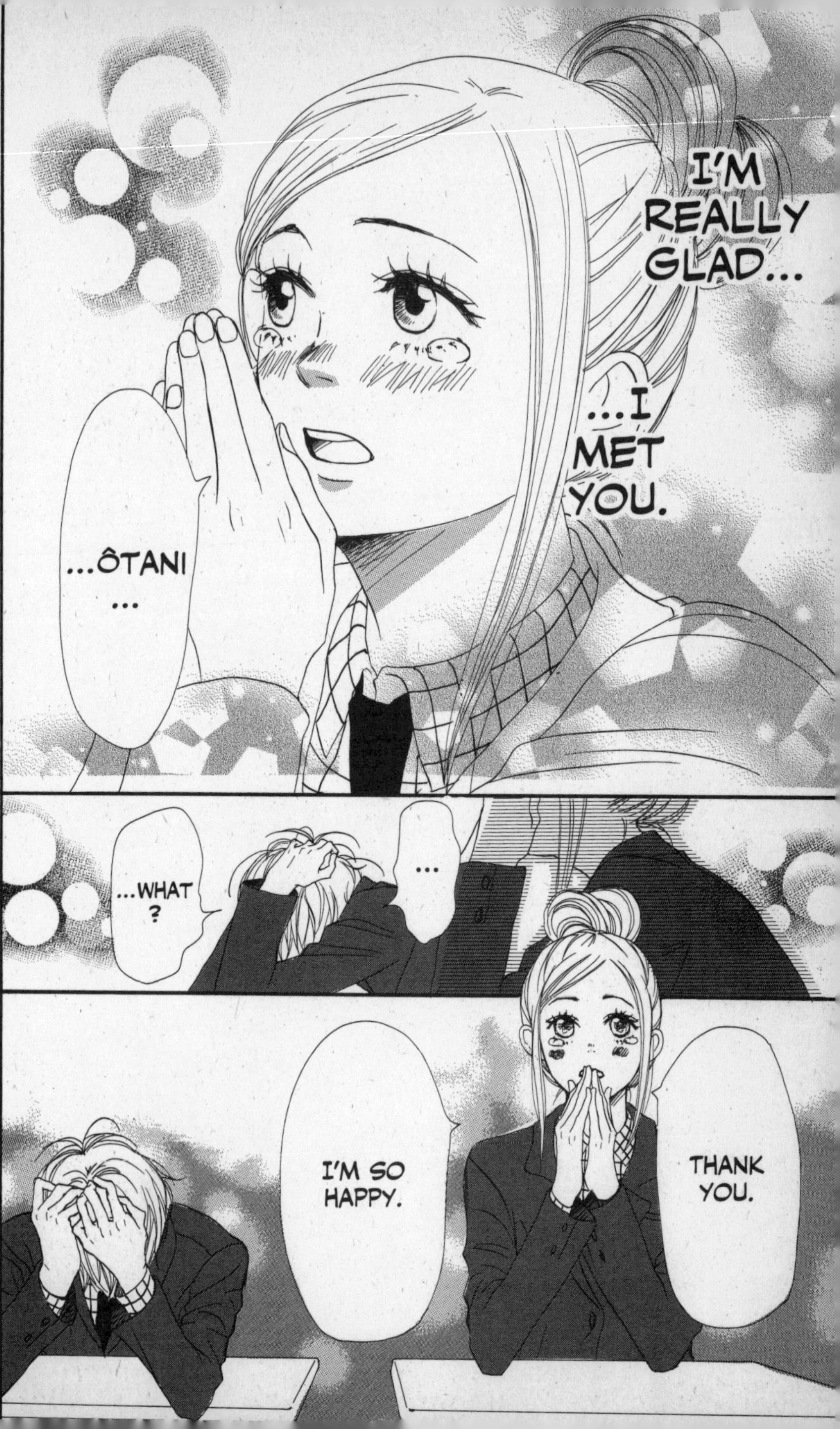
I'M REALLY GLAD...
...I MET YOU.
...ÔTANI ...
...
...WHAT ?
THANK YOU.
I'M SO HAPPY.

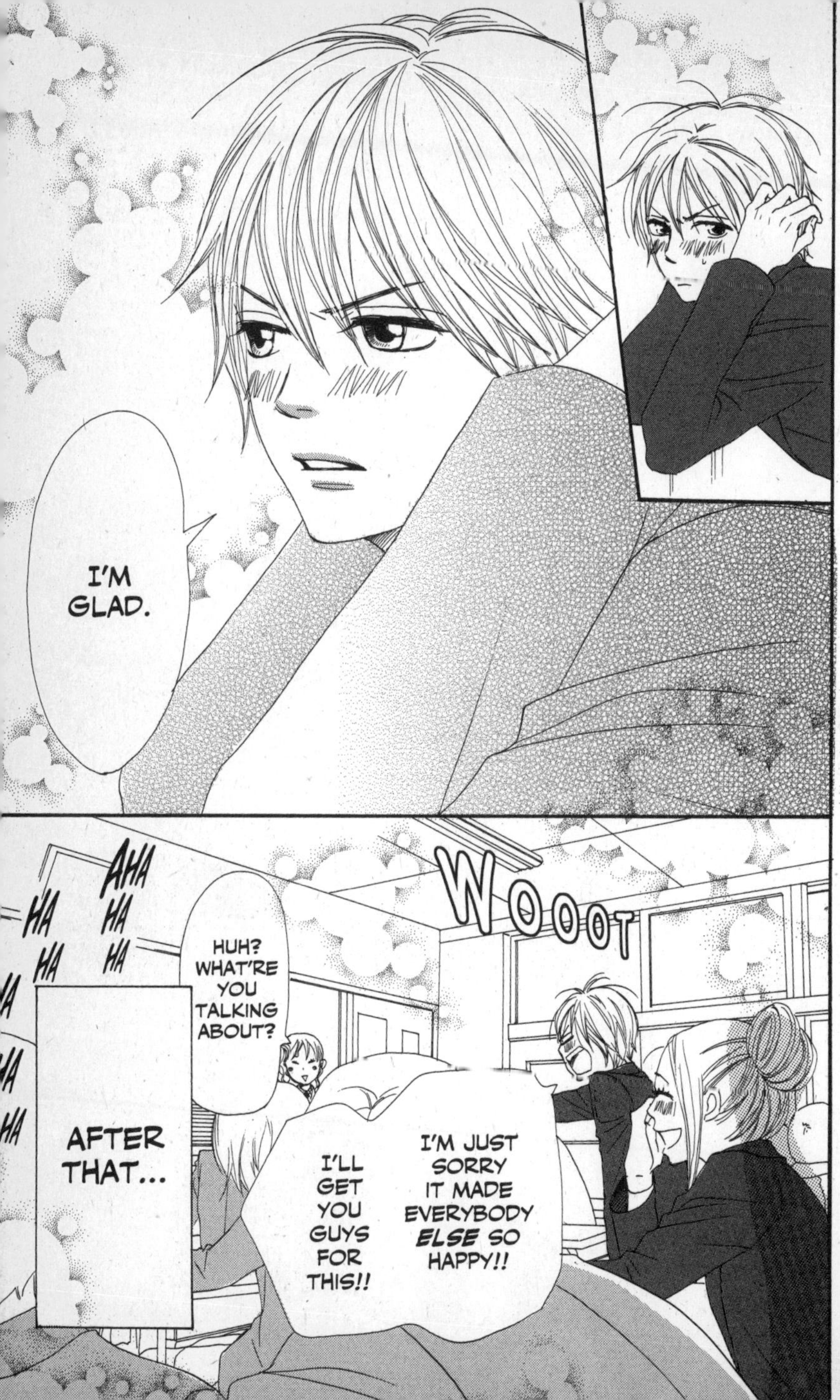
I'M GLAD.
WOOOT
I'M JUST SORRY IT MADE EVERYBODY ELSE SO HAPPY!!
I'LL GET YOU GUYS FOR THIS!!
HUH? WHAT'RE YOU TALKING ABOUT?
AHAHAHAHA
HAHA
AFTER THAT...

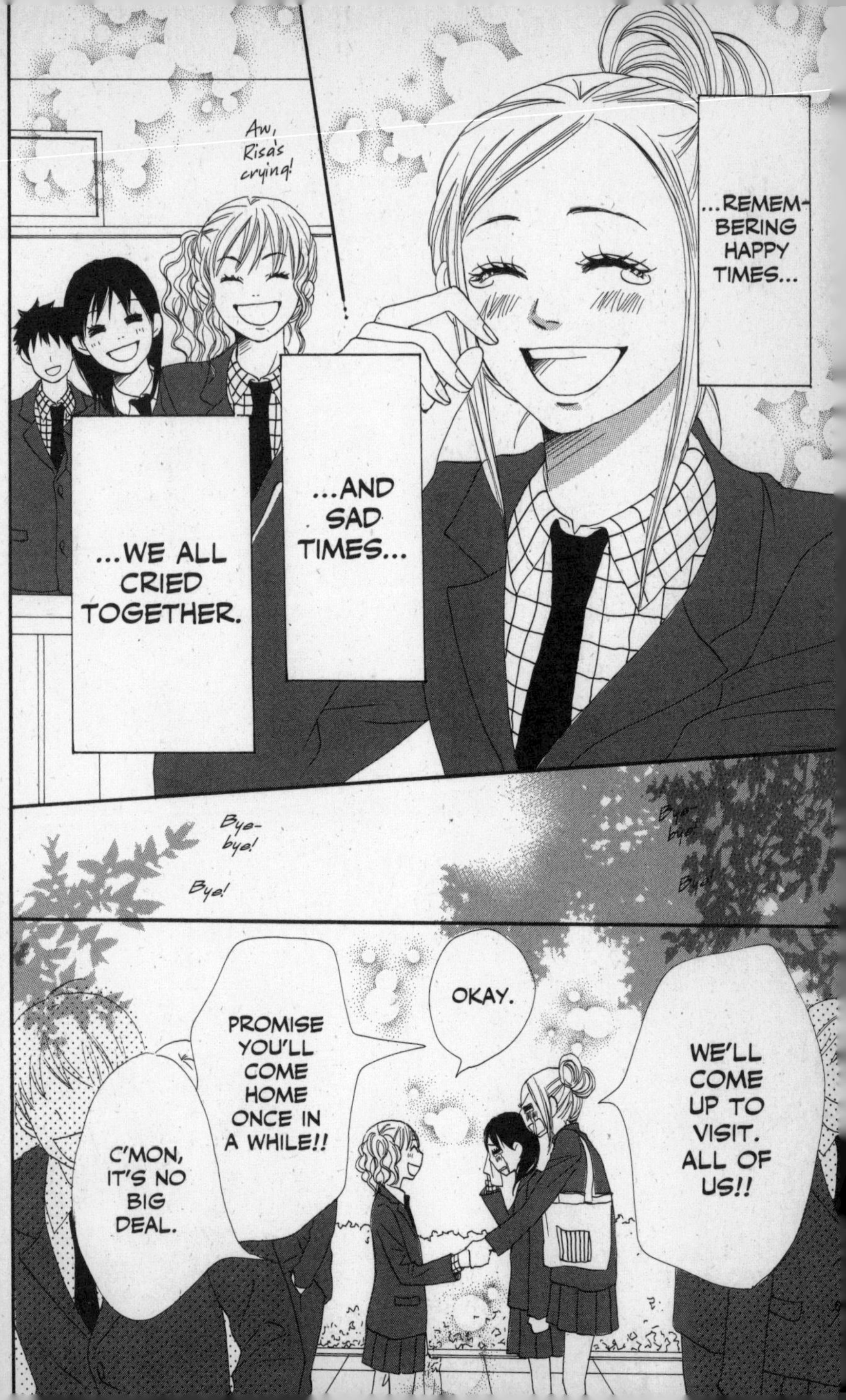

...REMEMBERING HAPPY TIMES...
...AND SAD TIMES...
...WE ALL CRIED TOGETHER.
Aw, Risa's crying!
Bye-bye!
Bye!
Bye-bye!
Bye!
WE'LL COME UP TO VISIT. ALL OF US!!
OKAY.
PROMISE YOU'LL COME HOME ONCE IN A WHILE!!
C'MON, IT'S NO BIG DEAL.

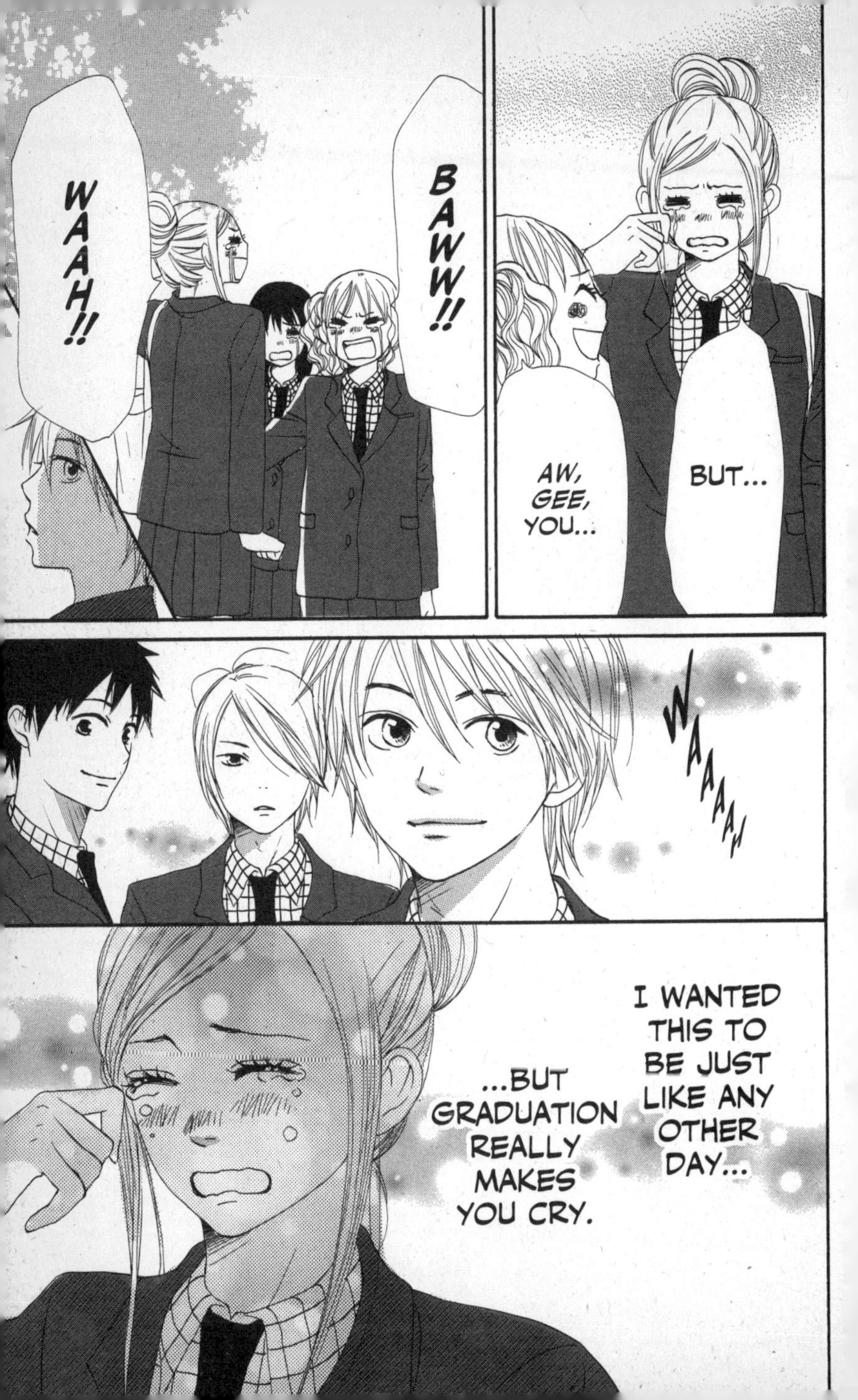
BUT...
AW, GEE, YOU...
BAWWW!!
WAAAH!!
WAAAAAH
I WANTED THIS TO BE JUST LIKE ANY OTHER DAY...
...BUT GRADUATION REALLY MAKES YOU CRY.

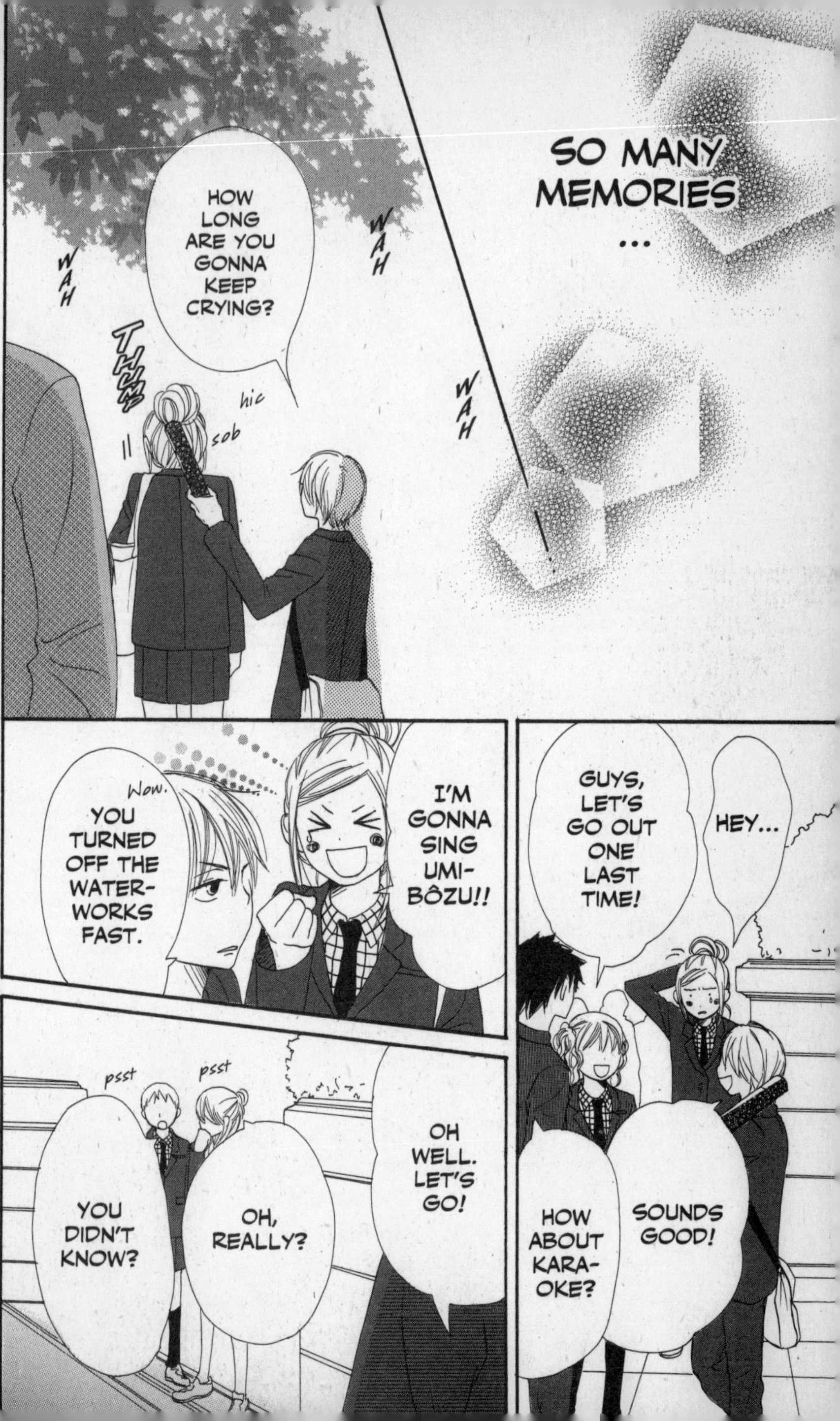
SO MANY MEMORIES ...
WAH
WAH
WAH
HOW LONG ARE YOU GONNA KEEP CRYING?
WAH
THUMP
hic
sob
HEY...
GUYS, LET'S GO OUT ONE LAST TIME!
SOUNDS GOOD!
HOW ABOUT KARA-OKE?
I'M GONNA SING UMI-BÔZU!!
Wow.
YOU TURNED OFF THE WATER-WORKS FAST.
OH WELL. LET'S GO!
psst
psst
OH, REALLY?
YOU DIDN'T KNOW?

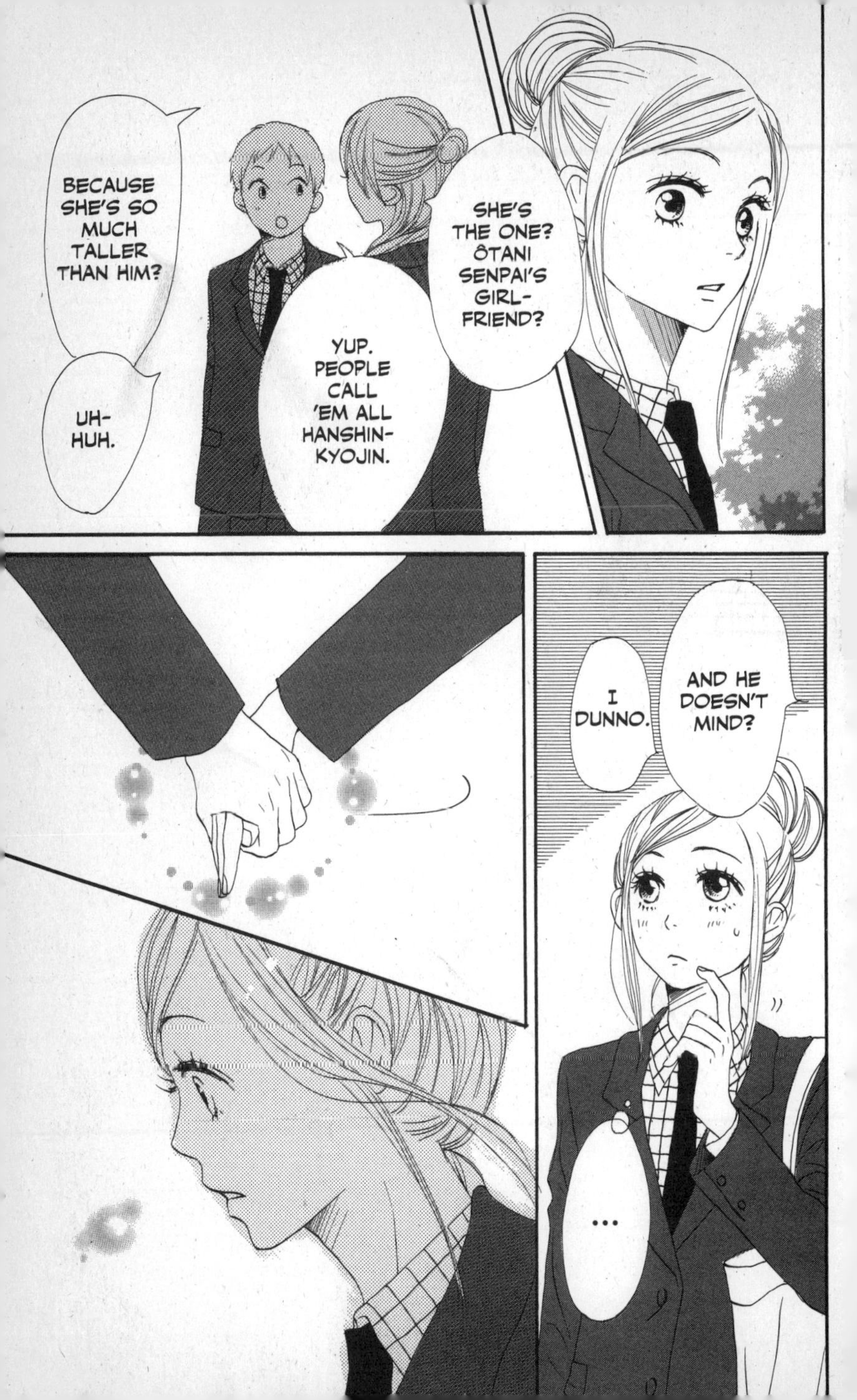
SHE'S THE ONE? ÔTANI SENPAI'S GIRL-FRIEND?
YUP. PEOPLE CALL 'EM ALL HANSHIN-KYOJIN.
BECAUSE SHE'S SO MUCH TALLER THAN HIM?
UH-HUH.
AND HE DOESN'T MIND?
I DUNNO.
...

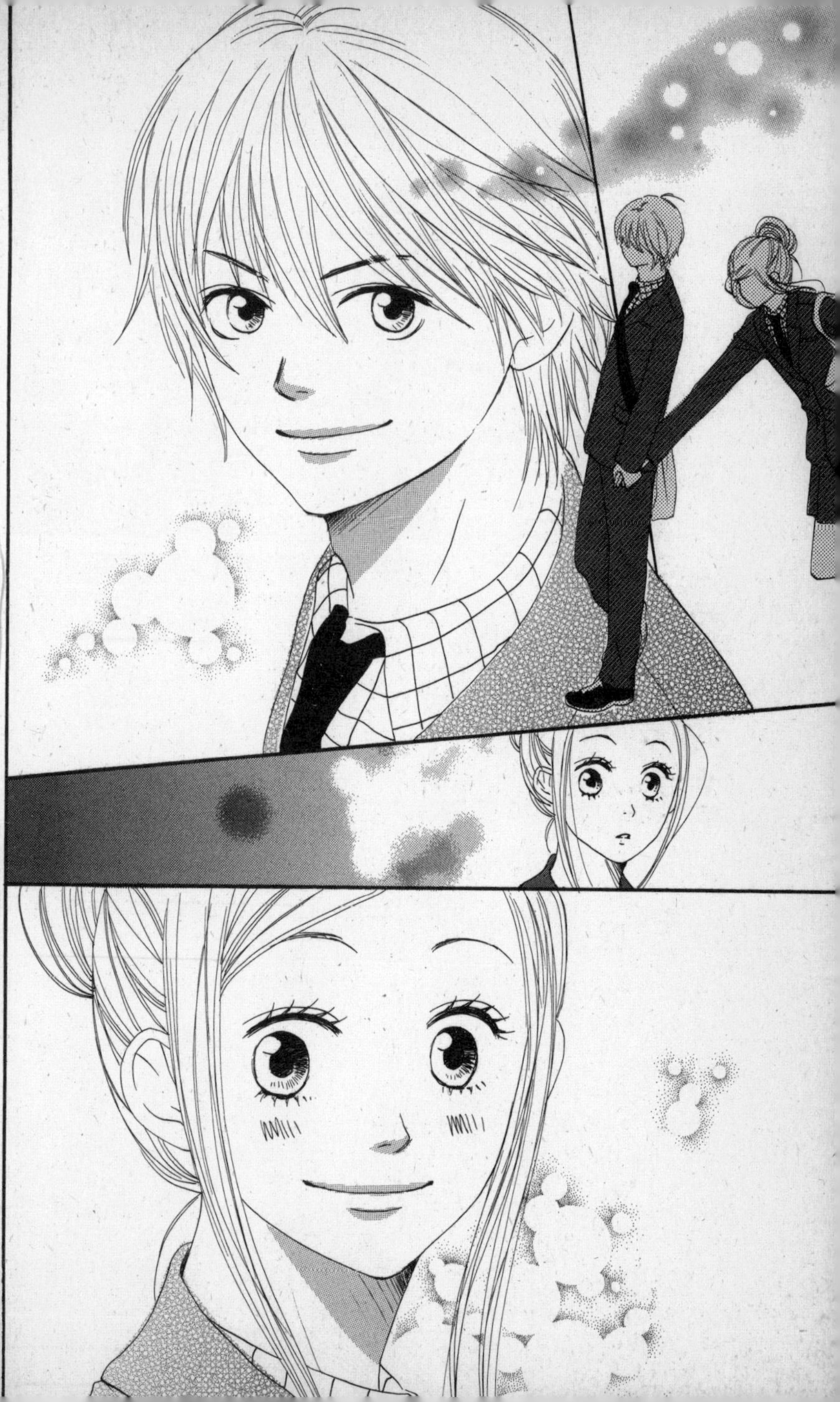

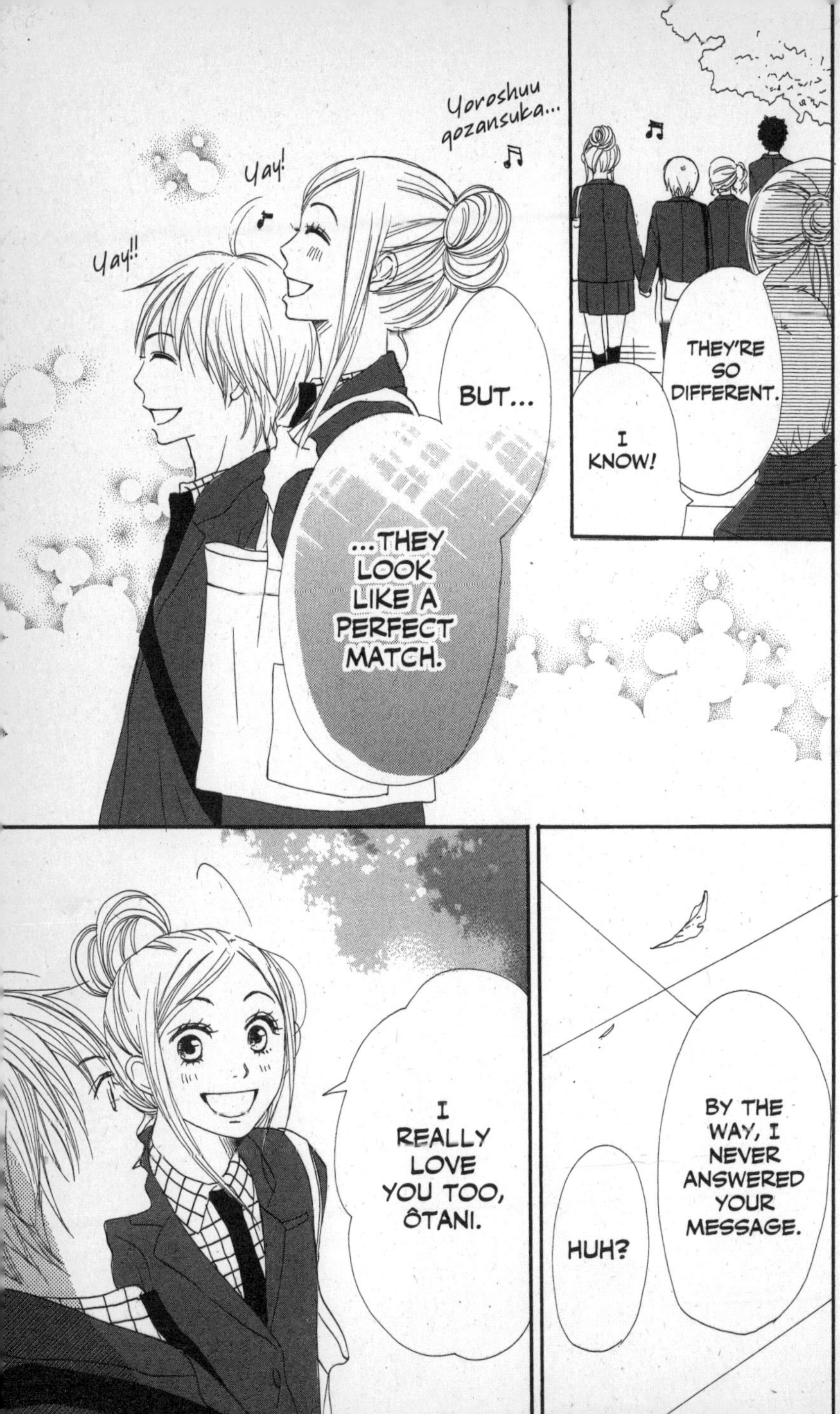
THEY'RE SO DIFFERENT.
I KNOW!
Yoroshuu gozansuka...
Yay!
Yay!!
BUT...
...THEY LOOK LIKE A PERFECT MATCH.
BY THE WAY, I NEVER ANSWERED YOUR MESSAGE.
HUH?
I REALLY LOVE YOU TOO, ÔTANI.

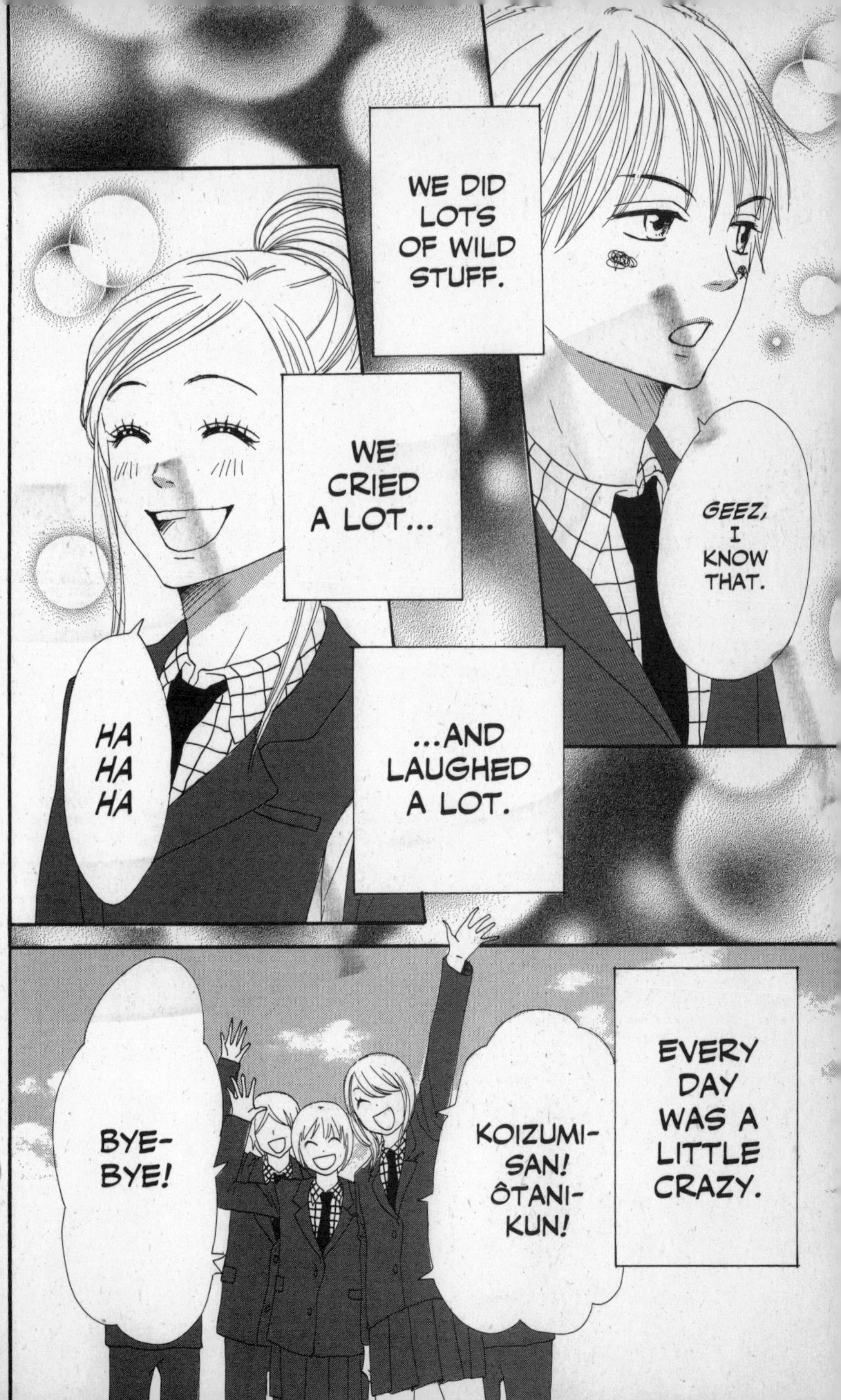
WE DID LOTS OF WILD STUFF.
GEEZ, I KNOW THAT.
WE CRIED A LOT...
...AND LAUGHED A LOT.
HA HA HA
EVERY DAY WAS A LITTLE CRAZY.
KOIZUMI-SAN! ÔTANI-KUN!
BYE-BYE!

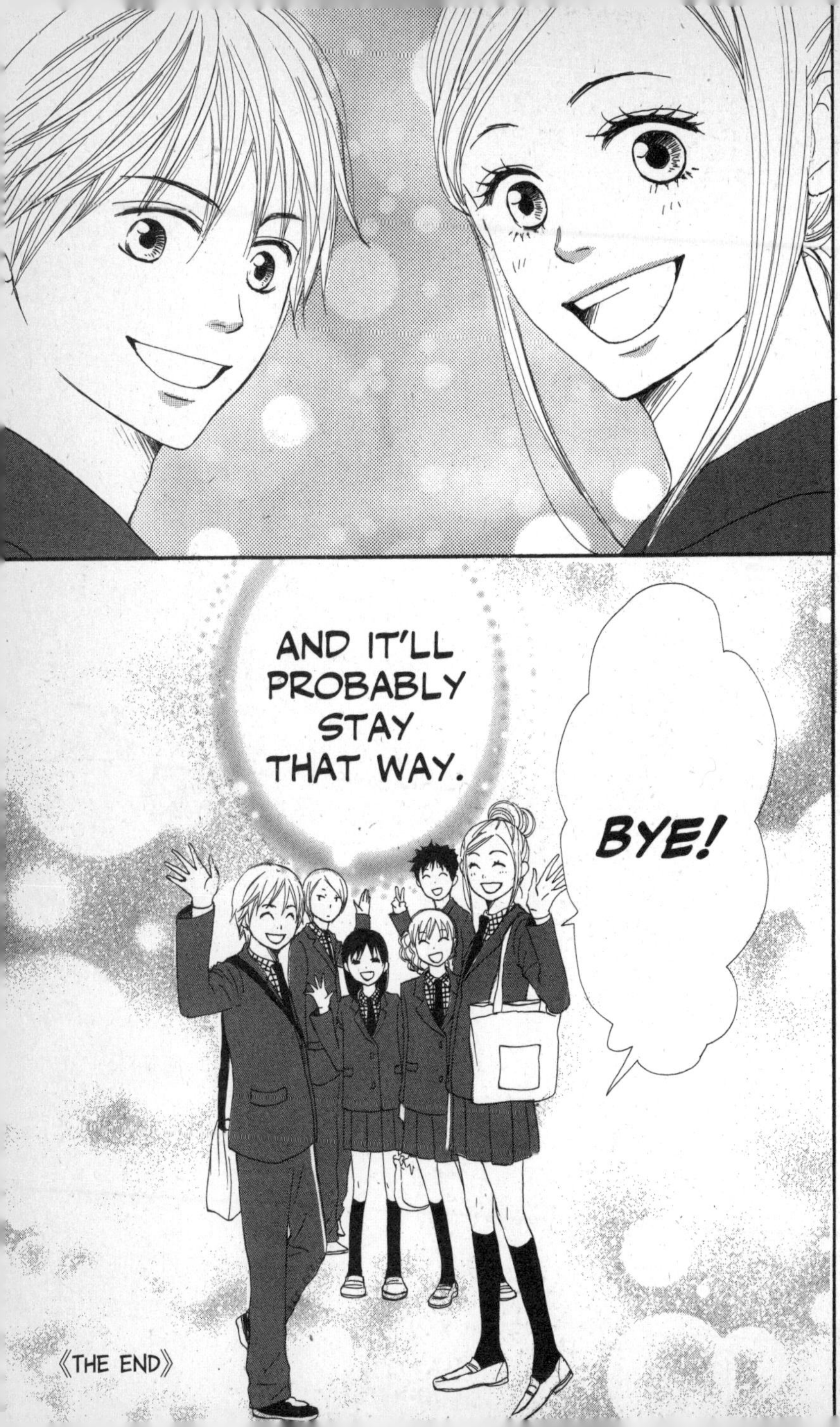
BYE!
AND IT'LL PROBABLY STAY THAT WAY.
《THE END》

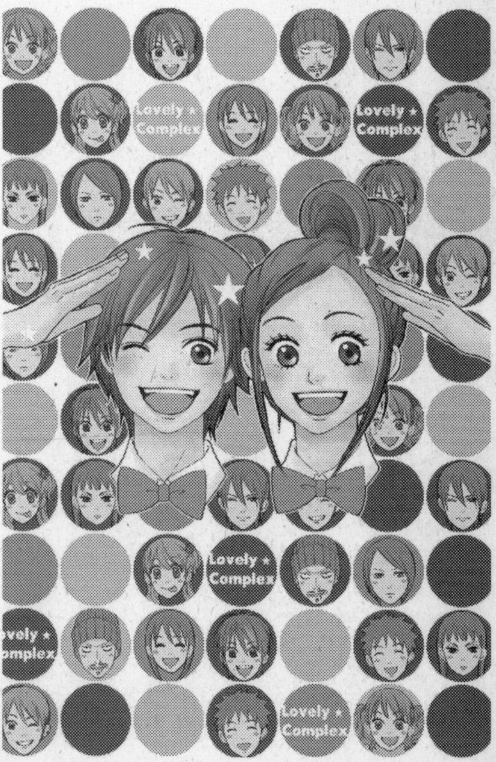
Lovely ★ Complex

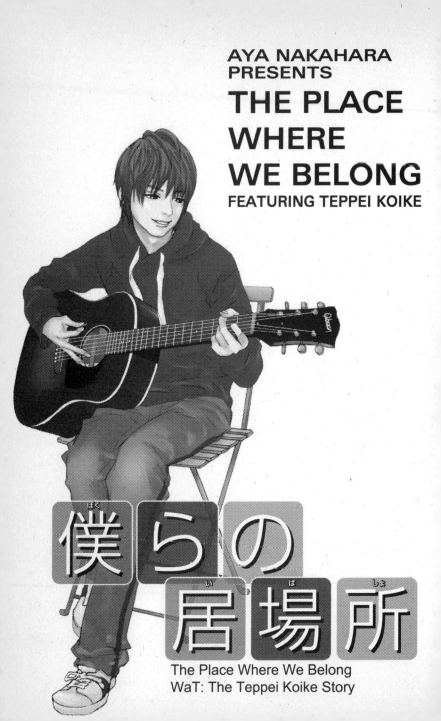

AYA NAKAHARA
PRESENTS

THE PLACE WHERE WE BELONG

FEATURING TEPPEI KOIKE

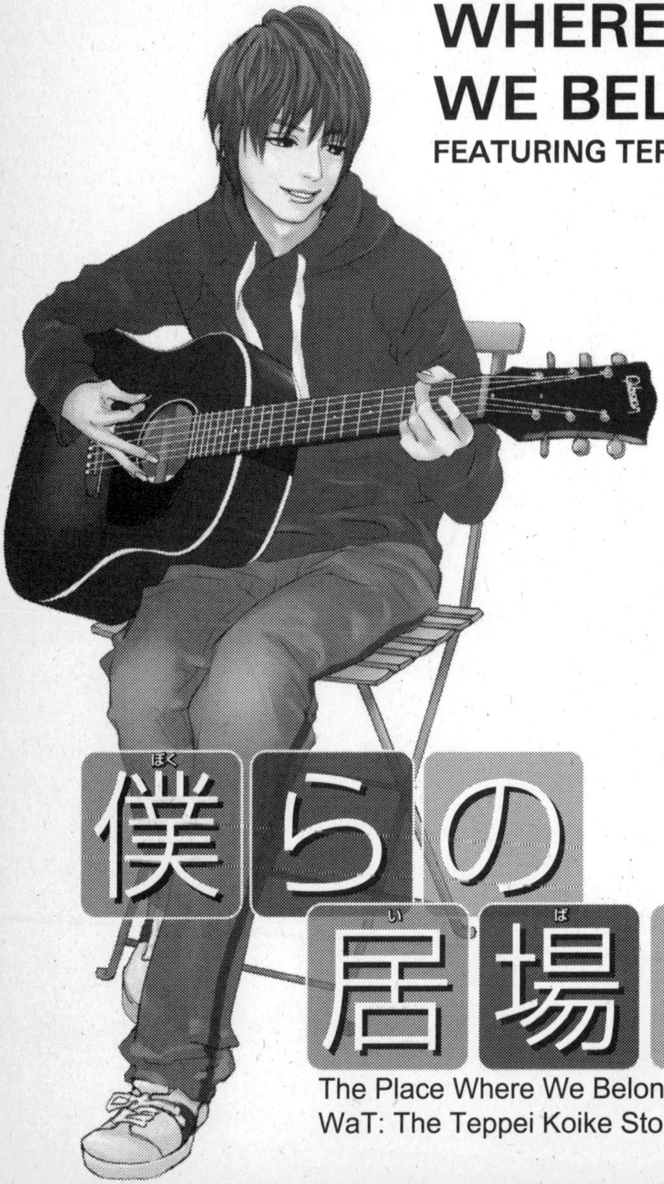

僕らの居場所

The Place Where We Belong
WaT: The Teppei Koike Story

← The story of WaT begins on the next page. I didn't want to draw anything false about actual, living people, so I really studied up on WaT (or maybe just turned into a fangirl). I came away with the feeling that the appeal of WaT is partly in their songs, and partly in the obvious friendship and bonding you see when the two of them are together. I tried very hard to bring out that part of them in my artwork.

Teppei is the main character in this story. Wentz-kun allowed me to portray him as someone Teppei tries to emulate. Teppei always described his friend and partner as a very cool person, so I did my best to convey that impression. Did it work? I felt like this was the first time in my manga career that I drew a totally cool character. It was a nice change.

My main characters are usually pretty introverted, so it was also refreshing to portray someone like Teppei, who's always positive and outgoing. It's not like he explained every little feeling to me, so I was a bit nervous about adding dialogue and thoughts. But I tried to keep it close to the way I thought the real Teppei would feel.

This was my first attempt at a manga about a real person. It was a fun, exciting experience. I'm very grateful to the people who gave me this opportunity. Thank you very much.

To all the WaT fans out there, and to those who aren't familiar with WaT, I hope you enjoy this manga.

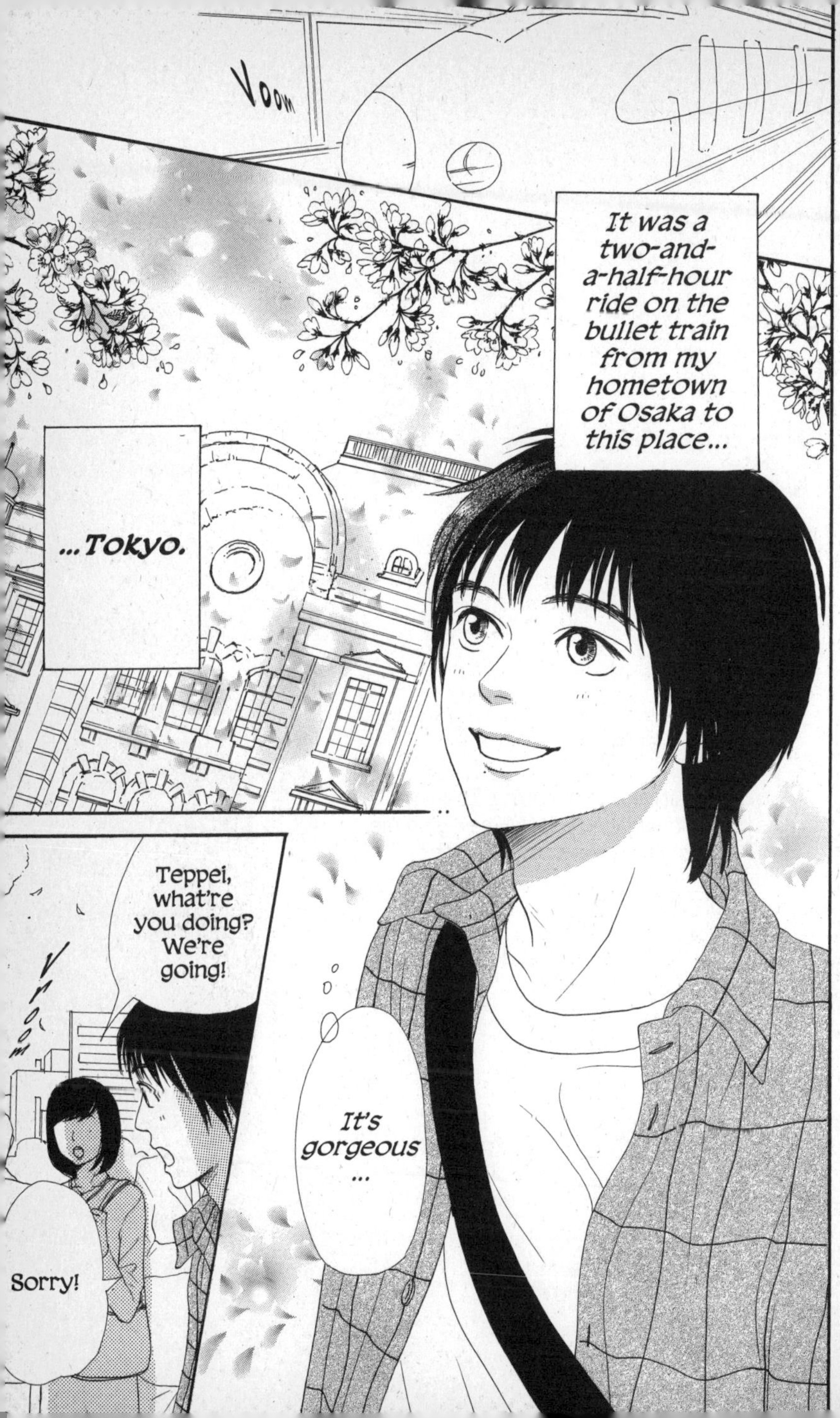
Voom
It was a two-and-a-half-hour ride on the bullet train from my hometown of Osaka to this place...
...Tokyo.
It's gorgeous...
Teppei, what're you doing? We're going!
Vroom
Sorry!

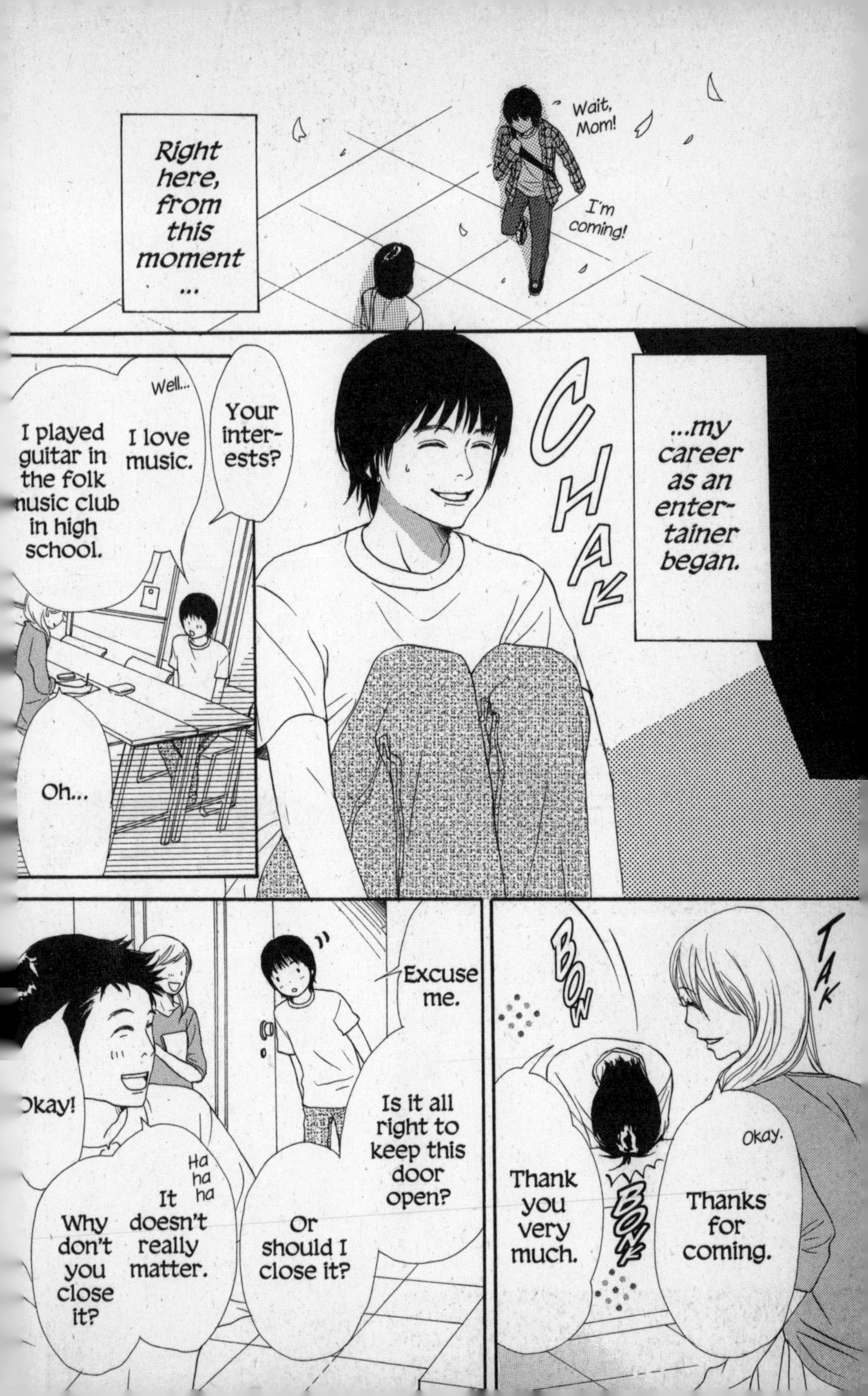
Wait, Mom!
I'm coming!
Right here, from this moment ...
...my career as an entertainer began.
CHAK
Your interests?
Well...
I love music.
I played guitar in the folk music club in high school.
Oh...
TAK
BOW
Okay.
Thanks for coming.
Thank you very much.
BOW
Excuse me.
Is it all right to keep this door open?
Okay!
Or should I close it?
Ha ha ha
It doesn't really matter.
Why don't you close it?

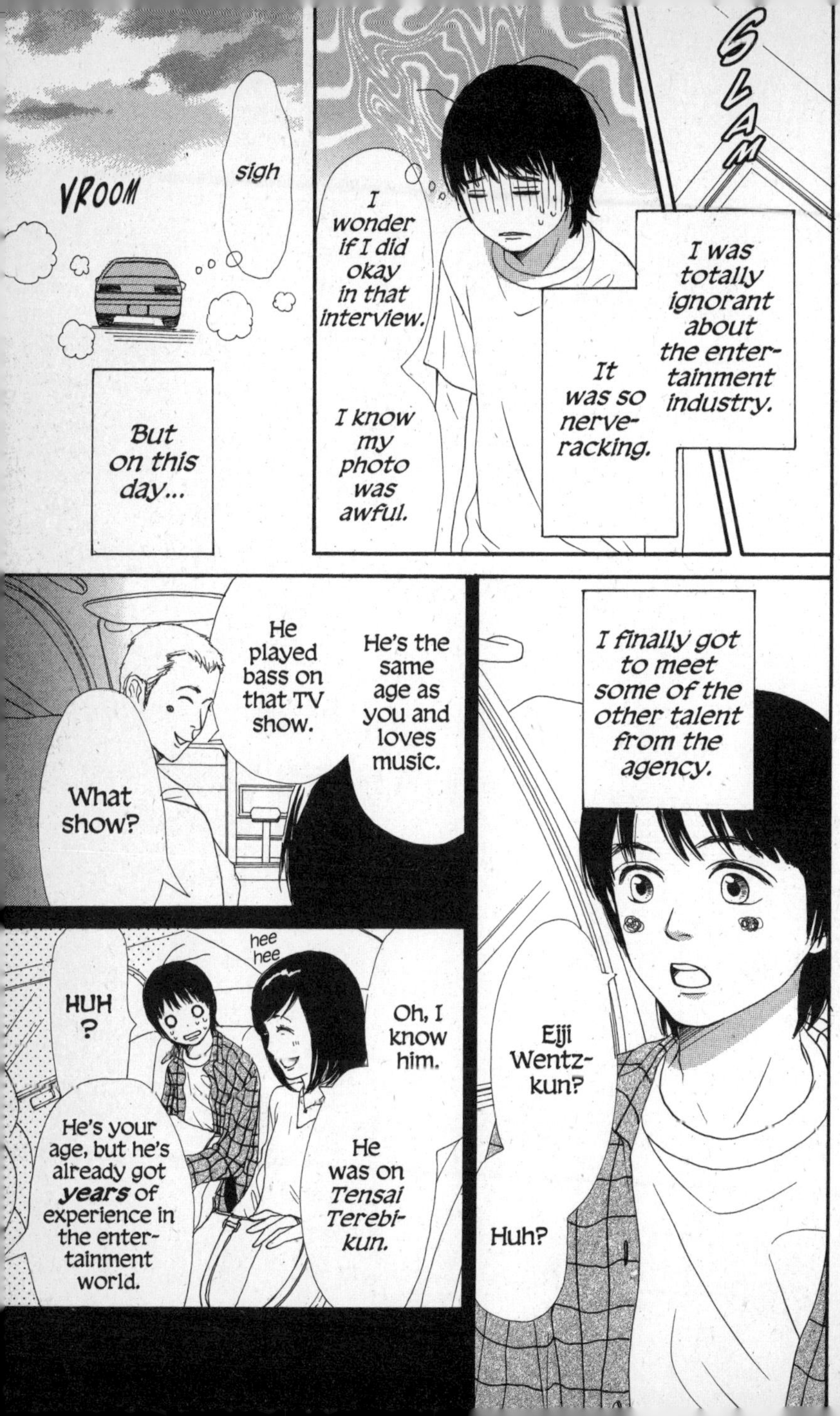
SLAM
I was totally ignorant about the entertainment industry.
It was so nerve-racking.
I wonder if I did okay in that interview.
I know my photo was awful.
sigh
VROOM
But on this day...
I finally got to meet some of the other talent from the agency.
Eiji Wentz-kun?
Huh?
He's the same age as you and loves music.
He played bass on that TV show.
What show?
Oh, I know him.
He was on Tensai Terebi-kun.
hee hee
HUH?
He's your age, but he's already got years of experience in the entertainment world.

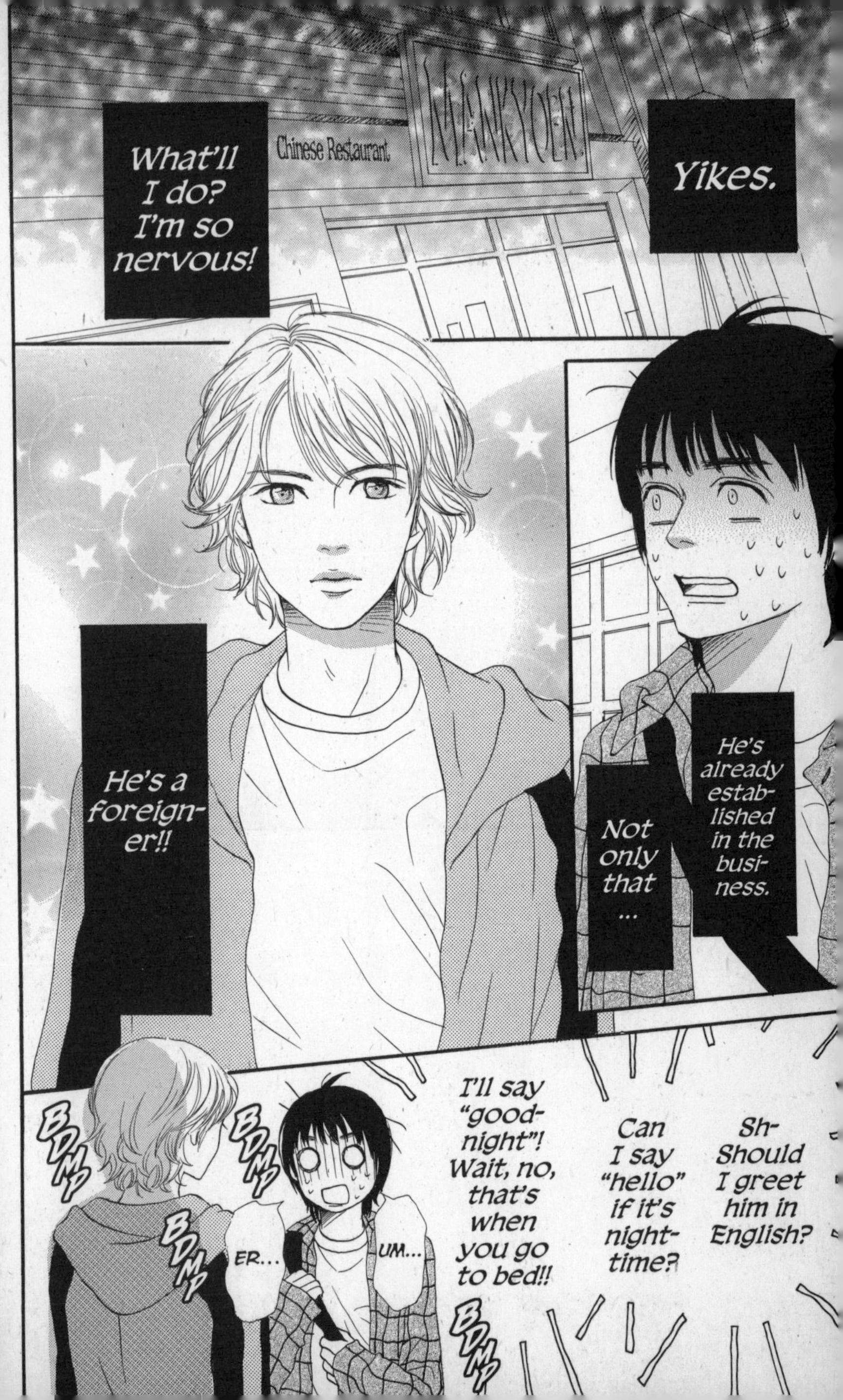
Yikes.
What'll I do? I'm so nervous!
Chinese Restaurant
He's already established in the business.
Not only that...
He's a foreigner!!
Sh-Should I greet him in English?
Can I say "hello" if it's night-time?
I'll say "good-night"! Wait, no, that's when you go to bed!!
UM...
ER...
BDMP
BDMP
BDMP
BDMP

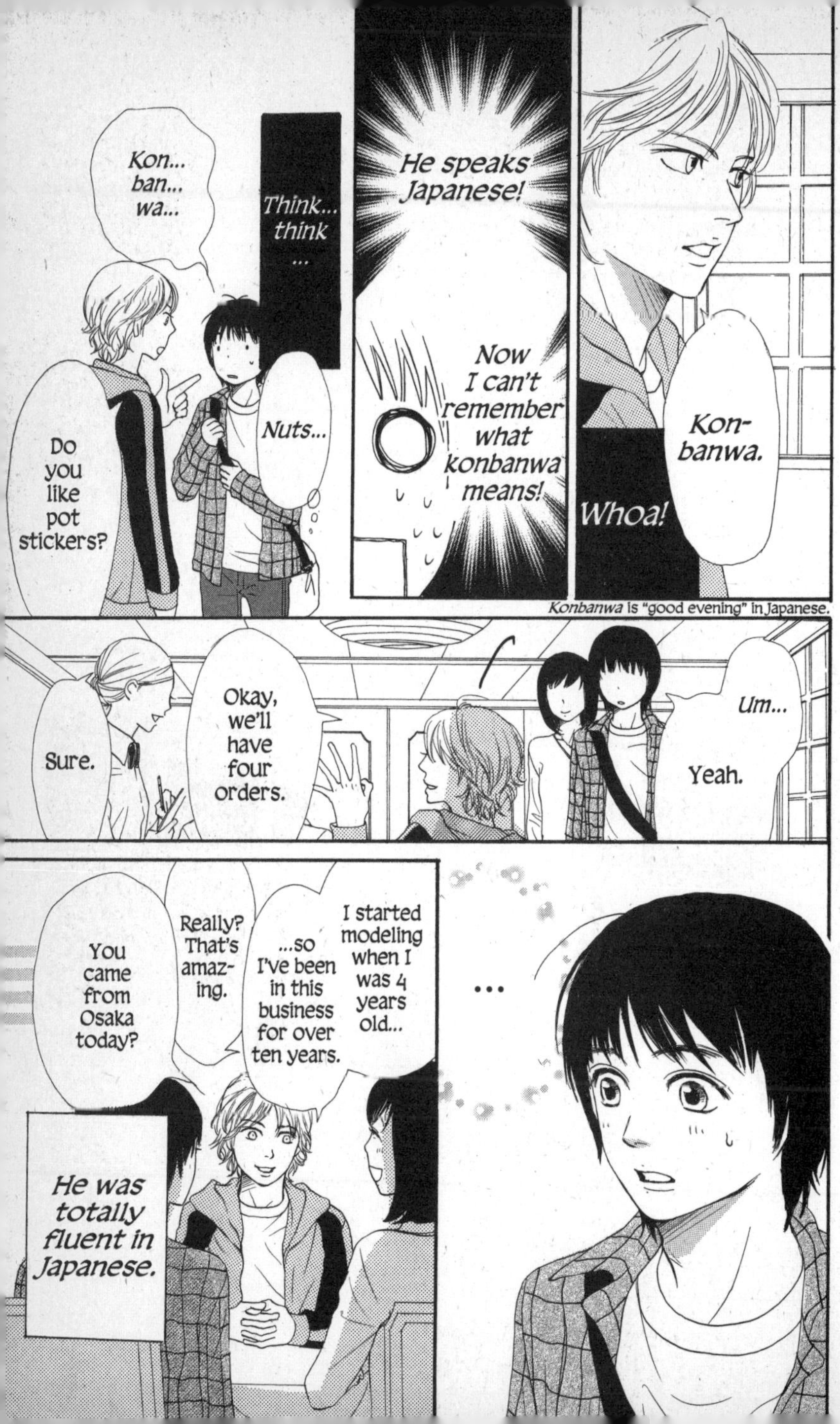
Kon-banwa.
Whoa!
He speaks Japanese!
Now I can't remember what konbanwa means!
Think... think ...
Kon... ban... wa...
Nuts...
Do you like pot stickers?
Um...
Yeah.
Okay, we'll have four orders.
Sure.
...
I started modeling when I was 4 years old...
...so I've been in this business for over ten years.
Really? That's amazing.
You came from Osaka today?
He was totally fluent in Japanese.

Konbanwa is "good evening" in Japanese.

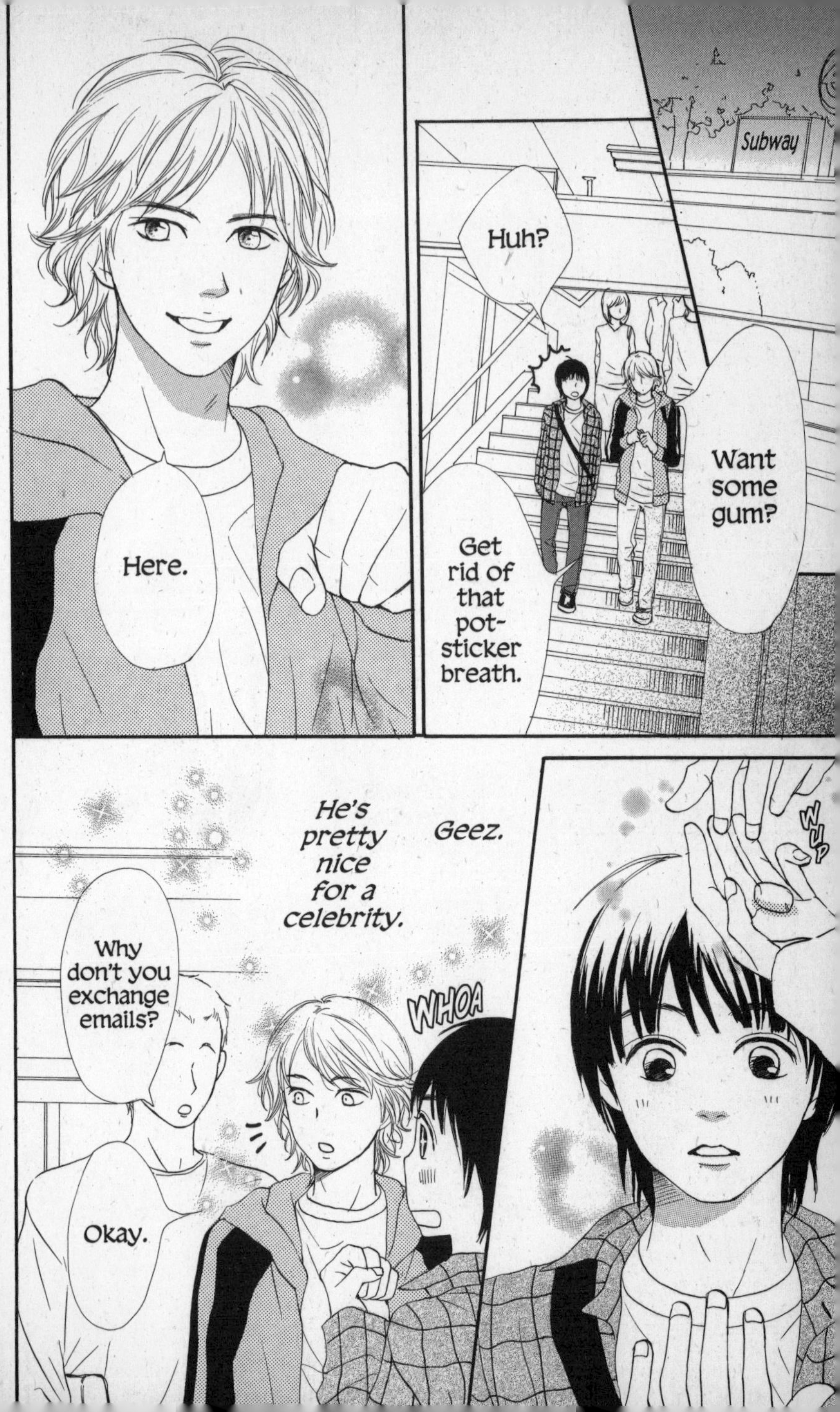
Subway
Want some gum?
Huh?
Get rid of that pot-sticker breath.
Here.
WUP
Geez.
He's pretty nice for a celebrity.
WHOA
Why don't you exchange emails?
Okay.

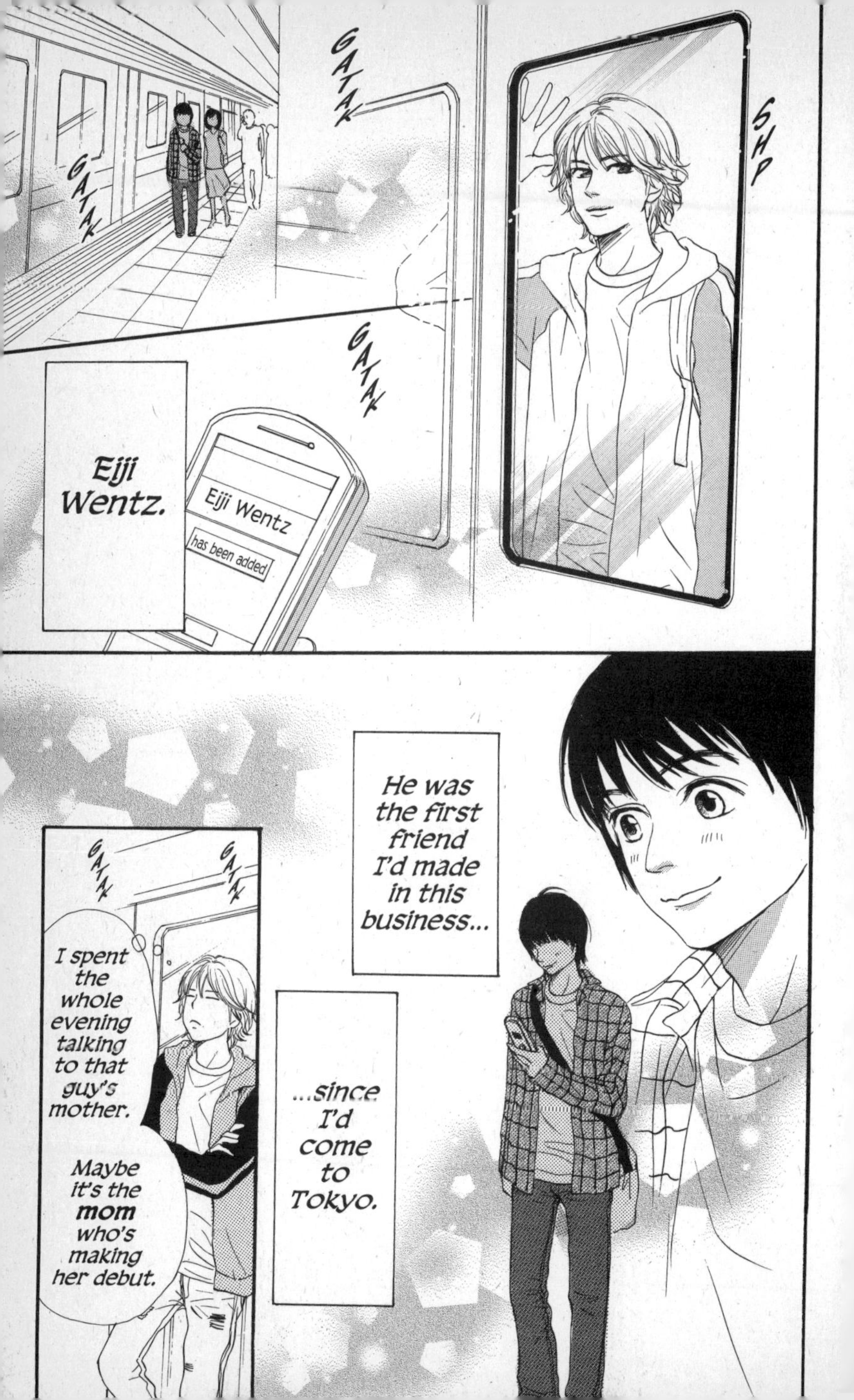
SHP
GATAK
GATAK
GATAK
Eiji Wentz.
Eiji Wentz
has been added
He was the first friend I'd made in this business...
...since I'd come to Tokyo.
GATAK
GATAK
I spent the whole evening talking to that guy's mother.
Maybe it's the **mom** who's making her debut.

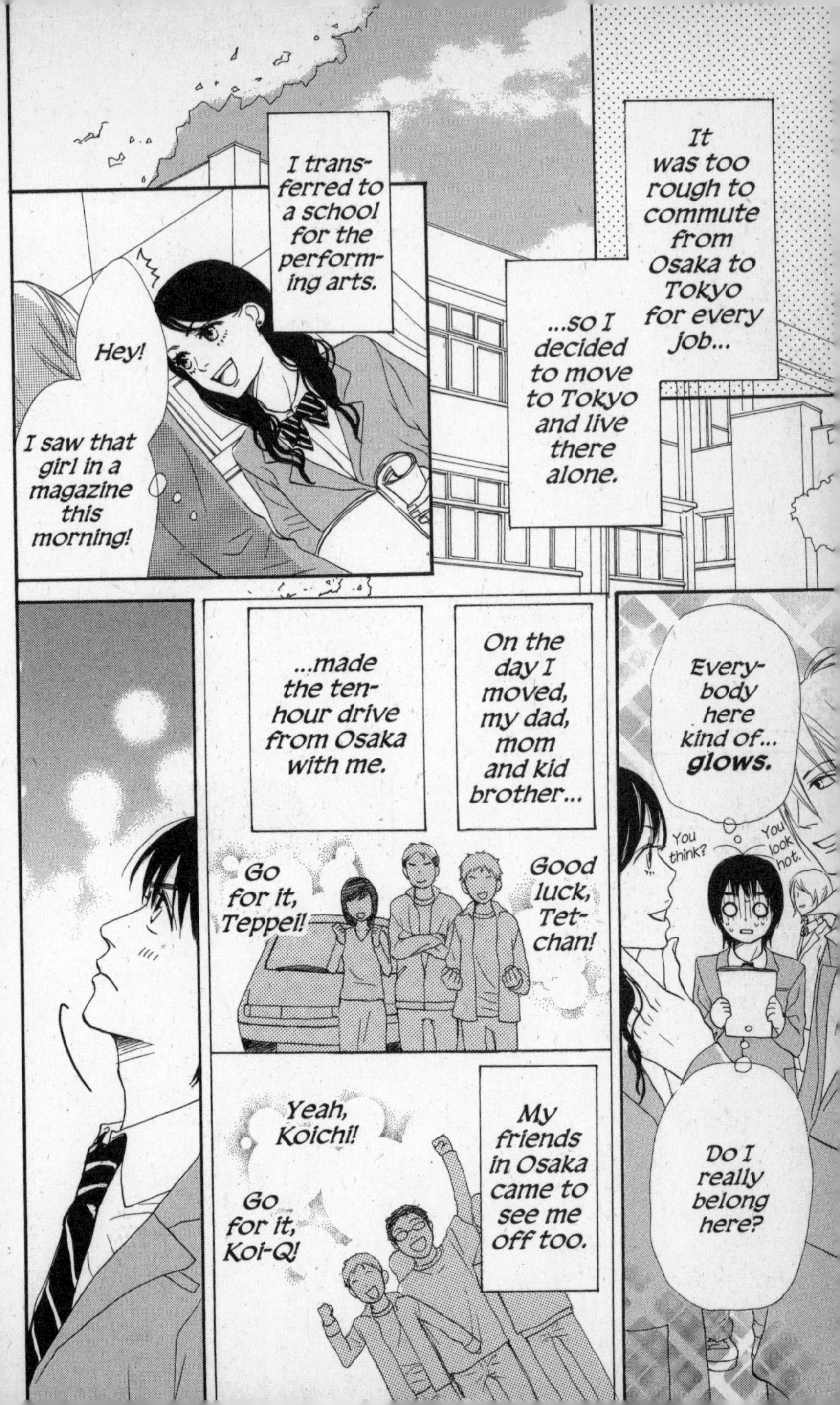
It was too rough to commute from Osaka to Tokyo for every job...
...so I decided to move to Tokyo and live there alone.
I transferred to a school for the performing arts.
Hey!
I saw that girl in a magazine this morning!
Everybody here kind of... **glows.**
You think?
You look hot.
Do I really belong here?
On the day I moved, my dad, mom and kid brother...
...made the ten-hour drive from Osaka with me.
Good luck, Tet-chan!
Go for it, Teppei!
My friends in Osaka came to see me off too.
Yeah, Koichi!
Go for it, Koi-Q!

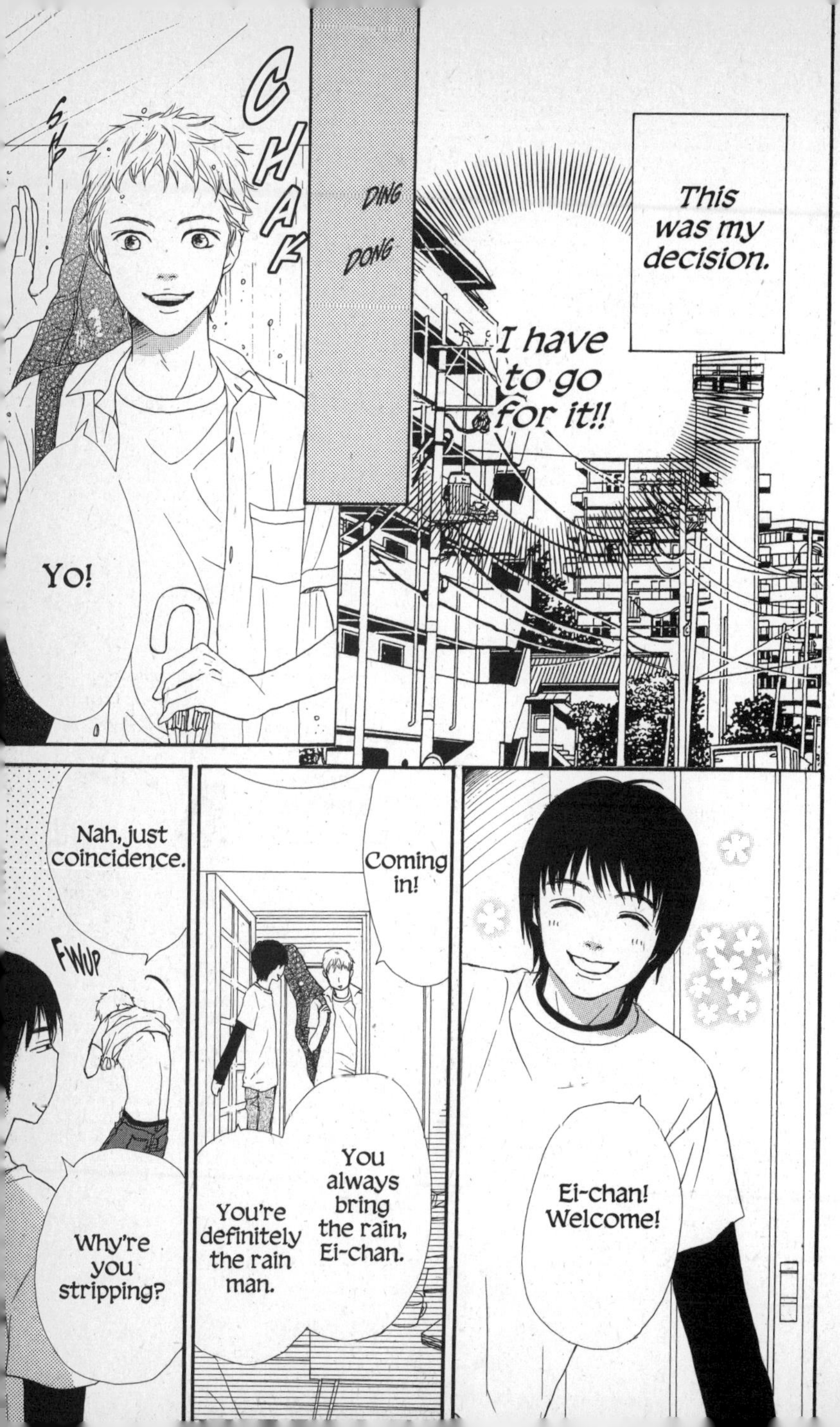
This was my decision.
I have to go for it!!
DING
DONG
CHAK
SHP
Yo!
Ei-chan! Welcome!
Coming in!
You always bring the rain, Ei-chan.
You're definitely the rain man.
Nah, just coincidence.
FWUP
Why're you stripping?

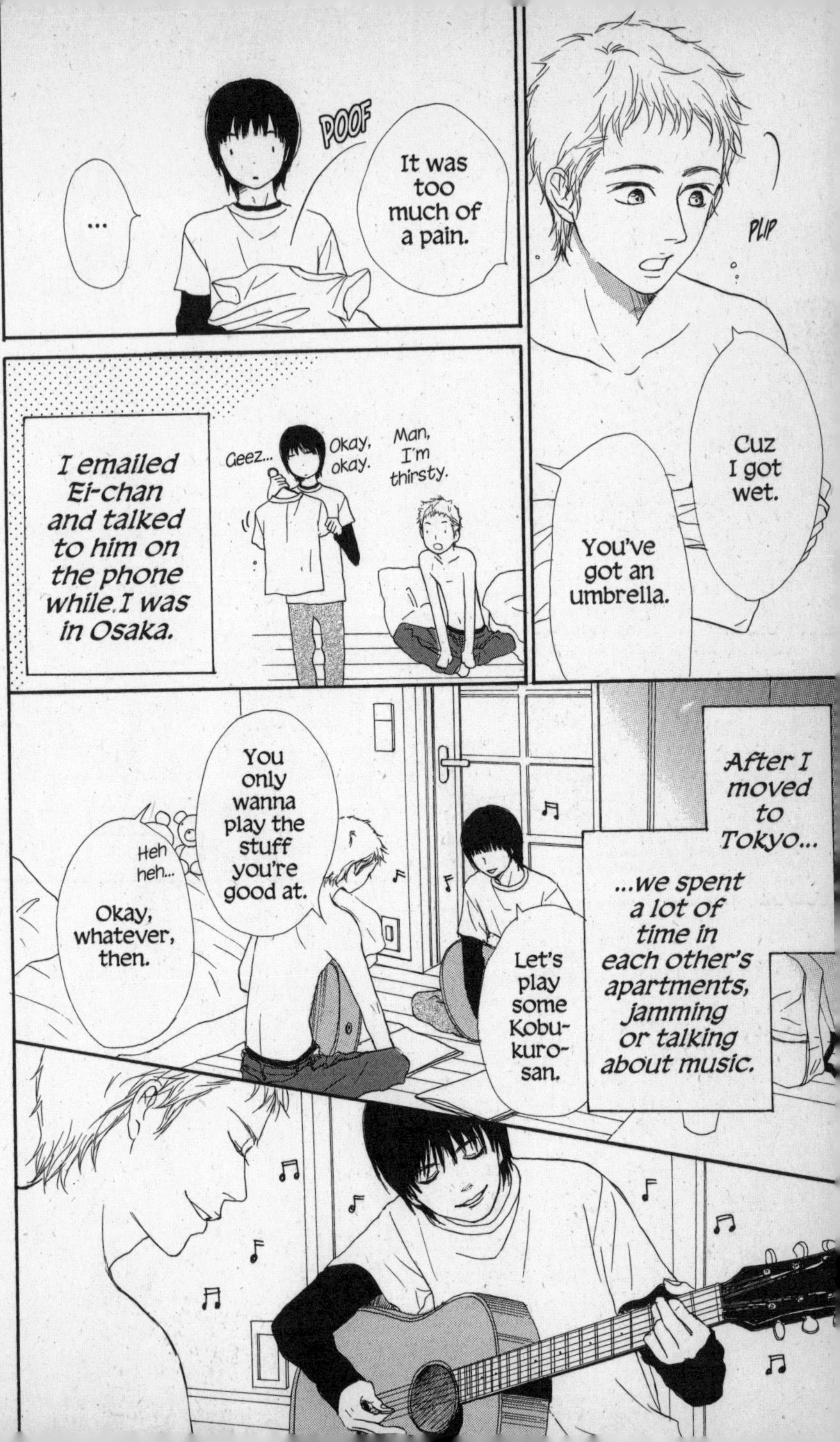
PLIP
Cuz I got wet.
You've got an umbrella.
POOF
It was too much of a pain.
...
Man, I'm thirsty.
Okay, okay.
Geez...
I emailed Ei-chan and talked to him on the phone while I was in Osaka.
After I moved to Tokyo...
...we spent a lot of time in each other's apartments, jamming or talking about music.
Let's play some Kobukuro-san.
You only wanna play the stuff you're good at.
Heh heh...
Okay, whatever, then.

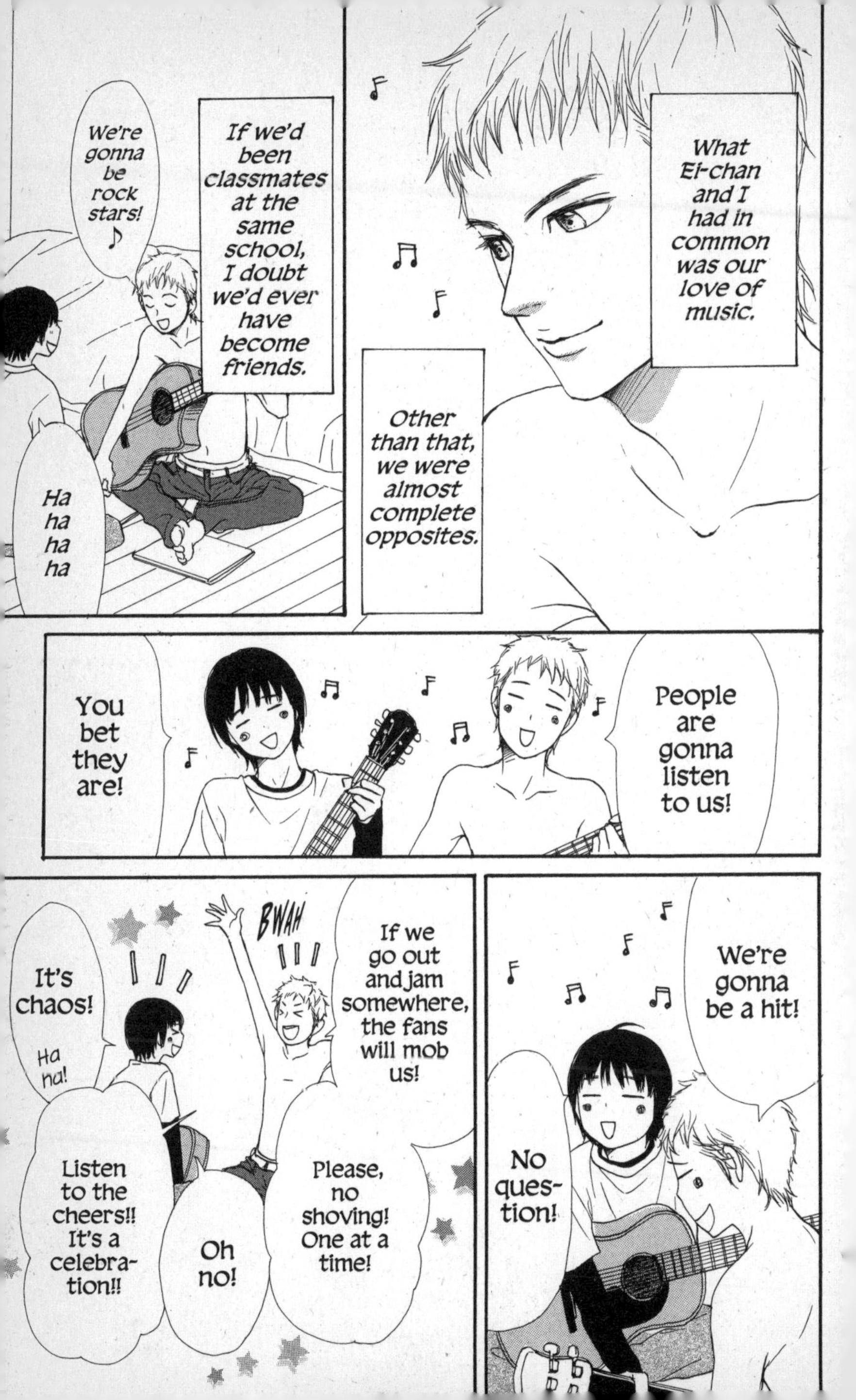
What Ei-chan and I had in common was our love of music.
Other than that, we were almost complete opposites.
If we'd been classmates at the same school, I doubt we'd ever have become friends.
We're gonna be rock stars! ♪
Ha ha ha ha
People are gonna listen to us!
You bet they are!
We're gonna be a hit!
No question!
BWAH
If we go out and jam somewhere, the fans will mob us!
It's chaos!
Ha ha!
Please, no shoving! One at a time!
Oh no!
Listen to the cheers!! It's a celebration!!

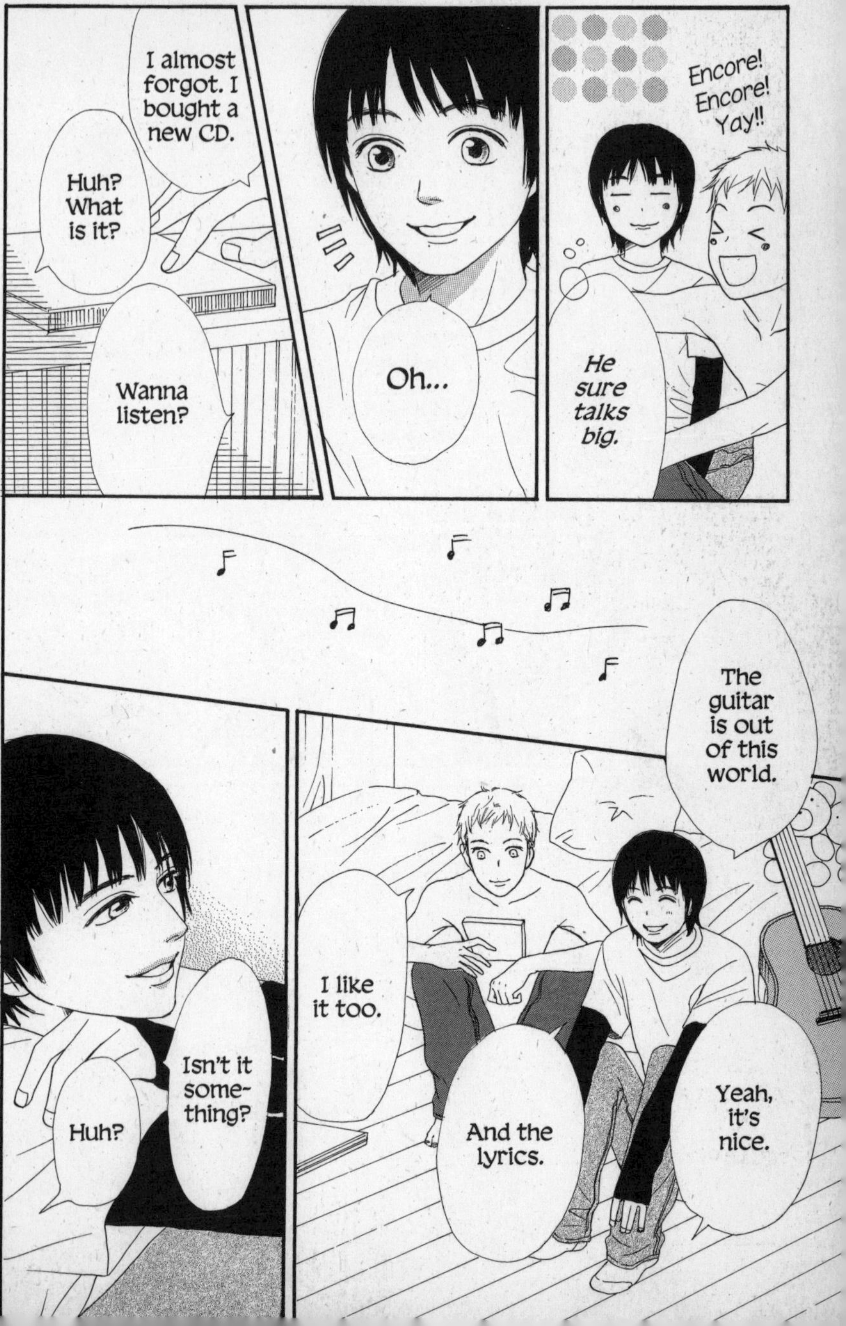
Encore! Encore! Yay!!
He sure talks big.
Oh...
I almost forgot. I bought a new CD.
Huh? What is it?
Wanna listen?
The guitar is out of this world.
Yeah, it's nice.
And the lyrics.
I like it too.
Isn't it some-thing?
Huh?

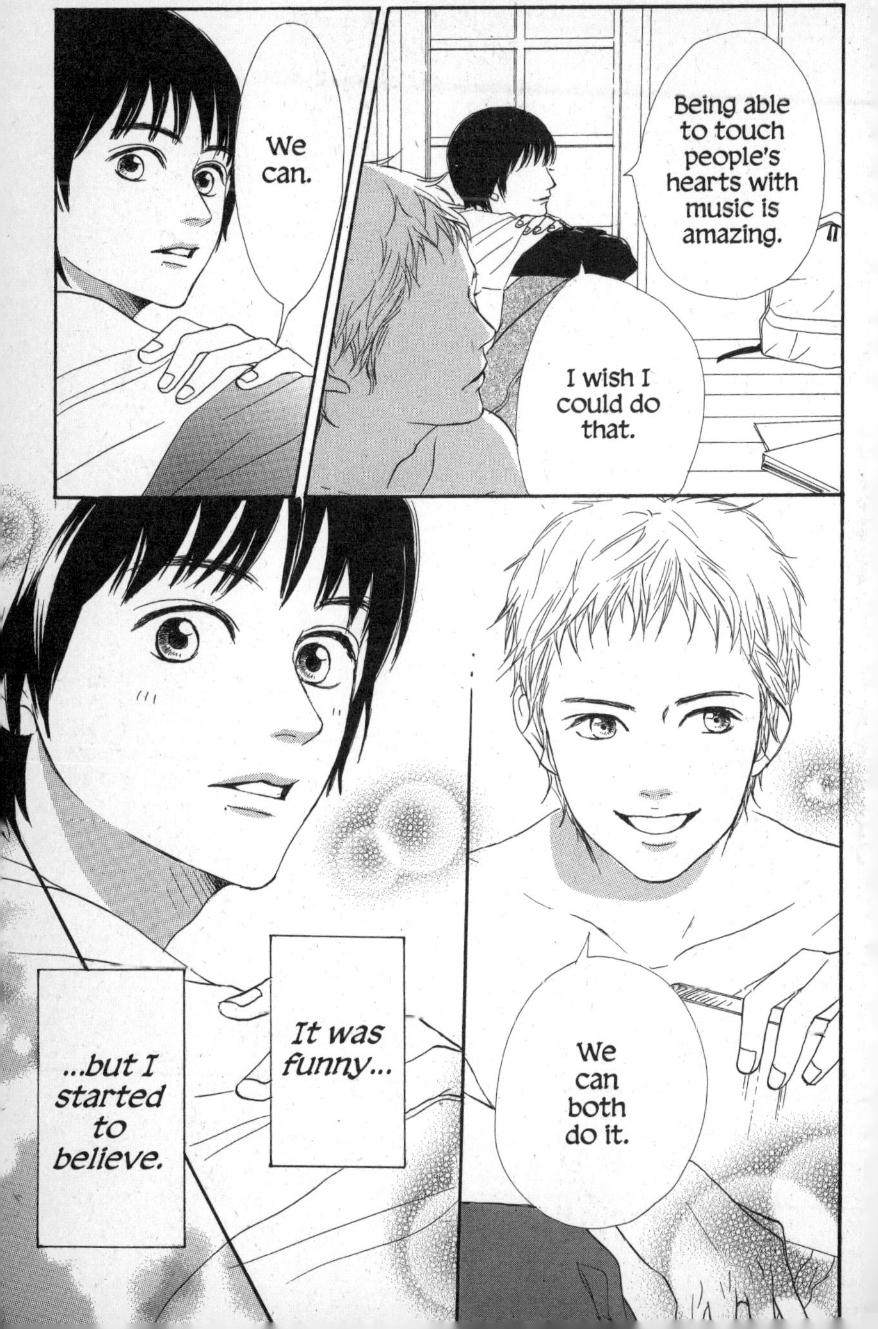
Being able to touch people's hearts with music is amazing.
I wish I could do that.
We can.
We can both do it.
It was funny...
...but I started to believe.

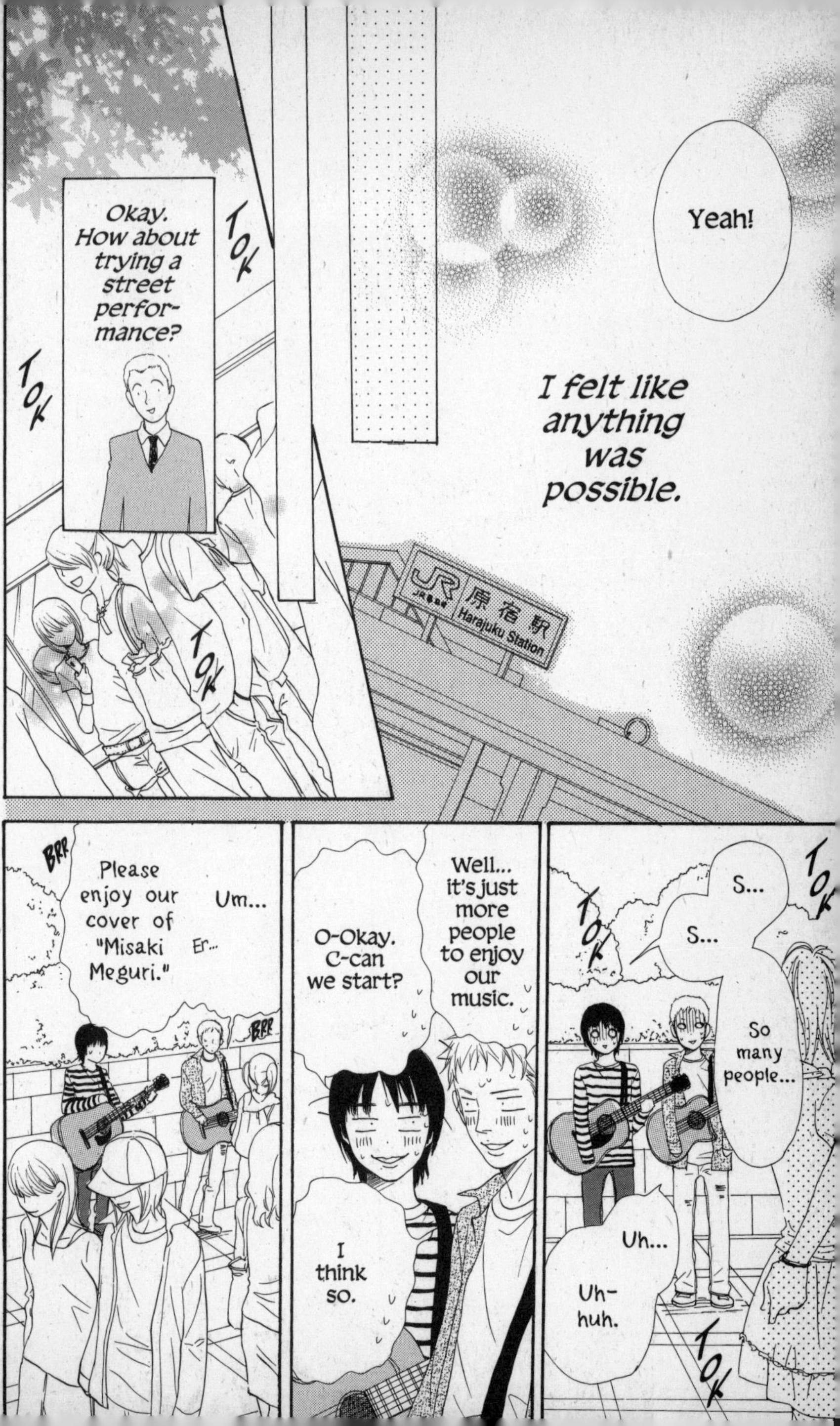

Yeah!
I felt like anything was possible.
原宿駅
Harajuku Station
TOK
Okay. How about trying a street performance?
TOK
TOK
TOK
S...
S...
So many people...
Uh...
Uh-huh.
TOK
Well... it's just more people to enjoy our music.
O-Okay. C-can we start?
I think so.
Um...
Er...
Please enjoy our cover of "Misaki Meguri."
BRR
BRR

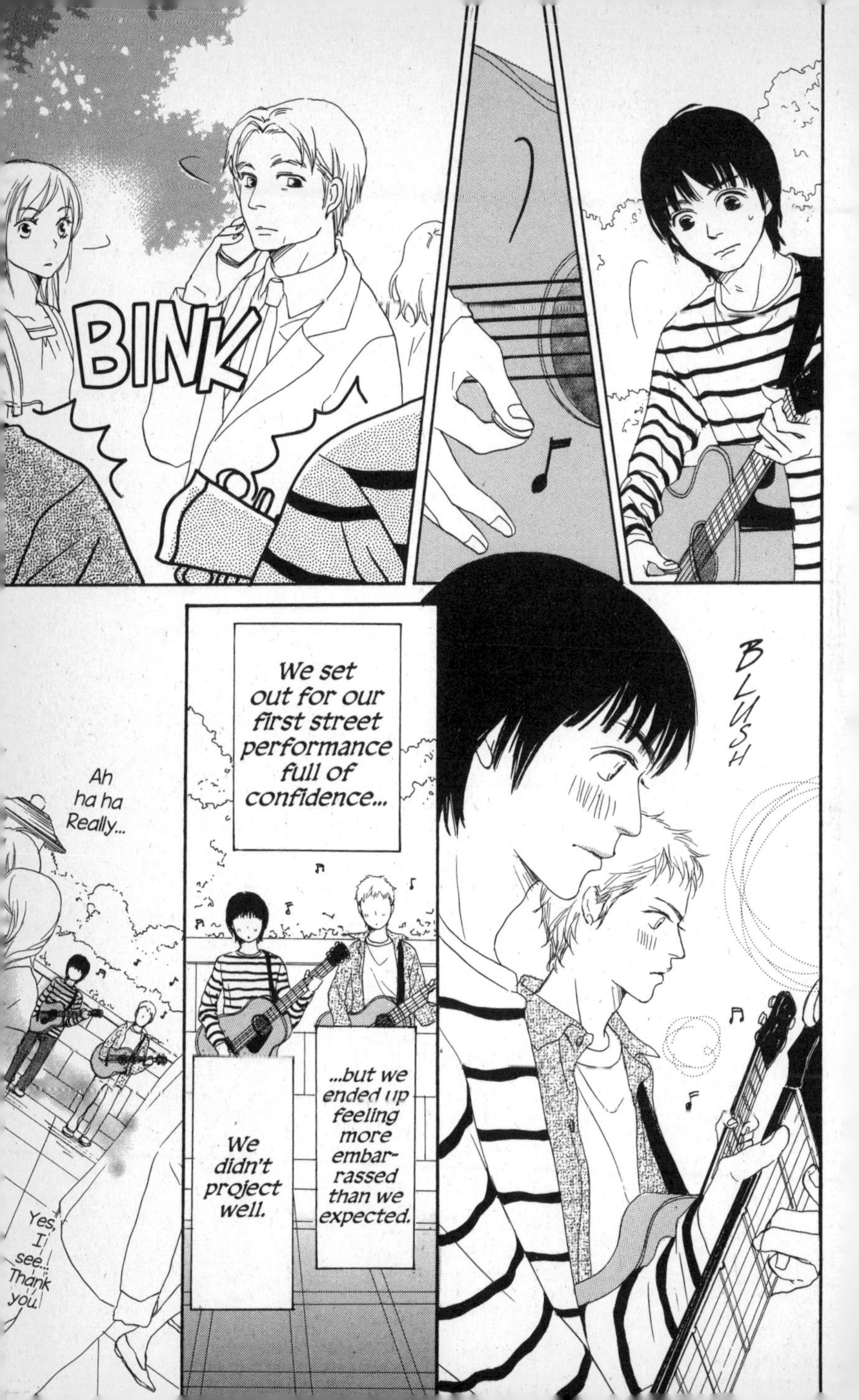
BINK
BLUSH
We set out for our first street performance full of confidence...
...but we ended up feeling more embarrassed than we expected.
We didn't project well.
Ah ha ha Really...
Yes, I see... Thank you.

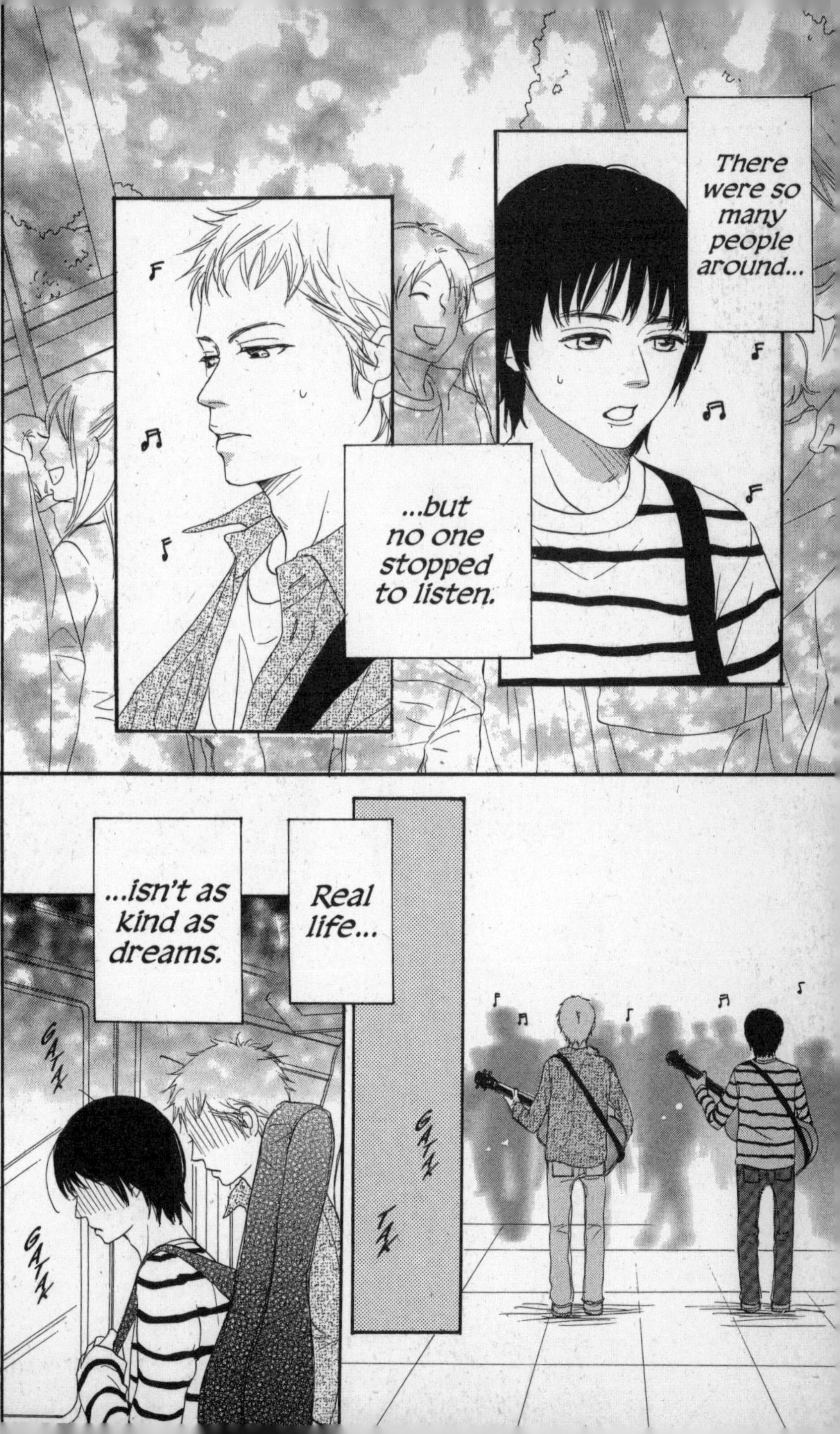
There were so many people around...
...but no one stopped to listen.
GATAN
TAN
Real life...
...isn't as kind as dreams.
GATAN
GATAN

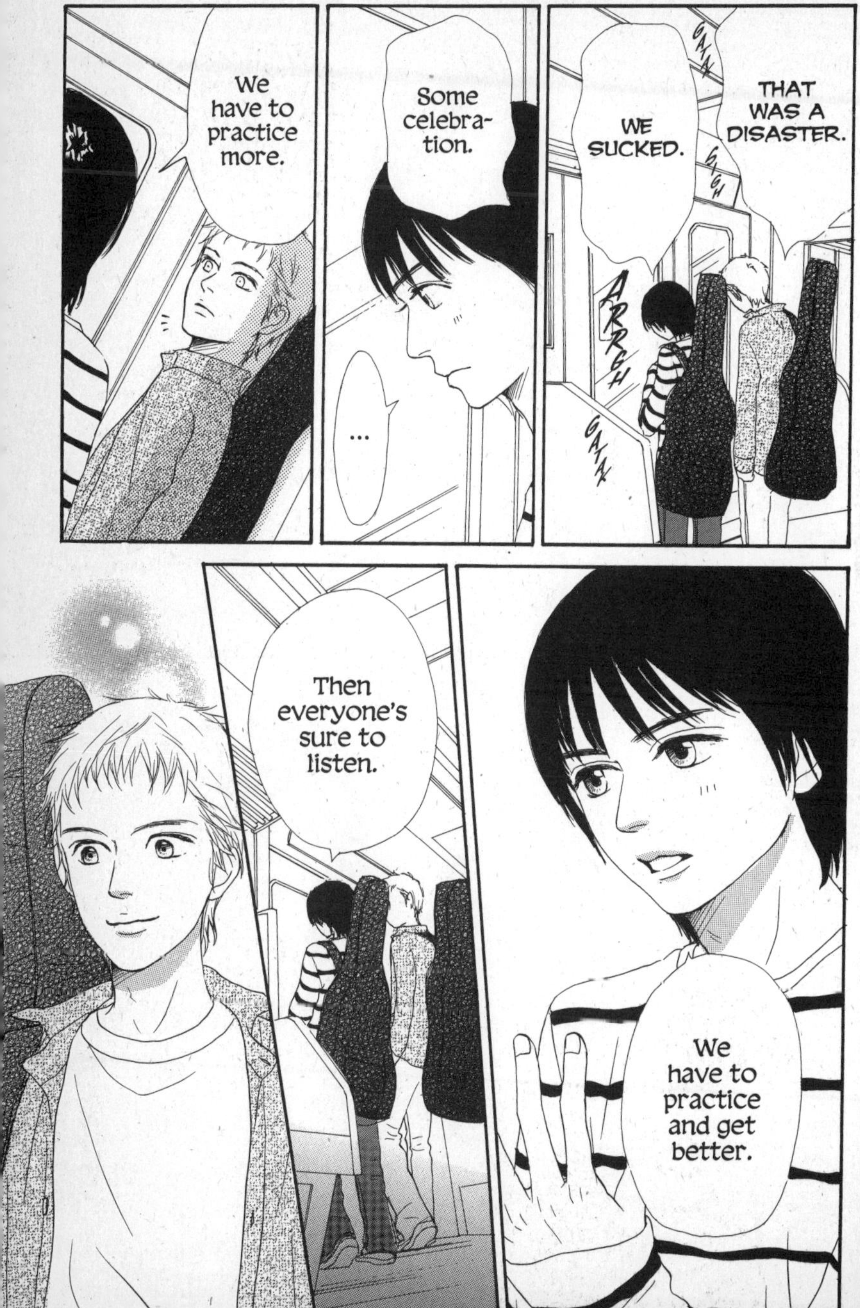
GATAN
THAT WAS A DISASTER.
SIGH
WE SUCKED.
ARRGH
GATAN
Some celebration.
...
We have to practice more.
We have to practice and get better.
Then everyone's sure to listen.

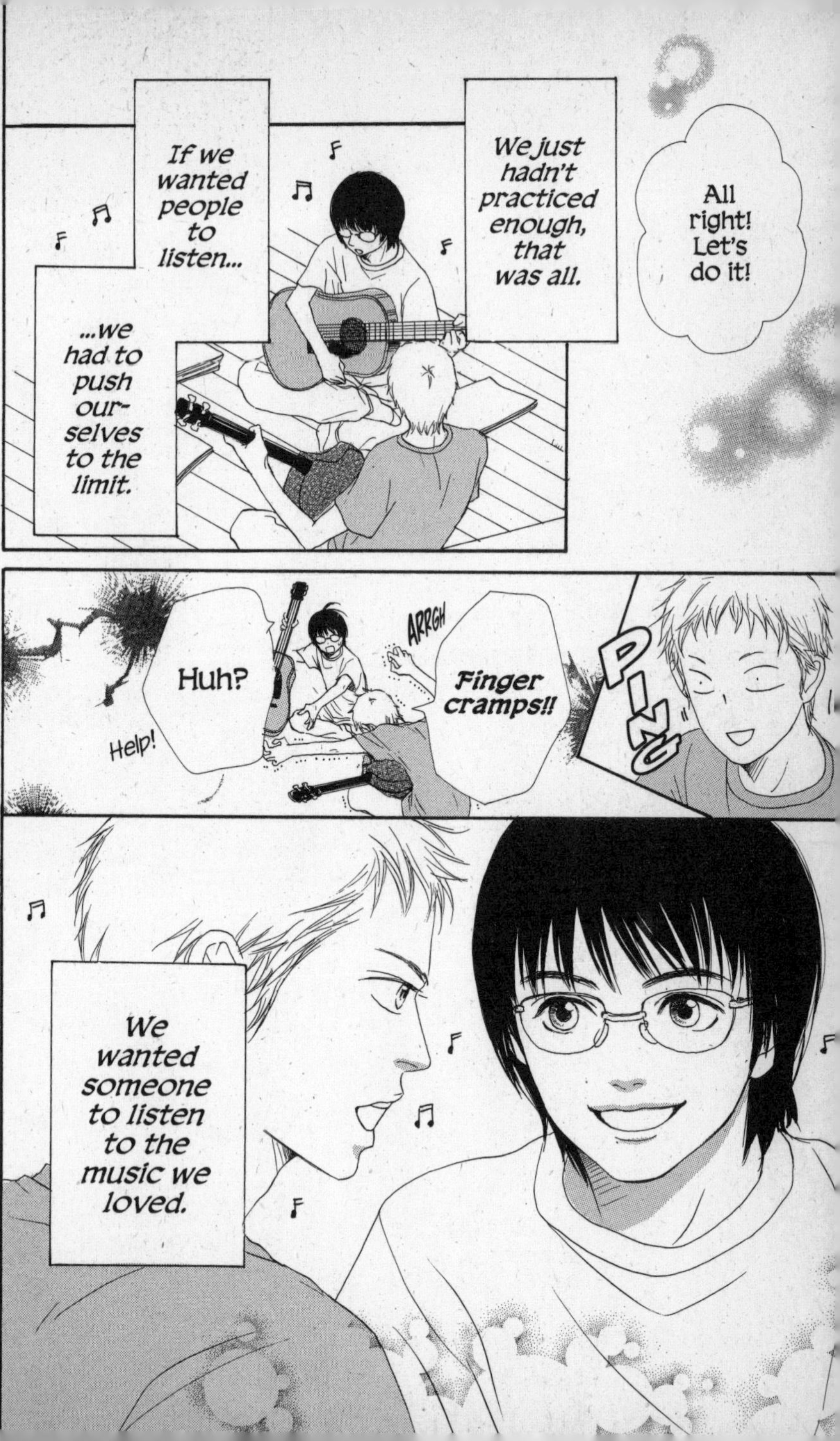
All right! Let's do it!
We just hadn't practiced enough, that was all.
If we wanted people to listen...
...we had to push ourselves to the limit.
PING
ARRGH
Finger cramps!!
Huh?
Help!
We wanted someone to listen to the music we loved.

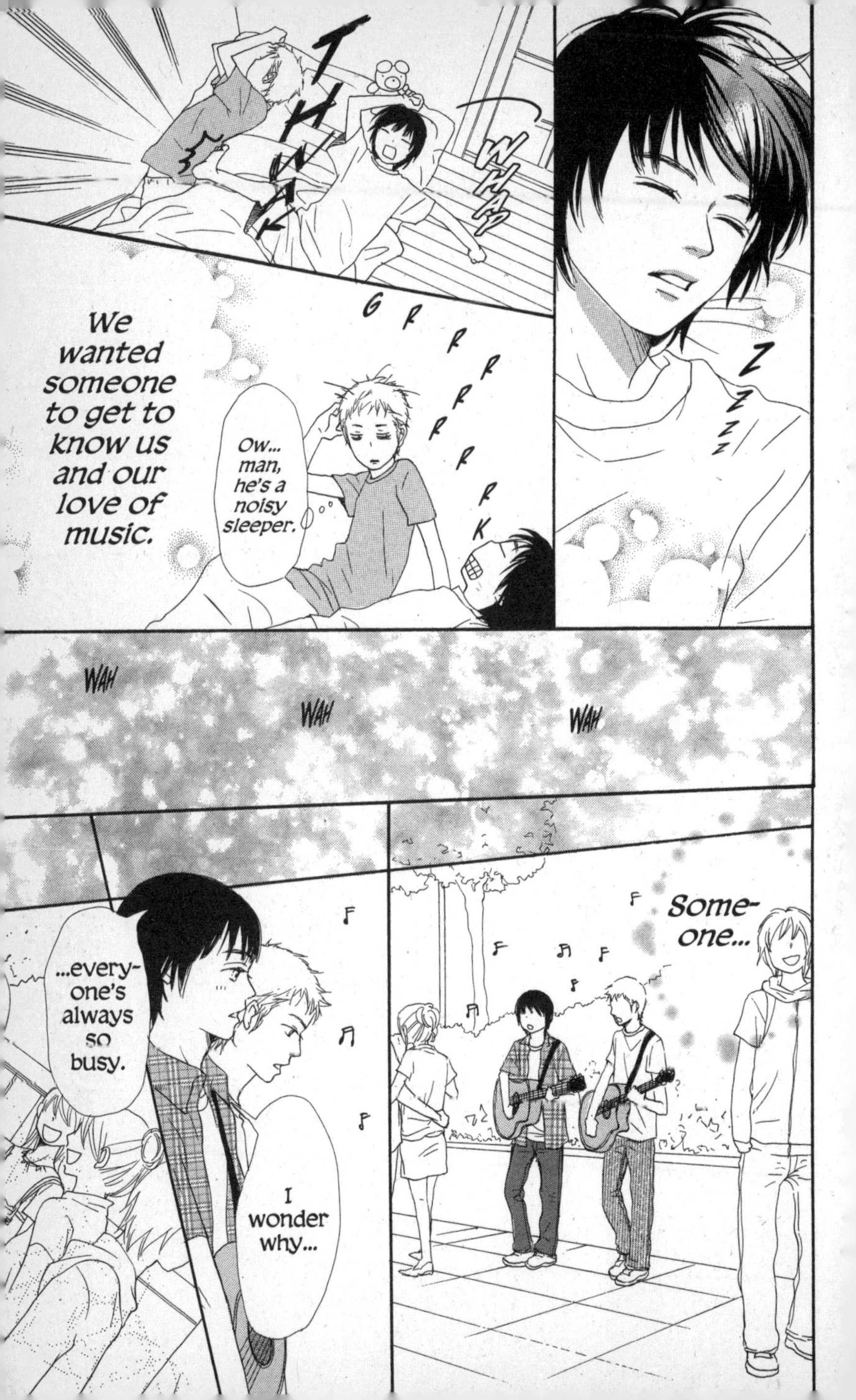
ZZZZ
WHAP
THWAK
GRRRRRRRK
Ow... man, he's a noisy sleeper.
We wanted someone to get to know us and our love of music.
WAH
WAH
WAH
Some-one...
...every-one's always so busy.
I wonder why...

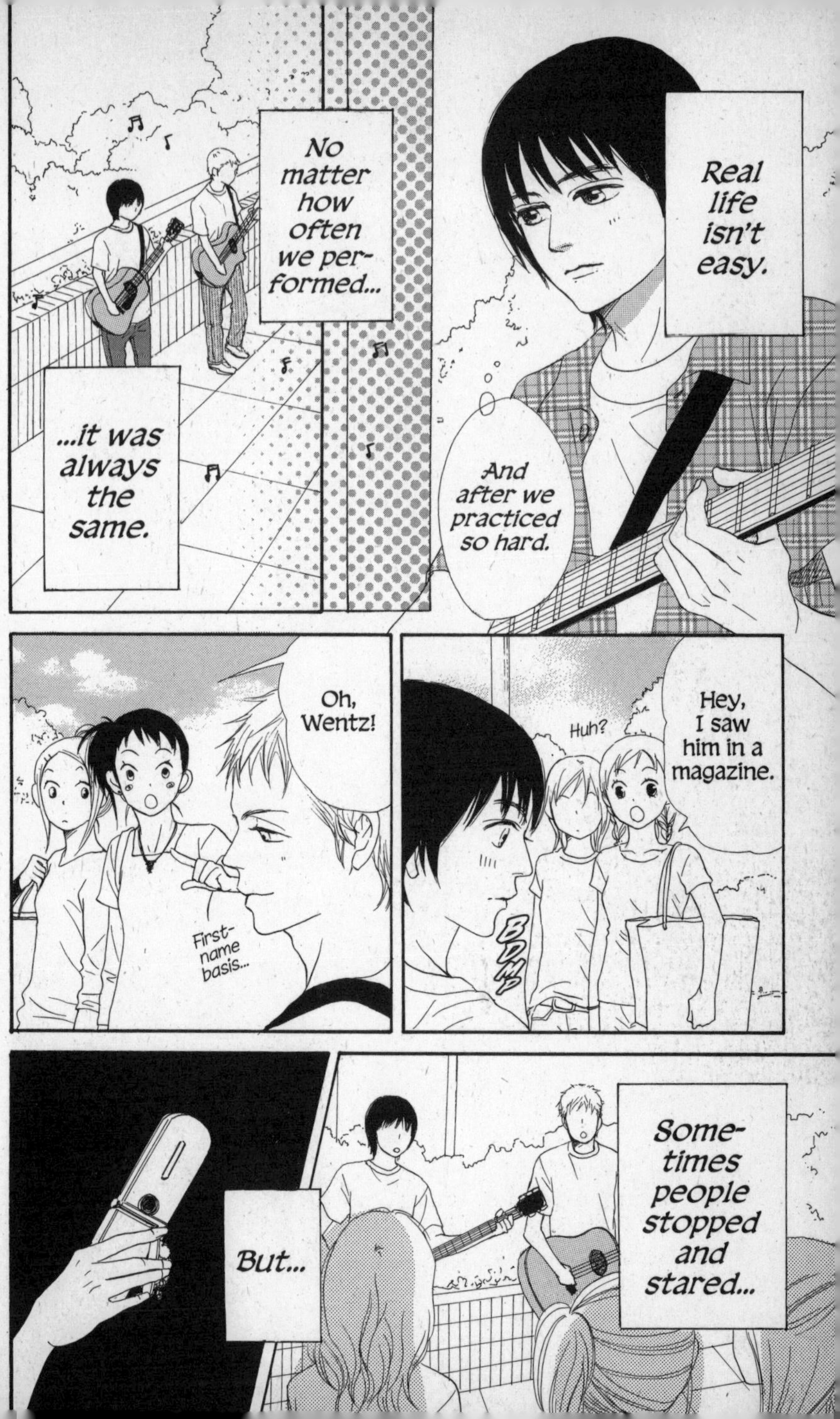
Real life isn't easy.
And after we practiced so hard.
No matter how often we performed...
...it was always the same.
Hey, I saw him in a magazine.
Huh?
BDMP
Oh, Wentz!
First-name basis...
Some-times people stopped and stared...
But...

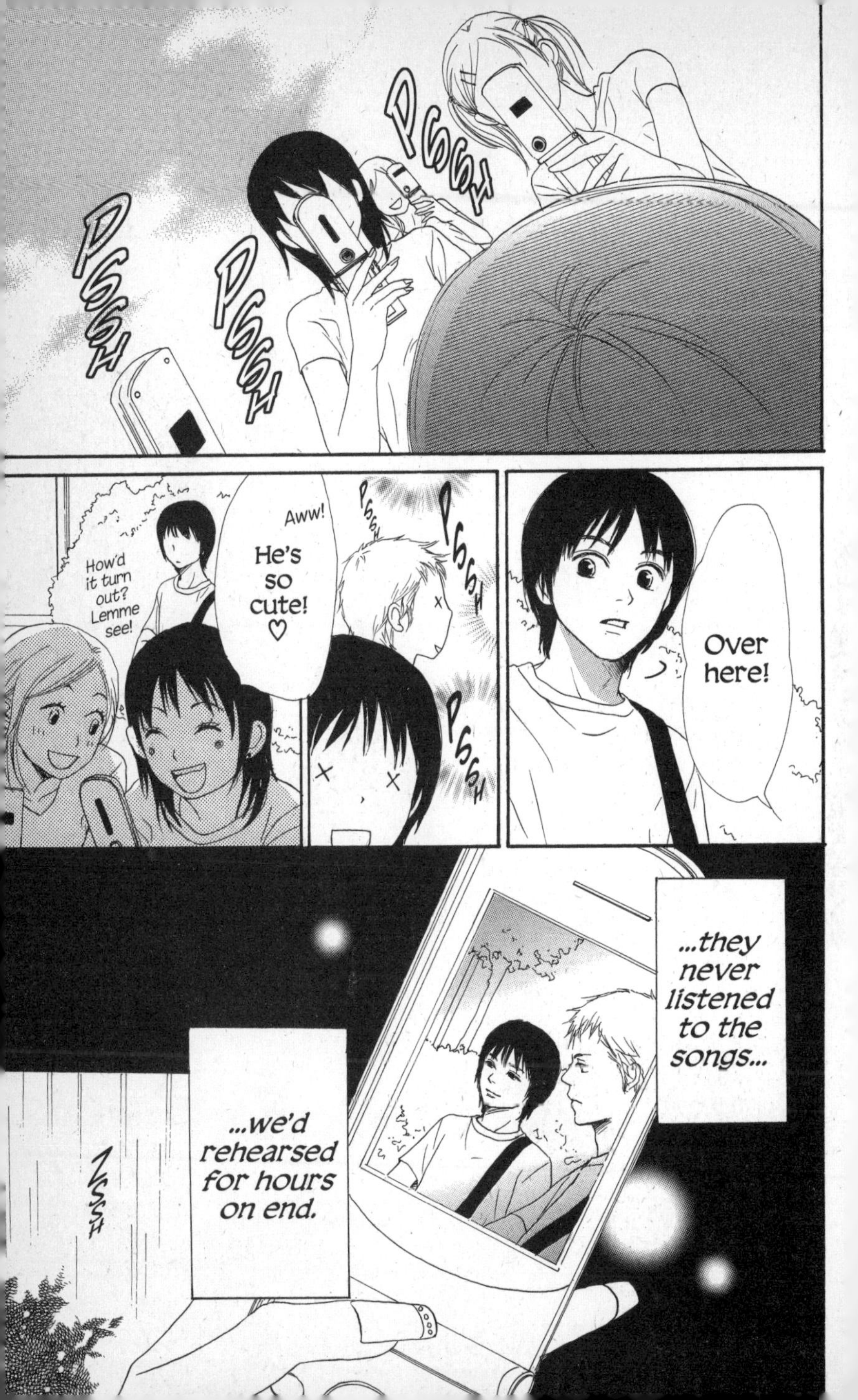
PSSSH
PSSSH
PSSSH
Over here!
PSSH
PSSH
PSSH
Aww!
He's so cute! ♡
How'd it turn out? Lemme see!
...they never listened to the songs...
...we'd rehearsed for hours on end.

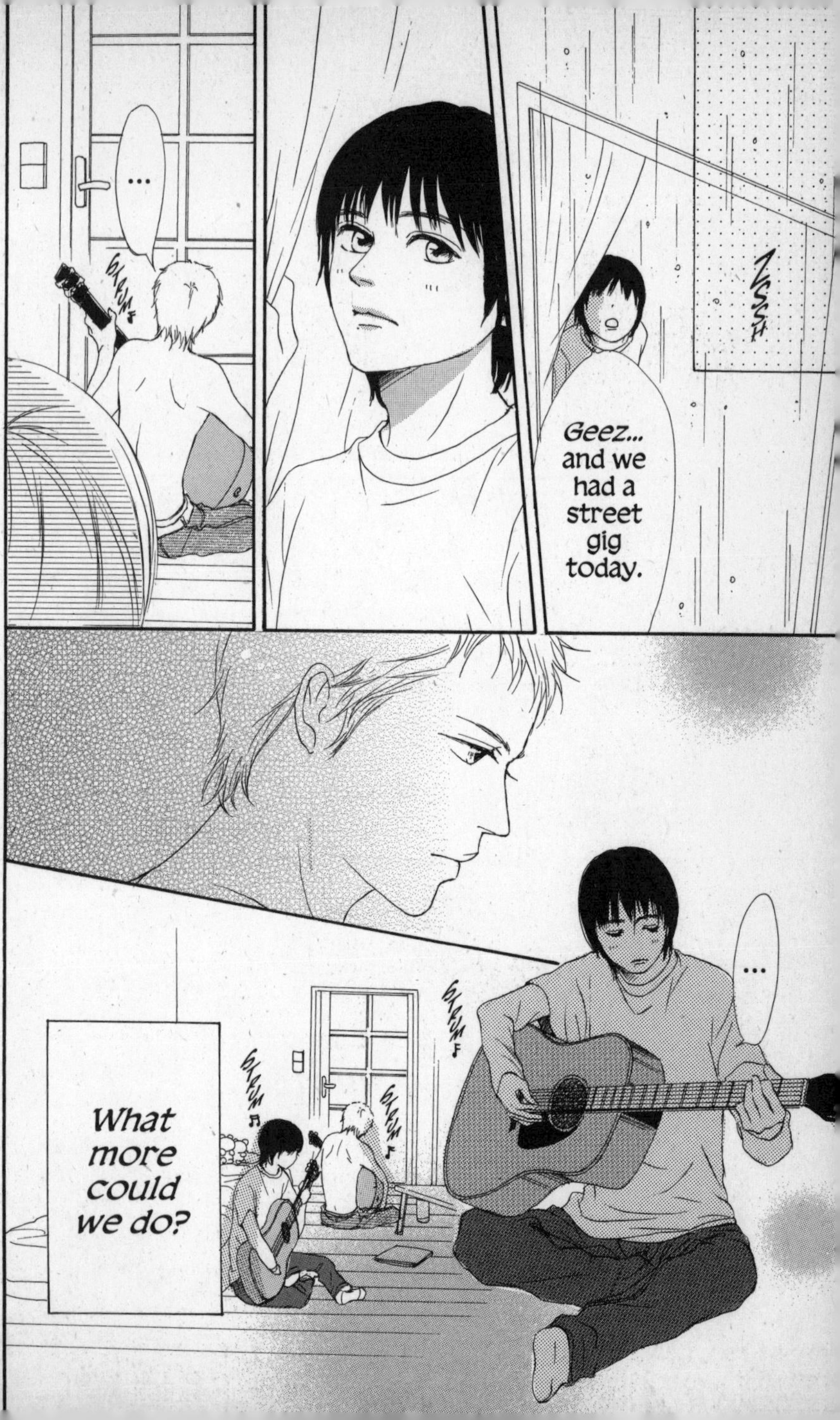
NSSH
Geez... and we had a street gig today.
...
STRUM
...
STRUM
What more could we do?
STRUM
STRUM

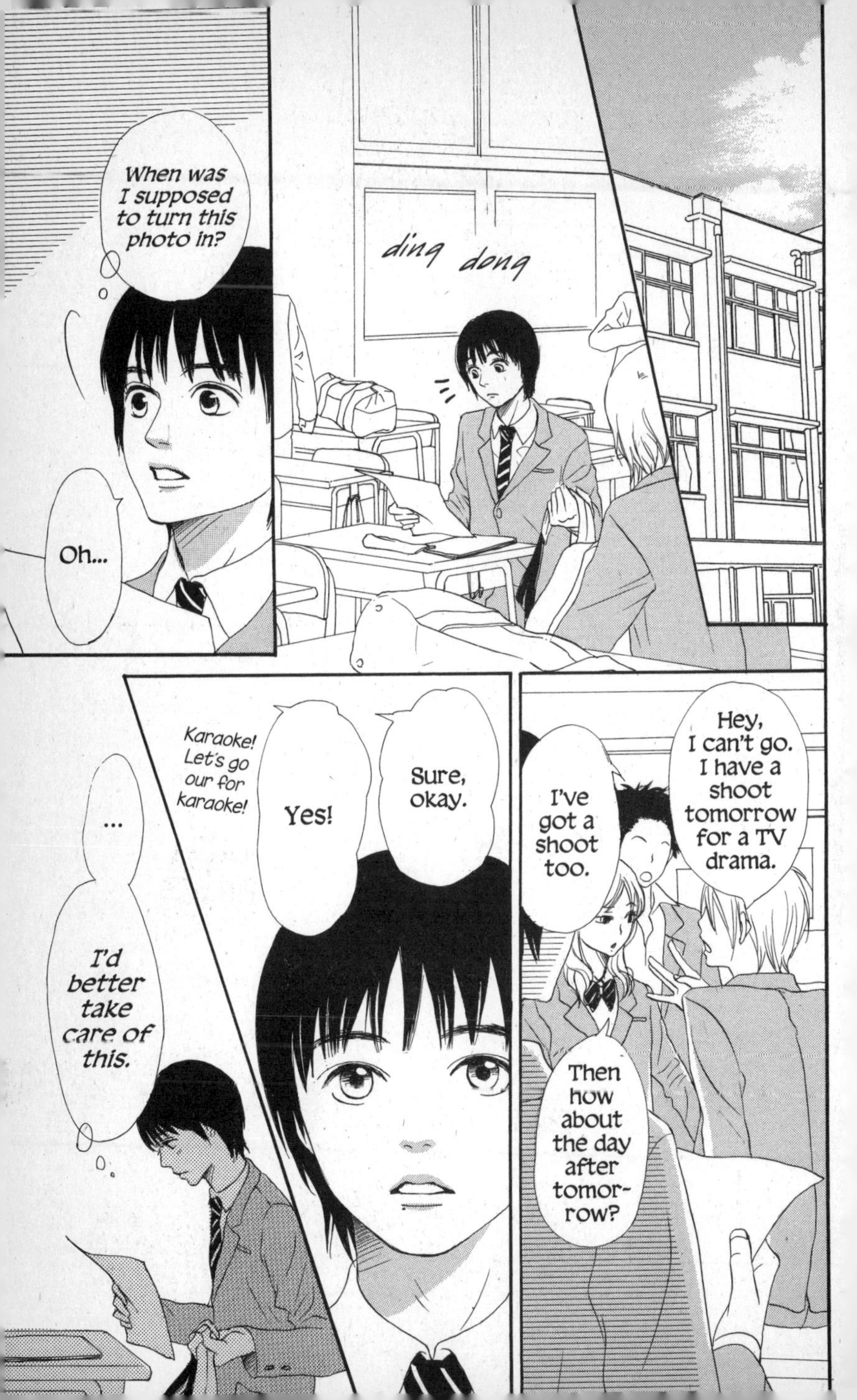
ding dong
When was I supposed to turn this photo in?
Oh...
Hey, I can't go. I have a shoot tomorrow for a TV drama.
I've got a shoot too.
Then how about the day after tomorrow?
Sure, okay.
Yes!
Karaoke! Let's go our for karaoke!
...
I'd better take care of this.

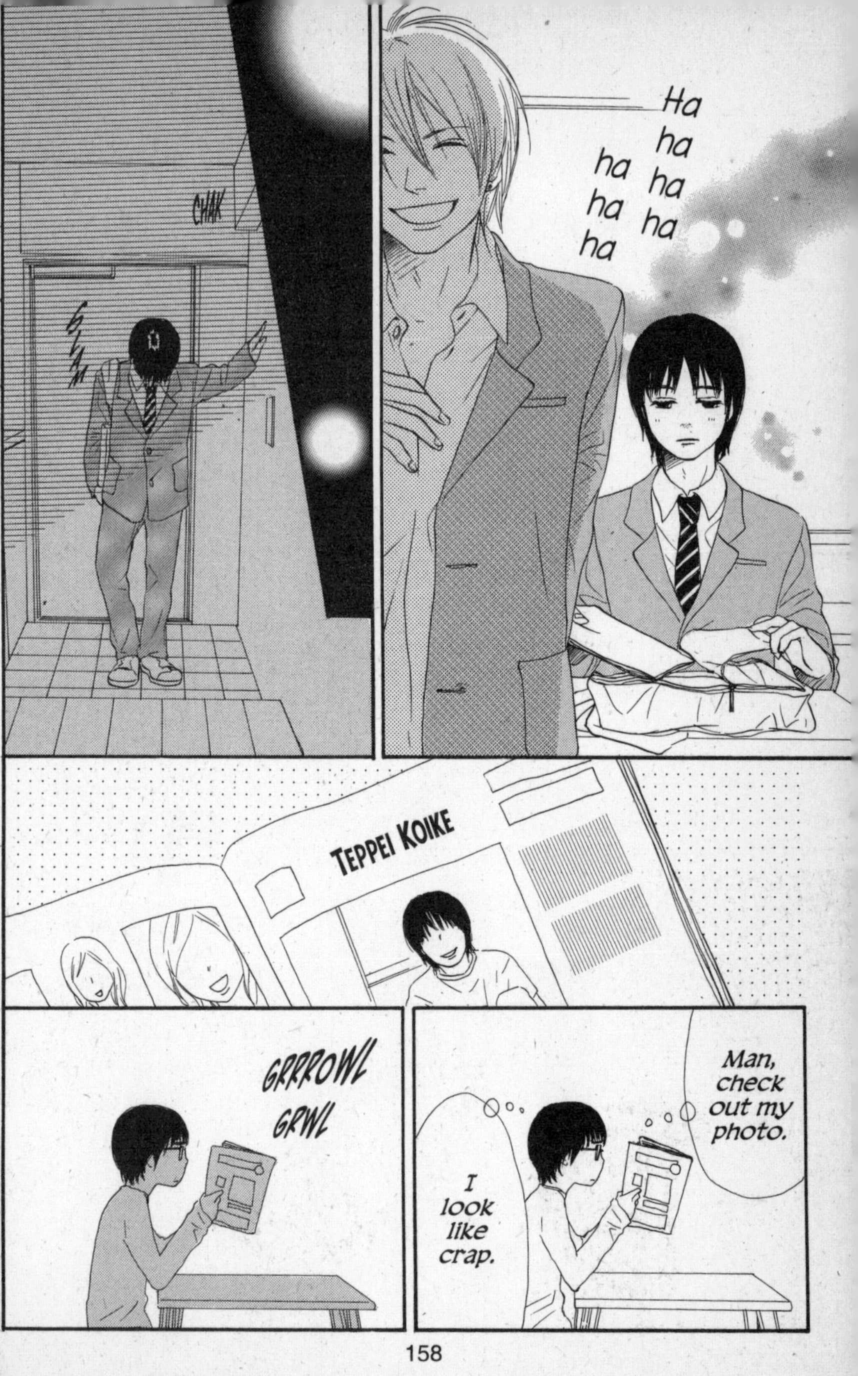
Ha ha ha ha ha ha ha ha
CHAK
SLAM
TEPPEI KOIKE
Man, check out my photo.
I look like crap.
GRRROWL
GRWL

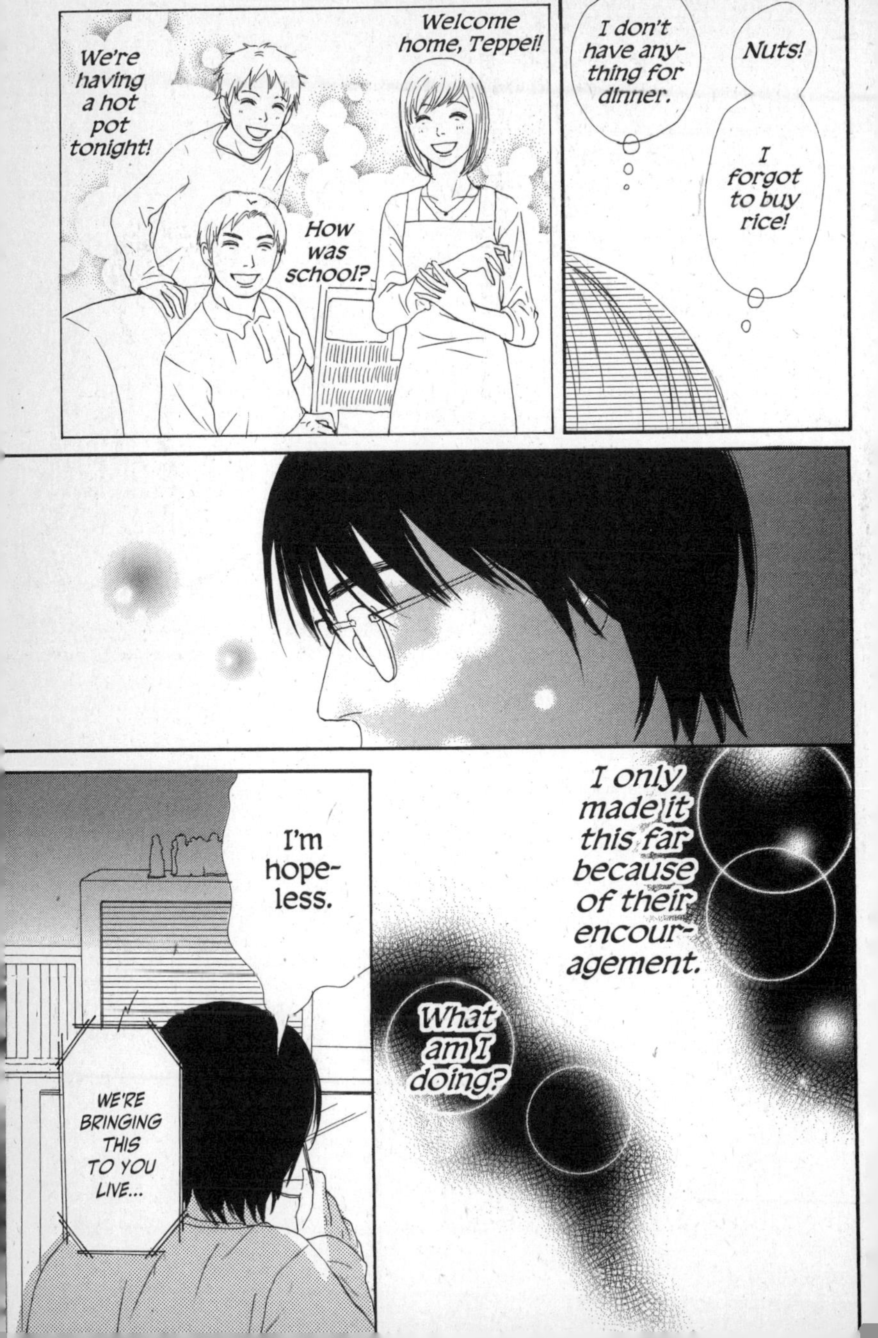
Nuts!
I forgot to buy rice!
I don't have anything for dinner.
Welcome home, Teppei!
We're having a hot pot tonight!
How was school?
I only made it this far because of their encouragement.
What am I doing?
I'm hopeless.
WE'RE BRINGING THIS TO YOU LIVE...

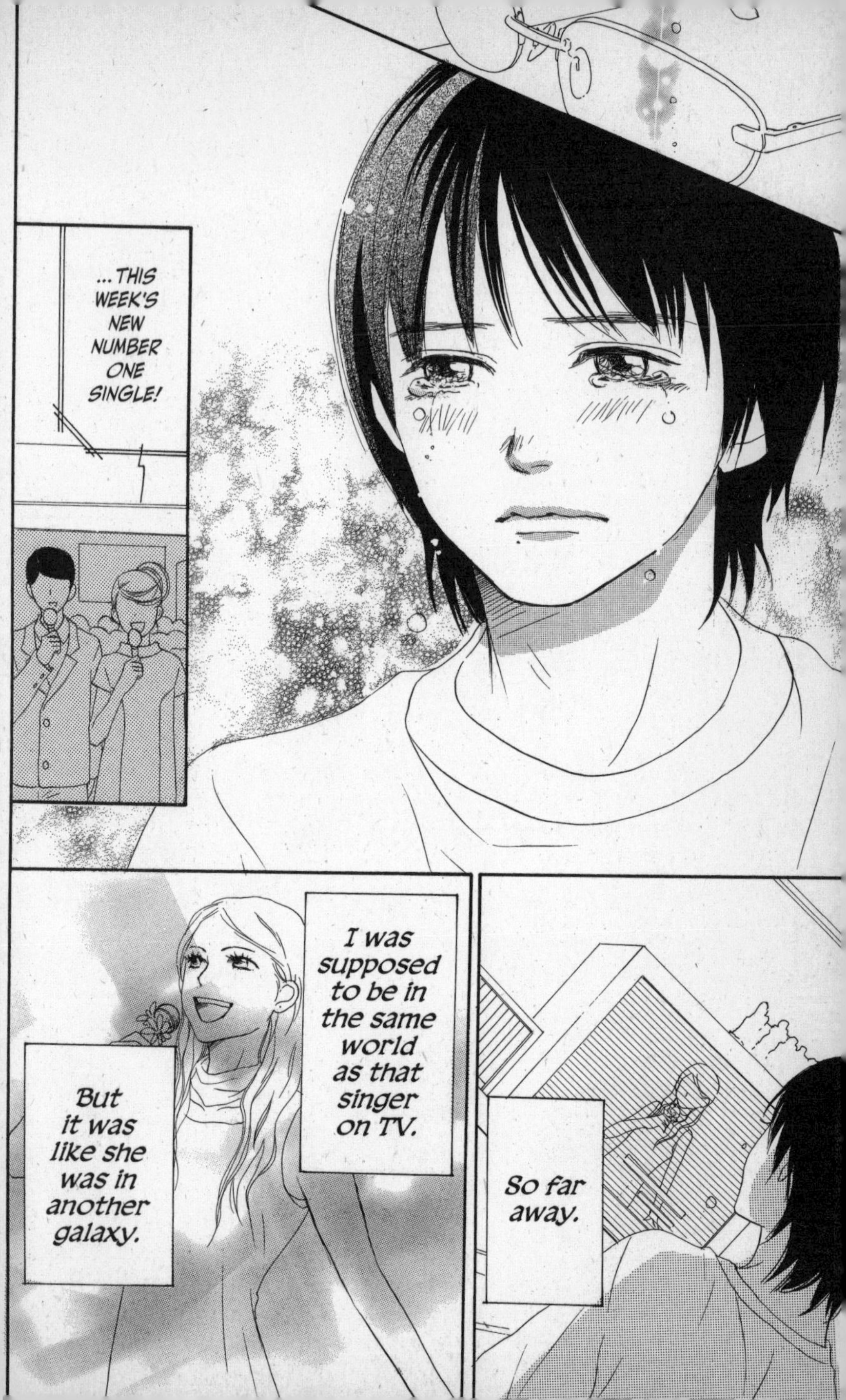
...THIS WEEK'S NEW NUMBER ONE SINGLE!
So far away.
I was supposed to be in the same world as that singer on TV.
But it was like she was in another galaxy.

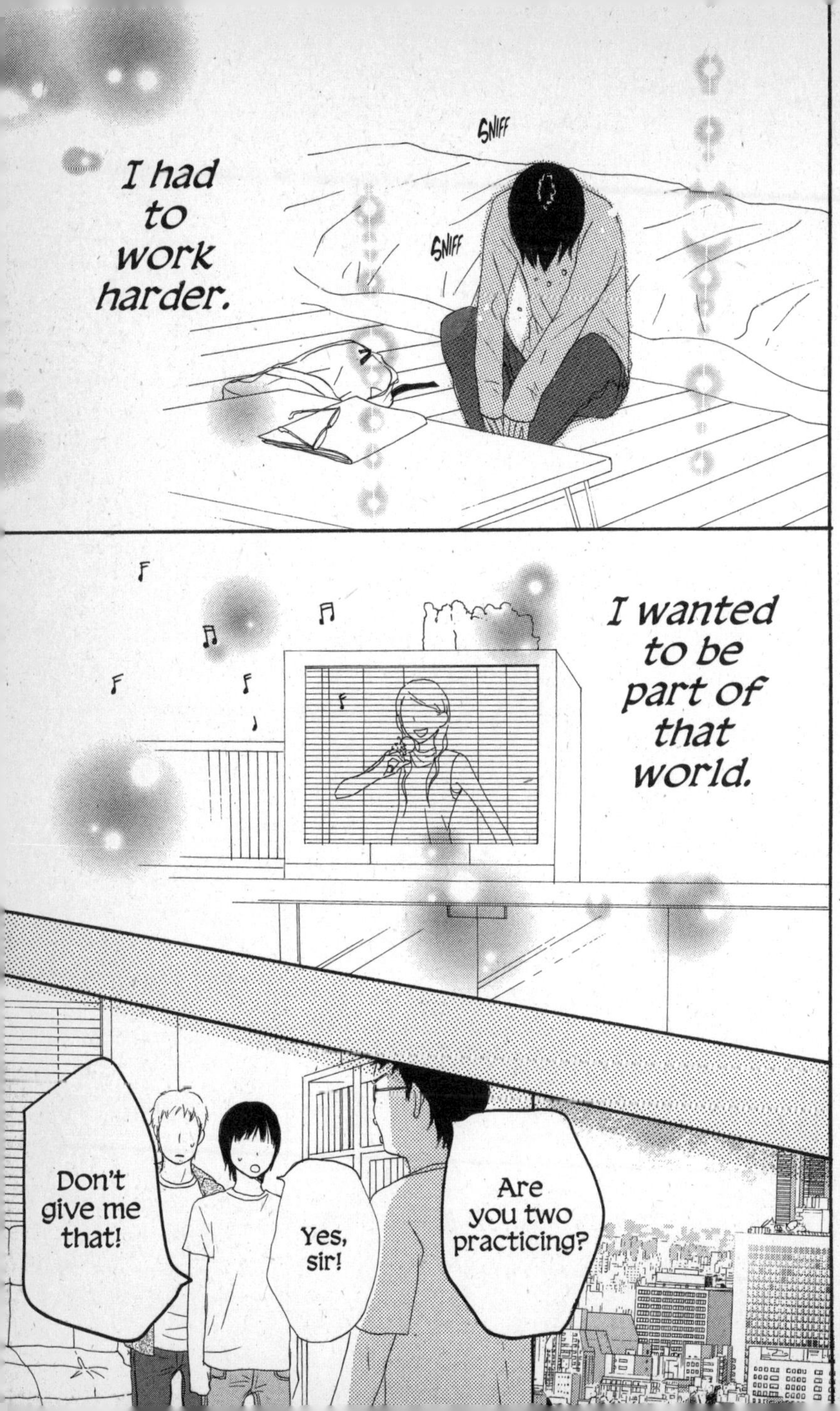
SNIFF
SNIFF
I had to work harder.
I wanted to be part of that world.
Are you two practicing?
Yes, sir!
Don't give me that!

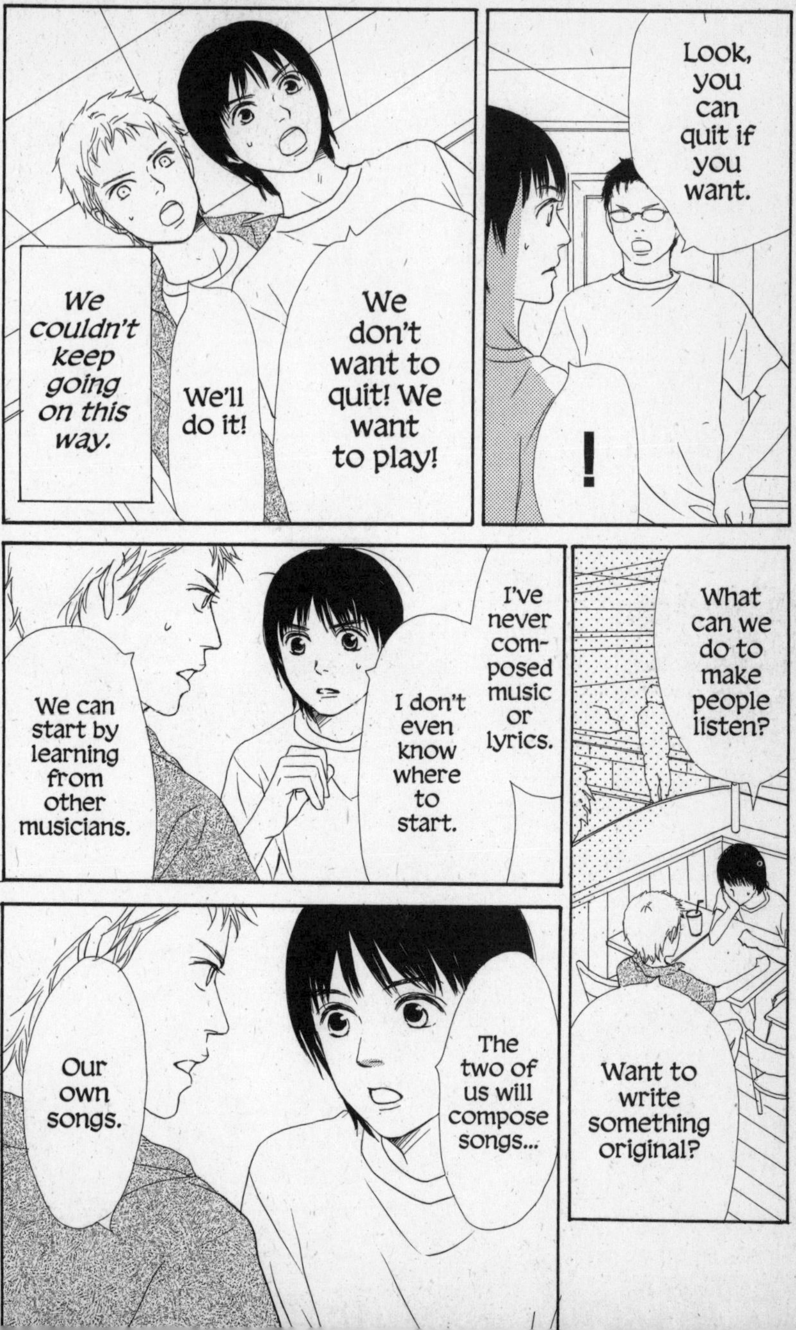
Look, you can quit if you want.
!
We don't want to quit! We want to play!
We'll do it!
We couldn't keep going on this way.
What can we do to make people listen?
Want to write something original?
I've never com-posed music or lyrics.
I don't even know where to start.
We can start by learning from other musicians.
The two of us will compose songs...
Our own songs.

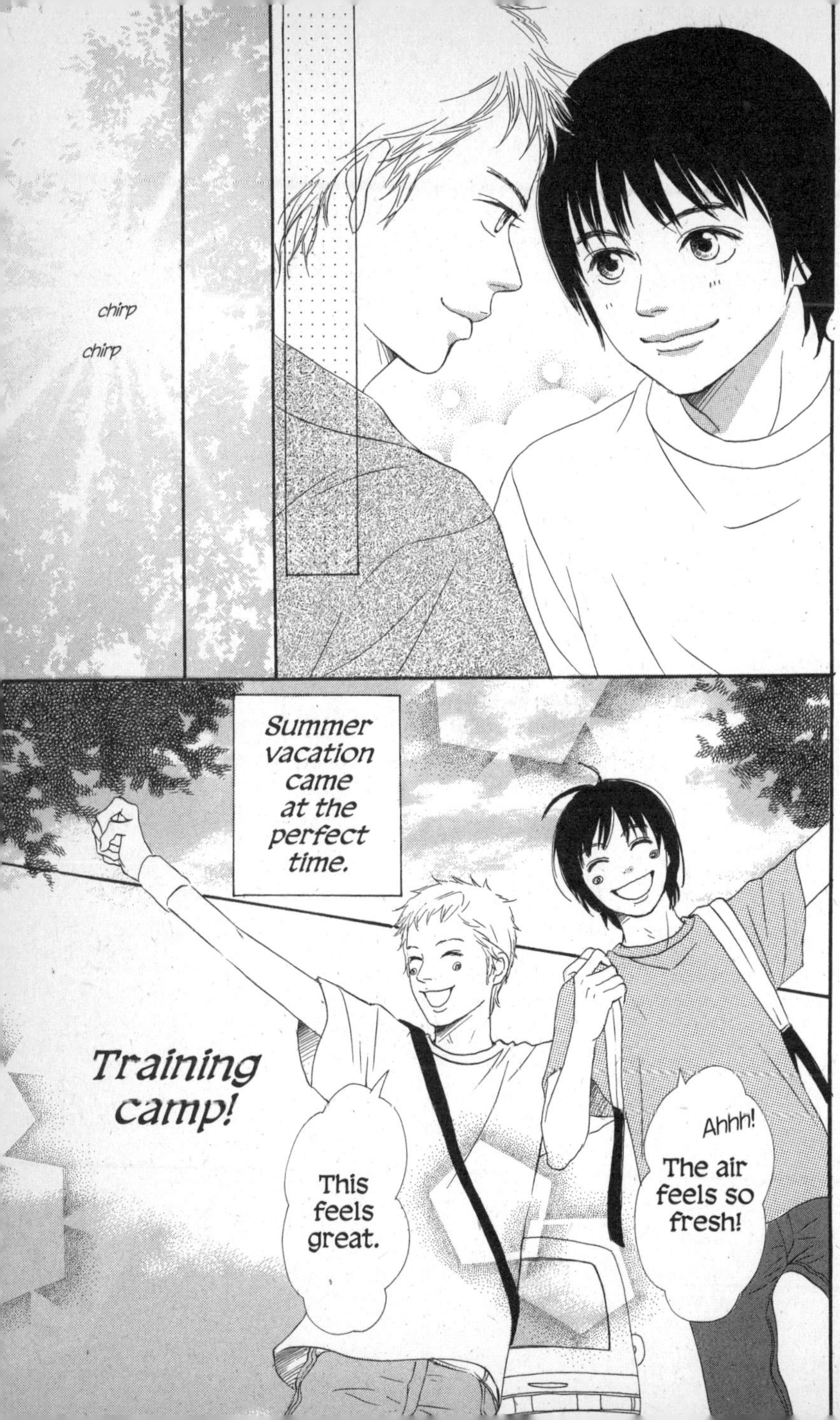
chirp
chirp
Summer vacation came at the perfect time.
Training camp!
Ahhh! The air feels so fresh!
This feels great.

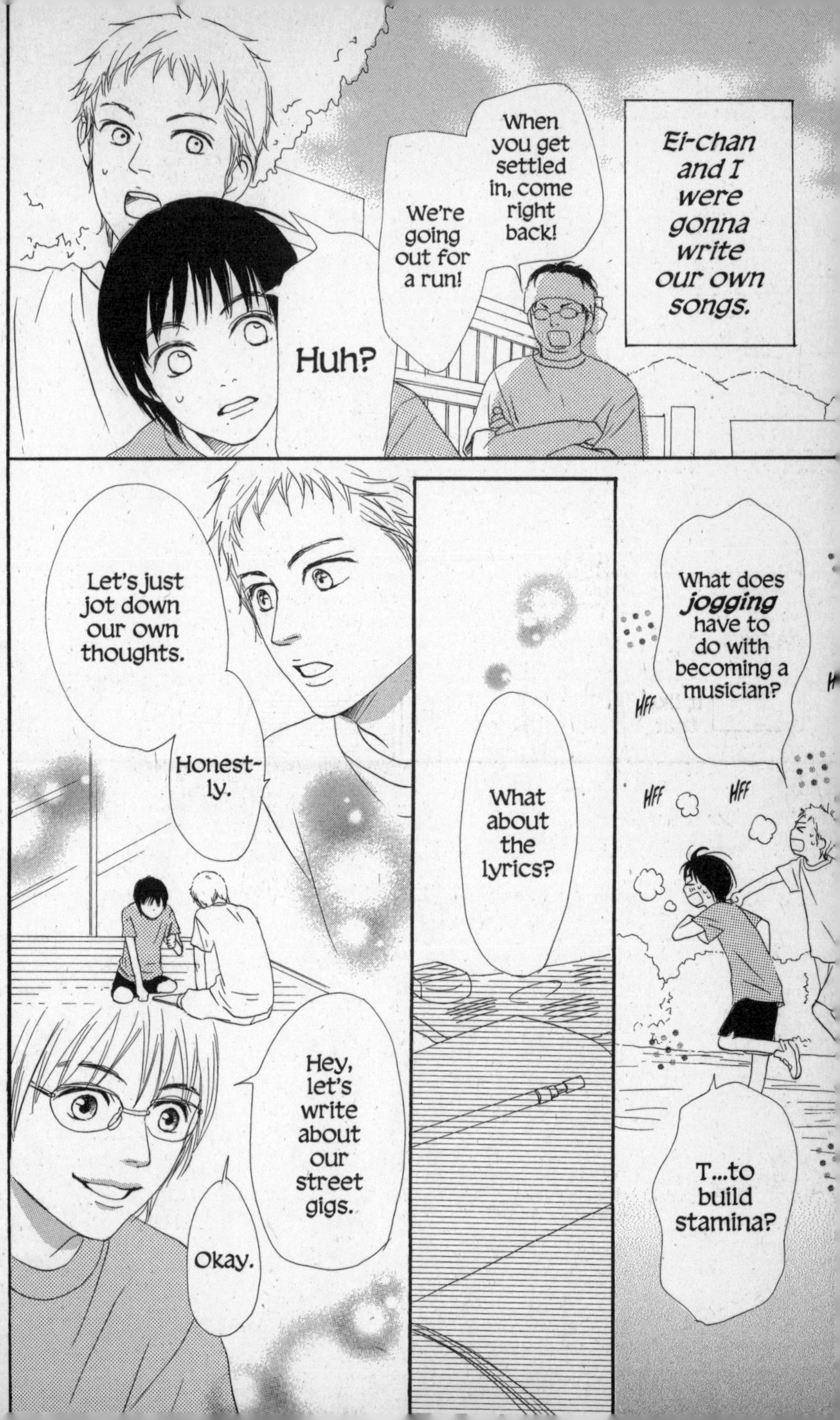
Ei-chan and I were gonna write our own songs.
When you get settled in, come right back!
We're going out for a run!
Huh?
What does *jogging* have to do with becoming a musician?
HFF
HFF
HFF
T...to build stamina?
What about the lyrics?
Let's just jot down our own thoughts.
Honest-ly.
Hey, let's write about our street gigs.
Okay.

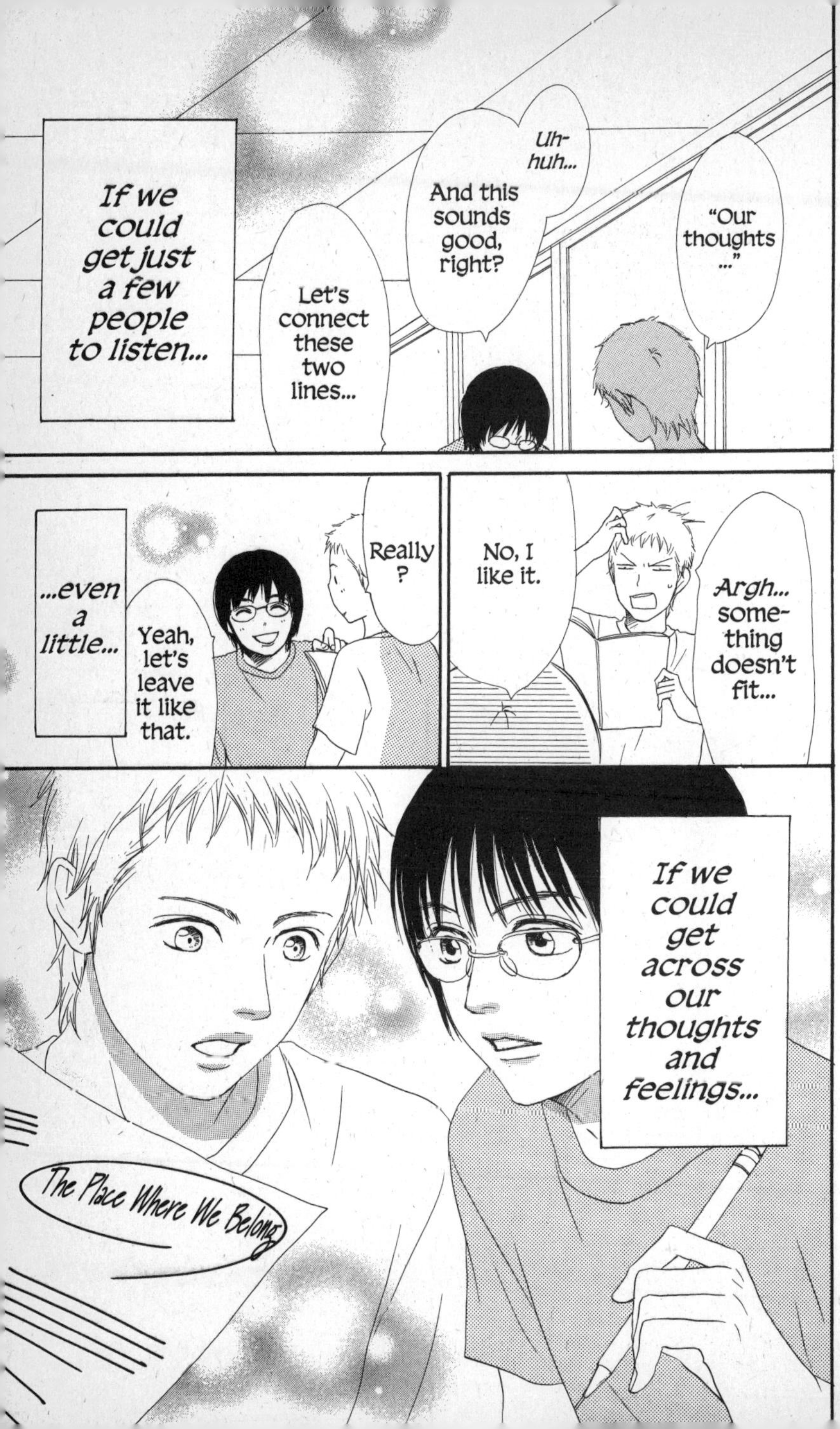
"Our thoughts ..."
Uh-huh...
And this sounds good, right?
Let's connect these two lines...
If we could get just a few people to listen...
Argh... something doesn't fit...
No, I like it.
Really?
Yeah, let's leave it like that.
...even a little...
If we could get across our thoughts and feelings...
The Place Where We Belong

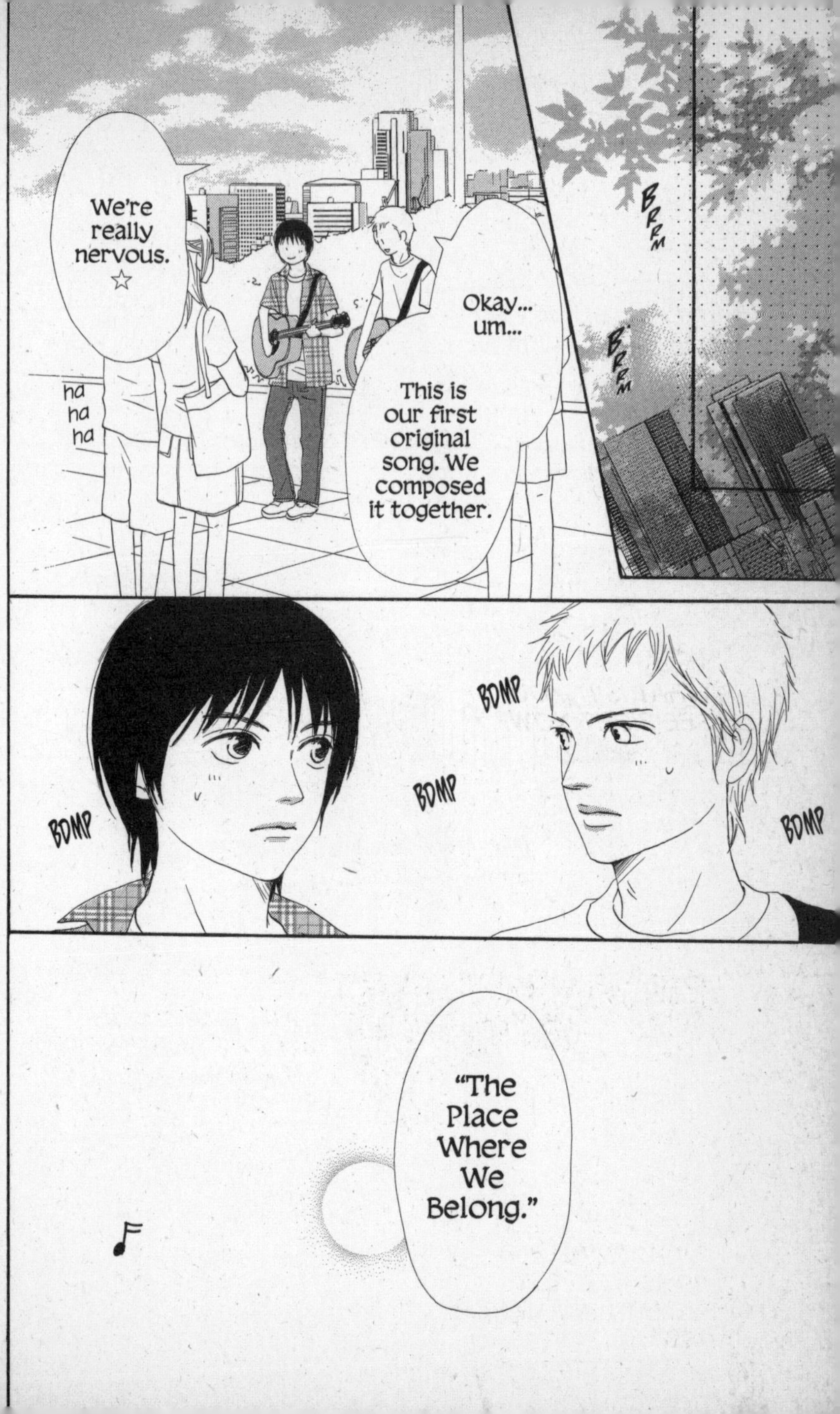
BRRM
BRRM
Okay... um...
This is our first original song. We composed it together.
We're really nervous. ☆
ha ha ha
BDMP
BDMP
BDMP
BDMP
"The Place Where We Belong."

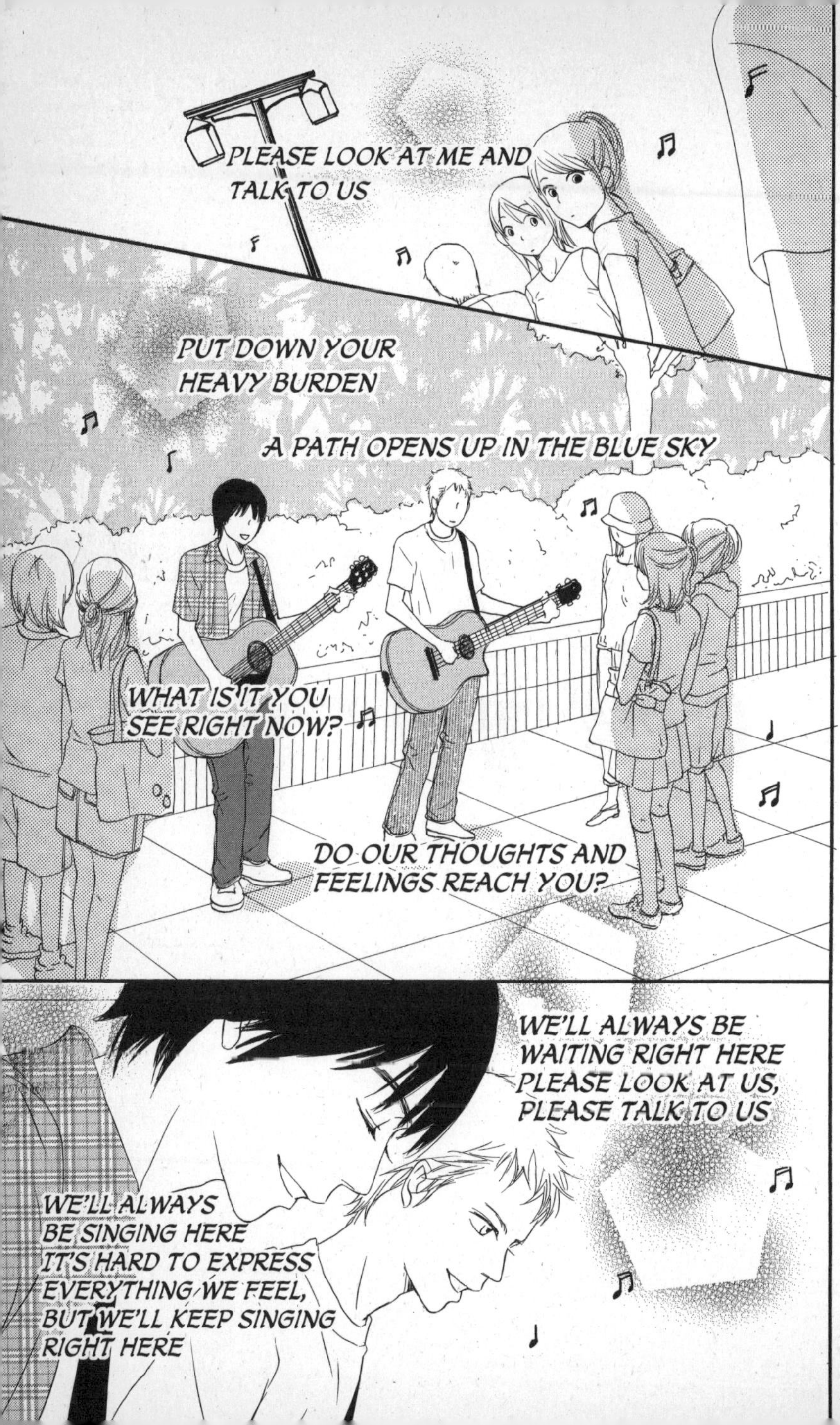
PLEASE LOOK AT ME AND TALK TO US
PUT DOWN YOUR HEAVY BURDEN
A PATH OPENS UP IN THE BLUE SKY
WHAT IS IT YOU SEE RIGHT NOW?
DO OUR THOUGHTS AND FEELINGS REACH YOU?
WE'LL ALWAYS BE WAITING RIGHT HERE PLEASE LOOK AT US, PLEASE TALK TO US
WE'LL ALWAYS BE SINGING HERE IT'S HARD TO EXPRESS EVERYTHING WE FEEL, BUT WE'LL KEEP SINGING RIGHT HERE

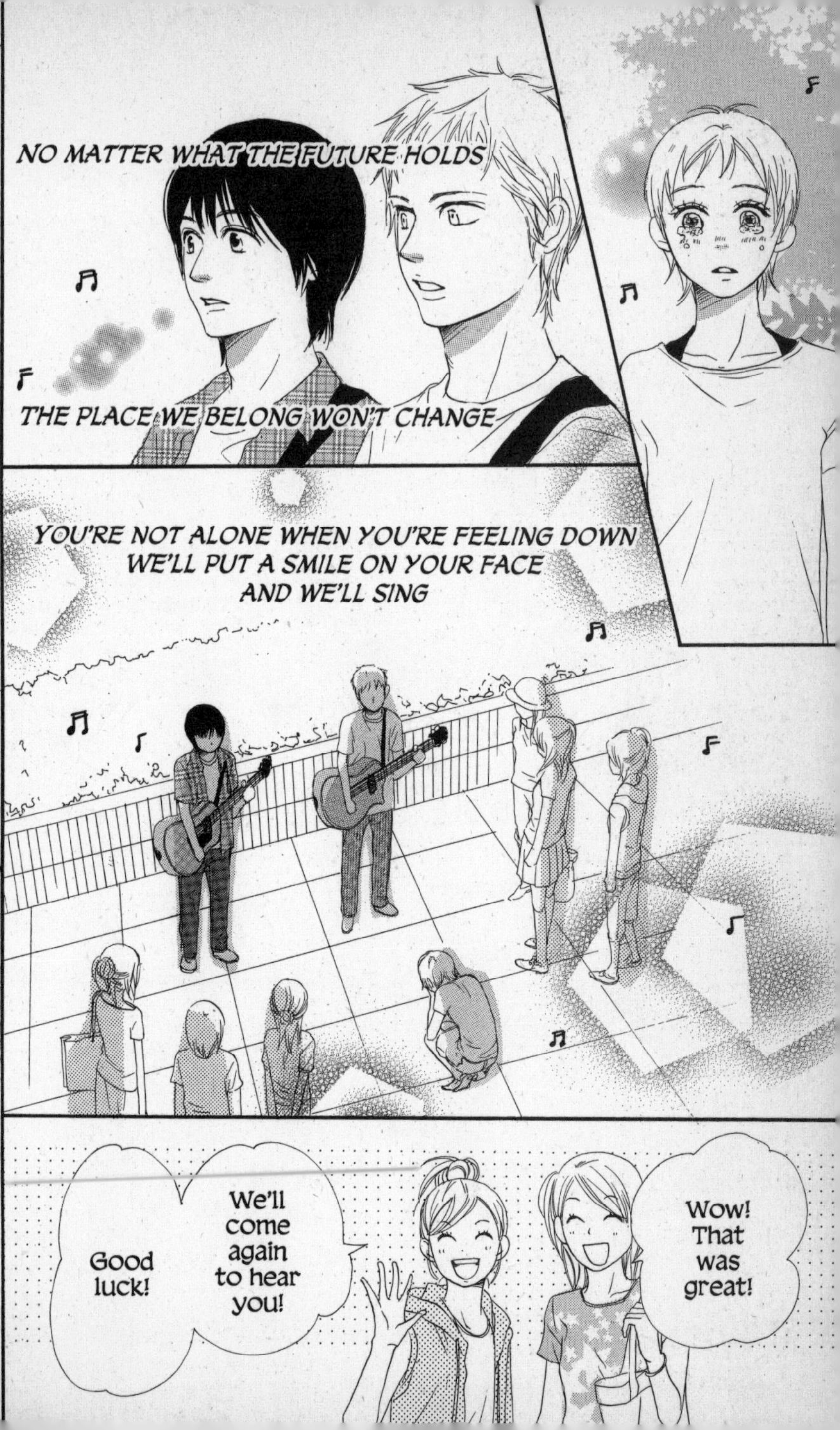
NO MATTER WHAT THE FUTURE HOLDS
THE PLACE WE BELONG WON'T CHANGE
YOU'RE NOT ALONE WHEN YOU'RE FEELING DOWN
WE'LL PUT A SMILE ON YOUR FACE
AND WE'LL SING
Wow! That was great!
We'll come again to hear you!
Good luck!

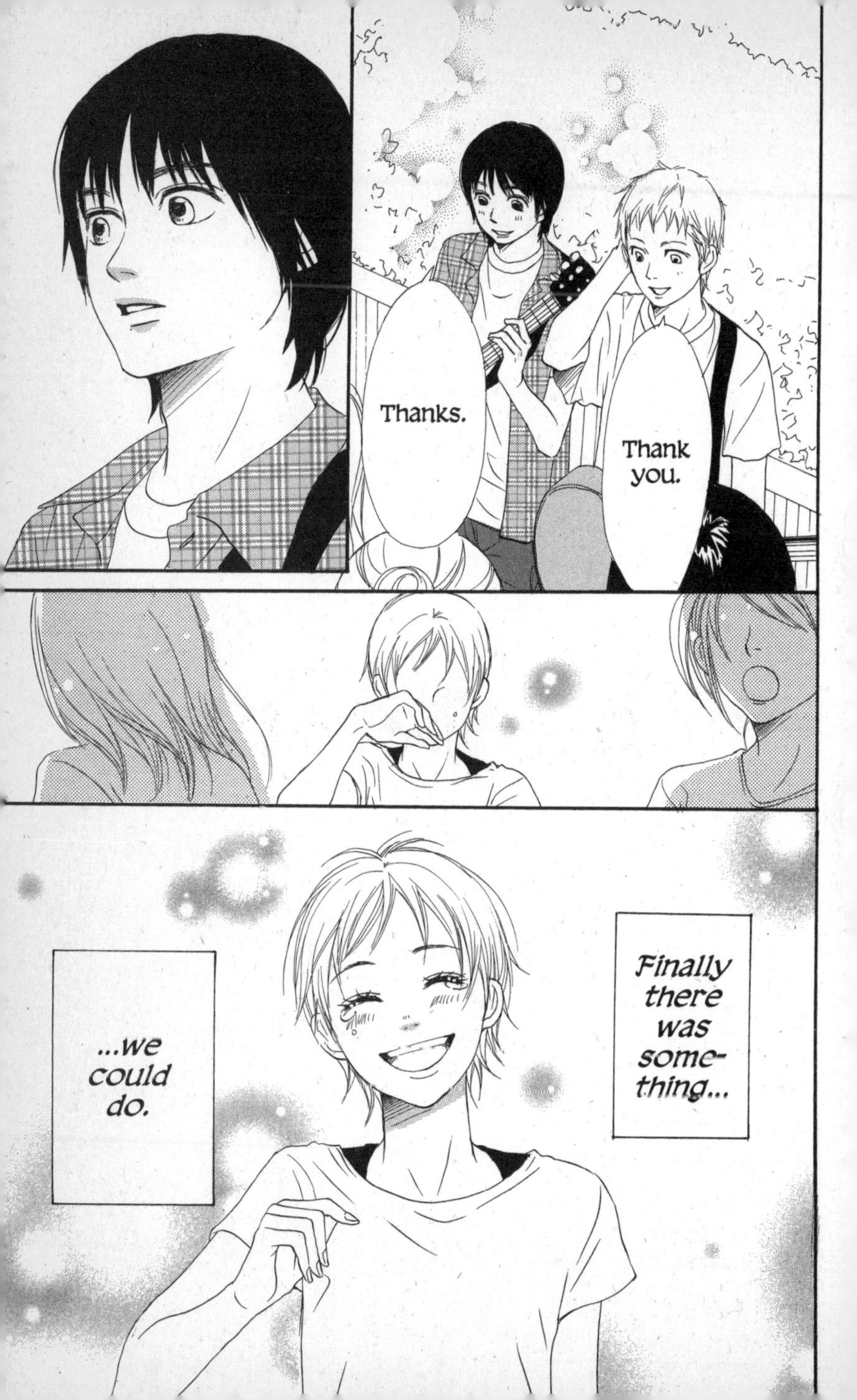
Thank you.
Thanks.
Finally there was some-thing...
...we could do.

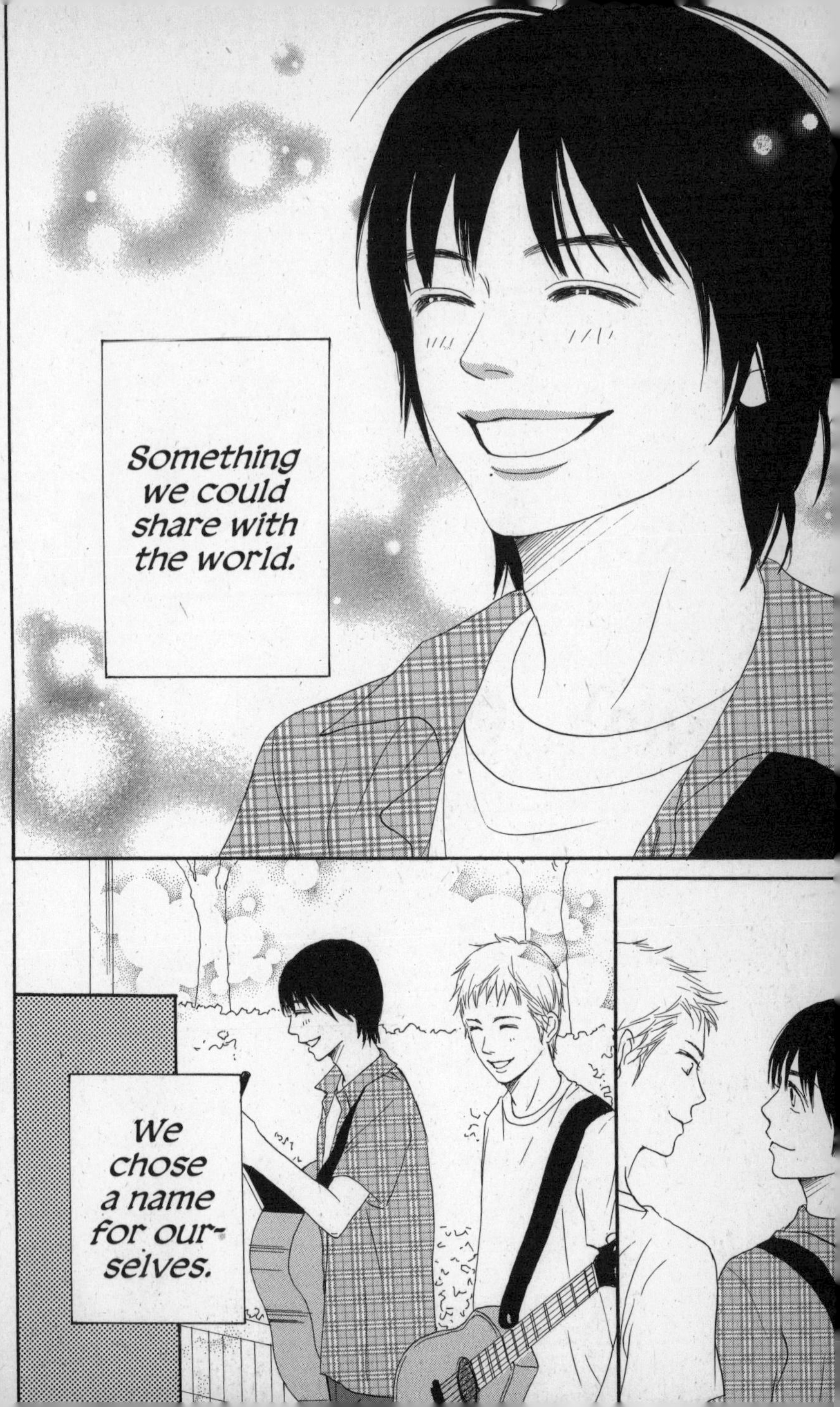
Something we could share with the world.
We chose a name for our-selves.

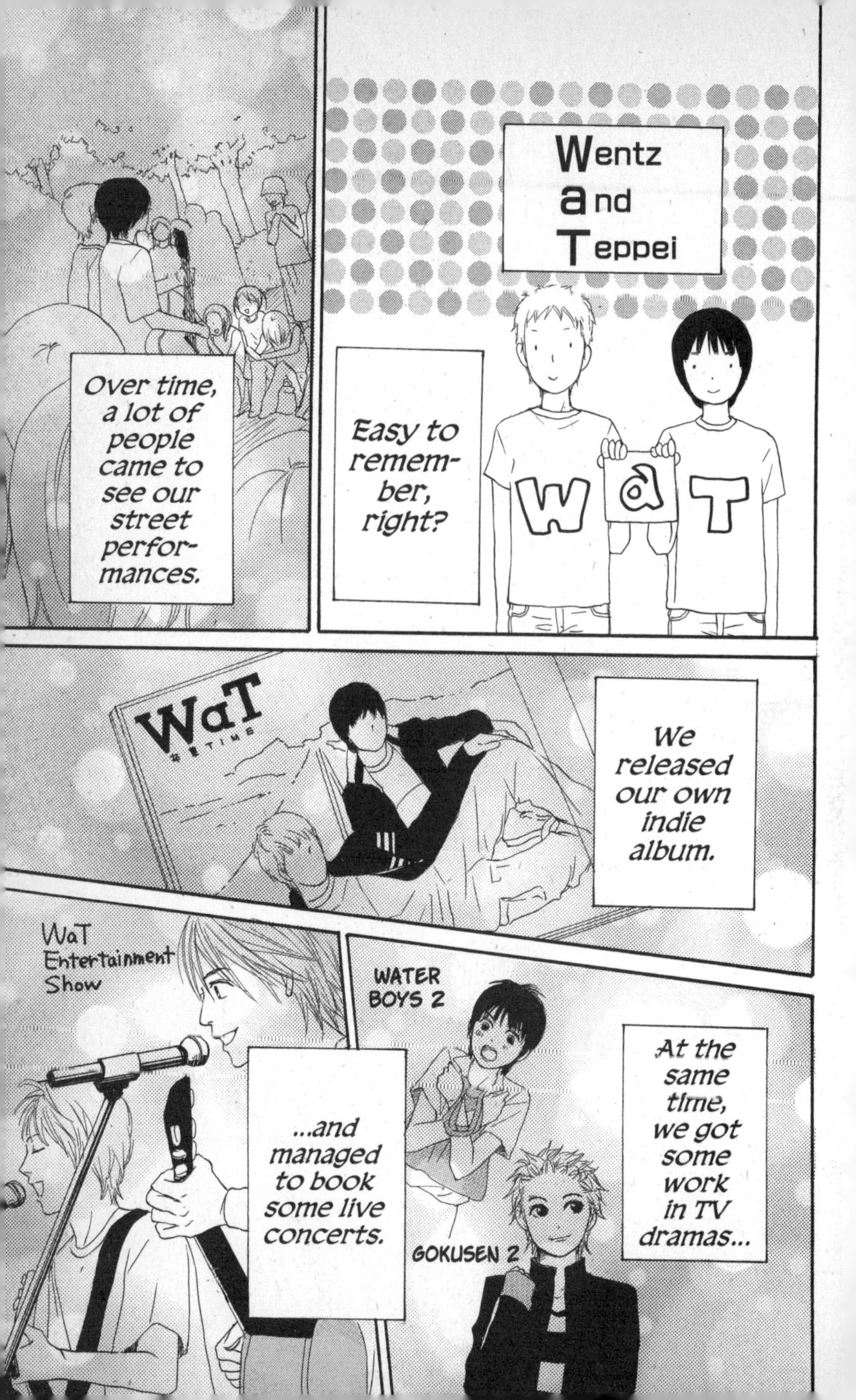
Wentz
and
Teppei
Easy to remember, right?
WaT
Over time, a lot of people came to see our street performances.
WaT
We released our own indie album.
At the same time, we got some work in TV dramas...
WATER BOYS 2
GOKUSEN 2
WaT
Entertainment
Show
...and managed to book some live concerts.

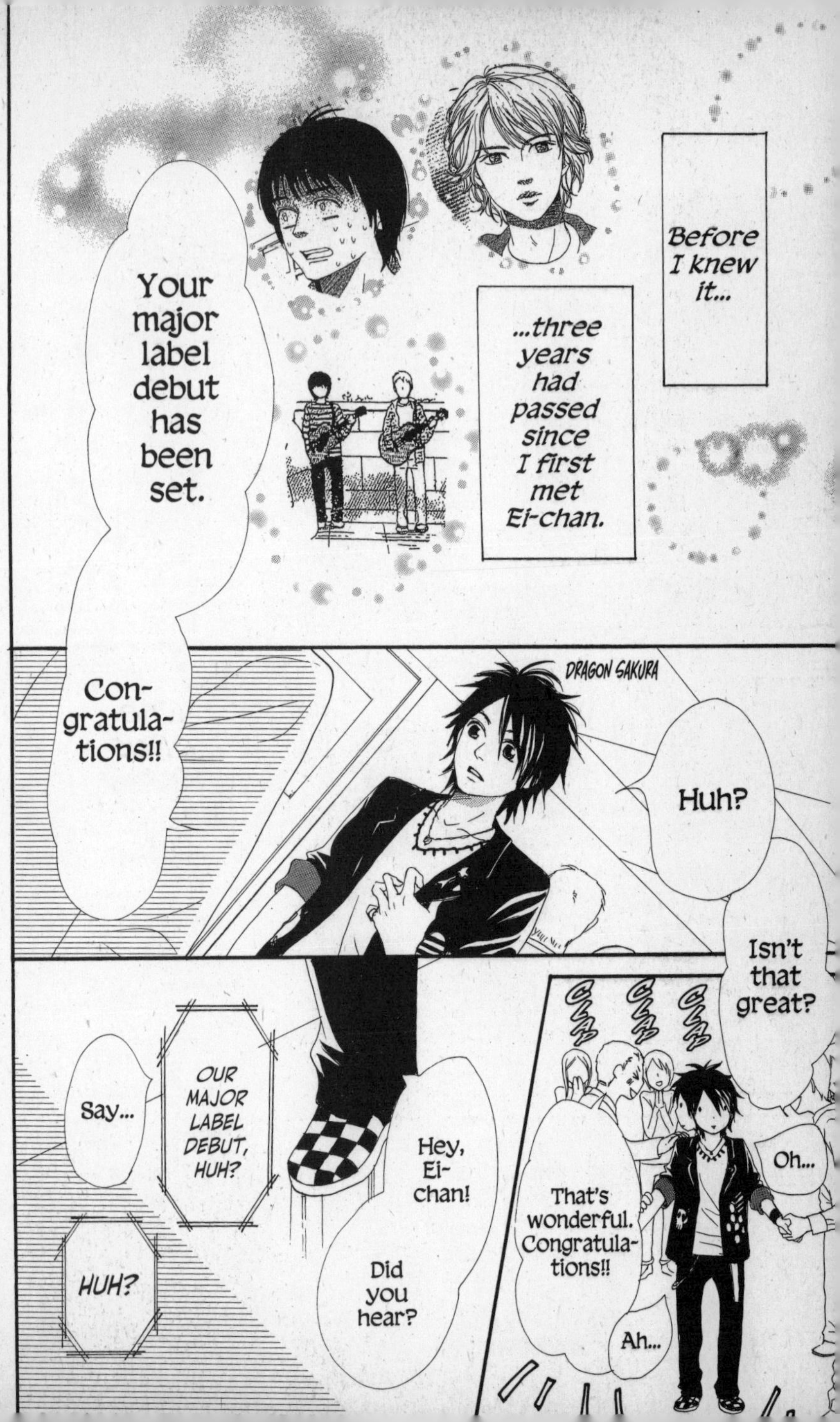
Before I knew it...
...three years had passed since I first met Ei-chan.
Your major label debut has been set.
Congratulations!!
DRAGON SAKURA
Huh?
Isn't that great?
Oh...
That's wonderful. Congratulations!!
Ah...
Hey, Ei-chan!
Did you hear?
OUR MAJOR LABEL DEBUT, HUH?
Say...
HUH?

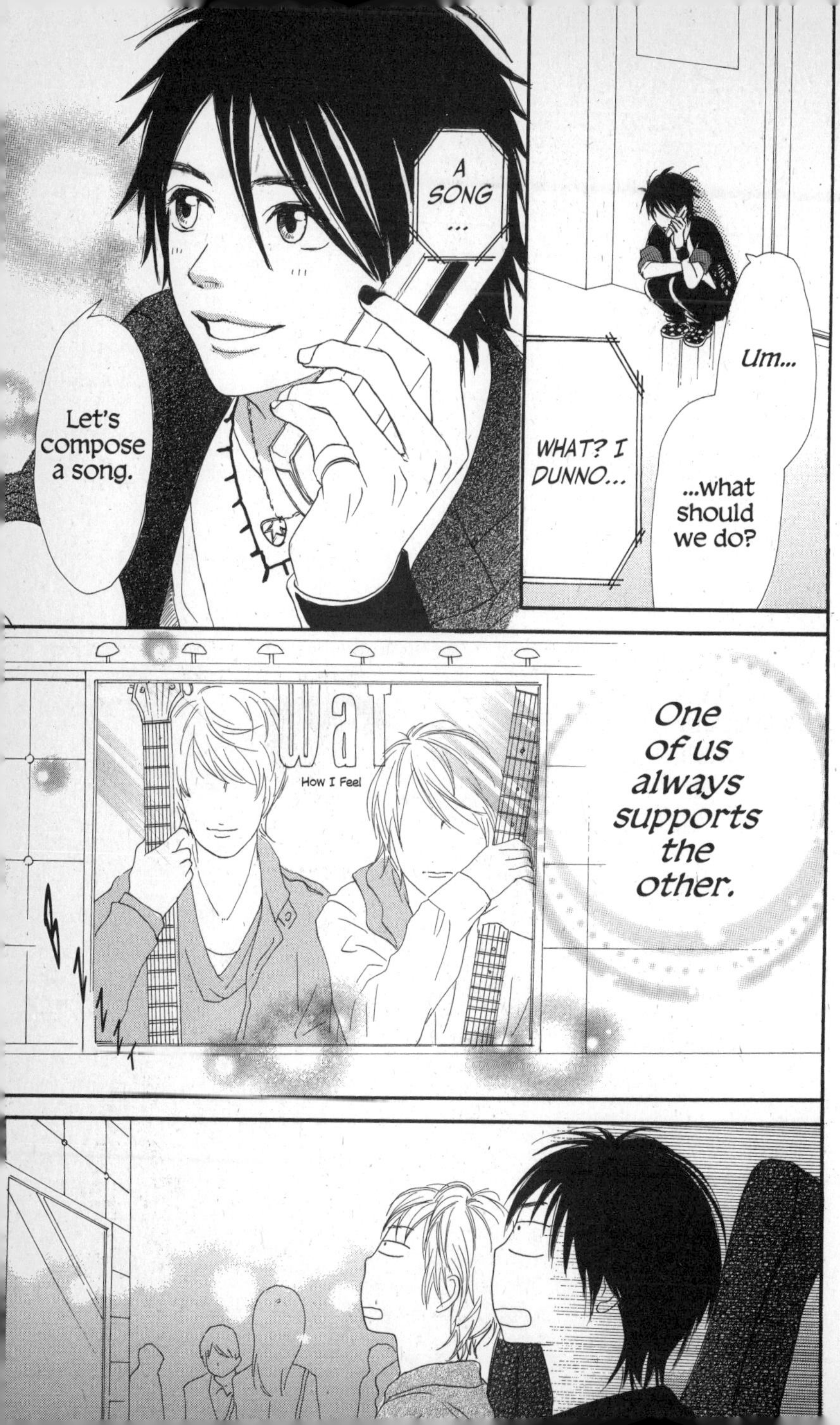
Um...
...what should we do?
WHAT? I DUNNO...
A SONG ...
Let's compose a song.
One of us always supports the other.
WaT
How I Feel

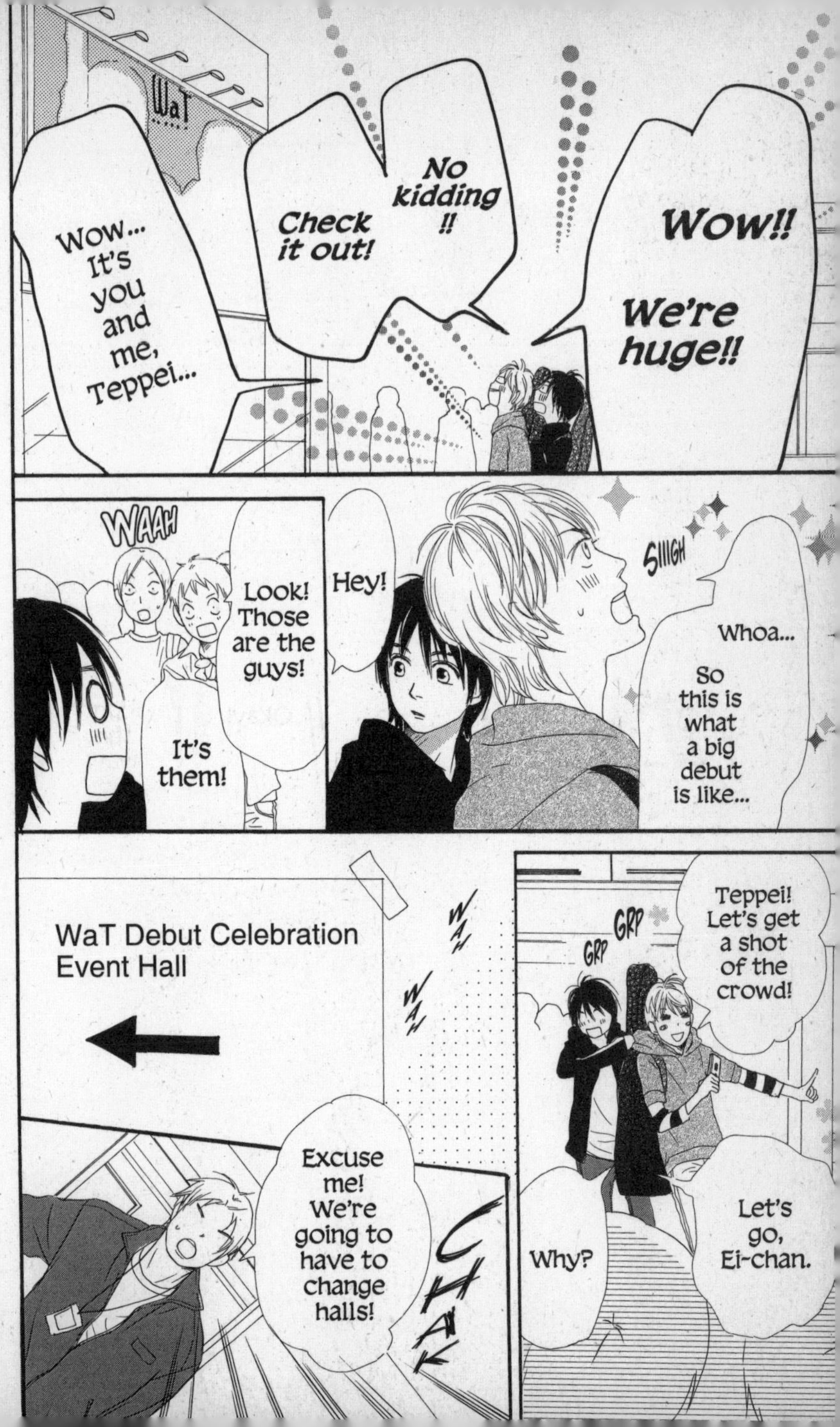
WaT
Wow!! We're huge!!
No kidding!!
Check it out!
Wow... It's you and me, Teppei...
SIIIGH
Whoa... So this is what a big debut is like...
Hey!
WAAH
Look! Those are the guys!
It's them!
Teppei! Let's get a shot of the crowd!
GRP
GRP
Let's go, Ei-chan.
Why?
WaT Debut Celebration Event Hall
WAH
WAH
Excuse me! We're going to have to change halls!
CHAK

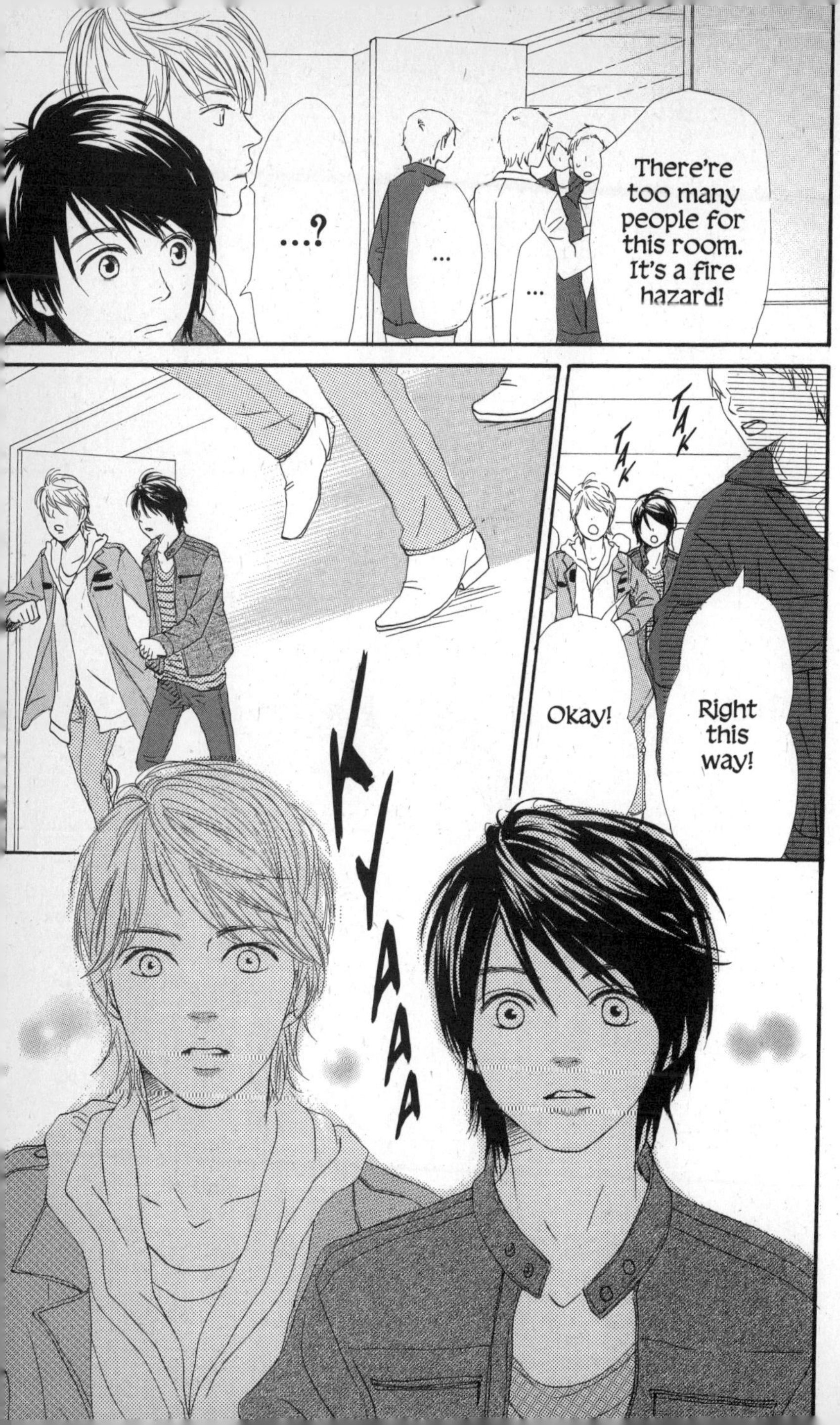
There're too many people for this room. It's a fire hazard!
...
...
...?
TAK
TAK
Right this way!
Okay!
KYAAAA

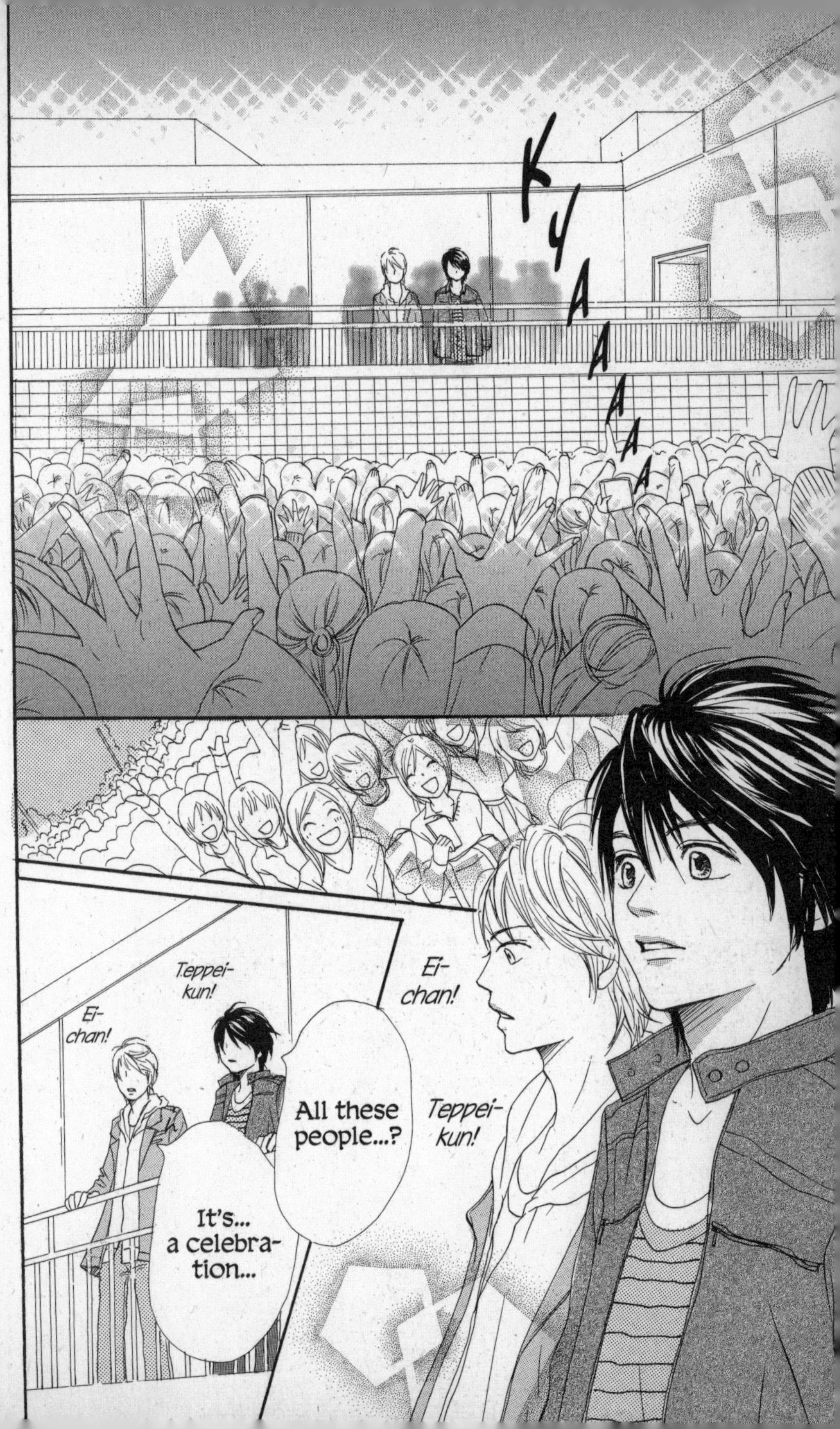
KYAAAAAA
Ei-chan!
Teppei-kun!
All these people...?
It's... a celebration...
Teppei-kun!
Ei-chan!

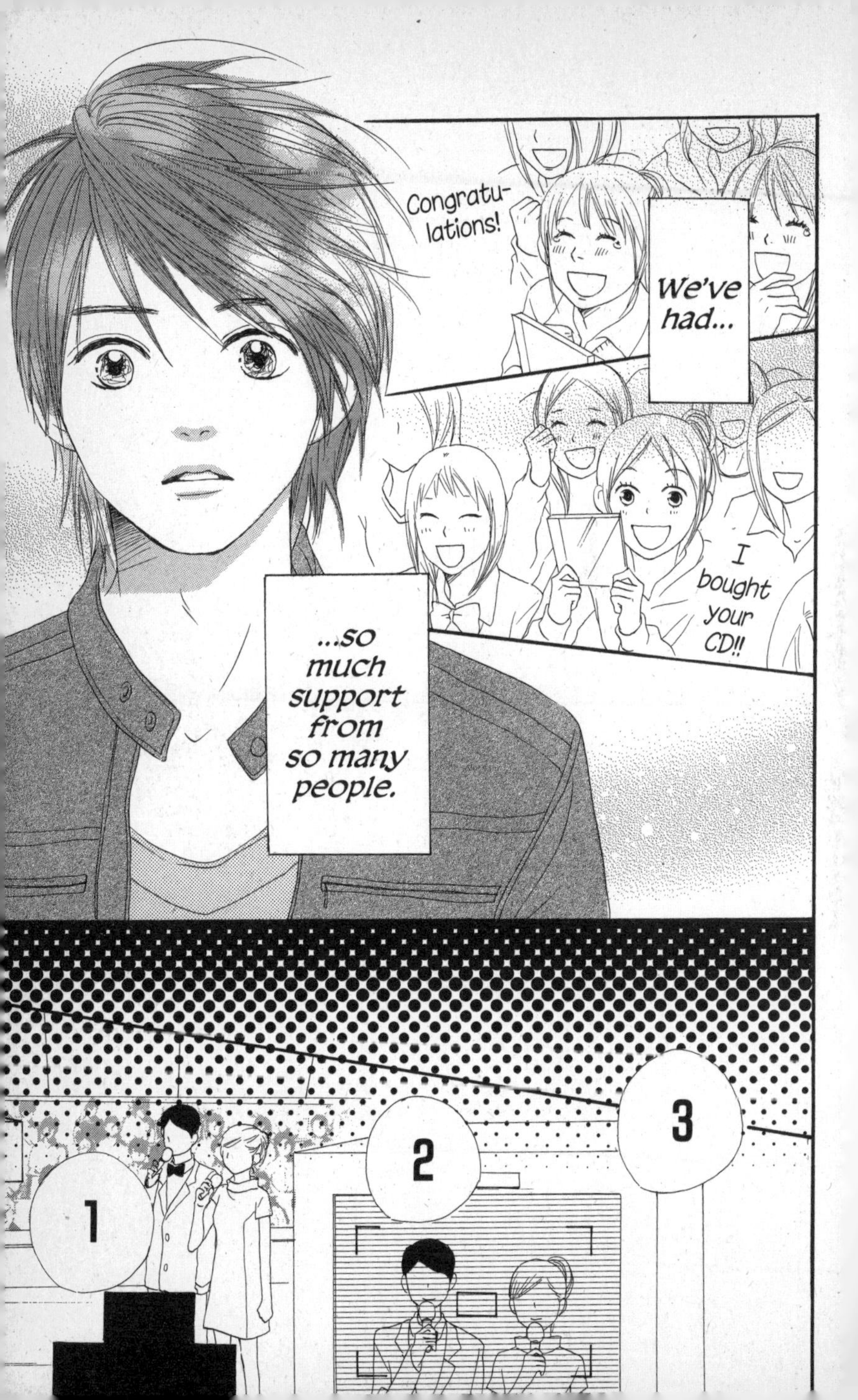
Congratu-lations!
We've had...
I bought your CD!!
...so much support from so many people.
3
2
1

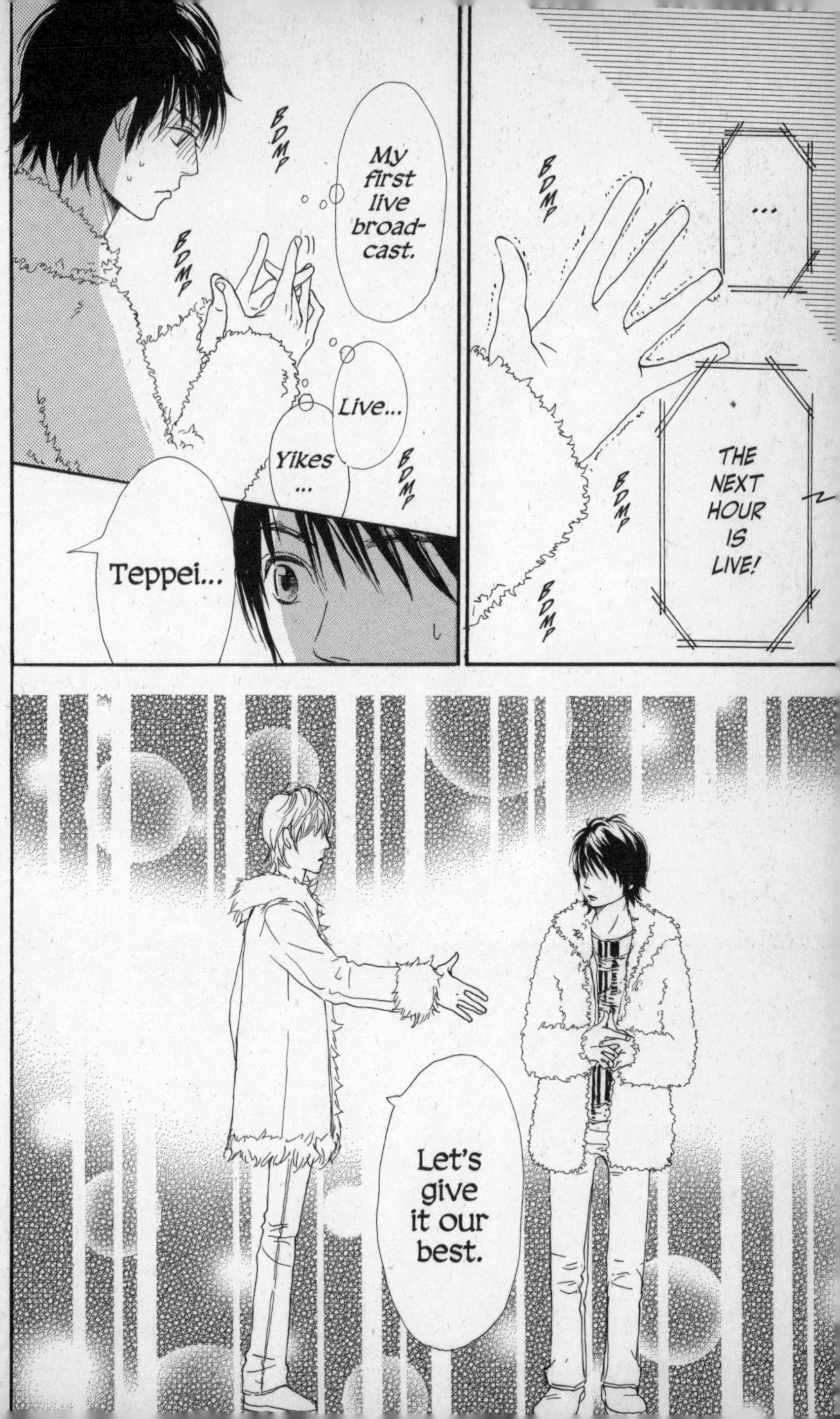
BDMP
...
THE NEXT HOUR IS LIVE!
BDMP
BDMP
BDMP
My first live broadcast.
BDMP
Live...
Yikes...
BDMP
Teppei...
Let's give it our best.

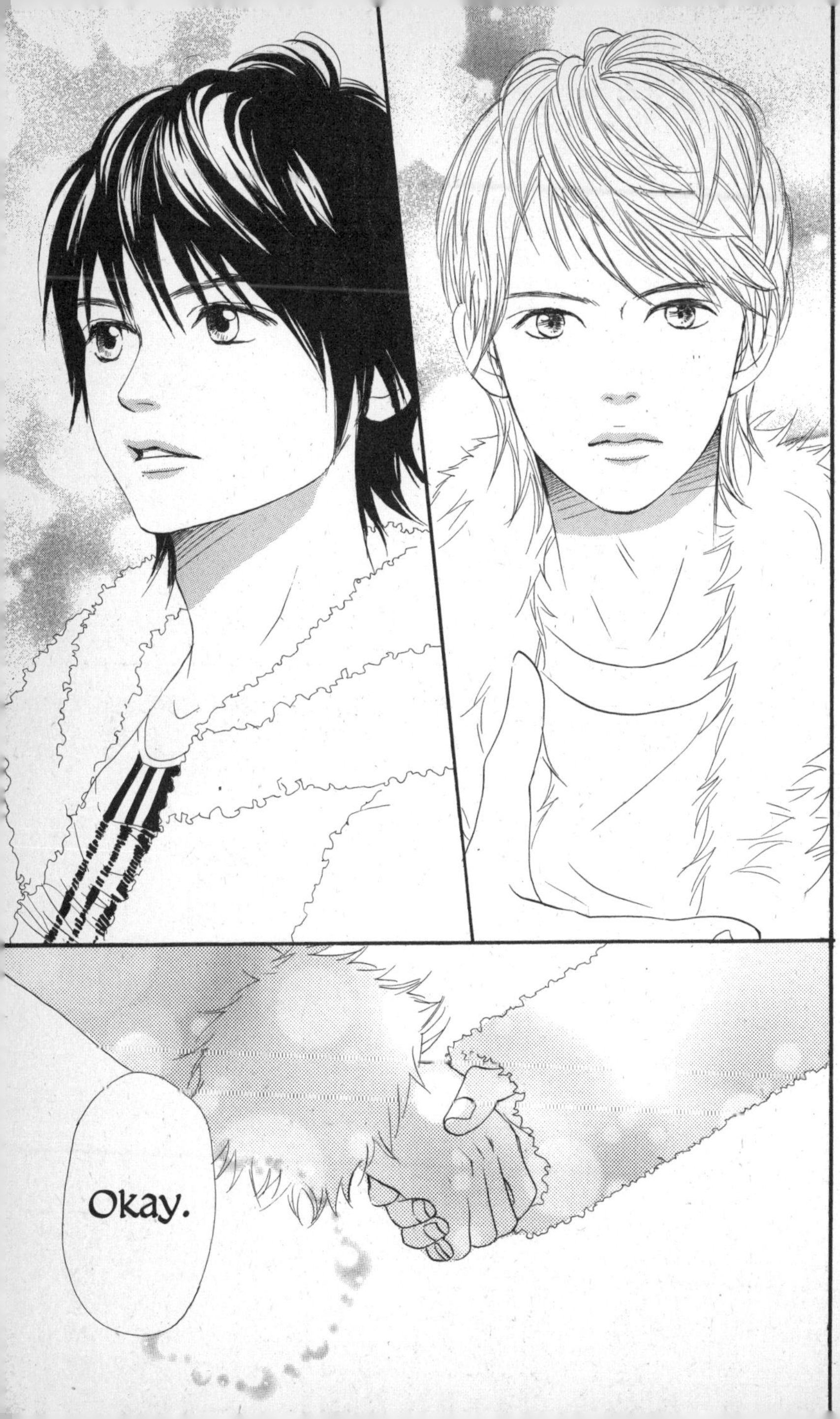
Okay.

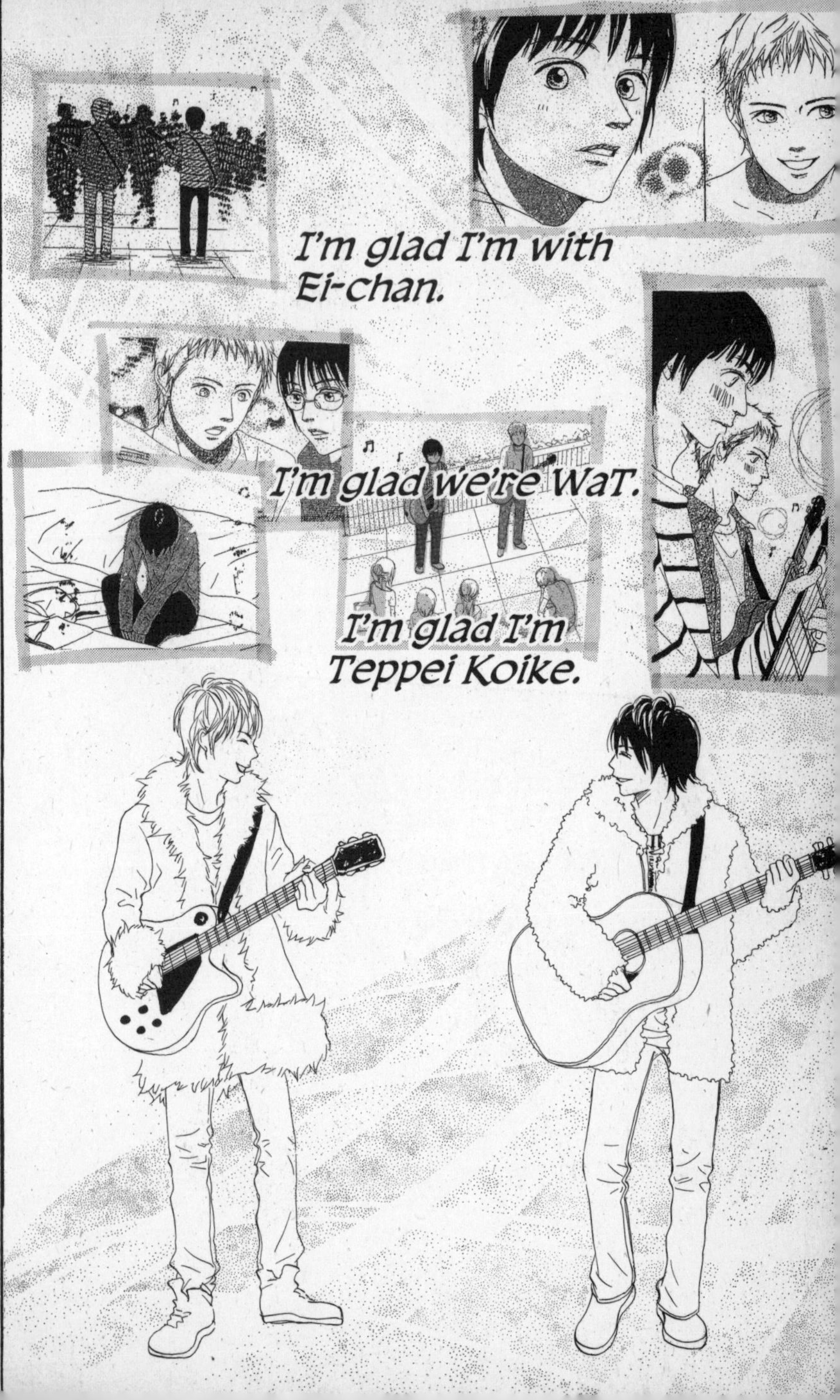
I'm glad I'm with Ei-chan.
I'm glad we're WaT.
I'm glad I'm Teppei Koike.

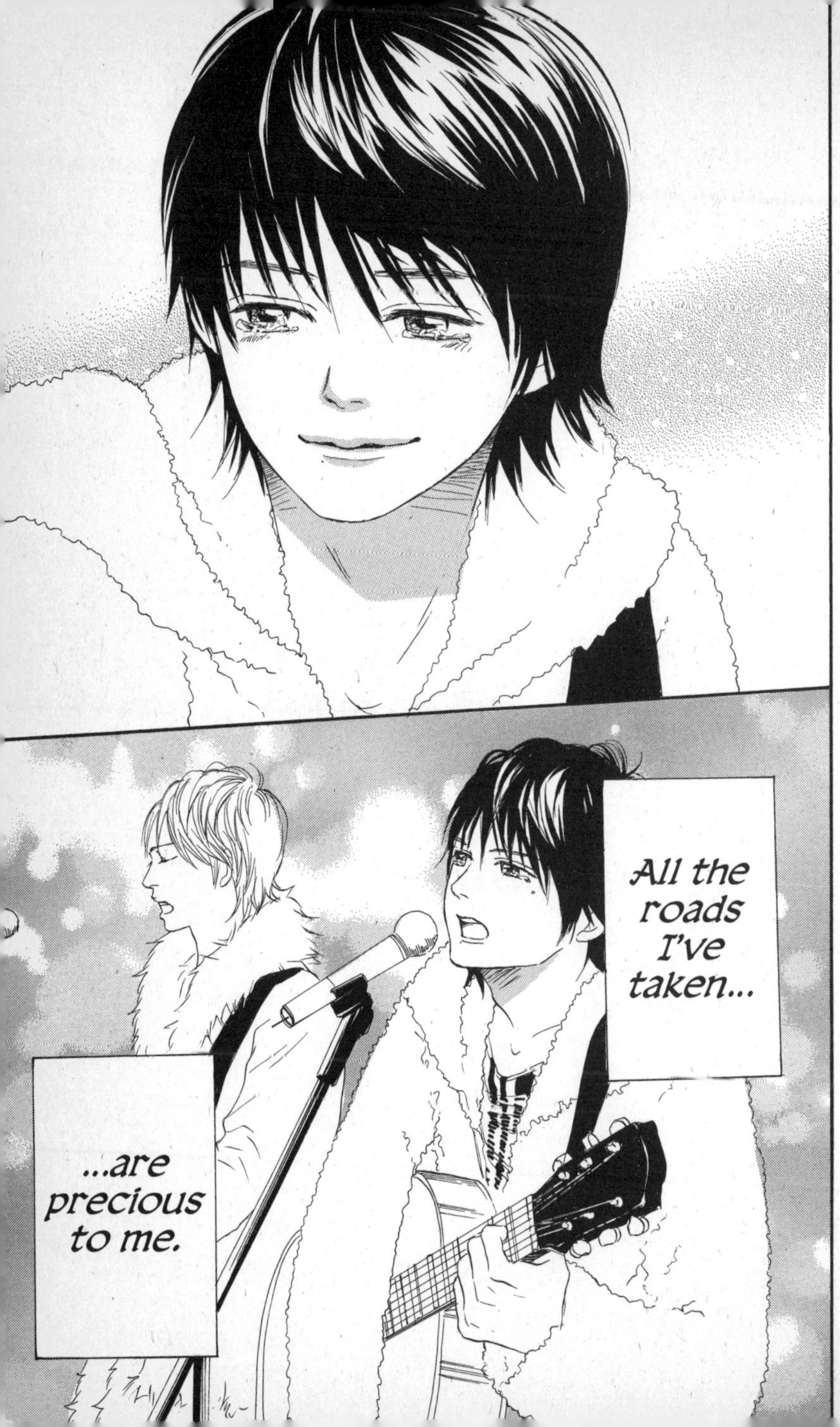
All the roads I've taken...
...are precious to me.

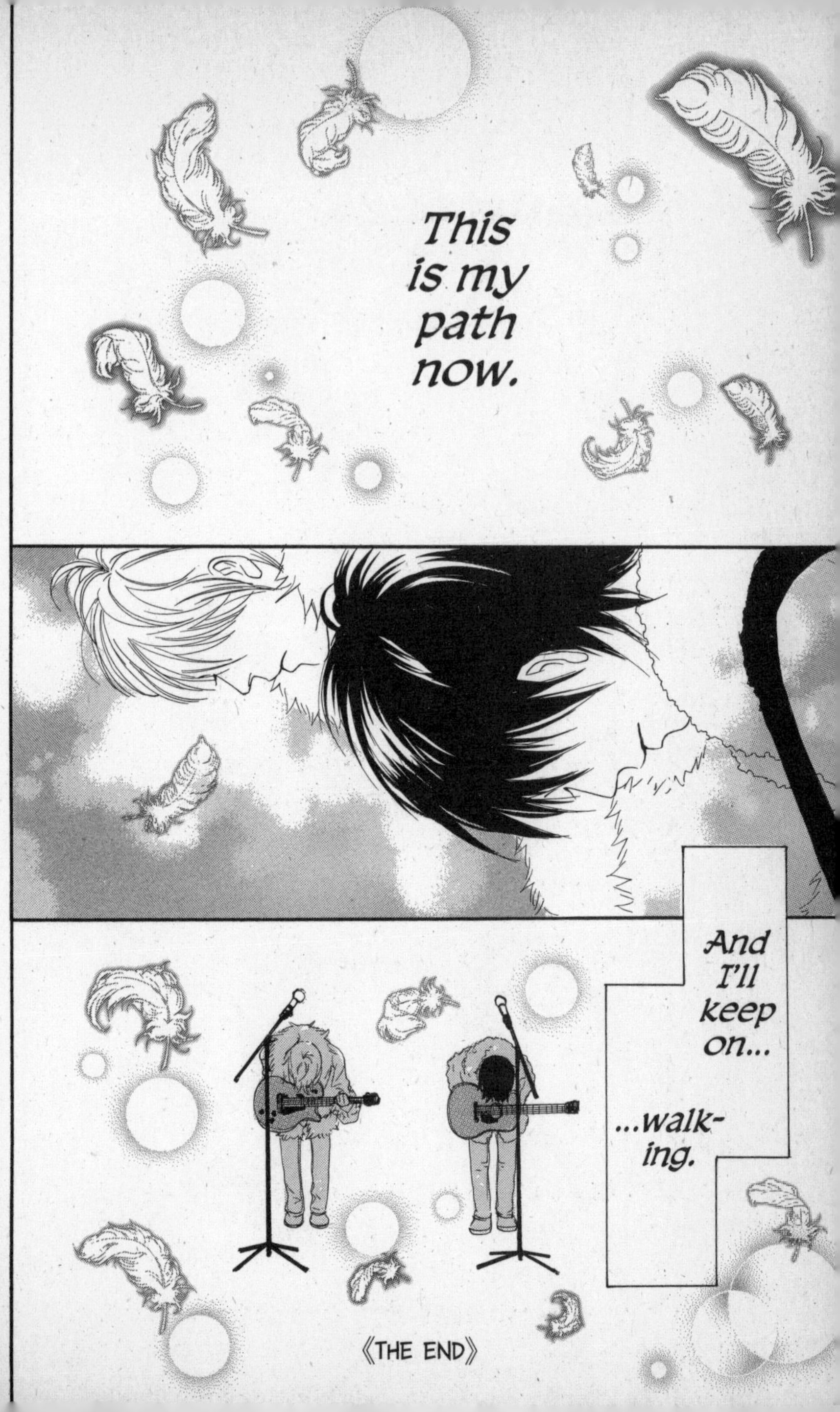
This is my path now.
And I'll keep on...
...walk-ing.
《THE END》

glossary

Page 7, panel 2: Good luck cat
The kanji character on the cat is *fuku*, which means good fortune/
happiness.

Page 10, panel 5: Issunbôshi
Issunbôshi is a Japanese folk tale about a tiny boy, similar to Tom
Thumb. (*Issun* is a unit of measure that equals approximately one
inch.) When he goes off to seek his fortune, Issunbôshi uses a soup
bowl for a boat and chopsticks for oars.

Page 80, panel 1: Matsuri
The kanji on Abe's jacket means "festival."

Page 96, panel 1: All Hanshin and All Kyojin
All Hanshin-Kyojin are a comedy team with a short guy (Hanshin)
and a tall guy (Kyojin). If you've been reading from volume 1, you
already know this!

Page 133: Teppei Koike
Teppei Koike is a singer/actor who had his first leading role as
Atsushi Ôtani in *Love★Com: The Movie.*

Page 137, panel 6: Tensai Terebi-kun
Tensai Terebi-kun was an NHK educational children's program. Eiji
Wentz played bass guitar on the show when he was 10 years old.

Page 144, panel 4: Kobukuro-san
Kobukuro-san refers to the musical duo of Kentaro **Kobu**chi and
Shunsuke **Kuro**da. The name of the band is derived in a similar
way to WaT (Wentz and Teppei)!

Page 171, panel 4: Water Boys 2 and Gokusen 2
These are both titles of TV dramas.

Page 172, panel 2: Dragon Zakura
Dragon Zakura is a TV drama from 2005.

This volume marks the end of our main story. But they're letting me do a few extra features and side stories, so there'll be one more volume after this. And the anime comes out in the spring! So I'd love it if you could keep *Love★Com* in your heart a little while longer.

Aya Nakahara won the 2003 Shogakukan Manga Award for her breakthrough hit *Love★Com*, which was made into a major motion picture and a PS2 game in 2006. She debuted with *Haru to Kuuki Nichiyou-bi* in 1995, and her other works include *HANADA* and *Himitsu Kichi*.

LOVE★COM VOL 16

Shojo Beat Manga Edition

STORY AND ART BY
AYA NAKAHARA

Translation/JN Productions
English Adaptation/Shaenon K. Garrity
Touch-up Art & Lettering/Gia Cam Luc
Design/Yuki Ameda
Editor/Carrie Shepherd

VP, Production/Alvin Lu
VP, Sales & Product Marketing/Gonzalo Ferreyra
VP, Creative/Linda Espinosa
Publisher/Hyoe Narita

Published by VIZ Media, LLC
P.O. Box 77010
San Francisco, CA 94107

10 9 8 7 6 5 4 3 2 1
First printing, January 2010

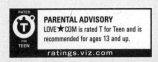

PARENTAL ADVISORY
LOVE★COM is rated T for Teen and is
recommended for ages 13 and up.
ratings.viz.com

www.viz.com

www.shojobeat.com

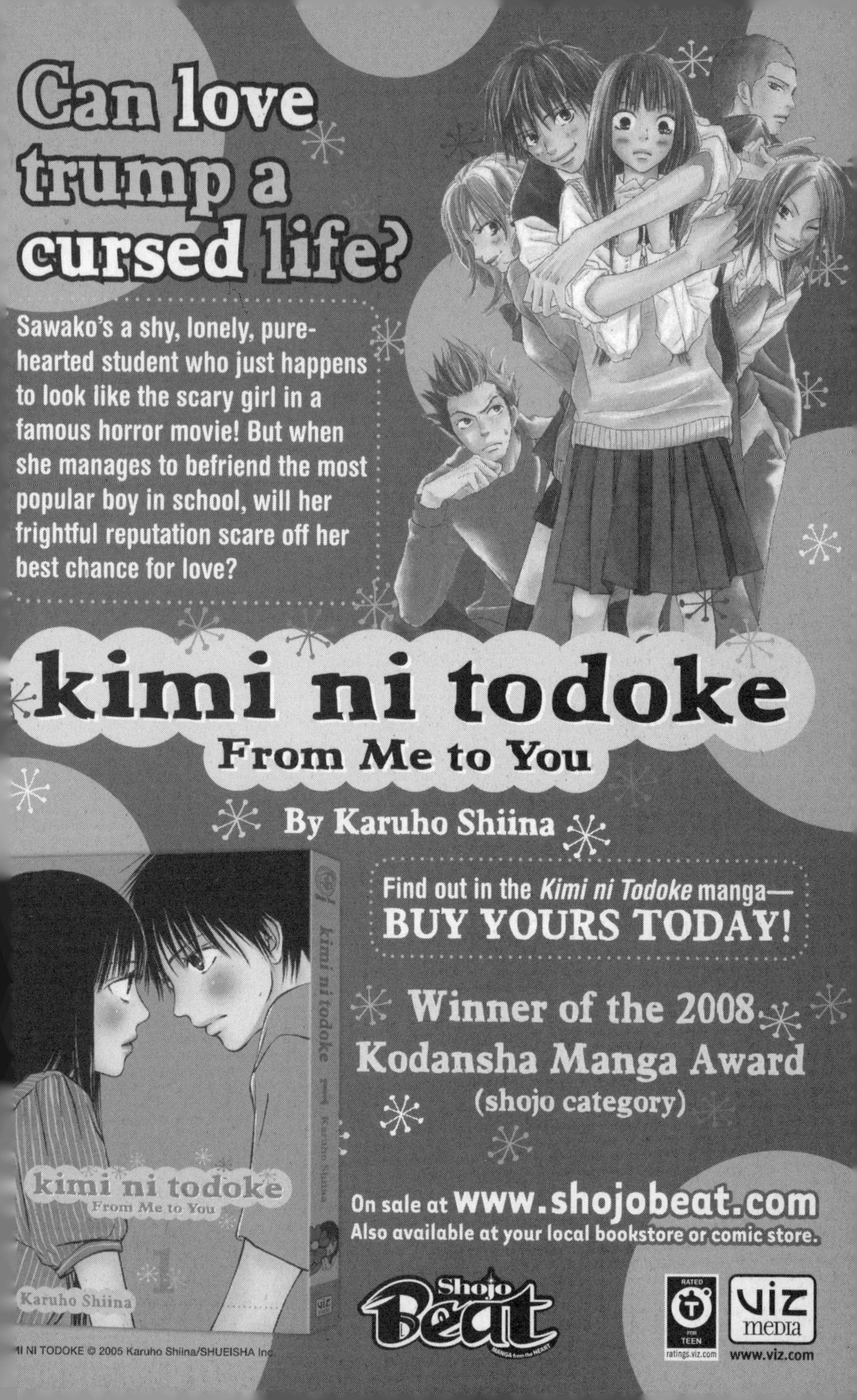
Can love trump a cursed life?
Sawako's a shy, lonely, pure-hearted student who just happens to look like the scary girl in a famous horror movie! But when she manages to befriend the most popular boy in school, will her frightful reputation scare off her best chance for love?
kimi ni todoke
From Me to You
By Karuho Shiina
Find out in the Kimi ni Todoke manga—
BUY YOURS TODAY!
Winner of the 2008
Kodansha Manga Award
(shojo category)
kimi ni todoke
From Me to You
1
Karuho Shiina
On sale at www.shojobeat.com
Also available at your local bookstore or comic store.
Shojo Beat
RATED T FOR TEEN
ratings.viz.com
VIZ media
www.viz.com
NI TODOKE © 2005 Karuho Shiina/SHUEISHA Inc.

Don't Hide What's *Inside*

OTOMEN

by **AYA KANNO**

Despite his tough jock exterior, Asuka Masamune harbors a secret love for sewing, shojo manga, and all things girly. But when he finds himself drawn to his domestically inept classmate Ryo, his carefully crafted persona is put to the test. Can Asuka ever show his true self to anyone, much less to the girl he's falling for?

Find out in the *Otomen* manga—buy yours today!

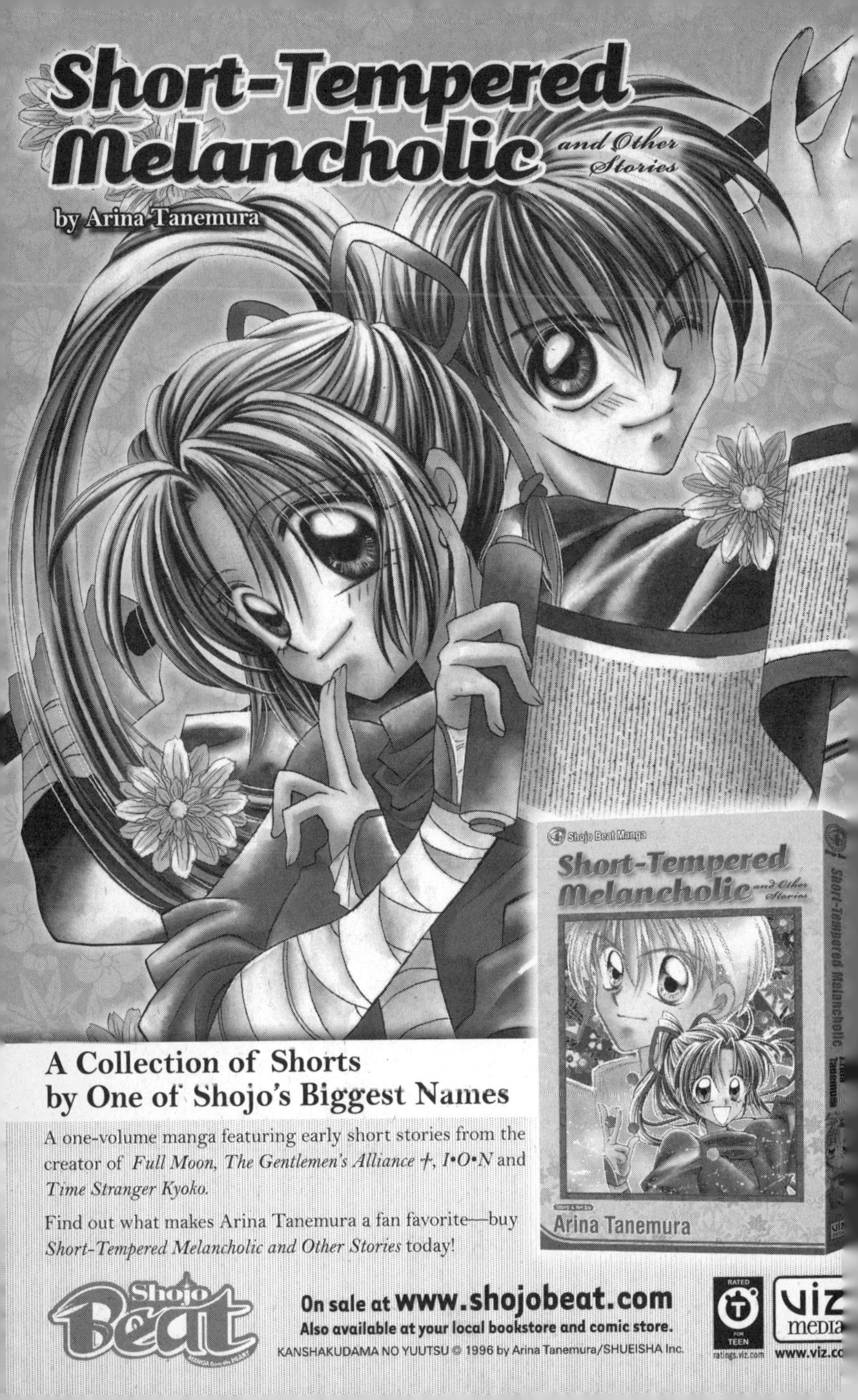
Short-Tempered Melancholic and Other Stories
by Arina Tanemura
Shojo Beat Manga
Short-Tempered Melancholic and Other Stories
Story & Art by
Arina Tanemura
A Collection of Shorts by One of Shojo's Biggest Names
A one-volume manga featuring early short stories from the creator of *Full Moon, The Gentlemen's Alliance †, I•O•N* and *Time Stranger Kyoko.*
Find out what makes Arina Tanemura a fan favorite—buy *Short-Tempered Melancholic and Other Stories* today!
Shojo Beat
On sale at www.shojobeat.com
Also available at your local bookstore and comic store.
KANSHAKUDAMA NO YUUTSU © 1996 by Arina Tanemura/SHUEISHA Inc.
RATED T FOR TEEN
ratings.viz.com
viz media
www.viz.co

Tell us what you think about Shojo Beat Manga!

Our survey is now available online. Go to:

shojobeat.com/mangasurvey

Help us make our product offerings better!